Library of
Davidson College

*THE INDIA
OFFICE,*
1880–1910

Sir Arthur Godley, later Lord Kilbracken Permanent Undersecretary of State for India, 1883–1909. Courtesy of the India Office Library.

THE INDIA OFFICE, 1880–1910

ARNOLD P. KAMINSKY

CONTRIBUTIONS IN COMPARATIVE COLONIAL STUDIES, NUMBER 20

GREENWOOD PRESS
NEW YORK • WESTPORT, CONNECTICUT • LONDON

325.3
K15i

Library of Congress Cataloging in Publication Data

Kaminsky, Arnold P.
   The India Office, 1880-1910.

   (Contributions in comparative colonial studies,
ISSN 0163-3813 ; no. 20)
   Bibliography: p.
   Includes index.
   1. Great Britain. India Office—History.
2. India—Politics and government—1857-1919.
I. Title. II. Series.
JV1043.K36 1986   325'.31'41   85-930
ISBN 0-313-24909-1 (lib. bdg.)

87-3957

Copyright © 1986 by Arnold P. Kaminsky

All rights reserved. No portion of this book may be
reproduced, by any process or technique, without the
express written consent of the publisher.

Library of Congress Catalog Card Number: 85-930
ISBN: 0-313-24909-1
ISSN: 0163-3813

First published in 1986

Greenwood Press, Inc.
88 Post Road West, Westport, Connecticut 06881

Printed in the United States of America

The paper used in this book complies with the
Permanent Paper Standard issued by the National
Information Standards Organization (Z39.48-1984).

10 9 8 7 6 5 4 3 2 1

For
Susan,
with love

Contents

Illustrations	ix
Foreword by Robin W. Winks	xi
Preface	xiii
Abbreviations	xvii
Introduction	3
1. Policy-Making and the Flow of Paper	11
2. The Council of India	35
3. The Secretary of State and His Council	63
4. External Responsibilities and Constitutional Relationships	89
5. The India Office and the Government of India	123
6. Pressure on the Periphery: Public Opinion, Special Interests, and Lobbies	159
7. Conclusion	191
Bibliography	205
Appendix A. Biographical Note on Sir Arthur Godley	227
Appendix B. Biographical Notes	235
Appendix C. Secretaries of State for India, 1858–1910	242
Appendix D. Permanent Undersecretaries of State for India, 1858–1909	244

Appendix E. Parliamentary Undersecretaries of State for
 India, 1858–1910   245

Appendix F. Chronological List of Members of the Council
 of India, 1858–1905   247

Appendix G. Committees of the Council of India, 1858–1905   252

Index   283

Illustrations

Sir Arthur Godley	*frontispiece*
1. Sir Arthur Godley	97
2. India Office interior: Council Chamber	98
3. India Office interior: Durbar Court	99
4. India Office interior: two staircases	100

Foreword
by Robin W. Winks

Empires thrive on bureaucracy. Administration creates its own rewards and comes to be an end in itself, and colonial bureaucracies generate collaborator groups in the classic mold—groups of people caught between the rewards, the predictive capacity, and apparent security of the imperial power and its presumed goal of even-handed justice and even-paced paper flow, and the imperatives of the indigenous culture. While this is true of all empires and to some extent of all colonies, it was especially so in Asia, where the British in particular often chose to administer their imperial possessions and protectorates through a locally created clerkly class. In India, Ceylon, and Malaya, administration became an end almost greater than the original goals of empire.

Even more so, then, did British administration in London play a significant role in shaping the nature of real government, as applied well below the level of policy, in the Asian subcontinent. It is fashionable to think of "pushing paper" as tedious, the work of unimaginative automatons who get satisfaction from minuting, annotating, and filing; yet knowing how to push paper, quickly to the right target, slowly or with deliberate inefficiency when the right target may, for reasons of internecine battle, be thought to be the wrong target, is one of modern civilization's more abstruse art forms. And colonial offices were particularly skilled bureaucracies.

Arnold P. Kaminsky has provided a lively example of how an office formulates, controls, and at time obfuscates policy. His work is in part a biographical study of an administrator/policy maker of considerable interest, Sir Arthur Godley, and in part a close study of how the India Office functioned in relation to other bureaucracies in the crucial decades at the end of the nineteenth and beginning of the twentieth centuries. The author examines the apparatus by which decisions were made, and he recognizes that procedure and convention are as important as personality to the dynamics of the India Office. In his examination he throws out a number of suggestions, some explicit though most by implication, for important and fresh studies that may yet be undertaken in India Office and related records. He distinguishes between the numbingly routine work of many junior clerks while recognizing that by their routines the junior clerks also fixed policy in place, and the work of those whom we would today call the decision makers. The result is a model study of how colonial government worked near the height of the British Empire, an account of how "the bad eyes brigade" of administrators, scholars, and registrars influenced the great, colorful events on which history more often, and perhaps too frequently, concentrates.

Preface

This study of the India Office in the latter nineteenth century attempts to describe and explain the formation of policy by the Home Government of the Indian Empire. In the course of my graduate study at the University of California, Los Angeles (UCLA), there were so many shadowy figures in Whitehall and numerous but inexplicable shifts in the final form of Indian policy that I was stimulated to investigate further and try and unravel the guild secrets of the India Office. In the process I discovered a hitherto virtually unknown world whose inhabitants, indeed, whose very existence, affected the course of the history of India in the late nineteenth century.

As I embarked on my project, I was given special inspiration and direction by Donovan Williams of the University of Calgary, whose own work on the India Office in its first decade set the high standards and goals for my own project. His encouragement and support of my pursuit of this topic was unflagging, as is my debt to him. There are many others to whom I have incurred debts of gratitude over the years. My mentor, Stanley A. Wolpert, offered guidance and support as a teacher and friend over the years. His invaluable insights and commentary have continuously challenged me in my work. A number of individuals were kind enough to read earlier drafts of this work and make valuable suggestions—N. Gerald Barrier (University of Missouri), Oliver Pollak (University of Nebraska, Omaha), Joseph O. Baylen (Georgia State University), and Donovan Williams. I am indebted to a number of individuals whose advice and encouragement stimulated me to undertake this effort: John S. Galbraith (University of California, San Diego); Dick Sisson (UCLA); Frank Conlon (University of Washington); Neil Rabitoy (California State University, Los Angeles); Edward Moulton (University of Winnipeg); and Peter Robb (SOAS). I owe a very special debt too for the encouragement offered over the years by D. R. SarDesai (UCLA), and James F. Tent (University of Alabama in Birmingham)—they were great sources of strength.

It would have been impossible to complete this book without the cooperation and help provided by the staffs of the India Office Library and Records Office (formerly headed by the late Stanley Sutton and later headed by Joan C. Lancaster) and the British Library. I am especially grateful to Martin Moir, Deputy Librarian and resident expert on the holdings of the IOLR, and Dr. Richard Bingle, Supervisor of European Manuscripts at the India Office, who were most generous with their time and the resources at their disposal. I would like to thank Lords Scarsdale, Cross, Elgin, and the Dufferin and Richards families for their cooperation in citing selections from the Curzon, Cross, Elgin, Dufferin and Richards collections respectively. I am also indebted to the librarians and staffs of the Public Records Office, Printing House Square, the British Library of Political and Economic Science (London School of Economics), the School of Oriental and African Studies, and the National Library of Scotland. Each was cordial and most helpful in arranging access to manuscript collections necessary for this project. I would be remiss not to mention that Charlotte Spence, former Indo-Pacific Bibliographer at the UCLA University Research Library, aided me considerably in obtaining materials for use in the United States.

Other individuals graciously granted me access to privately owned archives. The Earl of Kimberley kindly granted me permission to consult the Kimberley Papers, which have been removed from general circulation. This collection was at the time located in Sherborne, England, under the custodianship of Lieut.-Colonel N. Ireland-Smith, who was a most accommodating host during my visit. I owe a special debt to the grandchildren of Lord Kilbracken: the current Baron Kilbracken of Killegar, the Rt. Honorable W.A.H. Godley, Mr. Patrick Rice, and Mr. Arthur Coleridge. Each was magnanimous in sharing his personal reminiscences and personal correspondence with Lord Kilbracken.

Several agencies provided the necessary financial support to complete my study. The Shell Companies Foundation and the Department of History at UCLA provided me with support during my initial field work, and subsequent research was funded by the Faculty Research Council of the University of Alabama in Birmingham and the American Philosophical Society. Without their aid the completion of this book would have been considerably delayed. While it was being written, sections dealing with the India Office establishment, relations between India and London, and various pressure groups appeared in earlier versions in *Asian Profile*, the *Journal of Indian History*, and in *British Policy in India and Sri Lanka, 1858–1912: A Reassessment* (edited by Robert I. Crane and N. Gerald Barrier).

For her assistance in editing this manuscript, my thanks to Ms. Margaret

Tent. I also appreciate the endeavors of Ms. Jeanne Holloway in preparing the typescript of the book. My deep affection and gratitude go to my children, Michael and Sarah, who never quite understood my many moods and the long weekends I spent at the office. And finally, to my wife, Susan, who never wavered in her encouragement, spirit, and support, I owe the most.

Abbreviations

Abbreviations used principally in the references.

ADC	Aide-de-camp
BL	British Library
G.B.	Great Britain
GOI	Government of India
GG	Governor-General
ICS	Indian Civil Service
IO	India Office
IOL	India Office Library
IOR	India Office Records
INC	Indian National Congress
L/AG	Accountant-General Department Papers, India Office Records
L/F	Finance Department Papers, India Office Records
L/MIL	Military Department Papers, India Office Records
L/P&S	Political and Secret Department Papers, India Office Records
L/PO	Private Office Papers, India Office Records
PRO	Public Records Office (London)
Proc.	Proceedings
SS	Secretary of State

*THE INDIA
OFFICE,*
1880–1910

Introduction

For eighty-nine years the India Office was the Home Government of Britain's largest and most complex overseas possession. Yet there is a general lack of appreciation of the significance of the India Office role in the formation of Indian policy, especially in its first half-century. It is extraordinary that among the proliferation of administrative studies of U.K. departments of state since the late 1950s—the Colonial Office, the Foreign Office, the War Office, the Treasury, the Civil Service—the India Office has generally been ignored.[1] Moreover, Great Britain's largest administrative establishment in the late nineteenth century (the establishment cost of the India Office was roughly four and one-half times that of the Colonial Office) has not been included in the ongoing and enthusiastic debate about the conceptual framework within which the growth and development of British administration should be studied.[2]

The India Office was intimately involved in the formation of Indian and Imperial policy, and especially between 1880 and 1914. Yet no analytical investigation of the structure and function of the India Office exists for this critical period, and the personalities remain "statesmen in disguise."[3] Professor Donovan Williams of the University of Calgary has studied the origins and development of the India Office in its critical first decade. *The India Office, 1858–1869* (Hoshiarpur, Punjab, 1983) is a thorough and important study of the Office. S. A. Husain's University of London Ph.D. thesis focuses on the impact of Indian reforms and World War I on the India Office between 1910 and 1924; but until now, there has been no attempt to study the organization and operation of the India Office in the late nineteenth century. There are a few works which deal more generally with the India Office, including Sir Malcolm Seton, *The India Office* (London, 1926) and S. N. Singh, *The Secretary of State for India and His Coun-*

cil, 1858–1919 (Delhi, 1962), but they are superficial and offer little insight into the formation of policy in Whitehall.[4]

This absence of analysis of the manner in which Indian governmental business was processed and evaluated by Whitehall creates a historiographical "blindspot." British historians consider the India Office the "odd man out" because the office was funded out of Indian revenues for much of its existence, while historians of the Empire usually focus attention on events in India. Indian historians are equally remiss, lavishing attention on events and policy-making in India, with seemingly little interest in or appreciation of India Office involvement in the governance of the subcontinent.

Yet the India Office was a miniature Imperial government, self-contained in its part of Whitehall overlooking St. James's Park. It carried out administrative functions of every conceivable kind in the despatch of Indian business. Given its legal obligation to review Indian correspondence, the heavy concentration by historians on events and policy-making in India is puzzling. Reflecting on this imbalance, Donovan Williams has noted:

> There is a natural dichotomy in all history of empire, between the Home Government and the Colony itself. It is often a false dichotomy, yet necessity and convention sometimes force the historian to choose on which side of the dividing line he can best operate. The result is a lack of perspective. The flesh and gristle of the India Office is lacking. The Old Indians who are appointed to the Council of India seem to become less substantial. Personalities fade into the shadows and processes never emerge from the uniform pale gray shrouds of anonymity. While the heart of the "colonial" empire beats healthily and regularly, that of the Indian Empire generates concern for some historians.[5]

This imbalance is largely due to the great historiographical dedication to the East India Company exemplified by the works of Sir John Kaye and William Foster, and the massive amount of material in the India Office Records that have dissuaded many scholars from working on the Home Government of India.[6] There is also a tendency among South Asian scholars to study the subcontinent from the "bottom up" (i.e., district and regional studies), deeming studies of the upper echelons of British Indian Government unfashionable. As valid as this approach is for our understanding of British India, it does not bring to the fore the importance of the India Office for Indian governance at all levels.

Hence this study is an attempt to rectify this imbalance for the late nineteenth century. Given the diverse and multitudinous issues which could be grouped under the rubric "Indian policy," no attempt has been made to use a case study approach. I have attempted to clarify the structure and procedures of the India Office during the period 1880–1910, to emphasize some of the broader technical aspects of the India Office bureaucracy, and to bring into focus the mechanics and dynamics of the India Office decision-making process. By throwing light on the manner in which Whitehall formulated policy for India, I have sought to establish a frame of reference for future studies on a broad range of topics related to nineteenth-century British India.

In many ways the India Office conformed to the Weberian model of a "rational" bureaucracy, based on five concepts of legitimacy and eight principles of rational legal authority.[7] However, this study also demonstrates the limitation of applying the Weberian model to the Indian situation. For one thing, decisions in the India Office were affected by high government officials, viz., a Secretary of State and a permanent staff operating independently of the English Civil Service and Treasury until after World War I. There was also the Council of India, an enigmatic and often misunderstood cog in the machinery of the Home Government of the Indian Empire. It was charged with "conducting" Indian correspondence in the United Kingdom and hence played a key role in the formulation of Indian policy.[8] The Council provided the India Office with a certain Indian ethos that set its "paper empire" apart from departments of state dealing with peoples elsewhere. When the India Office chose to assess or devise Indian policy, it often had a much deeper appreciation of the reality of the Indian scene than either the Foreign Office or Colonial Office.[9] While this was not always a positive factor, it was nevertheless an important feature of the Indian policy-making process which has generally been ignored or glossed over by scholars working on the period.

To comprehend fully the importance of the India Office in the formation of Indian policy, one must understand the machinery of decision and policy-making, the legal responsibilities of the constituent parts of the Office, and its position within the Imperial framework. Thus this study begins with an analysis of the composition of the India Office bureaucracy, including a clarification of the "flow of paper" within the office—something which often dictated the timing, the extent of discussion, and even the outcome of Indian policy. This analysis includes a review of the permanent staff of the India Office, its departments, and the committees of the Council of India involved in the actual daily processing and formulation of Indian policy. It also seeks to identify the complicated legal framework within which the India Office operated. To this end, subsequent chapters deal with the constitutional relationships within the Office between the Secretary of State and the India Council, and between the India Office, the Government of India in Calcutta, Parliament, and other British departments of state. And since "extraconstitutional" groups, such as the Indian and English press, and various lobbies influenced the India Office and India policy, these have also been included.

This book covers parts of ten Indian Secretaryships, Lord Hartington to John Morley, and six viceregal terms, Lords Ripon to Minto. Largely as a result of more frequent communications with India during this period, the India Office played a greater role in the formation of Indian policy than during its first two decades. The specter of the East India Company, which had hovered over the India Office well into the 1870s, and dominated it in terms of procedures and personnel, had disappeared by 1880.[10] The changing internal organization of the India Office in this period enhanced the opportunities of the India Office bureaucracy to assess and create Indian policy. Significantly, many of the structural and procedural changes allowing the India Office to take a more active role in the formulation of Indian policy were effected by one man, Sir Arthur Godley, later Lord Kilbracken, who served as Permanent Undersecretary of State for India between 1883 and 1909.

Educated at Rugby and Balliol, Godley served as one of Gladstone's private secretaries between 1872 and 1874, and again between 1880 and 1882. During that service Godley was "saturated with Gladstonian tradition as to the earnestness in work,"[11] and had carte blanche responsibility in handling the Prime Minister's correspondence.[12] After a brief interlude at Inland Revenue, Godley assumed the Permanent Undersecretaryship at the India Office when only thirty-five years old. He remained at the India Office for twenty-six years, declining Permanent Undersecretaryships at the War Office, Colonial Office, and Foreign Office at home, and the Finance Membership of the Viceroy's Council and the High Commissionership of South Africa abroad.[13] Although he was not a serious contender, Godley was mentioned in Cabinet discussions as a possible candidate for the Viceroyalty in 1893.[14] His long service gave Godley command of the guild secrets of the India Office, and his position as Permanent Undersecretary afforded him many unique opportunities to affect the consideration and formulation of Indian policy.

Arthur Godley's devotion to duty was deeply rooted in his relations with Gladstone and Benjamin Jowett, Master of Balliol. It was duty which precluded Godley from taking any "actor part"[15] in party politics, and Godley felt that his politics were mostly like those of a nonpartisan "Ministerialist."[16] Nothing, however, could have been more desirable in a permanent official, for this allowed Godley to be a trusted adviser to both Liberal and Conservative chiefs in the India Office. It also accorded him great latitude to shape and mold the personnel and operation of the India Office and, consequently, the manner in which Indian policy was made. Godley was one of those late nineteenth-century Permanent Undersecretaries who was "notoriously self-possessed and wielded considerable power."[17] Asquith once described Godley as "the most distinguished Balliol man of his time."[18] He was the ideal "generalist," educated in the classics and inclined to keep things running smoothly. So great was his power that outside the India Office it appeared to knowledgeable politicians and bureaucrats that Godley "ruled India"[19] and was the "real Governor of India under a succession of Viceroys and secretaries."[20]

While it is doubtful that Godley "ruled" India, there can be no question

Introduction							7

that he virtually dominated the India Office for a quarter of a century. As Permanent Undersecretary, Godley made such crucial decisions as ordering a major military expedition in India, and at the same time dealt with such petty tasks as negotiating a charwoman's salary and reviewing designs for map drawers for the Geographical-Records Department. Because he was so integral to the structure of the India Office between 1883 and 1909, Godley's Permanent Undersecretaryship serves, in part, as a unifying theme in analyzing the India Office.

NOTES

1. For current publications on the Colonial Office, see the bibliographical notes in R. C. Snelling and T. J. Baron, "The Colonial Office and its Permanent Officials, 1801–1914," in Gillian Sutherland (ed.), *Studies in the Growth of Nineteenth-Century Government* (London: Routledge & Kegan Paul, 1972), pp. 139–66. For bibliographic material on the Foreign Office, see Zara Steiner, *The Foreign Office and Foreign Policy, 1898–1914* (Cambridge: Cambridge University Press, 1969), and Ray Jones, *The Nineteenth Century Foreign Office: A Study in Administrative History* (London: Weidenfeld and Nicolson, 1971). Recent scholarship on the Treasury is recorded in Henry Roseveare, *The Treasury* (London: Allan Lane, The Penguin Press, 1969) and Maurice Wright, *Treasury Control of the Civil Service* (Oxford: University Press, 1969). The War Office can be studied from W. S. Hamer, *The British Army: Civil-Military Relations 1885–1915* (Oxford: University Press, 1971). G. K. Fry, *Statesmen in Disguise* (London: Macmillan and Co., 1965), contains materials relating to the history of the Civil Service. Jill Pellew's *The Home Office, 1848–1914: From Clerks to Bureaucrats* (London: W. Heinemann, 1982), is a recent addition to the field. Gillian Sutherland's volume of collected essays on administrative history is an important beginning place for new researchers in the field.

2. A well-balanced summary of the debate over the conceptual nature of administrative history is found in Valerie Cromwell, "Interpretations of Nineteenth Century Administration: An Analysis," *Victorian Studies* 9:3 (March 1966), pp. 245–54. Cromwell outlines the basic arguments concerning "administrative growth," beginning with O.O.G.M. MacDonagh's "The Nineteenth Century Revolution in Government: A Reappraisal," *The Historical Journal* 1:1 (1958), pp. 17–34, and Jenifer Hart, "Nineteenth-Century Social Reform: A Tory Interpretation of History," *Past and Present* 31 (1965), pp. 39-61. Cromwell, "Interpretations" and Gillian Sutherland, "Recent Trends in Administrative History," *Victorian Studies* 13:4 (June 1970), pp. 408–11 and Roy M. MacLeod, "Statesmen Undisguised," *American Historical Review* 78:5 (December 1973), pp. 1386–405, contain more bibliography on recent works on administrative history and the conceptual debate.

3. The phrase is attributed to Sir James Stephen. See G. Kitson Clark, "Statesmen in Disguise," *The Historical Journal* 2 (1959), pp. 19–39.

4. See Donovan Williams, *The India Office, 1858–1869* (Hoshiarpur, Punjab: Vishveshvaranand Vedic Research Institute, 1983) and S. A. Husain, "The Organisation and Administration of the India Office, 1910–1924," unpublished Ph.D. thesis, University of London, 1978. Professor Williams has also produced a number of seminal articles while at work on the manuscript of this pioneering effort, among

them "The Council of India and the Relationship between the Home and Indian Governments, 1858–1870," *English Historical Review* 81:318 (January 1966), pp. 70–85, and "The Formation of Policy in the India Office (1858–1869): A Study in the Tyranny of the Past," *Journal of Indian History* (Golden Jubilee Volume) (1973), pp. 873–92.

5. Williams, *The India Office*, pp. xii–xiii.

6. See Williams, "The Tyranny of the Past," *loc. cit.*, and *The India Office*, pp. xi–xx.

7. See H. H. Gerth and C. Wright Mills (eds.), *From Max Weber: Essays in Sociology* (New York: Oxford University Press, 1958), pp. 196–244. For a penetrating analysis of the Indian bureaucracy within the context of various sociological models, see B. B. Misra, *The Bureaucracy in India: An Historical Analysis of Development up to 1947* (Delhi: Oxford University Press, 1977), pp. 1–37.

8. For an overview of the Council's legal functions, see Sir Arthur Godley, *Memorandum on the Home Government of India* [London: The India Office, 1901 (first published 1887)], pp. 12–15.

9. For a comparison of India Office and Colonial Office styles in an earlier period, see Williams, *The India Office*, pp. 455–62.

10. See Williams, *The India Office*, passim.

11. Quoted in A. T. Bassett, *The Life of the Rt. Hon. John Ellis, M.P.* (London: Macmillan and Co., 1914), p. 225.

12. For details of the complex procedures used in handling Gladstone's correspondence, see Lord Kilbracken, *Reminiscences* (London: Macmillan and Co., 1931), pp. 87–88. See also Godley to Ampthill, 12 August 1904, Ampthill Papers, IOL, MSS. Eur. E.233/37.

13. Curzon and Sir Edward Hamilton attributed Godley's refusal to change positions to the fact that for sixteen years the Permanent Undersecretary had had "a considerable voice in determining and controlling the policy of the Government of India, and would not leave his... post, except for something where he would be his own master entirely" (Hamilton to Curzon, 2 June 1899, Curzon Papers [hereafter cited as CP], IOL, MSS, Eur. F.111/158). Mr. Arthur Coleridge, Sir Arthur's grandson, attributes his refusal to shift to the simple fact that his grandfather hated to change *any* routine. (Interview, 1981.)

14. Godley had been "shortlisted" as a candidate for the Viceroyalty by the Cabinet (Gladstone Papers [Cabinet Notes], BL, Add. MSS. 44,648, f. 112). Kimberley, however, felt that Godley was "too bureaucratic" to be a viable candidate for India's Governor-Generalship (quoted in "Lord Kilbracken [Obituary]," *The Times*, 28 June 1932, p. 9). See also H. G. Hutchinson (ed.), *Private Diaries of the Rt. Hon. Sir Algernon West, G.C.B.* (London: John Murray, 1922), pp. 197–98.

15. Godley to W. T. Stead, 29 October 1888, Kilbracken Papers (hereafter cited as KP), IOL, MSS. Eur. F.102/1.

16. Godley to Curzon, 24 February 1899, CP F.111/158.

17. Roy M. Macleod, "Statesman Undisguised," *American Historical Review* 78:5 (December 1973), p. 1405.

18. The Earl of Oxford and Asquith, *Memories and Reflections, 1852–1929* (London: Cassell & Co., 1928), II, 202.

19. Lord Asquith, 25 May 1908, quoted in the Diary of Frederick Arthur Hirtzel,

IOL, Home Miscellaneous Series, No. 864, III, 50. See also O. T. Burne, *Memories* (London: Edward Arnold, 1907), p. 284.

20. Note dated 5 September 1922, cited in Asquith, *Memories and Reflections*, p. 202. See also "Note by Sir Arthur Godley concerning Sir A. McDonnell, February–April, 1905," KP F.102/62.

1

Policy-Making and the Flow of Paper

The multifarious work of the India Office was carried on in a carefully orchestrated manner by the Secretary of State, key permanent officials, the India Office departments and the Council of India. Reflecting on the distinction between the work of the India Office and that of other U.K. departments of state, Lord George Hamilton observed that

the India Office is a miniature Government in itself. There is not a branch of administrative or executive work connected with the big Government which is not represented inside the Office, and the great bulk of questions that come from the Government of India are not trivial or prosaic details of administration, but questions either of importance, or matters upon which there is difference of opinion or controversy, or connected with change or reform.[1]

In the face of such diverse responsibilities, some considered the India Office "intolerably cumbrous and dilatory,"[2] and Lord Kimberley, thrice Indian Secretary in the late nineteenth century, complained that the machinery therein was a "marvel of circumlocution."[3] Yet this great department of state managed to carry on the business of Indian governance without prolonged delays. In the latter nineteenth century this involved processing, evaluating, and generating well over 100,000 documents a year without typewriters or photocopiers. Hence the sheer mechanics of moving the vast and variegated amount of material necessary for the formation of policy was an important feature of the policy-making process. The physical configuration of the India Office, the logistical procedures, and the performance of subordinate personnel also influenced the timing and character of decision making in Whitehall. An even more decisive element in the review and formation of Indian policy in London was the distinctive division of responsibilities among the permanent officials, India Office departments and the Council of India, especially the committees of Council.

The Permanent Undersecretary of State was the linchpin in the daily management of this intricate machine. Because he was required to possess "professional or other peculiar qualifications not ordinarily . . . acquired in the public service," he could be appointed beyond the normal age and without a certificate from the Civil Service Commission.[4] The Permanent Undersecretary's interpretation of his role in the formulation of policy, his attitude toward the Secretary of State and Council of India, and his effectiveness in administering the Office and managing the subordinate staff directly influenced the extent to which the India Office involved itself in policy-making.

Arthur Godley was the fourth Permanent Undersecretary of the India Office and he held the position longer than all his predecessors combined. Sir George Russell Clerk was the first Permanent Undersecretary, and he served only two years before leaving to become Governor of Bombay. The procedures and duties of the fledgling office, which still mirrored those of the East India Company, were just beginning to change when Clerk left for India. This short term of office and Clerk's flamboyant and emotional style, militated against a successful tenure in the yet undefined position. Clerk did, however, return to become a forceful figure on the India Council in 1863.[5] John Herman Merivale succeeded Clerk and came to the India Office with considerable experience as Permanent Undersecretary at the Colonial Office. He arrived in 1860, and served fourteen years until his death in 1874. By and large, the India Office of the 1860s "was heir to a rather free and easy approach to administration," and Merivale "struck a nice balance between the increasing discipline (so necessary for a government office) on the one hand and inherited casualness on the other."[6] Merivale was an intelligent and highly competent administrator. During his tenure the centrality of the Permanent Undersecretaryship was steadily defined. In part this was due to the "kaleidoscopic" nature of the Parliamentary Undersecretaryship and also to the redirection of critical correspondence across his desk.[7]

The India Office's benevolent paternalism changed abruptly when Sir Louis Mallet assumed the Permanent Undersecretaryship in 1874. Mallet, whose name (it has been suggested) was singularly appropriate for the job, "was punctillious in his insistence on a high standard of official duty and etiquette and he practised what he preached."[8] Godley considered that Mallet had "an extraordinary gift of lucid exposition, both on paper and (what is still more uncommon) *viva voce*," and his rule of the India Office was austere and disciplined.[9] The transition from laxness to strict discipline and organization was completed when Arthur Godley assumed the Permanent Undersecretary's chair in 1883.

The transaction of business in the India Office was regulated by a set of rules initially prepared in Stanley's time and completed by Sir Charles Wood, with the aid of his Parliamentary Undersecretary, Thomas Baring, later Lord Northbrook and Viceroy of India, in 1859.[10] The reforms established a new working relationship between the permanent staff, departments and the Council of India in the initiation of despatches. Moreover, they made an important division of departmental responsibility between the Permanent and Parliamentary Undersecretaries of State. Wood's system established the following division of responsibility between the Undersecretaries:[11]

Permanent	Parliamentary
Political and Secret	Financial Matters
Military	Accountant-General
Revenue	Auditor
Judicial	Public Works
Administrator-General	Railway and Telegraph
Record and Statistical	Public Educational
Solicitor	Marine and Transport

The Permanent Undersecretary was also charged with the "general regulation" of the India Office, while the Parliamentary Undersecretary was required to superintend the preparation of Parliamentary Returns. Sir John Kaye, head of the Political and Secret Department of the office, hailed the scheme as a "Magna Charta,"[12] and although a slight modification (largely to accommodate the talents of Thomas Baring) was effected in 1860, a special departmental committee inquiring into India Office procedures reported the plan only slightly altered a quarter century later (1886).[13] Clerk, Merivale, and Mallet essentially divided the office work accordingly with their parliamentary counterparts.[14] This became increasingly more difficult in the late nineteenth century.

In the 1880s and 1890s Godley found the scheme deficient, largely because of the rapid turnover of Parliamentary Undersecretaries (there were eighteen during his tenure). Although he considered the India Office Undersecretaryships "exactly on the same footing and (so to speak) interchangeable," a careful survey of departmental "ladders" or routing slips reveals that Godley assumed primary responsibility for almost every department.[15] In part, the move was necessitated by the short terms of office, averaging one-half year, of the Parliamentary Undersecretaries; but Godley undoubtedly was influenced by the fact that he considered some of his colleagues "perfectly useless" in discharging the work of the office.[16] Of other more qualified colleagues, such as Sir John Gorst (1886–1891), Godley complained that he had "so many irons in the fire that we have not profited much by his abilities."[17] Gorst was upset at being passed over for a Cabinet post and a subordinate at the India Office noted that he "practically decline[d] to do any work . . . saying the position is too ignominious. So everything is left to Mr. Godley."[18] Occasionally a maverick Parliamentary Undersecretary would sympathize with the political opposition, e.g., G.W.E. Russell (1892–1894), on contagious diseases legislation for India. However, few showed either the determination or inclination to do open battle with the Indian Secretary in Parliament or the press.[19] Thus throughout his Permanent Undersecretaryship Godley assumed the major responsibility for reviewing draft materials even if they emanated from departments falling under the Parliamentary Undersecretary's charge. The only concession Godley made to this time-consuming task was the resurrection of the position of Assistant Undersecretary of State (removed from the civil list in 1872) to help supervise general correspondence and personal questions.[20] Horace Walpole, who doubled as Clerk to the Council of India, filled the position of Assistant Undersecretary between 1883 and 1907.

The machinery of India governance was equally complex in India and London. The complicated maze through which even elementary paperwork had to make its way sometimes shocked high Indian officials.[21] When the office was in its infancy, Sir Charles Wood complained about the Stores Department taking five months to report on a bricklaying machine,[22] but in 1885 Kimberley still complained of the "snail's pace" with which departments despatched simple matters.[23] The India Office departments played a central role in the consideration and formation of Indian policy in the late nineteenth century.

In the late nineteenth century there were essentially eight major divisions in India's Home Establishment. There were several technical departments, such as the Funds, Stores, and Auditor's departments. The Accountant-General's Department, in addition to acting as the Indian Empire's "paymaster," was the repository for all personnel matters in the India Office until 1924. The Accountant-General's Establishment Papers include many memoranda by Godley which, because of the constraints of time and the volume of the sources, have been largely unused prior to this work. There were also a number of "Miscellaneous Appointments" in the India Office who worked directly with the Permanent Undersecretary of State: the Librarian, Medical Examiner, Legal Adviser to the Secretary of State, and Surveyors. But two departments had the greatest impact on the ability of the India Office to handle the vast Indian correspondence—the Correspondence and the Registry and Record Departments.

After 1880 there were six separate divisions of the Correspondence Department, called "departments" in their own right: Financial, Judicial and Public, Military, Political and Secret, Public Works and Revenue, Statistics and Commerce. In the initial decades of the India Office, there had been considerable shifting about in the Correspondence Department. Revenue and statistical matters especially were shunted between the Financial and

Records Departments before their eventual grouping with Revenue and Commerce in 1879. The Judicial and Public Departments had once been separate, but were joined in the late 1870s and accorded additional charge of educational and ecclesiastical matters. No new realignments, however, were effected in the late nineteenth century.

The Correspondence Departments were the heart and soul of the India Office. Each was headed by a Secretary, and staffed by one or more Assistant Secretaries (depending on the size of the department) and a series of Senior and Junior Clerks. In the early years of the Office, when the correspondence departments were evolving, work was apparently distributed broadly within the department without regard to rank. By the 1880s, however, higher officials had lost confidence in their subordinate staffs, and one finds a much less universal distribution of work within the departments, with the Department Head or a senior Assistant Secretary usually drafting major despatches. Additionally, the earlier tendency of some clerks and subordinate personnel to specialize in certain subjects was checked in the late nineteenth century, and the scope for individual initiative within the subordinate ranks of the Office was severely circumscribed. This leveling process was due in part to the gradual disappearance of old East India Company hands in the subordinate ranks and also to the partial reconciliation of Lower Division Clerkships in the India Office with Civil Service Commission guidelines for other U.K. departments of state.

Procedurally, the India Office departments were responsible to the Permanent Undersecretary of State. Since Department Heads, or Secretaries, were supposed to complement the work of the India Council and its committees, their appointment was vital. In this sensitive selection process Godley was always concerned with the ratio of "insiders," those without Indian experience, to "outsiders," former Anglo-Indians, serving as Department Heads. Although he continued to recommend qualified candidates from India, Godley thought that the Council of India provided enough Indian experience, and he believed that promoting "insiders" would work to the office's advantage by providing incentives to Office personnel.[24] It was also essential to maintain some balance between the departments and the India Council because of the pivotal role Department Secretaries played in drafting as well as evaluating paperwork.

Initially the preparation of despatches in the India Office was done by the Council of India. While the departments produced preliminary drafts in continuation of the Court of Directors' policy, they simply could not contend with the experienced Councillors with their cumbrous and inefficient system inherited from the East India Company. Moreover, the elevation of the head of the India Office to a "pukka" Secretary of State in the Cabinet made the initiatory powers of the Council both anomalous and dangerous. The reforms initiated by Stanley and formalized under Wood were designed not only to streamline the flow of paper within the India Office, but also to establish the supremacy of the Secretary of State in his own house.

Wood's "Directions" formally assigned a new role to the departments, allowing them to draft despatches to India without submitting them to the Council first. These procedures, however, were not ironclad. Wood encouraged flexibility and considerable consultation took place within the Office between the departments and the India Council. In the early years of the India Office, intradepartmental policies are sometimes difficult to isolate because it is "usually impossible to put a 'chink' in the 'curtain of departmental privacy.'" Most subordinate clerks wrote under the explicit instructions of their Department Heads, with only a few specialists (e.g., C. R. Markham, on chinchona, or J. R. Melville, on political affairs) contributing readily identifiable efforts. Therefore, "one cannot be emphatic about who shaped and who pruned" despatches in the first two decades of the India Office, and it is best to regard the departmental Secretary as the "safest level to . . . dredge for the formulation of policy."[25] Some early departmental Secretaries, such as Sir John Kaye (Political and Secret) and H. L. Anderson (Judicial and Legislative), had served in India, were formidable forces who seized the new initiative with gusto during the 1860s. Others, like E. D. Bourdillon (Public) and Thomas Seccombe (Financial) were successful Department Heads without Indian experience. But all departments began to evolve a kind of "departmental atmosphere" which shaped their relations with the Council of India and the rest of the India Office in conducting Indian business.[26]

Unlike the first decade of the India Office, when it was difficult to identify authorship, in the last quarter of the nineteenth century the authorship of despatch writing became much clearer as the departments continued to exercise the initiative in drafting and assimilating Indian correspondence.For one thing, First and Second Class Correspondence Clerks in the departments were far less involved in drafting correspondence after 1880. Their primary function had become collating and copying materials for the Assistant Secretary and Secretary of their respective departments. They were no longer the carefree coterie who would attend to their business casually, or perhaps use the mantelpieces of their offices for pistol target practice.[27] In the mid-nineteenth century civil servants had been characterized as a "pack of mechanical loafers and shirkers"[28] and had been compared to the fountains in Trafalgar Square which play all day from ten to four.[29] Sometimes clerks were satirized in the press, pictured rejecting coffee "with horror," lest it keep them awake in the afternoon.[30] From the 1880s, however, Lower Division Clerks especially were a much more sober group.

But another reason for the assignment of only routine work to the subordinate Clerks in the Correspondence Departments after 1880 was the result of Godley's lack of confidence in the capacities of the junior men in the India Office. When Godley first arrived at the India Office, Kimberley confided to him his unfavorable opinion of the India Office staff as compared to those of the Foreign and Colonial Offices. "*Between ourselves only*," Kimberley said, "I cannot believe that the India Office Secretaries are harshly worked."[31] After a number of years in office, however, Godley qualified Kimberley's assessment: it was the *junior* men in the Office whose abilities he doubted, for he believed that the only reliable writing was indeed performed by department heads.[32] But the Permanent Undersecretary also doubted the competence of some Department Secretaries. While he acknowledged the expertise of such outstanding Secretaries as Henry Waterfield (Finance), F. C. Danvers (Registry and Record), Juland Danvers (Public Works) and William Lee-Warner (Political), and endorsed the Secretaries' administrative authority in select areas, in fact he personally directed the preparation of almost all important despatches during his tenure. After some time at the helm of the India Office establishment, Godley confessed that

one-third of my time here, at the India Office, is taken up in *seeing* people; mostly the Secretaries (heads of Departments). They are very much in the habit of coming up to speak to me about it, in order to see whether I shall agree with them. I encourage this, because it saves an immense deal of writing and rewriting at a later stage.[33]

If any encouragement for independent action was given to the departments, it was in the area of "demi-official" correspondence. As the need to solicit information grew unabated toward the end of the nineteenth century, some Department Heads began corresponding directly with India, soliciting information to aid in the formation of policy. Although the Council of India objected when some Secretaries began lacing demi-official letters with "official" language,[34] Godley, supported by the Legal Advisor's interpretation of the legality of demi-official correspondence,[35] approved of the practice and requested the Secretary of State to show confidence in such "information only" exchanges.[36] Still, the Permanent Undersecretary felt compelled to peruse many of these technical inquiries in addition to the extraordinary volume of paperwork that already crossed his desk daily. His compulsion to keep in constant contact with the India Office was so great that Godley issued strict regulations with respect to forwarding his mail to him when he left London on holiday.[37]

Godley further demonstrated his faith in the discretion of the Departmental Secretaries in helping to curb the "extra-official" activities of Subordinate Clerks. The Permanent Undersecretary was especially concerned when Clerks publicly aired India Office business, and severely chastised anyone writing for or to the press. Such activity, Godley decreed, had to be sanctioned by the Department Head, and he issued explicit rules that India Office staff were

> not at liberty to write to any newspaper, either in your own name or anonymously, on any subject connected directly or indirectly with India, or to write articles or read papers, or furnish information in any shape or form to the public or any member of the public upon any such subject, without the previous permission of the Under Secretary [or Department Head] in each case.[38]

Despite the relative independence of Departmental Secretaries within their own sections, difficult administrative problems had to be resolved by the Permanent Undersecretary of State. These were as diverse in nature as the India Office itself and problems ranged from handling minute issues like the personal appearance of Subordinate Clerks to more sophisticated situations like the protocol duties of the Political Aide-de-Camp responsible for visiting Indian dignitaries. Often they could be despatched painlessly; or, as in the case of Aides-de-Camp who acted too independently, it took twelve years to sort out.[39] In addition to closely monitoring the operation of the Correspondence Departments, during his tenure Godley actively concerned himself with all of the other India Office units. He routinely reviewed the correspondence of key departments responsible for large expenditures in England and India—the Accountant-General and Stores Departments.[40] But his determination to scrutinize personally huge quantities of paperwork had several ramifications. It involved Godley in the evaluation and formulation of policy to a much greater degree than had ever been imagined in the early days of the Office, and most assuredly more than his contemporaries at the Foreign and Colonial Offices. It also tended to moderate the initiative and independence of the departments, although it did not totally usurp their functions. Finally, it was decidedly wearing physically and emotionally on the Permanent Undersecretary, though this is often difficult to discern in official papers.

By far the most important department for controlling the flow of paper within the office was the Record and Registry Department. In general, the Registry Department had custody of records and parliamentary proceedings, and attended to the registry work and distribution of papers throughout the office. Hence, its efficiency was directly related to the timeliness of policy-making. The Department was formally constituted in 1859, and with only slight modifications during its first two decades, it continued procedures for the receipt and registry of letters used under the East India Company.[41] Individual departments, as well as the Registry, maintained registers of correspondence. The resulting complex system of "double registry," in which some documents were entered while others were not, often led to papers being spread all over the India Office. While there was no accurate means of ascertaining the actual number of documents, both Home and Indian, received prior to 1883, F. C. Danvers, the Superintendent of the Registry and Record Department, estimated that in 1878 a grand total of 81,720 pieces of mail passed through his Department. By 1884 the number of letters received in Registry and Records was 83,384. In 1893, however, the Department logged some 131,165 separate entries—an increase of 57 percent in one decade.[42]

Between 1878 and 1884 Danvers made several modifications aimed at reducing this duplication of effort by departments and the Registry.[43] But the situation was still muddled when Godley arrived in the India Office in 1883. One of Godley's first efforts in the India Office was to accelerate the reorganization of the Registry Department begun by Danvers. One week after taking his post, he sought and obtained approval from the India Council for an enlarged scheme of reorganization, merging the Record and Registry Departments and establishing a sophisticated Central Registry for the India Office. Under this new plan, departments could still maintain separate registers if they desired. But in 1884 the Central Registry was launched with three main branches: Despatch and Copying, Registry, and Record.[44] However the exceptional work of the "Secret" Department of the Political and Secret Department still required it to maintain a separate registry for "external" matters relating to India.

Several key subdivisions of the Registry and Record Department deserve special mention. The Parliamentary Branch—for most of its life part of the Records Department—was responsible for collating information to be used in Parliament and arranging collections of parliamentary materials. It attained special significance in the political culture of late nineteenth-century Britain, and in 1899 Godley redefined the responsibilities of the Parliamentary Branch to include the mechanical preparation and editing of Parliamentary Returns. The Branch was also required to screen all parliamentary questions to make sure nothing on Indian affairs was missing.[45] For the greater part of his service, Godley supervised this operation, which was supposedly the responsibility of the Parliamentary Undersecretary. He personally drafted replies to most parliamentary questions and superintended the preparation of Returns.

The formation of the Parliamentary Branch of the Registry and Record Department was no routine administrative reform. Indeed, it is a clear indication of the political maturity of the India Office and its intention to remain unfettered in the formation of Indian policy. The work of the Branch was directly related to the desire by the India Office to minimize parliamentary discussion of Indian affairs. In the late nineteenth century, agitation over placing the Secretary of State's salary on the British estimates, the clamor for periodic parliamentary reviews of Indian affairs, and even the highly publicized independent travels of Members of Parliament in India (e.g., George Curzon and Keir Hardie), gave Godley and other India Office officials a "wholesome dread of the interference of the House of Commons."[46] Acknowledging that Parliament had the technical wherewithal to scrutinize every detail of India Office procedure, Godley explained how the India Office coped with that situation when he wrote to Curzon:

You [Curzon] are wrong in thinking the authority of the H[ouse] of Commons over India matters has declined. Not a bit of it. When they are in earnest, they are the absolute masters of the situation.... True the H[ouse] of Commons has not often interfered of late years, but why? *Mainly because pains have been taken to keep a finger on their pulse, and to avoid doing anything that could excite them. On this subject I claim to speak with some knowledge.* [Italics added.][47]

In fact, the lobbying efforts of groups such as the British Committee of the Indian National Congress and the Indian Parliamentary Committee, upon which the India Office cast its watchful eye, were rarely effective. They lacked political cohesiveness and adequate funding, and were much too preoccupied with the problems of the Indian National Congress to mount the kind of dangerous parliamentary debate on India feared by India Office officials. Even so, the work of the Parliamentary Branch, and the great care exercised by the India Office in editing sensitive materials from Parliamentary Blue Books, made it easier to control the flow of information to the House of Commons and avoid controversial issues.[48]

Confidential printing in the India Office was also closely connected with the Registry and Record Department, and because of the peculiar arrangement of having to contract for "outside" help, it was one of the few areas really beyond the jurisdiction of the Secretary of State or his Permanent Undersecretary. The India Office printing section was housed in the basement of the building. This was a unique feature in Whitehall, and enabled the India Office to obtain quick and efficient copies of minutes and other important papers. Confidential documents under 150 pages in length were printed in the India Office, while longer papers were sent to the main offices of Messrs. Eyre and Spottiswoode who technically employed the printers until 1919.[49] The Head Printer retained copies of all work for one year for inspection purposes. Godley always seemed uneasy with this arrangement because confidentiality depended on the trustworthiness of the Head Printer.[50] But any potentially tense situation was avoided since for much of the late nineteenth century the Head Printer, a "Mr. Knott," was "a character efficient and cheerful, with strong religious principles. On his desk he kept before him a card with the inscription 'One man and God are always a majority.' "[51]

Finally, the work of Registry and Record Department and the Correspondence Departments as a whole was greatly improved by the introduction of the typewriter into the India Office in 1889. "Female manipulators," at seventeen to twenty-three shillings per week, could accommodate far more work than a larger number of more expensive male copyists.[52] During the early years of the typing section, because the employment of women was such a novelty, "many precautions were taken for the security of the lady...typists" and they led a "cloistered life."[53] The lady staffers were housed in "a small room at the top of the building, the door to which was normally locked, all work in and out going through a small hatch in the door."[54]

The complexities of the India Office departments were recognized by Secretaries of State. When John Morley left the Indian Secretaryship in 1910, he wrote to the Heads of Departments:

The complexity of the system of Indian government set up by Parliament in 1858, the dual spheres of administration and authority, the difficulties of the questions, the distance of the scene, the vast magnitude of the interests, all make a daily and almost hourly demand upon the varied capacity and resources of the India Office, which can only be realised by us who have worked in it through arduous times. No other department of State surpasses it in weight of responsibility; perhaps no other equals it. May I add that this feeling of mine is by no means limited to the higher officials among you. I do not forget those minor members of your establishment with whom my duties did not bring me into personal contact, yet with whose promptitude, readiness, and fidelity, in such unostentatious, but highly important work, as the custody of the registers, for instance, the accounting and all the rest of the detail unseen by the Secretary of State, I am well acquainted, and to whom I well know that my debt is heavy.[55]

Morley was correct in acknowledging the importance of the lesser ranks of the India Office to the smooth functioning of the unit. The subordinate staff shouldered a great burden because an effective system of locating and distributing papers by hand was essential to ensure that paperwork was efficiently handled. This was particularly complicated because the extensive network of offices and departments—almost 3 1/2 million cubic feet—filled three floors in its half of Whitehall (the Foreign Office occupied the other half).[56] In its first decade the India Office had been housed in the East India House, former headquarters of the East India Company, and then the Westminster Palace Hotel before ultimately being situated in the new Whitehall complex in 1867.[57] The new offices were spacious enough at first, but by the seventies overcrowding was apparent. By the 1880s the logistics of moving critical paperwork to its proper destination, and thus facilitating the timely disposition of paperwork, was considerably more complex. It required a large, highly regimented subordinate and supportive staff. Hence the physical arrangement of the India Office itself was unwittingly a large part of the relationship between policy and paperwork.

When Arthur Godley joined the India Office in 1883, he at once recognized the need to develop well-defined guidelines for the subordinate staff responsible for the distribution of paperwork within the office. Not only was the establishment growing and the Office becoming increasingly crowded, but the volume of work had increased dramatically during the last quarter of the nineteenth century. Godley could not help noticing the strain on interoffice communication carried on through a series of insufficient interconnecting "speaking tubes" (which continued in use even when superseded by the introduction of the telephone throughout all Whitehall offices in 1895) and an overstrained messenger system.[58] To rectify this situation, Godley "set himself to mould the comparatively juvenile office, to reform and simplify its procedure, and to establish its efficiency on a firm basis." His success is measured by a contemporary's observation that "it is not too much to say that the India Office . . . was largely his [Godley's] creation."[59]

Among the subordinate staff, both day and night messengers had designated stations and physical areas of responsibility.[60] Night messengers, for example, in return for free room and board, had to be on duty from 8:30 P.M. until the next morning to receive incoming telegrams and other messages. When these duties ended, the messengers would then "have to under the order of the office keepers during weekdays . . . sweep passages [and] wheel trucks of coal about" until 2:30 in the afternoon, when they could be free.[61] Messengers were usually appointed on the recommendations of Members of Council or other influential personalities. A contemporary described them as being

an odd lot; one of them, with a large family constantly grumbled at the inadequacy of his pay; another, pompous and ponderous, looked the ideal butler he had been aforetime. Those more fortunate sometimes supplemented their pay by serving at palace functions, when additional waiters were needed.[62]

Hall porters were assigned to monitor the movement of paper in the India Office. Prior to Godley's appointment, security procedures within the office were somewhat relaxed. Soon after Godley became Permanent Undersecretary, Kimberley issued a caveat to his new aide that it would be "well to remember that in everything we do or say that the India Office is *very leaky*."[63] After strictly regulating the allocation of keys to office personnel, Godley took steps to reduce the possibility of leaks and eliminate unsolicited visitations to the India Office by outsiders.[64] Hall porters were ordered to question, and if necessary, detain anyone entering the India Office until the nature of his business had been ascertained. If unsatisfied with either the "answer or demeanour" of the visitor, hall porters were to arrange for messengers to act as escorts throughout the India Office building.[65]

The work of Resident Clerks—whose responsibility was to receive and process despatches, telegrams, and incoming messages for the Correspondence Department, Undersecretaries, and Secretary of State—preoccupied Godley's attention immediately after he assumed office. Resident Clerks were usually appointed from the ranks of the junior Clerks in the Correspondence Department, with an occasional three-year appointment going to a senior Clerk in that service.[66] Responding to Kimberley's complaints about insufficient information regarding the receipt and despatch of telegrams, and the general unavailability of Resident Clerks, Godley issued a set of "Rules" in 1884 (which remained in effect through World War II) which codified the information to be provided on all telegrams, and strictly regulated the Resident Clerks' availability so essential to the proper flow of paper.[67] Godley's efficient office management did much to eliminate unnecessary delays in channeling paperwork to its proper destination; but even his stringent regulations gave way to an occasional adventuresome Resident Clerk, such as William Robinson, who, in 1894, "used to roller skate through the corridor of the India Office until prohibited."[68]

The general demeanor of India Office Clerks changed markedly in the last few decades of the nineteenth century. By far the most famous description of the clerks in the early days is attributed to Charles Lamb:[69]

> From ten to eleven
> Eat breakfast for Seven,
> From eleven to noon
> Think I'd come too soon;
> From noon till one
> Think what's to be done;
> From one to two
> Find nothing to do.
> From two to three
> Think it'll be
> A very great bore
> To stay till four.

Such slackness was not widespread when Godley arrived at the India Office; it is certain that none was evident when he retired twenty-six years later. One contemporary account of Godley portrays him as rather a tyrant to the subordinate levels of the India Office, extending the working hours from 10–4 to 10–5 daily and eliminating the staff's cherished Derby Day holiday. The luncheon room and kitchen of the India Office were also relocated from a lower to a higher floor, reportedly because the "nostrils of the Undersecretary of State were offended by the smell of cooking that pervaded the building."[70] But what the clerks at the India Office did not know, was just how much Godley sought to improve working conditions within the office. The India Office, at Godley's behest, was among the first Whitehall departments to switch from gas to electric lighting in order to relieve eyestrain among the many clerks and copyists.[71] The extension of working hours was not Godley's decision, but rather an attempt to bring India Office regulations into line with the recommendations of the Royal

(Ridley) Commission on the Civil Service and newly adopted Treasury pay scales.[72] Godley also negotiated with the Treasury for a reconciliation of the India Office's Second Class Clerks' salaries to a level on par with those of Second Division Clerks in the rest of the Civil Service.[73] (See Comparative Table of Salaries of Civil Establishment Clerks.)

The clerical staff of the India Office was divided into two groups, Upper Division Clerks (Senior and Junior) and Lower Division Clerks—the latter being called "Second Class Clerks" within the Office under an agreement with the Treasury.[74] When Godley arrived at the India Office, clerical salaries were well below those of other departments. In an effort to remain competitive with the other departments of state, Godley convinced the Secretary of State (Kimberley) to gradually increase India Office beginning salaries.[75]

Godley's efforts paid immediate dividends. When the Ridley Commission began its lengthy investigation of the Civil Service, Sir Reginald Welby, Godley's counterpart at the Treasury, attempted to compel the India Office to come into line on the reclassification of Second Class Clerks. By that time, however, such an action would have required the *reduction* of salaries. After all, Godley argued, "by giving them a somewhat more agreeable title [and] by giving them a slightly better salary we have invariably attracted the pick of the lot."[76]

Treasury control of the Civil Service has been the subject of several recent studies, but none has included the India Office in its discussion.[77] This is largely because the India Office was not subject to the usual Treasury "suggestions" on finance and budgetary matters as were other departments of state—that was a power reserved for Parliament, which rarely concerned itself with the accounts of office expenditure. The India Office also struggled vigorously to retain that independence at all costs, and generally succeeded until after World War I when the salary of the Secretary of State and certain establishment costs were absorbed by the Treasury through the estimates presented annually to Parliament.[78] In 1937 the remaining establishment costs were absorbed by the Treasury. The Office could muster impressive legal rhetoric in keeping the Treasury at arms' length, and when the Ridley Commission considered including the India Office in its review of Civil Service establishments, Godley and the then Secretary of State, Lord Cross, successfully argued that it was inappropriate given the statutory obligation of Parliament to supervise Indian expenses, including the India Office establishment.[79]

On another occasion, when the Treasury suggested that the power of promotions with the India Office be regulated by the Civil Service Commission and the Treasury, the Permanent Undersecretary of the India Office vehemently objected. He successfully argued that the internal management of the India Office was reserved for the Secretary of State for India alone under the provisions of the Government of India Act, 1858

Comparative Table of Salaries of Civil Establishment Clerks

	Initial Salary	Annual Increment	Maximum	Initial Salary	Annual Increment	Maximum	Initial Salary	Annual Increment	Maximum
	Class I Clerks			*Class II Clerks*			*Class III Clerks*		
Treasury	£1000	£50	£1200	£700	£25	£900	£250	£20	£600
Admiralty	900	50	1000	700	25	800	200	20	600
Home Office	900	50	1000	700	25	800	200	20	600
Colonial Office	900	50	1000	700	25	800	250	20	600
INDIA OFFICE	700	25	900	500	20	700	100	15	400
Foreign Office	900	50	1000	700	25	800	200	20	600
War Office	700	25	900	450	20	650	150	15	400

(ss. 3, 16).⁸⁰ But in 1891, after considerable tension and ill feeling had developed between the India Office and the Treasury and Civil Service Commission, the India Office agreed to draw its Second Class Clerks from the Lower Division lists of the Civil Service Commission. These Clerks could not, however, transfer to any other office. This prohibition (along with the different nomenclature) was designed to emphasize subordination to the Secretary of State for India. Godley informed the Civil Service Commission that *it* would have to impress upon any aspiring India Office appointees that "the man who takes it [an India Office position] will thenceforward become an India Office man [and] must live [and] die here."⁸¹

Salary and working hours for new junior Second Class Clerks were finally aligned with the Civil Service Commission's new guidelines in 1891.⁸² Henceforth, there was no further intrusion by the Treasury or Civil Service Commission into the internal operation of the India Office until the 1920s, and the new "Ridley Men" in the Office appealed in vain for equal promotion opportunities (comparable to other departments) as outlined in the Ridley report.⁸³ The entire promotion problem was thus left to the Secretary of State, who delegated it to Godley. The Permanent Undersecretary found the task so disagreeable that he felt an additional £1000 a year merely for that position "would be very moderate compensation."⁸⁴ Nevertheless, Godley accepted the delegated responsibility and strongly opposed both Treasury and Council of India involvement in the matter.⁸⁵ Internally, Godley specified that Clerks had to secure the recommendations of Department Heads before seeking promotion, and any deviation from the proper appellate process was regarded with extreme disfavor. As a rule, promotion was made "upon meritorious work alone,"⁸⁶ and confined to one's own division.⁸⁷

By and large, the India Office maintained cordial relations with the Civil Service Commission, especially in the examination and certification of Indian Civil Service candidates. Relations with the Treasury, however, were far less amicable. In 1892, when Gladstone suggested adding a Treasury representative to the India Council, Godley quickly protested that to do so required an act of Parliament, and this seemed to be a "serious objection," though perhaps not a fatal one.⁸⁸ The plan was eventually scrapped. In 1899 the Treasury again sought to impose its control over India Office expenditure. This implied increased parliamentary control. The move was successfully repelled, but the India Office strongly resented the attempt by the Welby Commission to use both Government of India and Indian National Congress witnesses in their abortive effort to wrest power from it.⁸⁹

The flow of paper and the formation of policy in the India Office were also intimately related to the Council of India's duty to "conduct" Indian business transacted in the United Kingdom.⁹⁰ Because of this fact, the Council had an opportunity to play a key role in the formulation of Indian policy. The Council represented a curious extension of "India in England,"

and the attitudes and behavior of its members, combined with its extraordinary legal powers, made the Council of India unique among the *gouverneurs* of the colonial empire.[91] While this was not always a positive factor, it was nevertheless an important feature of Indian policy-making processes that generally has been ignored or passed over. Hence the statutory relationship between the Secretary of State and his Council, the Council's committee system, and the working relationship between the Council and India Office departments are essential to understanding the way in which India was governed in the late nineteenth century.

NOTES

1. Lord George Hamilton, *Parliamentary Reminiscences and Reflections, 1868–1885* (London: John Murray, 1917), I, 68.
2. Quoted in Sir Malcolm Seton, *The India Office* (London: G. P. Putnam's Sons, 1926), p. 33.
3. Kimberley to Gladstone, 19 January 1893, Gladstone Papers, BL, Add. MSS. 44,229.
4. L. Abrahams, "Memorandum on the Financial Organisation and Procedure of the India Office," G.B., Parliament, *Royal Commission on Indian Finance and Currency*, Cd. 7238 (1914), XX, [Appendix XXXIV, p. 1019].
5. For more on Sir George Clerk's career as an Indian administrator, see Donovan Williams, *The India Office, 1858–1869* (Hoshiarpur, Punjab: Vishveshvaranand Vedic Research Institute, 1983), *passim*, (especially pp. 108–28).
6. Donovan Williams, "The Tyranny of the Past: The India Office, 1858–1870," unpublished paper delivered to ASPAC Conference, San Diego, 1974, p. 11.
7. Williams, *The India Office*, p. 120.
8. Bernard Mallet, *Sir Louis Mallet* (London: James Nisbet & Co., 1905), p. 39.
9. *Ibid.*, p. 40. For more on Mallet's activities as Permanent Undersecretary, see Edward Moulton, *Lord Northbrook's Indian Administration 1872–1876* (Bombay: Asia Publishing House, 1968), pp. 195–202, and Williams, *The India Office*, pp. 108–28.
10. Memorandum by Sir Charles Wood, "Directions for the Transaction of Business in the India Office," 17 November 1859, L/PO/Misc. 5. This document is reprinted as Appendix E in Williams, *The India Office*, pp. 571–75.
11. Wood, "Directions," p. 2, L/PO/Misc. 5.
12. Sir John Kaye to H. Merivale, 17 January 1874, IOR [unclassified],Sir John Kaye's Confidential Letter Book, p. 84.
13. "First Report of the Special Committee on India Office Procedure" [hereafter cited as "First Report"], 9 February 1886, L/PO/Misc. 5.
14. Lord George Hamilton, while Parliamentary Undersecretary, described the "voluminous" variety of "inordinately long minutes in which the Indian Official mind revels," and with which the India Office had to cope. He also noted that "Sir Louis Mallet and I made a division of the work to be done, he giving me my full share" (Hamilton, *Parliamentary Reminiscences and Reflections*,I, 69).

15. Godley to C. Ilbert, 19 February 1900, Elgin Papers (9th Earl of Elgin) [hereafter cited as EP], IOL, MSS. Eur. F.84/2.

16. Lord Kilbracken, *Reminiscences* (London: Macmillan and Co., 1931), p. 185.

17. Godley to Lansdowne, 9 June 1891, Lansdowne Papers [hereafter cited as LP], IOL, MSS. Eur. D.558/13. See also Godley to D. Mackenzie Wallace, 13 August 1886, Dufferin Papers [hereafter cited as DP], IOL, MSS. Eur. F.130/24b.

18. Ritchmond Ritchie, quoted in Mrs. R. Strachey to R. Strachey, 30 January 1890, Strachey Papers [hereafter cited as RSP], IOL, MSS. Eur. F.127/Box marked "Volumes 18–20." Gorst also caused problems for Cross and Salisbury by criticizing Lansdowne's Government for their handling of the Manipur crisis (Lord Newton, *Lord Lansdowne: A Biography* [London: Macmillan and Co., 1929], pp. 62–63); and Godley to Lansdowne, 26 June 1891, LP D.558/13.

19. Russell to Lansdowne, 24 October 1892, LP D.558/14. See also Arnold P. Kaminsky, "Morality Legislation and British Troops in Late Nineteenth Century India," *Military Affairs* (April 1979), pp. 78–83.

20. "Sixth Report of the Special Committee on Home Charges," 9 November 1888, L/F/9/1. Godley received much help throughout his tenure from Horace Walpole (Assistant Undersecretary, 1883–1907), whose appointment Godley had taken great pains to secure (Godley to J. Danvers, 27 November 1883, Kilbracken Papers [hereafter cited as KP], IOL, MSS. Eur. F.102/3). There were, however, a few brief interludes (c. 1872–1880) during which various retired Department Secretaries or Private Secretaries to the Secretary of State assisted the Undersecretaries.

21. Ampthill to Godley, 1 November 1905, KP F.102/39.

22. Williams, *The India Office*, p. 78.

23. Kimberley to Godley, 20 May 1885, KP F.102/3.

24. In 1902, the ratio of ex-Indians to "insiders" was 5:2; Godley felt that the proper ratio was really just the opposite (2:5) [Godley to Curzon, 22 April 1902, Curzon Papers (hereafter cited as CP), IOL, MSS. Eur. F.111/161]. No more perfect example of the dissension among "insiders" over choice appointments going to Anglo-Indians exists than the appointment of Sir William Lee-Warner to head the IO Political Department over the Assistant Secretary, Edmund Neel—who had run the department for several years. Neel took the Public Works Secretaryship as a second choice—but thereafter, Political Secretaries were selected from the India Office ranks (H. W. Garrett Collection, IOL, MSS. Eur. D.515/1, p. 9).

25. Donovan Williams, "The Formation of Policy in the India Office, 1858–66, with special reference to the Political, Judicial, Revenue, Public and Public Works Departments," unpublished D. Phil. thesis, Oxford, 1962, p. 375. See also, Williams, *The India Office*, p. 83. Williams is the first to point out the integral relationship between Stanley's efforts and Wood's reforms.

26. Williams, *The India Office*, p. 83ff.

27. Sir William Foster, *The East India House. Its History and Associations* (London: Lane, 1924), p. 234.

28. Morley to Minto, 7 October 1909, Morley Papers [hereafter cited as MRP], IOL, MSS. Eur. D.573/4.

29. Quoted in Algernon West, *Contemporary Portraits* (London: T. Fisher Unwin, 1920), p. 23.

30. *Ibid.*, p. 24.

31. Kimberley to Godley, 3 October 1883, KP F.102/3A.
32. Godley to Curzon, 13 February 1899, CP F.111/158.
33. Godley to Curzon, 16 June 1899, *ibid*.
34. See Sir William Lee-Warner, Political & Secret Department Letters from India [IOR, L/P&S/7/91/#467/1897], quoted in Martin Moir, "A Study of the History and Organisation of the Political and Secret Departments of the East India Company, the Board of Control and India Office, 1784–1919, with a summary list of records," unpublished thesis (archival administration), University of London, 1966, pp. 123–26. See also minute by Lee-Warner, 7 March 1898, IOR, Unclassified Political & Secret Department Memoranda Book I (1875–99), p. 350.
35. Minute by Charles Pontifex, 11 October 1887, IOR, Records Department, L/R&L/6/169/#669/1888, filed with #183/1897.
36. Godley to Cross, 26 October 1887, *ibid*.
37. See Godley's "Memorandum on Forwarding Mail," 11 July 1898, L/AG/30/27/34.
38. Godley to C.E.D. Black, 31 October 1888, KP F.102/1. See also related correspondence, Godley to Black, 19 May 1886, and Godley to Sir C. Bernard, 5 December 1894, *ibid*. For an associated ruling on extra-official employment as journalists outside the India Office, see Godley to Kimberley, 17 December 1883, memorandum on "Extra-Official Employment of India Office Personnel," (L/PO/Misc. 3). The problem reached its apogee when the outside activities of Black, acting as a subeditor of *The Times*, angered Godley enough for the Permanent Undersecretary to demand he resign one job or the other (L/AG/30/20/23, pp. 13–89; and L/AG/30/22/26, pp. 429–43 and 803–23).
39. Godley to Kimberley, 14 February 1884, Kimberley Papers [hereafter cited as KMP], private ownership, D/5. See also Moir, "Political and Secret Departments," p. 136.
40. For further clarification of departmental responsibility (including Correspondence Departments) as operable prior to World War I, see "Memorandum on India Office Administration," March 1919, L/PO/Misc. 5. Additionally from 1860 (memorandum by Merivale, 31 July 1860, IOR, Papers and Orders relating to the Registry and Records Department, L/R/5/2), the Accountant-General handled Home Establishment matters until the creation of the Services and General Department in 1924 (Joan C. Lancaster, "The India Office Records," *Archives* 9:43 [April 1970], pp. 130–41).
41. For an account of Registry procedures between 1858 and 1870, see Williams, "The Formation of Policy," pp. 40–50.
42. F. C. Danvers, "Statistics on Official Correspondence [Appendix]," "First Report," L/PO/Misc. 5; see also "16th Report of the special committee on Home Charges," L/F/9/1.
43. F. C. Danvers, "Memorandum of a Central Registry Department for the India Office," 30 March 1878, L/R/5/1, pp. 19–23; and "Recommendations of Special Committee," 5 July 1878, with Danvers, "Report on the Departmental Staff of the Record and Registry Department," L/R/5/3, pp. 78–105.
44. In 1885 the Map Department and Geographical Section of the India Office were transferred from the Revenue and Statistics Department to the Registry and Record Department (Godley to Lord Randolph Churchill, 15 August 1885, L/R/5/2, pp. 391–95). Oddly enough, the development of the Geographical Section of

the Office was due primarily to the efforts of Markham and C.E.D. Black, both of whom proved to be the source of endless exasperation for the Undersecretary of State. For background on the development of the Geographical Department, see Donovan Williams, "Clements Robert Markham and the Geographical Department of the India Office, 1867–77," *The Geographical Journal* 134:3 (September 1968), pp. 343–52.

45. Memorandum dated 6 February 1899, P&S Department Memoranda Book, p. 378.

46. Godley to Sir Henry Erle Richards, 1 July 1904, Richards Papers, IOL, MSS. Eur. F.102/3a.

47. Godley to Curzon, 26 February 1904, KP F.102/60.

48. For an extensive discussion of the British Committee of Congress and Indian Parliamentary Committee, see Margaret Duley Morrow, "The Origins and Early Years of the British Committee of the Indian National Congress, 1885–1907," unpublished Ph.D. thesis, University of London, 1977.

49. Godley to Kimberley, 22 October 1884, KP F.102/3. Kimberley was unhappy with the arrangement, but Godley concluded that if the contract—which allowed the IO more efficiency than other Whitehall offices—was to be used, "we have no choice but to give them our confidence unreservedly" (*ibid.*).

50. Godley to Hamilton, 14 June 1900, L/AG/31/22/32, p. 773.

51. Garrett Collection, D.515/1, p. 13.

52. F. C. Danvers to Godley, "Memorandum on Lady Type-writers and the Seven Hours Question," 6 July 1888, L/R/5/4, pp. 260–67. Also, hectography was used in the India Office until well after World War I. The process involved duplicating letters by placing a freshly typed letter, with a special "wet" ink, on a glycerin gel; this allowed copies to be made from the raised type, and was an extremely messy job. As to the type of machine used in the Office, Garrett recorded that Hammonds were used first, but S. J. McNally disagreed, arguing that Remingtons were used (S. J. McNally [Note on the Garrett Collection], IOL, MSS. Eur. D.515/2). Garrett, however, was right. Only in 1891, after visiting the War Office and seeing that Remingtons could make up to ten copies at a time, did Danvers move to purchase four Remingtons. The Hammonds were kept for hectography (F. C. Danvers to Godley, "Report on the system [typewriting] used in the War Office," 23 July 1891, L/AG/30/22/22, pp. 641–45.

53. Garrett Collection, D.515/1, p. 1.

54. S. J. McNally, "The India Office As I Knew It," IOL, MSS. Eur. D.801, pp. 39–40.

55. Morley to Heads of Departments, 7 November 1910, L/PO/Misc. 2.

56. The original architect's plan showing the relative position of rooms and messengers' stations (November 1867) is preserved in IOR, Accountant-General's Department L/AG/9/8/3 (vol. II), p. 400. For an overview of annual operating expenses of the India Office, see "16th Report of the Special Committee on Home Charges," 1 June 1893, IOR, Finance Department, L/F/9/1. Photographs of these plans are found in Williams, *The India Office*, p. 320.

57. For a discussion of the debate over the design of the new Whitehall offices, including the India Office, see Williams, *The India Office*, pp. 129–48.

58. See Arthur Hazlewood, "The Origin of the State Telephone Service in Britain," *Oxford Economic Papers*, Ser. 2, 5:1 (March 1953), pp. 13–25.

Policy-Making and the Flow of Paper   31

59. Quoted in Eveline C. Godley, "Arthur Godley," *Dictionary of National Biography (1931–40)* [London: Oxford University Press, 1940], p. 345.

60. See note 56, *supra*.

61. Godley to Hambrook, 4 February 1884, KP F.102/1.

62. Garrett Collection, D.515/1, p. 9. From 1902 requirements for messenger candidates were assimilated to those of other U.K. departments, thereby reducing patronage (L/AG/30/22/34, p. 379 and L/AG/30/22/35, p. 273). In order to reduce patronage even further, the India Office began using ex-Indian Army and Navy officers as messengers (L/AG/30/22/41, p. xiv).

63. Kimberley to Godley, 16 October 1883, KP F.102/3.

64. In 1902 the number of keys provided by Messrs. Chubb was fixed at eighty-five. Each key bore an imprint offering a "5s. reward" for its return to the India Office if lost, payable by the offending official (IOR, R&L, #566/1902, filed with Private Office [Miscellaneous Home Establishment Papers], L/PO/Misc. 3).

65. Godley also instructed hall porters to inspect all parcels carried into the India Office (memorandum by Arthur Godley, 7 April 1884, L/AG/30/27, p. 2).

66. For a detailed account of the rules and regulations regarding the appointment of Resident Clerks, see L/AG/22/41, p. xviii.

67. See Kimberley to Godley, 26 and 27 July 1884, KP F.102/3. For "Rules to Be Observed by the Resident Clerk," see Godley to Colvin, 6 August 1884, KP F.102/1.

68. Garrett Collection, D.515/1, p. 15.

69. Quoted in Algernon West, *Contemporary Portraits* (London: T. Fisher Unwin, 1920), p. 23. Garrett, however, offered a slightly adulterated version of the verse in his memoir on India Office life in the 1880s (Garrett Collection, D.515/1, p. 8).

70. Garrett Collection, D.515/1, p. 5. There seems to be an error in Garrett's recollection of events. According to Mr. S. J. McNally, Garrett's account was probably written after he left the India Office, and his memory was understandably vague. Regulations relating to official leaves (1909) show that Derby Day was still included as a day off for all eligible clerks, save for the typing pool, hectographers, and boy messengers. I am indebted to Mr. McNally, who joined the India Office staff in 1922 (rising to Assistant Accountant-General), for his kind assistance in sorting out the unused records of the Accountant-General's Department.

71. The Colonial and Foreign Offices had electric lights installed in 1895 (R. V. Kubicek, *The Administration of Imperialism: Joseph Chamberlain at the Colonial Office* [Durham, N.C.: Duke University Press, 1969], p. 14). As early as 1888 Godley made preliminary inquiries regarding the installation of lights in the India Office (Godley to Maitland, 16[?] February 1888, L/PO/Misc. 5). India Office departments, however, continued to use gas burners until the turn of the twentieth century and utilized candles during heavy fog (Garrett Collection, D.515/1, p. 1).

72. Great Britain, Parliament, *Report of the Royal Commission on Civil Establishments*: C. 5226 (1887), XIX; C. 5545 (1888), XXVII: C. 5748 (1889), XXI, C. 5748–1 (1889), XXI: C. 6172 (1890), XXVII; C. 6172–1 (1890), XXVII.

73. The rules governing the recruitment of Upper and Lower Division Clerks by open competition were established by the Order in Council, 4 June 1870. The extension of working hours by the India Office to reconcile itself with other U.K.

departments was approved by the India Office, 2 June 1891 (IOR, Unclassified Political and Secret Department Memoranda Book, p. 226).

74. For a summation of the various classes of civil servants, see Henry Roseveare, *The Treasury* (London: Allen Lane, The Penguin Press, 1969), pp. 210–16. For subsequent regulations regarding the recruitment and classification of India Office Clerks, see L/AG/30/22, Vols. 22, 28, 33, 34 and 35.

75. Godley charted the comparative starting salaries for other offices, emphasizing that candidates for the Civil Service chose their Office in order of merit, and that being the case, it appeared to him "absolutely necessary to make some changes in the direction which has already been taken by the other public offices, unless we are to be content with an inferior class of clerk for precisely similar work" (minute by A. Godley on the "Reorganisation of the Correspondence Department," L/AG/30/22/15, p. 615). The gaps in Godley's chart have been filled with statistics gleaned from the following Ridley Commission Reports: C. 5226 (1887), vol. XIX [Appendix, p. 429]; C. 5545 (1888), vol. XXVII [Appendix, p. 445]; C. 6172 (1890), vol. XXVII [Appendix, p. 173].

76. Godley to R. Welby, 28 November 1887, KP F.102/1. The special status of India Office Clerks evoked considerable discontent among Treasury Clerks; but Godley was unbending in his conviction that they be called "Second-Class Clerks" and the terminology remained in effect until after his retirement in 1909.

77. Roseveare, *The Treasury, passim.* See also Maurice Wright, *Treasury Control of the Civil Service, 1854–1874* (Oxford: Oxford University Press, 1969). For a more recent analysis of the Treasury's relations with other departments of state, see Maurice Wright, "Treasury Control, 1854–1914," in Gillian Sutherland (ed.), *Studies in the Growth of Nineteenth-Century Government* (London: Routledge & Kegan Paul, 1972), pp. 195–226.

78. For a summary of changes in the financial scheme of the India Office, see S. A. Husain, "The Organisation and Administration of India Office, 1910–1924," Ph.D. thesis, University of London, 1978, pp. 140–53.

79. Godley to Cross, 23 September 1886, KP F.102/1.

80. See file on India Office-Civil Service Commission negotiations on the Indian Civil Service, L/PO/Misc. 4.

81. Godley to W. Courthope, 27 April 1891, KP F.102/1.

82. Minute approved in Council, 2 June 1891.

83. See minute on "Second Class Clerks Scheme," L/AG/30/22/22, pp. 383–597. See also memorials by Second Class Clerks to Godley, L/AG/30/22/40, pp. 337–93.

84. Godley to C. Pontifex, 11 April 1890, KP F.102/1.

85. Kimberley to Godley, 14 October 1883, KP F.102/3. Godley also opposed Sir Louis Mallet's idea about the participation of the Council of India in India Office promotions. Godley felt that "it must lead to the Clerks looking to the Councillors instead of to their proper heads for promotion" (*ibid.*). In 1920 the India Office conformed, in part, to the recommendations of the Whitley Committee, 1917–18, to move grievances outside the India Office. See Husain, "The India Office, 1910–1924," pp. 146–47.

86. Godley to A. Hill, 20 February 1885, KP F.102/1. For a clarification of "due process" on India Office appeals, see Godley to P. Johnstone, 26 January 1885,

ibid.; and two letters from Godley to C.E.D. Black [Head of the Geographical Department], 21 July 1885 and 24 May 1886, *ibid.*

87. After the Treasury adopted the Ridley Commission's recommendations that Lower Division Clerks be allowed to move to the Upper Division Clerkships on a modified seniority basis, the India Office Second Class Clerks memorialized Godley, claiming that they would "be placed in a worse position" than the Lower Division Clerks in the Imperial Service. Godley rejected their pleas, arguing that the Secretary of State for India was not subject to outside rules regarding internal promotions (L/AG/36/22/24, pp. 1429–38).

88. Godley to Kimberley, 6 September 1892, filed with Kimberley to Gladstone, 10 September 1892, Gladstone Papers, BL, Add. MSS. 44,229. In his cover note Kimberley went further than Godley in noting that "the necessity for an Act of Parliament is a fatal objection."

89. Godley to Welby, 20 July 1899, KP F.102/1. See also Godley to Welby, 24 July 1899, *ibid.*

90. For an overview of the Council's legal functions, see Sir Arthur Godley, *Memorandum on the Home Government of India* (London: The India Office, [1901 (first published 1887)]), pp. 12–15.

91. See Donovan Williams, "The Formation of Policy in the India Office (1858–1869): A Study in the Tyranny of the Past," *Journal of Indian History* (Golden Jubilee Volume) (1973), pp. 873–92.

2

The Council of India

The Council of India is probably the most enigmatic and misunderstood cog in the machinery of the Home Government of the Indian Empire. It was charged with the responsibility to "conduct" Indian correspondence carried out in the United Kingdom, and thus had numerous opportunities to play a key role in the formulation of Indian policy.[1] In its first half-century especially, the Council of India had an intimate relationship with the permanent staff and India Office departments in the policy-making process. Yet there is a general lack of appreciation for the importance of the India Office role and hence that of the Council of India in the formulation of Indian policy in the period before World War I. Early studies on the Council, such as S. N. Singh's *The Secretary of State for India and His Council* (1962) and P. K. Chatterji's, *The Making of Indian Policy, 1853–65* (1975), have only scratched the surface of its role in policy-making. New insights into the working and organization of the India Office and Council of India in its first decade have recently appeared in Donovan Williams's *The India Office, 1858–1869* (1983), in which important constitutional issues, ideological predilections of establishment members and Councillors, and relations among the India Council, permanent staff, and India Office departments are assessed.[2] However, significant changes in the membership, organization, and function of the Council occurred in the late nineteenth century—changes which had a dramatic impact on the way in which Indian affairs were considered in Whitehall.

The Secretary of State's establishment was first constituted by an Order in Council of Queen Victoria following the traumatic upheavals of 1857 in India, and it was subsequently modified from time to time by additional Parliamentary Acts and Orders in Council.[3] The form of the proposed department of state elicited considerable parliamentary negotiation and debate.[4] What emerged was an office that was closely linked with the past and was in many respects a mirror image of the discredited John Company, both in terms of its personnel and operating procedures. The central issue in the debates and negotiations in and out of Parliament focused on the role of the proposed Council of India vis-à-vis the Secretary of State for India. Was the Council to be a deliberative body acting as a microcosmic Parliament or an executive body functioning like a Cabinet of sorts? The East India Company, in a petition drafted by John Stuart Mill, argued for the former role, contending that administrative details would be handled appropriately in India. In its last, futile attempt to delay dissolution, the Company argued that an essential characteristic of its long rule in India had been a Council "composed of men experienced in Indian affairs and personally independent of the minister, in order that they might be able effectively to oppose proposals founded in ignorance or self-interest."[5] The Company lost its bid to remain chartered, but its observations about the nature of the new Council were by and large accepted by Parliament. Ultimately it was decided that there would be a Council of fifteen, of whom seven would be elected by the Court of Directors of the Company and eight appointed by the Crown. Additionally, the new Office inherited most of the personnel of the defunct Company and was even housed in the East India House, the venerable Company headquarters in Leadenhall Street before ultimately being situated in Whitehall in 1867.[6]

Early in the negotiations over the Government of India Bill, Sir Charles Wood observed that "a [Secretary] of State and a Council would not . . . differ very much from a President [and] Court of Directors.[7] Lord Stanley, who became the first Indian Secretary, agreed and informed the Governor-General (Lord Canning) that "relations . . . remain what they were, the sole change being the substitution of the [Secretary] of State in Council for the Court of Directors. The new Council is really the Court revived under a new name."[8] This was only partially accurate, for there were changes in the structure of the new Office that would ultimately combine to affect intimately the formation of policy in the India Office in the nineteenth century. Constitutionally, the power of the Secretary of State for India was greater than that which had been enjoyed by the President of the Board of Control. Moreover, while it is safe to say that the new Councillors lacked some of the prestige and power of the Company men (particularly as they could not sit in Parliament), they had been legislatively fused to the new India Secretary, much as a Siamese twin, by the creation of the corporate entity, the Secretary of State *in Council.*

Of the Council's fifteen members, at least nine had to have appropriate "Indian qualifications"—they had to have served in India for at least ten years and must not have been absent from the subcontinent for more than ten years prior to their appointment to the Council. This Indian experience was mandated in order that the Council of India might function as an advisory body to the Secretary of State, supplying him with "that special departmental knowledge which it [was] utterly impossible for any public man, trained in the ordinary school of English administration, to possess upon purely Indian questions."[9] The Councillors were also appointed for life, and only Parliament could remove them from office in the first decade of the Council's life.

The outward appearance of the new India Office so closely resembled that of the pre-Mutiny days that less than a year after its establishment, John Bright observed that the Home Government of India "was changed in name only. It was scarcely changed in form, and has not been in the least changed in principle."[10] But Bright was not privy to the important changes going on within the Office in its initial years. Donovan Williams has painstakingly traced the changes in the India Office in the sixties as the Secretary of State, Council of India, and the permanent establishment all cast aside the static roles identified by Bright and developed a new set of internal relationships within the Office.[11]

The intent of the original legislation in 1858—to establish a system of effective "checks and balances" over the Secretary of State in the form of Parliament, Crown, and India Council—was never achieved.[12] After the bill became law, Parliament, "endemically indifferent to Indian affairs, relapsed into its former indifference leaving the Council to perform its function of control,"[13] and India became the " 'Great Bore' upon which no self-respecting Parliamentarian would pin his career."[14] Left alone to interpret both constitutional and assumed powers, the Council of India initially assumed dominance over an inexperienced India Office staff. The early Secretaries of State too were vulnerable when faced with the formidable collective experience of the Council. Sir Charles Wood, the second Secretary to hold the Indian seals of office, analyzed his position in the following way:

Can I, or any Secretary of State who has not been in India, pretend to set his opinion in detail against such men? Would it conduce to the transaction of business, if I was overruling them in expressions of opinion on details? I have insisted on the practical result being an approval of the course taken in the main.[15]

Although Queen Victoria initially chafed at the Council of India being "a check interposed between the Sovereign and the absolute government of India,"[16] several factors—including the sheer volume of Indian papers and the death of Prince Albert—enabled Stanley, Wood, and their successors to curtail markedly the involvement of the Queen in Indian affairs.[17] By and large, in the Office's first two decades, Victoria refrained from excessive interference in Indian matters, and in the late nineteenth century she interfered selectively (for example, in the selection of the Viceroy in 1893 and the award of honors).[18] However, to erect an additional buffer against any interference by the British Sovereign, the India Office strictly regulated information provided to the palace.[19]

The head of the India Office and principal adviser to the Crown on Indian affairs was the Secretary of State for India. He exercised on behalf of the Crown, "the powers formerly exercised by the Board of Control and the Court of Directors, and who, as a member of the Cabinet is responsible to and represents the supreme authority of Parliament."[20] Generally the Secretary of State was the ultimate governing authority over Indian officers. Special powers were reserved for him in the Secret Department of the India Office and, as President of the Council, he directed its business at weekly meetings.[21]

But the Secretary of State's powers were limited in two directions in addition to his constitutional responsibilities as a Crown Minister. First, he derived his authority from Parliament, and he was required to submit certain reports, such as the annual accounts for India revenue and expenditure, and nominations for certain Indian appointments, to the House of Commons. However, his salary and establishment costs were borne by Indian, not British, revenues and therefore it was not until 1919 that he had to face an annual parliamentary review of his establishment. Yet the Secretary of State's relations with Parliament were still critical, and are discussed below.

It was the second constraint on the Secretary of State that crucially affected the formation of policy and the processing of paperwork within the India Office: the statutory relationship between the India Secretary and the Council of India. He was required by law to work with the Council in despatching Indian correspondence.[22] As a Council of advice and deliberation, it differed from the Viceroy's Executive Council (with its portfolio system) and also from administrative boards such as the Army Council or Lords Commissioners of the Admiralty in England. The Council of India and Secretary of State formed a corporate entity—the Secretary of State *in Council*, which had only limited collective responsibility for its actions. In fact, while the Councillors had no individual accountability, they were meant to serve in both an advisory and judicial capacity as the final court of last resort on Indian questions.

The manner in which the Council discharged its duties was critical in the formation of nineteenth-century Indian policy at all levels. In its first two decades the Council's performance produced opposing impressions from Members of Parliament. Some felt that the Secretary of State's rule was as despotic as that of "Alexander and Darius or any other autocrat who ever existed, for, being a member of a Government which ruled by commanding a majority in [the] House, its shield was necessarily thrown over him."[23] Others saw the India Council essentially unchecked in its operation. In fact there was an uneasy truce between the Secretary of State and his Council in which neither side consistently dominated the other. It meant that policy debates and deliberations among the Council, departments, and Secretary of State were often extremely tense, but not impossible.

Initially the India Council was hampered in its efforts by persistent regional loyalties that often delayed considerations of legislation in the India Office. The regional interests of Councillors contributed to much infighting in Committee and Council meetings over the final form of Indian communications. This does not mean, however, that the Secretaries of State for India—especially in the first decade and a half—could override the Council, because the Secretary of State was also circumscribed by his obligation to conduct business as a corporate body, the Secretary of State in Council. The result, particularly in the 1860s, was a series of compromises and noncommittal "half and half letters" that delayed much required and progressive legislation from being enacted.[24] The immediate beneficiary of the factionalism in the Home Government was the Supreme Government in Calcutta, which could often present London with a fait accompli in Indian policy and go unchallenged.[25] In the long run the divisiveness in the Council tended to enhance the authority of the Secretary of State and permanent staff of the Office as organizational and procedural reforms were effected in the 1860s.[26]

An eventful dispute between the Council and Secretary of State occurred in 1867 over the Mysore succession question, and for the first time in the history of the young Office, the Secretary of State exercised his authority and overruled his Council.[27] The following year *The Times* emphasized the aging character of the Council and denounced its predilection to contradict the Secretary of State. The newspaper urged the Council's reorganization because from *The Times*'s vantage point "fresh blood" was needed in the rarefied air of the India Office, and because "the knowledge wanted in the Council is the knowledge of India as it is, not of India as it used to be."[28] High government officials, especially Lord Salisbury (who as Lord Cranborne had experienced the frustration of dealing with the Council), attacked the Council in Parliament. Salisbury was chagrined at the "curious machinery of the Council, so strangely selected and endowed with such anomalous power," which, he said, held the Secretary of State in "tutelage." The current Secretary of State, Sir Stafford Northcote, added that he could not tolerate a Council comparable to a "conclave of cardinals with a dying pope."[29] Something, they argued, had to be done to provide the Secretary of State with advisers who had more recent Indian experience. Both men were, of course, articulating their frustration with the Council and indeed with the entire policy-making process as it had evolved to that point. Ultimately Parliament did effect a change in the nature of Council membership.

Parliament enacted the Government of India Amending Act (32 & 33 Vic., c. 97) in 1869. This act limited Councillors' terms of office to ten years (with a possible five-year extension for special reasons) and repre-

sented a feeling on the part of Parliament that the Council was, after all, "a consultative not a controlling body."[30] Significantly, the act also included a provision that all subsequent appointments to the Council of India would be made by Crown nomination and *not* through election by the Councillors. An additional change in the composition of the Council was legislated by Parliament in 1876 (39 & 40 Vic., c. 7), allowing the Secretary of State to appoint persons having "professional or other peculiar" qualifications to the Council in order to help sort out the increasing complexities of Indian business. (This applied almost exclusively to a member of the London financial community who was regularly appointed to Council after this time.)[31]

The constitutional relationship between the Secretary of State and his Council was not well defined by the Government of India Act, 1858. This ambiguity led to three basic "constitutional" struggles within the India Office from its inception until World War I, each of which affected the consideration and formulation of Indian policy: (1) the debate over the Council's financial veto (s. 41 of the Act of 1858); (2) the disagreement over the Secretary of State's powers in the Secret Department of the India Office; and (3) the question of the degree to which the Secretary of State was obliged to listen to his Council and the circumstances in which he could overrule them.

The financial powers of the Council of India affected the expeditious discharge of business in the India Office most directly. Under the Act of 1858 (s. 41), the Council of India was delegated the following duty:

The expenditure of the revenue of India, both in India and elsewhere, shall be subject to the control of the Secretary of State in Council, and *no grant or appropriation of any part of such revenue, or any property coming into the possession of the Secretary of State in Council by virtue of this Act, shall be made without the concurrence of a majority of votes at a meeting of the Council.* [Italics added.][32]

The first major disagreement between the Secretary of State and his Councillors over the interpretation of section 41 and the extent of the Council's financial powers occurred in 1869. The ambiguity of the second portion of the clause—whether it applied only to orders for expenditures proposed by the Secretary of State to his Council, or to *all* spending authorities in India or elsewhere—was left unresolved. Many felt that the vagueness about the Council's financial powers was better defined by the "good sense of the Council and the Secretary of State" than by any specific interpretation.[33] Hence, even though Salisbury and his cohorts desired it, the amending legislation of 1869 did not address the question of the Council's financial powers. Not all Parliamentarians forgot the issue, however, and in 1880, regardless of how imperfectly they were understood outside the precincts of the India Office, the Council's broad technical powers were attacked in Parliament by that rascally "Member for India," Henry Fawcett.

The Secretary of State, Lord Hartington, successfully rebuffed the call for a Select Committee of Parliament to investigate the internal structure of the Office, but promised instead to refer the matter to a few prominent individuals. Hartington then requested the Council's premier jurist, Sir Henry Maine, to prepare a memorandum on the subject. Maine was the distinguished author of legal texts and had served as Professor of Law at both Oxford and Cambridge. Before joining the Council of India in 1871, Maine had been Legal Member on the Viceroy's Executive Council in India. He gladly accepted the task of reviewing the 1858 legislation, for Maine had long decried the shabby treatment of the East India Company, which he considered an "ignoble variety of the neglect which broke the heart of Cortez, and . . . the ingratitude which dishonoured or assassinated Labourdannais, Lally, and Dupleix."[34]

Maine concluded that the limited interpretation of the rule most accurately reflected Parliament's intentions. Since section 41 was enacted in the pretelegraph era, Maine reasoned that any reasonable budget system would be inoperable if the Council of India were required to scrutinize each item on the Government of India's budget. Maine also pointed out that part of the confusion over the scope of the Council's powers was due to the technical parliamentary word "appropriation," which had been inserted into the act in addition to the more suitable term "grant" (expressing alienation of property).[35] Maine rejected the clamor to revise the Act of 1858 and section 41 because in fact he felt strongly that the "actual practice of the Indian Government, both in England and in India [was] in harmony with the true intentions of Parliament, however imperfectly they [were] expressed in section 41 of the Act."[36] Maine's arguments successfully answered parliamentary critics, and the power of financial review by the India Council was again left unaltered. He proceeded to provide the following penetrating description of the Council's financial power:

The power of the Council, which is both great and real, is of a very different kind, and is almost independent of any formal authority given to it by statute. It is simply the power of experience and knowledge in a given subject, or rather a mass of subjects, of the greatest extent, of the greatest difficulty, of the greatest complexity, and in some branches of business of ever-growing technicality. So technical indeed have some departments of Indian business become, that, it appears to me, the ablest English statesman, brought into the India Office, and finding no Council to consult, would be very much like a layman of great natural ability brought suddenly into the Court of the Queen's Bench, and set suddenly to administer the Crown jurisdiction according to his own sense of right and justice.[37]

The tension within the India Office over the proper relationship between the Secretary of State and Council of India was crucial in the transaction of Indian business. The India Council's powers of financial review were central in defining that relationship and were thus debated continuously throughout the 1880s and 1890s. The most concentrated attack on the Council's financial powers came during Lord Curzon's Viceroyalty (1898–1905). Throughout his tenure Curzon was in conflict with the India Council, and in 1901 he proposed revision in the Council's power of financial review. He sent his plan to Sir Arthur Godley, Permanent Undersecretary of State for India from 1883–1909, maintaining that

I have always respected the candour just as I have always believed in the correctness of your [Godley's] analysis of the inner working of that peculiar machine which you assist to drive. But do you believe that the Act of 1858 can last forever? I certainly do not. I believe that two hours in the House of Commons with a good speaker who knew his case would blow the whole thing to smithereens.[38]

The veteran Whitehall mandarin agreed, and even offered that "probably no one could coach the said speaker better" than himself. But Godley deferred from endorsing any changes in the Act of 1858 because he knew quite well that any new legislation would pass through Parliament "with amendments which would make the remedy worse than the disease."[39] Godley summarized his feelings about the system imposed by the Act of 1858 when he told Curzon:

The Act of 1858, which I spend my life administering as best I can, is one of the worst Acts ever passed through Parliament; it is like Dr. Johnson's leg of mutton, ill-designed, ill-drawn and ill-amended. . . . [It is] an illogical compromise . . . [and] can only be worked at all by an elaborate system of shams, arrangements, acquiescences and occasional illegalities: if everyone stood on his rights, the machine would come to a stop in 24 hours.[40]

Besides, added Godley, though he had also had his temper tried frequently on small matters, he accepted the fact that "the Constitution of the India Office is not worse than the British Constitution," and advised Curzon that "it may be said of both that we must be content to worry along and make them work somehow."[41] Curzon was not amused and his personal relations with the Council of India deteriorated as his Viceroyalty continued. Thus he eagerly accepted a suggestion by Balfour, the Prime Minister, that he submit proposals to revise the Act of 1858 (especially s. 41)[42] and he prepared a memorandum entitled *Amendment of the Government of India Acts*.[43] He submitted a draft of his memorandum to Godley at the India Office because, Curzon reasoned, by virtue of his long tenure as Permanent Undersecretary he knew better than anyone the inconsistencies and tribulations of the Council's financial deliberations. Some years earlier Godley had confided to the then Viceroy, Lord Elgin, that "nobody values the Council as a consultative body more than I do; but . . . their 'vote' (for of course in financial matters they have a veto) is an almost intolerable nuisance compared with which the vote of the House of Lords is a purely beneficient contrivance."[44] Still, Godley informed Curzon that his personal relations with the Council, "though profoundly influenced by the existence of this veto, have been uniformly good [and] friendly for many years past, [even though it] was not always so."[45]

Curzon emphasized the "peculiar" circumstances under which the India Office had been set up, with one eye fixed on the East India Company. He made various recommendations regarding the size of the Council, method of appointment and qualifications of the Councillors, and revisions in the length of their service. Curzon's attack on the Council's veto power was predicated on his belief that it elevated the Council of India to an uncontrollable position of supremacy over the Government of India, Secretary of State, and even His Majesty's Government. After all, argued Curzon, almost every case before Council in some way involved the disbursement of funds, and this, he maintained, meant that the Council—not the Secretary of State or India Office departments—ruled the roost:

The Secretary of State for India is expected to be, and is popularly regarded as being, as much a master in his own house as other Secretaries of State are in theirs. The Council are intended to be, and are popularly regarded as being, his advisers; and if it were known that he (apart from personal influence and prestige) had no power except the casting vote, greater than the least of them, and that in fact they are not advisers but masters, the statement would, I believe, be received with general incredulity.[46]

Above all, Curzon deplored the effect of the Council's veto power over legislation submitted by the Government of India. Such proposals could take up to as much as one and a half years of preparation—sometimes at the instigation of the Secretary of State himself—and could be swept away in Council by a solitary vote.[47] It was incongruous to Curzon that the veto power lay with the Council instead of the head of the India Office. While he acknowledged that checks and balances were essential to the British Constitution, Curzon insisted that the Secretary of State should have ultimate veto power in his domain. In fact, proclaimed Curzon, the Indian Secretary did not even possess the power to force a resignation as did the Prime Minister when faced with an errant Cabinet member. Hence Curzon claimed that the Secretary of State for India was the "only head of a great Imperial Department who is destitute of this power, and who is the servant, therefore, instead of the master of his subordinates."[48]

Although there was considerable tension in the India Office between the Secretary of State and his Council over this power of veto, Curzon's evaluation of the relationships within the India Office contained several basic flaws. First, Curzon had not proven that the Council of India had in fact abused its powers—only that he, as Viceroy, was offended because of a number of matters rejected by the Council. Even Godley advised Curzon that this "veto" had *not* been abused by the Council.⁴⁹ Second, the powers of "persuasion and prestige" employed by the Secretary of State weighed heavily in the Secretary of State's relationship with the Council of India. This was far preferable to the operation of the War Office or Admiralty (lavishly praised by Curzon) where disgruntled Councillors publicly aired disagreements with their respective Secretaries when they were overruled.⁵⁰ This was particularly true of the War Office. St. John Brodrick, later Lord Midleton, who had recently shifted from the War Office to the Indian Secretaryship, informed Curzon that if the Indian Councillors acted like the old soldiers at the War Office, "we should have treble the number of questions of Indian Government dragged before Parliament that are brought there at present. This I believe you will agree with me in thinking disastrous."⁵¹

Godley was a much more seasoned observer of the Council's behavior than Brodrick. He admitted that the work of the office was done "at a considerable sacrifice of time [and] trouble, which would not be necessary if the Council were really a Council, [and] not a controlling force."⁵² And though he considered that "no official . . . would benefit more by the change than the Permanent Under Secretary," Godley agreed with St. John Brodrick as to the inadvisability of introducing any new legislation into Parliament.⁵³ Moreover, Godley was adamant that he "must not be understood to be a party to any hostile criticism of the use which Members of Council have made of the powers that they now possess."⁵⁴ Over the years successive Permanent Undersecretaries had established a favorable modus vivendi with the Councillors, and Godley considered that in his time they had, "on the whole a good record, and have always (so far as I know) loyally acquiesced in the views of the Cabinet even when they did not agree with them."⁵⁵

But the source of real danger in any alteration of the Council's powers was interference by the House of Commons in the administration of India. Only by attacking the Council in open debate could any new measures be pushed through Parliament. Curzon was willing to take that chance; the paladins of the India Office, however, shared Godley's belief that the Councillors' "vote" was preferable to that of Parliament under any circumstances.⁵⁶ There was clear evidence to this effect. Soon after Godley assumed the Permanent Undersecretaryship at the India Office, the independence of the Secretary of State, or apparent lack of it, was attacked both in Parliament by John Slagg, senior Member for Manchester, and outside the Commons by a pamphlet campaign directed by William Birkmyre of the Cobden Club.⁵⁷ The India Office was particularly sensitive to these public attacks because they coincided with the appearance of the Indian National Congress and the institutionalization of Indian nationalism. It simply would not do to have Slagg go about calling the Council of India "a sort of *vehmgericht* or Secret Council,"⁵⁸ or to have Birkmyre accuse the Council of being "a secret conclave of ancient pensioners, recruited from the class who nearly brought the Empire to ruin" thirty years earlier.[59] Hence the officials at the India Office assiduously worked to short-circuit questions in Parliament. This included a complete redesign of the Office's Parliamentary Branch to monitor parliamentary questions closely and prepare public answers to them carefully.[60]

Another potentially divisive issue within the India Office was the debate between the Secretary of State and Council of India over "secret" correspondence. The problem was that the Supreme Government in India possessed broader powers of marking papers "secret" than did the Secretary of State for India. Section 28 of the Government of India Act, 1858, provided a loophole that spelled out certain situations in which the Secretary of State could legally withhold information from the India Council. Although it was rather evasively phrased, any despatches to Great Britain could be withheld from Members of Council which "if this Act had not been passed, [might otherwise] have been addressed to the Secret Committee of the Court of Directors."[61] The Councillors feared that the Secretary of State would bypass them on critical issues relating to levying war, making peace, or negotiating treaties with native states by marking such correspondence "secret" according to sections 29, 20, and 41 of the Act of 1858. They also agonized over the Government of India's ability to mark "secret" any despatch "concerning the Government of the said territories and acquisitions (33 George III)." But the real fear of the Councillors was that somehow the Secretary of State would circumvent the India Council and unilaterally undertake large expenditures in India. It was a gray area within the India Office, and one that occasionally led to anomalous situations wherein the Government of India's correspondence to London was withheld from the Council, while the Secretary of State's answer had to be laid on the Council table. The Councillors' anxiety most often centered on the question of sedition, for it was here that the Secretaries of State tried to use this vaguely defined set of rules to their advantage.

In the early years of the India Office, the Secret Department and its assorted ad hoc committees were anomalies inherited from the East India Company. It was the "private face" of the Political and Secret Department of the India Office.[62] Generally the Secret Department dealt with British India's external relations (both in Asia and Europe) while the Political Department and Political Committee of Council handled all questions dealing with Native States of the subcontinent.[63] From 1858 to 1874 the Political and Secret Department was headed by Sir John Kaye, who possessed enormous prestige and power vis-à-vis the India Council because he had command of the guild secrets of the department. This does not mean that the Political Committee of Council was completely overshadowed by Kaye or by his successor in 1875, Sir Owen T. Burne. (Burne would, in fact, later join the Council of India.) The "public face" of the Political and

Secret Department was a spirited debating society in which a wide range of crucial issues was debated openly by prominent former Anglo-Indian administrators who were self-assured in the extreme about their vision of India's post-Mutiny configuration. More than any other group in the early years of the India Office, the Political Committee of Council was wrenched to and fro by advocates of two opposing philosophical schools regarding British India's future—those steeped in what Donovan Williams has called the "Dalhousie tradition" ("reactionists," deeply committed to Britain's divine mission in India and implacably opposed to concessions to Indians) and the "Malcolm tradition" ("traditionalists," inclined to have more sympathy and trust for Indians and their customs and institutions).[64]

These larger-than-life figures involved in the political decisions in the India Office during the 1860s and on into the 1870s were no longer present as the 1880s unfolded. Distinguished individuals participated in both the Political Department and the Political Committee of the Council; but they were less committed to any particular doctrine or philosophical school and had not personally been involved in the pre-Mutiny conquest and consolidation. They tended to be more clinical in their assessment of Indian policy. However, they shared with their predecessors a concern over the Secretary of State's use and potential abuse of powers in the Secret Department. The Council's concern over the growth of secret correspondence with India that bypassed the Council table corresponded to the increased proclivity of the Government of India to send home papers related to sedition marked "secret." Tension within the India Office mounted when increasingly in the 1890s the Secretary of State began answering them in the same manner.[65] This was particularly vexatious because topically sedition fell within the jurisdiction of the Judicial and Public Department—an anomaly that continued until the Special Branch of the Thuggee and Dacoity Department was transformed into the Central Criminal Intelligence Department under the Political Branch of the Government of India's Home Department in 1904. As a result, the Judicial and Public Department also had to form its own "secret" branch, which caused further concern among Councillors.[66]

The situation reached the crisis stage in 1899 when the Government of India and the Secretary of State exchanged information about the political activities of the Natu brothers in Bombay in the Secret Department.[67] Several Councillors finally objected formally to the correspondence because it circumvented the Council of India. Since it fell within a gray area legally, Lord George Hamilton asked his Political Secretary, Sir William Lee-Warner, an old India hand, to prepare a detailed analysis of the legal position. He did so, and Lee-Warner argued for a broad interpretation of the Secretary of State's powers, presenting an extensive list of previous examples of secret papers which had been withheld from Council on the issue of sedition. When the Lee-Warner thesis was supported by the India

Office Legal Adviser, Sir Arthur Wilson (who reversed his earlier position) and a leading Member of Council, Sir John Edge (1898–1908), Hamilton concluded that he had enough support to enunciate the policy that the Secretary of State could answer *any* despatch marked "secret" by the Government of India in the secret department.[68] However, no attempt was made to formalize this broad interpretation until 1915, and in 1916 the nature of secret communications was extended to include "the public safety" and "defence of the realm."

Godley was uneasy about the open-ended nature of Lee-Warner's proposition. He was especially concerned that it might upset generally smooth relations between the Political Committee of Council and India Office departments and lead to a reversion to the early days of the Office when suspicion rather than trust dominated.[69] In some ways he preferred the cautious approach suggested a few years earlier by Sir Henry Maine, who had argued that the wording of the Act of 1858 referred only to orders which "might legally" have been addressed to the Court and thus had to be seen by the Council. Godley also discounted most of Lee-Warner's evidence. Although he did not interfere when Hamilton adopted the bold position, Godley advised the Secretary of State not to challenge the Council openly in the matter of secret correspondence. Godley observed that

there seems ... to be no use in calling the attention of Council to the existence of this power. It certainly does exist, and I think you are bound to use it as your predecessors (all except the more recent ones) certainly did. If, on any occasion, your action is challenged, you will have a complete defense [in Lee-Warner's minute]. *But, until it is challenged, I do not see why you should say anything about it.* [Italics added.][70]

From the late nineteenth century a new series of problems emerged with the expanded use of the telegraph in urgent communications with India on issues ranging from sedition to matters relating to increased nationalist activities. Here, too, the Secretary of State had the option, according to the Act of 1858, to bypass Council and record his reason for doing so at a later date. Official, secret, and private telegrams increasingly flowed between the centers of Indian governance without reference to Council. However, Godley arranged an understanding with the Council of India whereby this telegraphic correspondence could go on without incurring the wrath of Councillors over any infringement of their rights of "perusal." This issue could have been a serious impediment to the prompt consideration of Indian policy—since India's security was a persistent topic of correspondence between Calcutta and London—had it not been for Godley's perceptive establishment of a modus vivendi among the Political Committee of Council, the Secret Department, and the Secretary of State, in which it was "usual but not necessary" for the latter to communicate "secret" documents to the Political Committee of Council.[71] Essentially, in these matters and indeed in the overall relationship between the Secretary of State and Council of India in the late nineteenth century, relations were helped considerably by the ultimate realization by each Secretary of State (with Godley's encouragement) that "everyone, and above all a corporate body like a Council, likes to have a hand in initiating a desirable change."[72]

The third great constitutional struggle within the India Office in the nineteenth century involved the Secretary of State's power to overrule his Council. Given the vital role assigned to the India Council in the governance of India, it was a serious matter for the India Office Secretary to overrule a decision. The Act of 1858, mandated that this could be done only in extreme emergency, and required the Secretary of State to record the reasons for his action. This was, indeed, one of those issues where the machine could have ground to a halt if everyone had chosen to stand on his constitutional rights.

The Council of India was required by the Act of 1858 to meet at least once a week and usually convened on Tuesday afternoons. The Secretary of State or the Vice-President of the Council (a position which usually rotated according to seniority) presided over the session, which had an average attendance of nine Councillors.[73] The procedure in meetings was well established. Thus:

After an initial statement as to whether the Secretary of State or the Vice-President was presiding, telegrams and letters to the Viceroy and other officials were read. Then the resolutions were listed regarding the papers laying upon the table. One by one each committee submitted to Council its draft of relevant letters and resolutions which were read and subsequently approved or disapproved after discussion. Where a resolution was not unanimous, the ayes and nays were recorded in the Council Minute Book.[74]

Only the Secretary of State could initiate business at Council meetings, and his power over procedural questions was absolute. In Council deliberations, Members had to stand and speak, but "were allowed to do so once on the same sin [question]."[75] Voting in the Council was by a show of hands, with the Secretary of State usually abstaining unless a "casting vote" was necessary to break a tie. On any issue (apart from those specific instances in which a majority vote of Council was required), the Secretary of State could overrule his Councillors.[76] India Secretaries rarely utilized this power (section 23 of the Act of 1858) during the first fifty years of the India Office. In fact, eighteen Secretaries of State for India "negatived Council" only seven times in that period.[77] Councillors who disagreed with a decision taken at a meeting they had attended could request their opinion recorded in the Council Minutes. But the impact of a Councillor's dissent was minimal, for most dissentient opinions rarely left the India Office, and most Members of Parliament were ignorant of the very existence of the Council Minute Book. The dissents of the India Council were also screened from the Government of India. Although an occasional dissent was "leaked" to the press or included (by the Secretary of State) in a Parliamentary Blue Book, by and large they remained a strictly internal matter.

As a result, India Office decisions always appeared unanimous. Godley explained that this was because it was imperative that all decisions "go forth with the full authority of the Secretary of State in Council," with the reasons behind the decision remaining on record purely for "domestic consumption."[78] As to the public airing of dissent, Godley cautioned the Councillors that any attempt to get dissents published, directly or indirectly, would be acting in a manner bordering on disloyalty and "calculated to impair the working of our official machine."[79] Over the years Councillors had few opportunities to record their dissents, although they retained the legal right to do so. The predilection of individual Councillors to try to circumvent official procedures was more pronounced in the early years of the Office than after 1880. By 1886 Godley considered that the practice had "all but fallen into disuse" and was "cumbersome and useless."[80] In part this occurred because of the dead end to which dissents were relegated in the Office; it was also due in great measure to Godley's advocacy that a Councillor's vote, not the official record of his arguments, was a true dissent.[81]

The peculiar relationship between the Secretary of State and the Council of India intimately affected the conduct of business in the India Office. The Secretary of State could not ignore the India Council in the formation of India policy, and there could be no "uncontrolled autocracy" by the India Office chief. For its part the Council could not hope to ride roughshod over a Cabinet Minister in spite of regular shifts in the Indian Secretaryship. This delicate balance was difficult to sustain in the first decade of the office as the internal relationships among permanent officials, Councillors, and India Office departments experienced considerable realignment, reorganization, and redefinition of responsibilities. From the 1880s on activity was more formalized.

Despite periodic estrangements after 1870, the Council of India tended to avoid any serious clashes with the Secretary of State for India and retained substantial powers in the formulation of Indian policy. It continued to consider correspondence at several key junctures. For example, a financial letter would be received in the Registry Department, opened, and sent to the Finance Department. The Finance Department, after minuting on the letter, would send it forward with a draft reply to the Undersecretary of State, the Secretary of State, and finally the Finance Committee of Council. The Committee would approve the draft, amend it, or reject it. Procedures for Council amendments were so refined that it was specified as to how to use the margins of documents. The draft was then sent back to the Undersecretary who in turn either referred it back to the Secretary of State or the full India Council. Finally, the Council, under the presidency of the Secretary of State, would approve or reject the despatch.[82]

The Members of Council were free to discuss materials referred to them by the Secretary of State, either in committee or individually. As a body, the Council never challenged this format, although an occasional reminder on procedure was issued to both Department Heads and Councillors.[83] In the assessment of correspondence and the formation of policy, the committee system of the Council of India was the very heart of the nineteenth-century India Office. Indeed, Donovan Williams concluded his study of the India Office in the first decade by labelling Indian governance as "Government by Committee."[84] This remained so in the late nineteenth and early twentieth centuries, although the nature of committee activity was far more technical and less emotional than during the early, formative years. What then was the nature of the Council's committee system, and what was the nature of Council membership in general, and in particular, the method by which Councillors were selected and slotted to particular committees?

Several truncated analyses of the membership of the India Council do exist.[85] The biographical data therein, however, rely for the most part on the India Office Lists for service records. A more critical shortcoming is the unduly heavy reliance on the often biased *Dictionary of National Biography* for evaluating the many Councillors' performances in the nineteenth century. A clear departure from this trend has been Donovan Williams's use of policy minuting over a number of years and on a number of issues to create ideological profiles of the Councillors of the period up to 1870. Although the task remains a full study in itself, some generalizations about Councillors and their selection after 1880 can be made.

Several factors influenced the Secretary of State's selection of his Councillors. First, it was imperative to have an assorted expertise among Members. During the late nineteenth century, for example, there was always one Councillor selected from the London financial world.[86] Obviously, when the "financial member" retired, the Secretary of State had to replace him with a man with similar qualifications. The same need dictated the presence of a "law member," as well as political, military, and public works experts with Indian experience on the Council. Additional factors in a Councillor's selection included the area of India in which he had served, his political philosophy and, in the case of Indian appointees after 1907, acceptability to both educated Indians (Hindus and Muslims) and the Anglo-Indians. By carefully evaluating the service files of candidates and consulting the Permanent Undersecretary prior to making appointments to his Council, the Secretary of State could achieve the proper provincial mix in his Council and have reasonable assurance that he was getting men with whom he could work.

But the Permanent Undersecretary of State was the real watchdog over appointments to the Council of India. Although the Viceroy was always consulted when a vacancy occurred, there was very little correlation between viceregal recommendations and actual appointments to the Council. Occasionally, a member of the Indian Civil Service (ICS) actively lobbied for a position on the Council of India; such direct contact, however, was largely unsuccessful.[87] So the task of "vetting" potential Councillors went to Godley for some twenty-six years.

From the very beginning of his tenure, Godley provided background information and personal evaluations on the suitability of candidates for these critical appointments. Godley stressed that regional balance, recent Indian experience, and political philosophy (especially as regards adherence to such personality cults as Lyttonian, Lawrentian, or Curzonian were factors in filling vacancies on the Council).[88] This tended to make the Council of India a broadly based group. By and large they shared a common "establishment" education and service in the ICS. Regional assignments lent a certain desirable diversity to Councillors (which proved far less vexatious than in the early years of the office), and some Councillors had "all-India" experience, having served on the Viceroy's Executive Council before going to the India Office. Appendix G (a list of committee assignments between 1858 and 1905) provides detailed information on the Councillors and their deputed functions within the Office in the period 1858–1905.

There are serious questions about the role of the Council of India in the formation of policy. Was the Council basically an obstructive and conservative group? What factors allowed either individuals or the Council as a whole to influence the course of Indian legislation and Indian history? These questions are best answered by examining specific case studies that scrutinize the role not only of the India Council but also of all the constituent parts of Indian governance, both external and internal, as they interacted in a given set of circumstances. It is beyond the scope of this study, and a worthy project for other historians. Understanding the nature of the Council, its membership, and its role in policy-making will open new avenues of investigation on a wide range of subjects. But as a necessary prelude to this type of analysis, the operating procedures and opportunities of the Council of India in examining paperwork and influencing policy must be clarified.

When Godley joined the India Office in 1883, the weekly meetings of the Council were not at all conducive to the processing of large amounts of paperwork. The Undersecretaries usually attended Council meetings but did not participate unless specifically requested to do so.[89] Sir Alfred

Lyall, a Member of the Council of India during the period 1887–1902, found the Council "rather depressing" and noted that all its members had "the look of old hulks laid up in the dock and are men who have said goodbye to active service."[90] This was, if true, certainly a great contrast to the larger-than-life figures who sat on the Council in the 1860s, men like Sir George Clerk and John Lawrence. And even in the 1880s this characterization seems to be belied by the tremendous activity of the India Council on the committee level.

In accord with the Act of 1858, the Council was initially divided into three committees: the Finance, Home and Public Works Committee; the Political and Military Committee; and the Revenue, Judicial and Legislative Committee. At first, committees of Council were allowed to work over and revise each despatch *prior to* submission to the Undersecretaries or the Secretary of State, and thus they retained substantial authority and initiative in the preparation of despatches. Reforms initially formulated in Stanley's tenure and formally instituted by Sir Charles Wood in 1859 substantially altered the initiatory powers of the committees of Council. The reforms altered the number of committees in order to create a closer alignment with the India Office departments, and appropriated for the Secretary of State the power to appoint chairmen of the committees.[91]

The new committees of Council were: Finance and General Revenue; Public Works and Railways; Military; Political; Land and Revenue, Judicial and Legislative; and Public/Educational, & c. In 1866 Public Works was divorced from the Railway and Telegraphic Committee, and the Public Educational group was merged with the Revenue and Judicial body. From 1867 until 1873 a Sanitary Committee existed, and also in 1867, Revenue reemerged as a separate committee. In 1874 Railways and Telegraph problems became the responsibility of the Public Works Committee, and a Statistics and Commerce Committee first appeared. A Stores Committee was also established in 1874. When Godley arrived at the India Office, eight committees of Council were operative. Each subset of the Correspondence Department of the India Office—Finance, Judicial, Military, Political, Public Works, and Revenue—had a committee of Council to peruse its business. Additionally two Council committees reviewed matters relating to Stores and Statistics.

Procedurally the Secretary of State realigned committee assignments once a year. The key factor in the composition of committees was the division of responsibility according to expertise. Military men obviously went to the Military Committee, political experts to the Political Committee, and so on. In reality, the committee assignments were rarely changed, except for adjustments to accommodate new Members with outstanding expertise in a given field. Occasionally "in house" politics was a force in committee assignments. This happened when the Secretary of State or his

Undersecretary felt that a "safe" vote was required on a certain committee in anticipation of specific issues predicted to arise that year.

The committees' performance in reviewing policy papers was conditioned by three factors: their ability to get papers quickly, their specialized assignments compared with the Council as a whole, and the relationship between committees of Council and the India Office departments. Papers were often referred to two or more committees, to a joint committee, or to a special committee of Council. The decision as to which committee would deal with a given subject was quite distinct, and often two committees would offer differing viewpoints on a single issue. It was not, however, a case of committee number two "overruling" the initial report, because the two recommendations went on an equal footing to the Council, where the *Secretary of State in Council* considered them.[92] In order to accomplish this work, Councillors had to have access to papers of all kinds during the week, and they had to be diligent in reading them. Facilitating this task was also the Permanent Undersecretary's responsibility. Godley's predecessors in office had been concerned with the problem and made various efforts to make the system more effective.[93] But serious problems persisted which had to be addressed as both the character and pace of India Office business intensified in the late nineteenth century.

Sir Arthur Godley respected the Council of India, and considered Indian experience an invaluable aid in the formation of Indian policy. He himself never went to India, and unlike the early years of the office, few members of the permanent establishment had Indian experience. By this time there was little interchange of personnel between Whitehall and the subcontinent (e.g., Sir George Clerk going from Permanent Undersecretary to the Governorship of Bombay to the Council of India). Although he was occasionally frustrated by delays caused by the obligatory references of paperwork to the Council, Godley never questioned its constitutional authority to review Indian policy. Instead, he concerned himself with streamlining the review procedures of the Council. The Permanent Undersecretary argued that the large number of Councillors (fifteen) established by Parliament in 1858 had been "experimental" and the primary motive for its adoption, viz., to give adequate representation to the East India Company, was outdated. Since the Acts of 1858 and 1869 had provisions to deal with reductions in the Council, Godley urged that the number of Councillors be reduced for the more efficient functioning of committees.[94] Godley recommended that a Council of no less than nine members be formed; each member would then be asked to serve on three of the eight three-man committees (except for the larger Revenue and Finance Committees) of the Council. In order to retain sufficient Indian experience, at least seven members were to retain the "Indian qualification" under the proposals.

The recommendations were considered by a special departmental committee on India Office procedure in 1886. That committee concluded that despite obvious delays owing to the difficulty of Indian subjects, the necessity of consulting one or more departments and Members absent on leave or in India, the Council had managed to circumvent any *prolonged* tieups.[95] The Committee also identified several impediments to the Council's ability to discharge its business promptly. For example, papers often missed the weekly meetings and were put aside an entire week before being considered by the full Council. To surmount this problem, the Committee suggested that a box be circulated containing the papers to be considered at the next meeting. Unless Members voiced their objections to these papers, approval was implied and the business was completed. Next, as the full Council met only once a week, papers awaiting final approval might be set aside up to two weeks or more if the documents had the misfortune to miss a meeting and had to be placed on the Council reading table for an additional week. To eliminate this delay, the Special Committee, headed by Godley, suggested that papers be placed on the Council table for two clear days and promptly considered at the next full meeting. With minimum dissent these proposed "Rules for the Conduct of Business" in the India Council, drafted by Godley, were put into effect in 1887 and remained the standard procedure until the Government of India Act, 1935, transformed the Council of India into the Secretary of State's Advisers (and even then the basic procedures were only slightly modified).

In 1888 Godley chaired a Committee on Home Charges which again recommended a reduction in the number of Councillors in order to streamline the functioning of the committees, where the real work of the Council continued to take place.[96] He succeeded this time. The Council of India Reduction Act (52 and 53 Vic., c. 65), passed in 1889, empowered the Secretary of State to reduce the number of Councillors to ten, reflecting Godley's belief that the committees could function better if the number of participants was reduced. In practice, however, Council membership never dropped that low, and, in anticipation of the addition of Indian members to the Council of India, another Act of Parliament in 1907 (7 Edw. VII, c. 35) established the permissible limits to between ten and fourteen.

The relationship between the Council of India and the India Office departments is a fascinating story. Unlike the fluid and often tumultuous relations of the first decade, in this period it was quite effective for the efficient consideration of Indian papers. In part, the fact that several key Department Heads (e.g., Henry Waterfield in the Finance Department) had held office for several decades reduced the potential for friction and jealousy between the Council and the departments. More significant, however, is the fact that Godley acted as an effective liaison between the two divisions of the India Office. For over a quarter of a century, he actively involved himself in the drafting of Indian correspondence in the departments, and he had daily intercourse with the committees of Council while

Indian business of all kinds was being scrutinized and finalized. This enhanced his own position as a key adviser on Indian policy to the Secretary of State for India, but it also smoothed out the eddies in the sea of red tape within the Office.

Given the large volume of paper with which the committees of the India Council had to deal, the Councillors did very well, considering the circumstances. Not that they always impressed their superiors in the India Office—Lord George Hamilton felt that the Councillors during his long tenure (1895–1903) could not compare "in reputation or intellect" with the Councillors of the 1870s.[97] Several modern Indian historians have perpetuated this negative image of the Council of India by calling it a "reactionary body" which operated solely at the Secretary of State's discretion.[98] But the composition of the India Council became increasingly specialized after 1880; facilitated by reforms in the conduct of business introduced by Godley, its performance in the policy-making process differed substantially from its behavior in the first two decades of the India Office. The Council was still intimately involved in the perusal and formation of Indian policy and therefore cannot be ignored as an anomaly, or peripheral to events in India. There were many outstanding individuals who served on the Council between 1880 and World War I, such as John and Richard Strachey, A. C. Lyall, J. L. Mackay, William Lee-Warner, D. M. Stewart, J. B. Peile, and Alexander Arbuthnot. Godley emphasized their contribution to the formation of Indian policy when he told Curzon:

I am bound to say that my estimate of the value of our Council has distinctly risen during the 20 years I have been here; also, I consider that, *for the practical working of the office*, we have a far better team now than we had in the old days when there were several distinguished names on the list, and when we had far more oratory and note-writing. [Italics added.][99]

Godley's assessment is substantiated by the record. This is not a value judgment as to the Council of India's contribution to Indian policy. However, given the volume of Indian correspondence and business that came to the India Office after 1880 and the legal obligation of the Council of India to review large portions of it, the India Council put on a creditable performance. Blanket criticism of the Council's obstructiveness to the development of representative institutions in India tends to distort its role in the governance of India. While it occasionally initiated policy in its early years, it ceased to do so by and large in the late nineteenth century and confined itself to discussing only those matters presented to it by the Secretary of State or specific Indian expenditures. This was no small undertaking, and it still gave the Councillors significant opportunities to modify, shape, and prune Indian policy. Again, this remains a mystery; and Godley was in no small way responsible for our lack of knowledge about the

Council's operating procedures as well as the resultant harsh evaluations of its performance. The Permanent Undersecretary believed that the Secretary of State in Council was a corporation, and like the inner working of any public concern, "we . . . must conceal our machinery as much as we can."[100] Hence the composition of the Council committees, like its record of dissents, was not publicized outside the Office and remained, until now, hidden in the Council's Minute Books.

Although the Permanent Undersecretary set the professional standards and regulated the operating procedures within the India Office, its tenor at any given time was also reflective of the personality of the Secretary of State. During the sixties and seventies, the office of Secretary of State had enhanced its position vis-à-vis the India Council. This was in part due to reorganization and reforms within the structure of the Office—particularly the usurpation of the initiatory powers of the Council—and in part to the simple fact that the Secretaries of State did, after all, carry with them the authority of the Cabinet. On the other hand, the Council retained its financial veto and the legal obligation to peruse large quantities of Indian correspondence. They also represented on-the-spot experience as opposed to Secretaries of State representative of political parties at home, who more often than not assumed the Indian seals with little or no knowledge of the subcontinent. Hence the personal style of the Secretaries of State was also a factor in the policy-making process of India's Home Government in the late nineteenth century.

NOTES

1. For an overview of the Council's legal functions, see Sir Arthur Godley, *Memorandum on the Home Government of India* [London: India Office, 1901 (first published 1887)], pp. 12–15.

2. Hoshiarpur, Punjab: Vishveshvaranand Vedic Research Institute, 1983.

3. See Williams, *The India Office*, pp. 20–50. See also Williams's "The Council of India and the Relationship between the Home and Supreme Governments, 1858–1870," *English Historical Review* 81:318 (January 1966), pp. 56–73. P. K. Chatterji, *The Making of Indian Policy, 1853–65* (New Delhi: Orient Longman, 1975), *passim*; S. A. Husain, "The Secretary of State for India and His Council: An Analysis of Organisation and Procedure, 1858–1919," *Bangladesh Historical Studies* 4 (1979) pp. 64–79.

4. For an overview of the debate regarding the GOI Act, 1858, see Williams, *The India Office*, pp. 1–19, and H. H. Dodwell (ed.), *The Cambridge History of India* (Cambridge: Cambridge University Press, 1932).

5. G. B., *Hansard's Parliamentary Debates*, 3rd ser., vol. 148 (1857–58) [Appendix]. The concept that the men who helped govern India should be free from ministerial influence dated from the Company's rule in the eighteenth century. For a discussion of this ideal, see Lucy S. Sutherland, *The East India Company in Eighteenth Century Politics* (Oxford: The Clarendon Press, 1952), pp. 279, 379.

6. The India Office operated from East India House, and then from what became the Westminster Palace Hotel. In 1867, after considerable parliamentary and architectural debate, the India Office moved into a new edifice adjacent to the Foreign Office on King Charles Street. See Williams, *The India Office*, pp. 129–48.

7. Sir Charles Wood to Roger Ellice, 6 October 1857, quoted in Williams, *The India Office*, p. 5.

8. Stanley to Canning, 5 October 1858, *ibid.*, p. 18.

9. Lord Stanley, G. B., *Hansard's Parliamentary Debates*, 3rd ser., vol. 150 (1858), col. 1674.

10. John Bright, 7 March 1859, *ibid.*, vol. 152 (1859), cols. 1362–63. Bright, orator and statesman, served as M.P. for both Manchester and Birmingham during his career. See also contemporary writers such as H. S. Cunningham, *Earl Canning* (Oxford: The Clarendon Press, 1892), pp. 170–71.

11. For an overview of the reorganization, reform, and evolution of new relationships within the Office in the first decade, see Williams, *The India Office*, pp. 20–128.

12. See H. H. Dodwell, *A Sketch of the History of India from 1858–1914* (London: Longmans, Green and Co., 1925), p. 30.

13. Cited in Donovan Williams, "The Formation of Policy in the India Office, 1858–1866, with special reference to the Political, Judicial, Revenue, Public and Public Works Departments," D. Phil. thesis, Oxford, 1962, p. 10.

14. E. Bell, *The Great Parliamentary Bore* (London, 1869), Preface, p. iii, cited in Williams, *The India Office*, p. 25.

15. Wood to Canning, 9 January 1861, quoted in C. H. Philips, H. L. Singh, and B. N. Pandey (eds.), *The Evolution of India and Pakistan 1858–1947: Select Documents* (London: Oxford University Press, 1962), pp. 11–12.

16. Stanley to Wood, 14 July 1859, cited in Williams, *The India Office*, p. 31.

17. See "Minute approved by the Queen on the Conduct of Business," 27 November 1858, with Wood to Stanley, 4 June 1859, Halifax Papers, IOL, cited in Williams, *The India Office*, p. 31.

18. For a detailed account of the Queen's select involvement in Indian affairs—particularly questions of honor and the selections of the Viceroy—see J. Chandran, "Queen Victoria and the Viceroyalty of India, 1893–1894," *New Zealand Journal of History* 3:2 (October 1969), pp. 175–89.

19. See confidential memorandum, "Instructions As to Sending of Papers to the King," 20 June 1901, IOR, Private Papers [Miscellaneous Home Establishment Papers], L/PO/Misc. 3. Documents were sent to the Crown "For information only," and were carefully vetted by IO departments. Department heads could signify their suggestions on a *detachable piece of pink or red paper, while urgent messages were placed on green paper. The King received only lists of despatches, edited telegrams, and final, sanitized (never draft) papers.*

20. Sir Courtney Ilbert, *The Government of India* (Oxford: The Clarendon Press, 2nd rev. ed., 1907), p. 109.

21. Godley, *Home Government of India*, pp. 3–10.

22. For a list of subjects required by law to be brought before Parliament, see "Memorandum on India Office Administration [Appendix I]," March, 1919, L/PO/Misc. 5.

23. Col. Sykes, 11 July 1863, G.B., *Hansard's Parliamentary Debates*, 3rd ser., vol. 172 (1863), col. 786.

24. See Williams, *The India Office*, passim.

25. In June 1862 Wood admitted to Elgin that "I have sanctioned many things in the last three years which I did not approve, because they were done" (Wood to Elgin, 25 June 1862, quoted in Williams, "The Council of India," pp. 68–69).

26. See Williams, *The India Office*, pp. 51–77.

27. On the Mysore succession question, see Donovan Williams, "The Adoption Despatch of 16 April 1867: Its Origins and Significance," in Donovan Williams and E. Daniel Potts (eds.), *Essays in Indian History in Honour of C. C. Davies* (New York: Asia Publishing House, 1973), pp. 222–43.

28. *The Times* (London), 25 April 1868, p. 9. For an expanded discussion of the events surrounding the Act of 1869, see S. N. Singh, *The Secretary of State and His Council, 1858–1919* (Delhi: Munshi Ram Monohar Lal, 1962), pp. 22–28.

29. Lord Salisbury, G. B., *Hansard's Parliamentary Debates*, 3rd ser., vol. 194 (1869), col. 1074; and Northcote to Macnaghten, 26 September 1868, cited in Singh, *The Secretary of State*, p. 22.

30. Sir Charles Dilke, quoted in Williams, "The Formation of Policy," p. 11.

31. Three distinguished Members of Council appointed under this provision were H. S. Maine, Henry Yule, and Richard Strachey. For a convenient summary of legislative acts affecting the Council of India to 1914, see "Memorandum on the Constitution, Powers, and Duties of the Secretary of State in Council and His Establishment" (by T. W. Holderness), *Royal Commission on Indian Finance and Currency* (Appendix 35), Parliamentary Papers, Cd. 7238 (1914) [reprinted in L/PO/Misc. 5].

32. "Memorandum by Sir Henry Maine on the Powers and Responsibilities of the Secretary of State as regards the Council of India," 8 November 1880, L/PO/Misc. 5. The document was produced at Lord Hartington's request when Parliament, sensitive after the Afghan War, wanted to review the Council's financial powers. Previous Secretaries differed sharply on the extent of these powers, and Maine attempted to clarify the situation. The minute was so edifying that the Permanent Undersecretary forty years later (T. W. Holderness) had it reproduced for use in considering legislation after World War I.

33. Lord Chancellor Hatheley, quoted in Singh, *The Secretary of State*, p. 26.

34. Sir M. E. Grant Duff (ed.), *Sir Henry Maine: Life and Speeches* (New York: Henry Holt & Co., 1892), pp. 16–17. For an examination of Maine's "guiding philosophy," see Brian Smith, "Sir Henry Maine and the Government of India (1862–87)," *Journal of Indian History* 41:3 (December 1963), pp. 565–75.

35. Maine, "The Secretary of State and Council of India," p. 4.

36. *Ibid.*

37. *Ibid.*, pp. 4–5.

38. Godley to Curzon, 7 August 1901, Curzon Papers [hereafter cited as CP], IOL, MSS. Eur. F.111/160.

39. Godley to Curzon, 19 September 1901, *ibid.*

40. Godley to Curzon, 11 January 1901, *ibid.*

41. *Ibid.*

42. Curzon to Godley, 5 June 1904, Kilbracken Papers [hereafter cited as KP], IOL, MSS. Eur. F.102/22. For an overview of the events leading up to Curzon's

proposals, see Heather Coughlan, "The Role of the Council of India, 1898–1910," unpublished Ph.D. thesis, Duke University, pp. 145–65.

43. 1 December 1904, CP F.111/440, ff. 33–36.

44. Godley to Elgin, 29 November 1894, Elgin Papers (9th Earl of Elgin) [hereafter cited as EP], IOL, MSS. Eur. F.84/24.

45. Godley to Curzon, 26 June 1904, CP. F.111/440, ff. 41–44.

46. *Curzon Memorandum*, CP F.111/440, ff. 33–36.

47. *Ibid.*

48. *Ibid.*

49. Godley to Curzon, 26 June 1904, CP F.111/440, ff. 41–44.

50. In fact, the War Office Council hardly ever met: 1891 (11 times), 1892 (8 times), 1893 (7 times), 1894 (4 times), and in 1895, prior to Rosebery's resignation, the Army Council did not meet at all. The Council was reorganized in 1895 and again in 1901. See W.S. Hamer, *The British Army: Civil-Military Relations, 1885–1915* (Oxford: Oxford University Press, 1971), pp. 145–47 and 165–70.

51. Brodrick to Curzon, 22 December 1904, CP F.111/164.

52. Godley to Brodrick, 8 August 1904, KP F.102/2.

53. *Ibid.*

54. *Ibid.*

55. *Ibid.*

56. Godley to Elgin, 29 November 1894, EP F.84/24.

57. John Slagg, "Parliament and the Government of India," *Contemporary Review* 45 (February 1884), 210–23. See also William Birkmyre, *The Secretary of State for India in Council* (London: Cassell & Company, 2nd ed., 1886).

58. Slagg, "Parliament and the Government of India," p. 219.

59. Birkmyre, *The Secretary of State for India in Council*, p. 8.

60. See pp. 25–27, *supra*.

61. For a clarification of the acts relating to "secret" and "urgent" communications, and the Secretary of State's power to withhold such from the Council, see memorandum on the "Powers of the Secretary of State and the Government of India in the Secret Department," IOR, Political and Secret Department Memorandum D.75.

62. See Williams, *The India Office*, pp. 186–208.

63. Internal and External divisions in India were not formalized until 1914, and in the India Office until 1930. See Martin Moir, "A Study of the History and Organisation of the Political and Secret Departments of the East India Company, the Board of Control and India Office, 1784–1919, with a Summary List of Records," unpublished thesis (archival administration), University of London, 1966, pp. 126–29. See also Owen T. Burne to Godley, 7 March 1887, L/PO/Misc. 1.

64. See Williams, *The India Office*, pp. 209–94.

65. A Special Branch, responsible for the "collection of intelligence on political, social and religious movements" in India—under the direction of the General Superintendent for the Suppression of Thuggee and Dacoity—reported to the Secretary of State through the GOI Foreign Department (Moir, "Political and Secret Departments," p. 177). See also Sir Percival Griffiths, *To Guard My People. The History of the Indian Police* (London: Ernest Benn, 1971), pp. 121–37.

66. Moir, "Political and Secret Departments," p. 178.

67. For a detailed account of the issue concerning the Natu brothers and British

fears about sedition in India, see "Powers of the Secretary of State in the Secret Department," Political and Secret Department Memorandum D.149 [in continuation of D.75].

68. Lord George Hamilton, unbound file (Political and Secret Home Correspondence) 2458/1899, filed with Godley to Hamilton, 9 February 1901, L/PO/Misc. 5.

69. Walpole to Godley, 25 July 1900, L/PO/Misc. 5.

70. Godley to Hamilton, 9 February 1901, *ibid.*

71. Godley, *Home Government*, p. 5. This is corroborated by the IO *Urgent Book* [List of Orders or Communications made under clause 26 (Urgency) of Act 21 & 22 cap. (*sic*) 106 with the Reason Recorded by the Secretary of State for Making the Same, 1873–1920], IOR, C/133. In 1886, an IO committee reviewed this procedure and recommended that the practice be dropped; however, it continued de facto beyond this point.

72. Hamilton to Curzon, 21 May 1902, Hamilton Papers, IOL, MSS. Eur. C.126/4.

73. In the summer months it was difficult to achieve the quorum of five, and much business was delayed until October (Morley to Minto, 29 August 1906, Morley Papers, IOL, MSS. Eur. D.573/1). See also Hamilton to Curzon, 26 August 1903, Hamilton Papers, IOL, MSS. Eur. C.126/4.

74. Coughlan, "Role of the Council of India," p. 18.

75. Owen T. Burne, *Memories* (London: Edward Arnold, 1907), p. 286.

76. Godley, *Home Government of India*, p. 12.

77. See handwritten memorandum (1913?), filed with Government of India Act, 1858 (s.23), IOR, Council of India, C/143.

78. Godley to William Lee-Warner, 14 July 1905, KP F.102/2.

79. Godley to Horace Walpole, 15 June 1905, *Ibid.*

80. "First Report of the Special Committee on India Office Procedure," [hereafter, "First Report"] 9 February 1886, L/PO/Misc. 5, p. 4. The Committee included Godley, Lord Harris (Parliamentary Undersecretary) and Councillors Henry Maine and Richard Strachey.

81. Godley to Lee-Warner, 15 June 1905, KP F.102/2.

82. Godley, *Home Government of India*, pp. 12–15.

83. Godley to Heads of Department, March 1889, P&S Department Memoranda Book, I, 210a. Godley added that "I shall be glad if Heads of Departments will bear in mind that all alterations which Committee may desire to suggest, in the drafts submitted to them by the Secretary of State or by his orders, should be written in the margin as suggestions; and that no cancellation or insertion under any circumstances be made in the body of the draft or on behalf of the Committee."

84. Williams, *The India Office, passim*, especially pp. 453–81.

85. See Singh, *The Secretary of State*, pp. 162–72, and Coughlan, "The Role of the Council of India," pp. 26–67. Williams, *The India Office*, provides several appendices unveiling Council assignments for the first decade.

86. L. Abrahams, "Memorandum on the Financial Organisation and Procedure of the India Office," *Royal Commission on Indian Finance and Currency* (Appendix 34, p. 1019), Cd. 7238 (1914), XX.

87. See Bradford Spangenberg, *British Bureaucracy in India* (Columbia, Mo.: South Asia Books, 1976), p. 49.

88. See Godley's recommendations on Council appointments, Godley to Kimberley, 7, 13, 20, 23, and 28 January, 1888, Kimberley Papers, Private Ownership, D/17.

89. A. T. Bassett, *The Life of the Rt. Hon. John Ellis, M. P.* (London: Macmillan and Co., 1914), p. 225.

90. A. C. Lyall to James Lyall, January 1888, quoted in Sir Mortimer Durand, *Life of the Rt. Hon. Sir Alfred Comyn Lyall* (Edinburgh: William Blackwood and Sons, 1913), pp. 322–23.

91. Sir Charles Wood, "Directions for the Transaction of Business in the India Office," L/PO/Misc. 5.

92. Godley to Cross, 21 July 1891, L/PO/Misc. 5.

93. See Williams, *The India Office, passim.*

94. Godley to Kimberley, 18 February 1884, L/PO/Misc. 5. Godley was opposed to Louis Mallet's view that a large Council could more easily be divided against itself and that lowering the number of Members would increase their power vis-à-vis the Secretary of State. Godley countered that lower numbers would *increase* efficiency in policy-making and servicing paperwork (Godley to Kimberley, 24 July 1884, Kimberley Papers D/8).

95. See "First Report," p. 1.

96. See draft correspondence on proposed "Rules for the Conduct of Business" drawn up by Godley (L/PO/Misc. 5). Except for Sir A. Eden, who feared a decrease in the Council's power, the main objections were over the proposed regulations on official leaves—which were eventually adapted to the Council's liking, and the Rules went into effect and were essentially unaltered up to independence. The recommendations of the Committee on Home Charges, 1888, are located in their "Sixth Report," IOR, Finance Department, L/F/9/1. The flow of papers "Before Council" is detailed in a Godley memorandum dated 25 March 1900, L/PO/Misc. 3. Interestingly, these recommendations did not go as far as the proposed Council of India Bill of 1914 whereby Lord Crewe would have essentially "departmentalized" the Council by attaching one member to each India Office department. For the debate over the Council of India Bill, 1914, see S. A. Husain, "The Organisation and Administration of the India Office, 1910–1924," unpublished Ph.D. thesis, University of London, 1978, pp. 214–47.

97. Hamilton to Curzon, 5 April 1900, cited in Singh, *The Secretary of State*, p. 156. See also Lord George Hamilton, *Parliamentary Reminiscences and Reflections, 1868–1885* (London: John Murray, 1917), II, 26.

98. See Singh, *The Secretary of State*, p. 69; and R. S. Jain, *The Growth and Development of [the] Governor-General's Executive Council (1858–1919)* (Delhi: S. Chand & Co., 1962), p. 174.

99. Godley to Curzon, 11 March 1904, CP F.111/163.

100. Godley to Curzon, 1 January 1904, *ibid.*

3

The Secretary of State and His Council

The Secretary of State for India—irrespective of his personal strengths, weaknesses, or political convictions—maintained a cautious and well-conceived *modus operandi* in dealing with the Council of India in the late nineteenth century. This internal relationship was particularly well defined between 1883 and 1909, largely because of Arthur Godley's presence in the Office. But it also derived from the realization by successive Secretaries that the complexity of India business could only be dealt with effectively and efficiently if major disruptions were avoided. By and large office management was left in the Permanent Undersecretary's hands and Godley was remarkably consistent in his methodology. Moreover, in his crucially situated position as Undersecretary, in which huge quantities of paper flowed across his desk, Godley was an effective arbitrator among the Secretary of State, India Office departments, and the Council of India on numerous issues. He provided the link between nine successive administrations and the Council (see Appendix C), and he was largely responsible for enlightening these men as to the mysteries of the India Office and its internal mechanisms. Still there was enough flexibility in the Office's operation that the personality of the Secretary of State could indeed change the character of the institution and dictate the atmosphere within which Indian business was conducted. Far too often India Secretaries of the nineteenth century are viewed as either mere figureheads or autocrats. In truth they were neither; each quickly learned the parameters within which he could operate, and this had a direct impact on the manner and form of policy-making, especially with regard to relations with the Council of India.

Broadly speaking, India Secretaries in the first decade of the Office concentrated on the reform and reorganization of the Office and refrained from any overt attempt to dominate or bypass the India Council.[1] This is in no small way related to the domineering personalities on the Council and the corresponding consideration by Stanley and Wood of administrative reforms as the higher priority. After 1869 several pressure groups within the Council, who were advocates of an aggressive "forward policy" in Central Asia, progressively exhibited their independence during the Secretaryships of Cranborne (later Lord Salisbury), Northcote, and Argyll.[2] Tension between the Secretary of State and his Council increased in the mid-seventies, until an open rift between them occurred during Salisbury's second term of office (1874–1878) and that of Cranbrook (1878–1880). The disagreements between these Secretaries and their Councils eventually spilled over into public attacks on the Council in Parliament, which effected several amendments to the legal relationship between the Secretary of State and Council of India—although not to the extent that the Secretary of State eliminated either the Council's de jure or de facto role in the policy-making processes.[3] It was, nevertheless, an ominous note of discord which could, if not repaired, complicate the day-to-day functioning of the India Office. The Marquess of Hartington's assumption of the Indian seals in 1880 reinstituted peace with the India Council; the situation remained, however, potentially explosive and debilitating to the Office. The arrival of Godley and Kimberley at the India Office a few years later signaled the beginning of a pattern of operation within the Office which would dominate the late nineteenth and early twentieth centuries.

Having declined the Viceroyalty two years earlier, Kimberley assumed the Indian Secretaryship in 1882.[4] At once Kimberley faced difficulties with his Council over the Ilbert Bill. Mindful of his inexperience in Indian affairs and the warnings of more experienced colleagues to avoid any open rift with the Council lest it provoke a parliamentary inquiry,[5] Kimberley resisted the Viceroy's pleas to ignore the India Council on this and several other matters.[6] Kimberley, who served as Secretary of State for India three times, chose instead to place himself on a firm constitutional footing and work around the Councillors. This was a slow process. Only a few months after his appointment, Kimberley confided to the outgoing Permanent Undersecretary, Sir Louis Mallet, that "I am beginning to understand them (the Indian questions) a little, and I am proportionally stronger, but I shall probably be turned out of office before long, and then another Secretary of State may be appointed who has to learn his business."[7] A short time later Kimberley did leave office and his prophecy materialized. However, an unanticipated development moderated the potentially unsettling effects of this semiregular occurrence. Few people anticipated that the new Permanent Undersecretary would occupy his place for a quarter of a century; but because of the length of time he held office, and his unmatched command of the legalities and conventions of Office procedure, Godley was able to facilitate the education of new Secretaries of State. He familiarized them with the constitutional and practical relationships within the India Office and thus smoothed the various transfers of authority.

Godley considered Kimberley "a good second" to Gladstone in the performance of official duties, and thought him "extraordinarily quick, shrewd and businesslike in his application of his knowledge [of social, economic and political questions] to his official work."[8] Although a concise and master draftsman, Kimberley's proclivity for excessive conversation was well known in government circles. Officials on the India Office staff confirmed that "he was very particular as to phrases in despatch-writing, and was essentially what is called a safe man while wrapt up in his work" who often required long "official" hours.[9] As a member of the Council of India, Sir Alfred Lyall noted that Kimberley was "celebrated for talking incessantly at official interviews instead of listening to the man he ha[d] sent for;" nevertheless, he was considered by all "a very strong man," very much in control of the India Office.[10]

Kimberley's relations with the Council of India presaged a pattern which was consistent during the late nineteenth century and early twentieth century in the India Office. Following his third term of office, *The Hindu*, a prominent Indian newspaper, evaluated Kimberley's performance as Secretary of State:

Our London correspondent thinks that Mr. Fowler is an improvement on Lord Kimberley as the head of Indian affairs in England, and that while willing to pay every deference to the Members of the Council and the permanent officials, he will not consent to be simply their mouthpiece. Well, this is good news, so far as it goes. Not that Lord Kimberley was always the mouthpiece of the Members of Council and the permanent officials. During the short time he was Indian Secretary in the present ministry, he overruled the Council in two important matters. But these matters involving the relation between the Ministry and its followers in Parliament, as it is a maxim that party interests, large or small, are to be preferred to every other interest, Lord Kimberley threw the Council overboard in view to the interests of his party. But whenever no party interests were involved, Lord Kimberley was, it may be said, a tool in the hands of the old officials in the India Office and was perfectly use less [sic] in initiating any reform or putting down any abuse. We hope Mr. Fowler will prove himself to be made of a different stuff, and the present radical Secretary will show greater sympathy with and confidence in the Indian people than did his predecessor whose Radicalism was only skin-deep and concealed a hard mass of Whiggism beneath.[11]

Certainly Kimberley gave more than a passing consideration to party issues and Parliament.[12] This was a fact of life in the India Office. But within the confines of the Office itself, Kimberley never ignored the Council and often utilized special committees of Council to review thorny problems. Kimberley, with Godley's help, also streamlined India Office procedure. Even Kimberley's overthrow of his Council's vote involved the means of implementing a despatch rather than any disagreement on the substance of the order. Kimberley had not yet refined the tactics of his successors, notably Lord George Hamilton, in neutralizing any negative Council reaction by informally transmitting draft measures to Members, holding individual conferences, and making concessions on smaller matters. Nevertheless, Kimberley had a firm hand on the rudder of the India Office machine—firm enough to guide it most ably among the strong ebb and flow of parliamentary, Indian, and international currents.

When Kimberley's successor, Lord Randolph Churchill, arrived at the India Office in 1885, he was known as an ultraconservative with a penchant for personally attacking Gladstone in the House of Commons. Privately, however, some politicians were concerned that Churchill might actually adopt a liberal view of Indian affairs. Shortly before he assumed the Indian Secretaryship, Churchill visited India and experienced first-hand the "Manichean duality of Riponism versus Lyttonism" which pervaded the Indian scene. Indeed, there was a general expectation that he would follow a line reminiscent of Ripon's Liberalism rather than Lytton's repression. This never materialized, for Churchill's close personal friendship with Lytton and deeply seeded conservatism progressively convinced him that increased Indian representation and responsibility were incompatible with his evolving "aristocratic idea" of Indian government.[13]

Churchill's impending arrival at the India Office created an air of expectancy in Whitehall, especially for Godley. The Permanent Undersecretary received condolences when the appointment was announced. Although they knew each other from school days at Oxford, on the face of it, Churchill's appointment did not bode well for one of Gladstone's ex-private secretaries. However, Godley knew what most outsiders did not—that the "taming and moderating effect of accession to office" called for a different tack, one that often ran counter to one's previous public posture.[14] Like Kimberley in his first term, Lord Randolph Churchill came to the India Office generally ignorant of Indian affairs (in spite of his travel to the subcontinent in 1885) and relatively inexperienced in administration. At the start of their relationship, the Viceroy, Lord Dufferin, confessed that "somewhat like a horse mounted by a new rider . . . [he] felt at first the effects of a somewhat uncertain and wayward hand."[15] However, he and Godley soon agreed that the new Secretary of State was in fact master in his own house. Owen T. Burne described Churchill's arrival at the India Office as follows:

Lord Randolph Churchill came into the India Office with the character of a reformer who was going to tear the carriage wheels off the rusty old office coach, and to toss councillors, secretaries, and clerks into some unknown abyss. An unfriendly reception was therefore in store for him, but in a marvellous manner he soon gained to his side his would-be opponents, and proved while in office a wise and earnest worker, who took short cuts through Blue-books and official papers and burnt all the red tape he could find.[16]

Churchill's relationship with his Council was cordial largely because he adopted a successful method of dealing with them and with the Office staff. He often disarmed opposition by admitting his inexperience; after his first Council meeting, Churchill confessed that he felt "like an Eton boy presiding at a meeting of the Masters."[17] It was a clever tactic endorsed by Godley and it allowed Churchill to quickly master Council procedures and the idiosyncrasies of the individual Members. This, in turn, enhanced the Secretary of State's effectiveness when he desired to influence his Councillors on specific issues.[18] Within the office this behavior was well received, and subordinate staff felt that Churchill exhibited a profound "receptivity" and candor, always willing to listen to a well-reasoned argument.[19] They responded by according him great respect and hard work. Thus a recent biographer summed up Churchill's attitude:

Lord Randolph Churchill genuinely liked Departmental work, and the power vested in the Secretary of State for India was stimulating for him. There was much of the autocrat in Lord Randolph; in the India Office "I would"—to use his own phrase—but in the Cabinet things were different: "the dull men always won the day," he complained to Herbert Gladstone many years later. The truth was that he was a great leader but a bad colleague.[20]

Perhaps more than any other Secretary of State in this period, Churchill subordinated Indian domestic policy to external considerations, and all Indian policy to its acceptance by the English electorate. Within the India Office his progressively Lyttonian proclivities led him to support Lord Roberts (an unregenerate Lyttonian with "Russia on the brain"), Sir Peter Lumsden (an ardent advocate of a "forward policy" who had been recalled from duty on the frontier—and whom Churchill subsequently helped onto the Council of India), and Lepel Griffen (the so-called hammer of the baboos who championed Lytton's repressive press laws and whose recurrent "indiscretion, rudeness, importancy and ostentatious carrying-on with 'light-skirted women' " earned him Dufferin's sustained invective.)[21] In the same vein A. W. Moore, a senior man with Indian foreign policy experience, served as Churchill's private secretary and exercised substantial influence on his chief. In fact, it was one of the few times Godley was ever challenged in his preeminent position as the Secretary of State's primary adviser. But even though Godley described Moore as "quite as much Secretary of State as his Master," Moore never came close to supplanting Godley, the permanent staff, or the Members of the Council of India in the policy-making process.[22] One interesting by-product of Churchill's evolving conservatism on Indian affairs was that he increasingly became philosophically reconciled with the India Council.

After Churchill's death in 1895, Godley confided to the Viceroy, Lord Elgin, that in many respects, and certainly for *"getting a thing done,"* Lord Randolph was the best Secretary of State he had known.[23] Although he was among the youngest to hold the Indian seals (Godley, at thirty-eight, was older than both Churchill and Lord Harris, the Parliamentary Undersecretary), Churchill quickly perceived that effective office management, and a willingness to concede smaller matters to the Council of India, could in a number of instances circumvent the complex constitutional relationships within the Office. Thus he was able to have considerable impact in the deliberations revolving around crucial issues such as Indian finance, military organization, trade and frontier policy (relating to both Russia and Burma). Outside the India Office Churchill's wholesale retreat from Riponism, his unabashed endorsement of English mercantile interests, and his implacable hostility to the fledgling Indian National Congress were vigorously criticized by Indian critics, who accused him of "being ignorant of India, utterly wanting in common candour, [and] reckless of assertion." He was castigated as "a cuckoo, only repeating the cry of his Council," and as Lord Lytton reincarnate—"a second-rate poet employed to work out the visionary plans of a second-rate novelist in India."[24] But Churchill did not kowtow to the whims of his Council; nor did he ride roughshod over them. It was the usual give and take of any Indian Secretaryship, perhaps outwardly distorted by Churchill's unusual sensitivity to the immediate pressures and electoral priorities of Great Britain.

Kimberley returned to the India Office in early 1886. With an air of quiet confidence, and with Godley's assistance, Kimberley initiated an intensive review of the office's organization and of the committee system of the India Council. Some of the Special Committee's more important recommendations (considered below) were incorporated into the Council of India Act, 1889. However, Kimberley's second term of office was uncharacteristically short and after only four months in harness, Richard A. Cross assumed the Indian seals for the next six years. Cross (later Viscount Cross) came to the India Office with considerable administrative experience, having served as Home Secretary in two Conservative governments. Although disdained by some younger politicians and critics as "Mother Cross," as fastidious as an old codger, as Home Secretary he had earned great popular acclaim by authoring several factory, sanitation, and licensing acts.[25] A light-hearted jingle of the day reflected his popularity:

> For he's a jolly good fellow
> Whatever the Rads may think;
> For he has shortened the hours of work,
> And lengthened the hours of drink.[26]

Godley described Cross, a fellow Rugbeian, as "a very pleasant, kindly old gentleman, perfectly capable of doing all that was required of him."[27]

Cross, although on excellent terms with all the "inmates" of the India Office, relied extensively on the official machine—particularly Godley—to get things done. After working with him for only a week, Godley reported to India that "our new Secretary of State is very businesslike and hard working—[he] looks into *everything* for himself, like Lord Salisbury—and will, I think, do well."[28] But Godley soon changed his estimate and a year later reported to Lord Dufferin considerable uneasiness within the India Office. Cross, reported the Permanent Undersecretary, concealed his innermost thoughts and while he was "amiable and friendly," he was

by nature rather suspicious, and is conspicuously wanting in the power of putting himself at ease with those with whom he has to do business. You may imagine what sort of man he is in this respect from a very small fact:—he still, after nine or ten months of the most intimate official relations, addresses his Private Secretary as "Mr. Maitland"![29]

Cross's performance was atypical of late nineteenth-century Indian Secretaryships. While he maintained cordial relations with his Council, leaving Godley to draft "Rules for the Conduct of Business [in the Council of India],"[30] it seemed to the Permanent Undersecretary that he had "taken the India Office without any particular enthusiasm, and seldom did any work that he was not obliged to do."[31] This tendency to pass the buck was corroborated in the testimony of a contemporary who noted that "Cross' minute on papers referred to him sometimes took the form 'consult Mr. Godley.' "[32] His aversion for decision making was also apparent to Lord Lansdowne, who throughout his Viceroyalty showed considerable initiative in dealing with exceptional domestic and foreign problems, e.g., the expansion of the Indian Councils and Afghanistan respectively.[33] This does not mean that Cross shirked all his responsibilities. He overruled his Council on several notable occasions, such as on the issues of ICS age limits and Cantonment [Contagious Diseases] legislation, when he was subjected to considerable pressure from special interest groups to pursue a certain course of action. These included the English press, specialized lobbies, and even the Cabinet.[34] However, he temporized on several important issues at the end of his tenure, and it fell to Kimberley when he returned to the India Office for a third time to sort them out. Overall, Cross's conduct at the India Office was the exception to the trend toward Whitehall's growing supremacy over Simla and Calcutta in the direction and formation of Indian policy.

Two years later (1894), Henry Fowler (later Lord Wolverhampton) arrived at the India Office. Godley considered him a "new departure" from previous Secretaries of State. He was unfamiliar with business conducted through despatches, telegrams, and private letters, and someone who would require "some special help and suggestions at first."[35] According to Fowler's daughter and official biographer, her father's promotion to the India Office

was deservedly popular. The invariable justice of public opinion approved, and the sun shone for him most brightly upon the period when he was at the India Office than during any other portion of his career. The intense interest of that great Department consumed and claimed his whole intellectual being, and the great demand called for his great supply of power in response. He learned the lore of the India Office, he grasped its technique, he mastered its material, and he dominated its counsels in an amazingly short time.[36]

This judgment, however, is much too extravagant. While Fowler possessed some very useful qualities in an exceptional degree, Godley did not consider him a first-class statesman.[37] Fowler had a tendency to make quick decisions after he thoroughly studied a problem, but was at the same time "remarkably cautious." Some years later Lord Kilbracken concluded that the most distinctive characteristic of Fowler's reign was "his habit of looking all round a question, and of considering consequences, including the effect upon Parliament and on public opinion of any proposed course of action."[38] This was certainly important in the political milieu of the day. However, it is an observation that must be qualified by the fact that during his tenure Fowler made some momentous decisions on the relationship between Whitehall and the Government of India.

In the daily operation of the India Office, Fowler displayed great confidence in the permanent staff, and his relations with his Council were generally friendly and pleasant. In this respect he was fortunate that Kimberley, his immediate predecessor, was the one who had to overrule the India Council on the Cotton Duties and Cantonment Acts legislation—difficult issues left open-ended at the end of Cross's service. But Fowler was no passive tool in the hands of the Council; nor was he simply a slumbering figurehead as India Secretary. It was he that reaffirmed and clearly defined the principle that the Cabinet and House of Commons ultimately governed India. It was during Fowler's Secretaryship that the supremacy of the Home Government over the Government of India, and that of the India Office over the Viceroy's Executive Council, was clearly and unequivocally articulated.[39] (See Chapter 4.) The political exigencies of the day—the exaggerated sensitivities of the political parties to "public opinion" and the pleas of special interest groups—imposed themselves upon Fowler's tenure at the India Office more than any previous Secretary of State. Amidst the confusion, the Secretary of State outlined the existing constitutional and real relationship between the centers of Indian administration. The Home Government's dominance over the Government of India crystallized in Fowler's Indian Secretaryship, and was extended in the subsequent terms of Hamilton, Brodrick, and Morley.

Godley played a large role in helping to refine and communicate this posture to the Viceroy, Lord Elgin, and the Government of India. The Permanent Undersecretary also continued to be an intermediary between the Council and the Secretary of State. For example, Godley helped develop the compromise solution of a countervailing excise duty on Indian goods in the cotton duties question between the Home and Indian governments. This issue directly stimulated debate over the Home Government's authority to mandate a certain course of voting by official members of the Viceroy's Council. Fowler acknowledged his debt to Sir Arthur in handling this and many other complex issues, always allowing that his own mastery of Indian affairs "was in a great measure due to the initiation and instruction which he received from so able and distinguished a man as Lord Kilbracken."[40] Although the Indian press was ruthless in its condemnation of both Fowler and Elgin and withdrew its earlier optimism about the Secretary of State,[41] Elgin acknowledged that the overall feeling in India was "that no [Secretary of State] had acted more fearlessly [and] strongly for the best interests of India."[42]

Fowler's successor, Lord George Hamilton, headed the India Office for eight and a quarter years, longer than anyone else during Godley's tenure, and only reluctantly vacated his office in 1903 after a Cabinet dispute involving Free Traders and the advocates of preferential tariffs in Imperial administration and trade.[43] Hamilton was an experienced administrator, having served as Parliamentary Undersecretary at the India Office from 1874 to 1878, and two terms as First Lord of the Admiralty, before taking over the Indian seals. Provoked in part by Hamilton's recent opposition in Parliament to Indian interests in the cotton duties debate, the periodical *India*, voice of the Indian National Congress in England, speculated that "neither [the Earl of Onslow] nor Lord George Hamilton is likely to give much trouble to the permanent officials at the India Office or to the bureaucrats in India."[44] Several recent studies have considered Hamilton's India Office career, but generally limit their remarks to Hamilton's relations with the volatile George Curzon in India.[45] There is a tendency to overlook the fact that Hamilton had been Secretary of State for nearly four years before Curzon went to India. It was during that time that Hamilton developed and finely tuned his skills in dealing with the Council of India, using tried and tested techniques. Hamilton, always attentive to Godley's learned advice, continued to discuss problems with individual Councillors and often provided them with proposals in draft form. Hamilton's approach in attempting to neutralize or evade Council opposition to schemes he favored was also modelled on the successful approach used by his predecessors. Essentially, as noted before, "everybody, and above all a corporate body like a Council, likes to have a hand in initiating a desirable change."[46]

Hamilton's relations with Elgin proved to be an invaluable training period for the turmoil which would characterize Curzon's Viceroyalty. In a number of areas—cotton duties, cantonment legislation, plague rules, frontier policy (especially Chitral), famine and agricultural policy—Hamilton was in conflict with the Government of India.[47] Soon after Curzon's accession to the Viceroyalty relations between the Secretary of State and Viceroy, as well as between their respective Councils, deteriorated. The continuous dialogue over the relationship between the Home and Indian Governments during Hamilton's tenure provides the clearest picture of the harmonious relationship between the Secretary of State and his Council.

Hamilton disclosed some of the details of the daily intercourse between the Secretary of State and India Council. On the use of private telegrams to the Governor-General, Hamilton revealed that far from being suspicious, the Councillors often encouraged that the Viceroy either be appraised privately of impending legislation or that "unofficial" recommendations be forwarded for consideration in connection with certain despatches.[48] The Council remained, however, much more reluctant to grant these same privileges to "secret" correspondence. Additionally, the Secretary of State and Council reached an understanding on the scope of independent action which the India Office chief might take on subjects legally within the Council's authority if it would expedite some uncontroversial types of business.[49] Hamilton rarely defied tradition in dealing with the Council of India. Unlike most members of the Cabinet, who seldom perused or completely digested highly concentrated summaries of problems, the India Councillors usually thoroughly read and familiarized themselves with their papers. Although Godley continued to revise and expedite the flow of paper within the Office, neither Hamilton nor any Secretary of State ever accused the Councillors of dragging their feet.[50] That would have invited the anger of the Council, which would quickly point out that the volume of Indian paperwork was simply too great for such a small group.

S. N. Singh's assertion that "it was not until late in the 19th Century, particularly from Hamilton's term, that the Secretary of State's influence became paramount" over the Council, errs on two counts.[51] First, Hamilton adopted techniques well entrenched in the India Office before his arrival there; he only refined and formalized them. Second, despite his confidence in dealing with the India Council, and even on occasions when he was supported by Curzon and the Government of India, Hamilton remained "chary" of being overruled by the Council.[52] Hamilton's most elaborate espousals about his relations with the Council of India were in defense of that body from Curzon's attacks. Hamilton acknowledged the ability of an individual Councillor—well-respected and an authority in a given area—to influence the Council and at the very least, to slow down the decision-making process. Therefore, because a majority of the Council was absolute—and it was not easy to overrule a really strong member with "personal knowledge" of a question—Hamilton often promoted compromise solutions to difficult problems.[53] Sometimes Hamilton attempted to maneuver in and around the Council by appointing special committees to review especially complex situations.

The importance of individual communication between the Secretary of State and Councillors was well understood by Lord George Hamilton. Like his predecessors in office, Hamilton frequently consulted Councillors on specific cases and on prospective Indian appointments. The Councillors also recognized the advantage of this open channel to the Secretary of State—and occasionally directed informal personal notes or minutes to him arguing their case. Hamilton's belief in exchanging information with the Council became so much a fixture within the India Office that Clinton Dawkins, former Finance Minister in Curzon's government who had taken up a post in the War Office, reported to the Viceroy that the Secretary of State was decidedly weak in the face of his Council. Dawkins reported that Hamilton, in presenting the Northwest Frontier Bill to the Council, had done so in "the baldest and most colourless" language. What was needed, offered Dawkins, was a "strong and determined Secretary of State who will insist on his own way and riddle the present system with ridicule."[54] Hamilton, however, tenaciously adhered to these very low-key techniques disdained by Dawkins as those best suited for getting his way with the Council. In return for this consideration and for defending the Council against attacks by the Government of India, Hamilton generally received the support of his Council. The major exceptions—when Hamilton did not carry his Council—concerned agricultural, famine, and plague policies.[55]

Like his predecessors, Hamilton was susceptible to Cabinet and parliamentary pressures. For example, dealing with the question of Imperial Famine Grants and Coronation expenses, the Government of India was able to play to the press and Cabinet and effect a counterpoise to the combined strength of the Secretary of State and Council of India.[56] All in all, Hamilton steered an even course between the often vituperative charges of the Viceroy of India and antagonizing his Council lest Parliament be stirred into action. It was this last consideration which dominated Hamilton's thinking—for he considered the "amount of waste and the disorganisation" which would attend a parliamentary investigation an "evil inseparable from Parliamentary control, ... an evil ... at times expanding into a danger."[57] Because the inner workings of British officialdom were hidden from the public, Hamilton received generally unfavorable treatment by the India press when he left office. A more contemporary assessment perpetuates this negative image of Hamilton, noting that he was "a staunch tory of the Victorian era, [whose] political imagination was limited by his attachment to the Imperial *status quo.*"[58] What is more significant, however, is that in this light his tenure was no different from any other late nineteenth-century Secretary of State, who, while representing India to

Her Majesty's Government, was often forced to remind the Indian Government of its subordinate role to the India Office and ultimately to Parliament.

When Balfour reconstructed his Cabinet in September 1903, St. John Brodrick (later Lord Midleton) moved from the War Office to the India Secretaryship. A close personal friend of Curzon, Brodrick had experienced a controversial and emotionally charged term as Secretary for War, especially in his attempts to introduce Army reform during the Boer War.[59] In the midst of controversy, a relieved Curzon expressed confidence in Brodrick as "a resolute man [with] . . . much strength of character as well as rectitude of purpose."[60] Curzon and Hamilton both had been reserved in their criticism of Brodrick in those halcyon days; this restraint, however, dissipated almost totally in the summer of 1903 when Brodrick placed Hamilton and the Government of India in an awkward position by virtually committing India to bear one-half the expense of maintaining troops in South Africa as a reserve in case of war with Russia—*before* hearing the Government of India's answer to the proposal. Brodrick had been tactless before, and now Hamilton chided that "this clumsy method of dealing with a difficult question is one peculiar to Brodrick," and concluded that his "never-failing 'gaucherie' will prevent him from ever becoming either a popular or a really capable minister."[61] Fortunately, the Government of India's plea to drop the plan as too impractical and expensive was strengthened by Lord Kitchener's concurrence when he arrived in India as Commander-in-Chief. Ironically, a few months later Brodrick replaced Hamilton at the India Office.

Although Curzon had maintained an active correspondence with Brodrick since 1880, he lamented the "new and . . . painful experiment" of having to start with a new Secretary of State almost at the end of his term.[62] Curzon expected their relations to be "of the most confidential and satisfactory character," although Brodrick would have to demonstrate

some change of clothes before he can be generally recognised as the whole-hearted champion of Indian interests. The War Office point of view is not the India Office point of view, or even if it is that, it is most certainly not the point of view of the Government of India.[63]

Curzon also expected an unfavorable reaction in India when the appointment was announced. After all, he argued, "if he is transferred from the War Office, it will be because he is not thought to have succeeded there, and no Department is particularly overjoyed at receiving the failures of another." Still, Curzon expressed a hope that India could eventually help Brodrick retrieve his tarnished reputation.[64]

Brodrick, for his part, promised Curzon he would "never differ from you if I can possibly help it, and I have perhaps an exaggerated view of the necessity of trusting the man on the spot."[65] No other words could possibly have elicited more agreement from Curzon. Brodrick was greatly impressed with the complexity of the India Office business and procedure.[66] Furthermore, he was delighted at the capabilities of the India Office staff, and in particular, learned rather quickly how invaluable an asset Godley was in running the Office. Godley found that Brodrick treated him with "friendliness and confidence,"[67] and Brodrick, for his part, promised to adhere strictly to the Permanent Undersecretary's advice on India Office procedures.[68] Godley continued to fulfill important functions which had become his duty over the previous administrations—advising the Secretary of State on committee appointments within the Council of India, attending committee meetings in order to minimize substantial changes in draft legislation, and acting as general counsel on a wide range of complex constitutional issues.[69]

Brodrick obviously lacked the experience which Hamilton had gained in eight years of working with the Council, and he unhesitatingly adopted the basic formula for dealing with that body: he utilized individual expertise, held individual consultations, utilized Godley's "good office" and persuasiveness to assist in securing votes, and above all displayed a respect for the Council of India as both an institution and valuable source of experience.[70] Nevertheless, Brodrick's relations with his advisers were strained by Curzon's relentless attacks on the Council of India. The Secretary of State confessed that he had more difficulty in "manipulating" members of Council than had Hamilton, and that he had to work overtime with great diplomacy and careful "management" to get the Council to approve a majority of Curzon's proposals.[71] Like his predecessor, Brodrick "toned down" most proposals to the Council and tended to "lie by for a bit rather than run other chances of defeat."[72] However, the Secretary of State's reports to Curzon came only after one and one-half years of very strained relations between the Council and Viceroy, and Brodrick's confessions to Curzon must be suspect.

In fact, the entire Curzon-Brodrick correspondence was permeated with "dishonesty" by both men. Brodrick learned from Walter Lawrence, Curzon's Private Secretary, that the Viceroy had the Secretary of State's letters printed in Calcutta—a long-established procedure so that the Viceroy could have easy access and reference to the large and diverse correspondence generated by the Government of India. Brodrick refused to "open up" his innermost thoughts because of this, and despite Curzon's assurances that nothing leaked in India, Brodrick resented the "sort of veiled reproach [from the Viceroy on] the dullness of my letters, to which I am not insensible."[73] By 1905 Curzon, too, refrained from communicating his "innermost feelings" because he recognized that "such frankness was not desired, and . . . I have deliberately confined my letters, upon the analogy of your own, to the more commonplace incidents that were not likely to provoke disagreement."[74] Brodrick charged that it was not Curzon's frankness to which he objected, but the "tone of denunciation which made the weekly receipt of your letters a positive pain to me."[75] Eventually Curzon ceased all correspondence with Brodrick and Godley, so that the India Office had to turn to the Governors of Bombay and Madras for information about the actions of the Government of India.

During Brodrick's tenure Curzon became increasingly incensed with the Council of India, and he turned his frustration on the Secretary of State. He wrote to Clinton Dawkins that Brodrick's Council was "delighted to have got a new man, who does not know anything of India, and they knock the spots off us with the keenest satisfaction."[76] Brodrick, Curzon maintained, had reneged on his earlier promise to let the "man on the spot" take decisive action (especially in foreign affairs) and finally admitted to Godley that: "I am regarded with jealousy and dislike by an Indian Council in England who are conscious of derogation from their former authority, and that I am even a source of disquietude to a Secretary of State who is anxious to assert his own individuality."[77] It was then that Curzon introduced his proposals to amend the Government of India Act mentioned earlier. The proposals, however, were eventually turned down by the India Office and Cabinet. But it was not that the Council found Brodrick a weak Secretary of State and opted to exert their powers more than they had under Hamilton; rather, Curzon had begun to make proposals on issues in which the Council of India, and often the Secretary of State himself, felt the Viceroy had gone too far, too quickly, and their constitutional role as a "brake" on such excessiveness was at once accentuated.[78]

Brodrick and the Council of India enjoyed their greatest rapport in dealing with the military administration question—the so-called Curzon-Kitchener Dispute. The controversy itself has been reviewed elsewhere in depth.[79] What needs attention, however, is how the India Office dealt with the issue and the role played by the Secretary of State and his Council. Again Brodrick followed the example of his predecessors in establishing a special committee of Council to deal with an especially difficult problem. The committee also included prominent individuals from outside the India Office.[80] The dispute revolved around the division of military responsibility between the Indian Commander-in-Chief, who did not sit on the Viceroy's Council, and the Military Member, who did. In the end the special committee ruled against Curzon, and the Viceroy became obsessed with the idea that the Council, Cabinet, and Secretary of State were all against him. In particular, he saw Brodrick as a weak and incompetent Secretary of State (especially as compared to Hamilton) who was trying to "score off an old friend in private, and humiliate the Viceroy in public."[81]

The political exigencies of the day combined to force Curzon's resignation. In a pencilled note composed late in his life, Curzon placed the blame for all that happened squarely on Brodrick:

St. John Brodrick was a greater friend of mine at Balliol and in after life than at Eton. He was in some respects my closest friend in public life until in an evil hour he became Secretary of State while I was Viceroy. In two years he succeeded in entirely destroying both my affection and my confidence. Burning to distinguish himself at the India Office as the real ruler of India, as distinct from the Viceroy, egged on by my superior successes in public life—a feeling of which all our friends were cognisant—phenomenally deficient in tact, and tortuous and mean in his actual procedure—he rendered my period of service under him one of incessant irritation and pain, and finally drove me to resignation.[82]

Godley, on the other hand, believed that Brodrick was "a really kindly-disposed, good-hearted fellow," but with "abnormal sensitiveness." He had, according to Godley, "literally strained every nerve to the last, according to his limits, to avoid a row" with Curzon.[83] Inasmuch as he favored Kitchener's position, Godley too eventually parted ways with Curzon over the military administration question. In fact, Godley's relations with Curzon were markedly cool and, on the occasion of Curzon's death, he recounted a story told to him by authoritative sources. The sources conveyed that "his [Curzon's] first wife on her death-bed made him [Curzon] solemnly promise never to be reconciled to three individuals whom she named—Balfour, Midleton and myself [Godley]."[84]

In 1905 the Earl of Minto succeeded Curzon in India and, following the Liberal victory in December, John Morley (later Viscount Morley of Blackburn) accepted the India Secretaryship.[85] Recent scholarship on John Morley at the India Office has provided us with a cross section of opinion about Morley's tenure generally, and his role in the development of the so-called Morley-Minto Reforms in particular.[86] Morley and Godley were old acquaintances, sharing a close relationship with Gladstone which had helped stimulate both their political careers. Godley, in fact, had declined to author Gladstone's biography following the Grand Old Man's death and had recommended Morley for the task.[87] Godley considered Morley "the most intellectually brilliant" of the Secretaries under whom he served.[88] When he drafted despatches, they were lucid and pleasurable reading. Morley's weakness, however, seemed to be his uneven temperament. This emotionalism prompted his Parliamentary Undersecretary, J. E. Ellis, to characterize the Secretary of State as "a man of moods."[89] This moodiness was often reflected in Morley's correspondence with officials in India, and Lord Ampthill, Governor of Madras, confided to Godley that the Secretary of State's letters made him a bit "creepy" and seemed "stern and cold and they lack[ed] the 'human' element which characterized the letters of his predecessors."[90]

Morley's relations with Godley were far from ideal. The new Secretary of State, concerned with what he perceived to be an unimaginative and conservative bureaucracy, considered the Permanent Undersecretary of State the ultimate buffer between himself and the Government of India.

He was especially critical of Godley's "categorical" assessments which rarely seemed to go beyond the black-and-white of an issue. Morley had experienced a similar difficulty with Gladstone, and he attributed Godley's like behavior to his former chief's influence.[91] In large part it was their common "tendency to autocracy" which most often strained their official relationship.[92] Still, Morley required Godley's knowledge of the guild secrets of the India Office, and Godley continued in harness throughout most of Morley's term of office.

Most observers felt that Morley, although a nonconformist in many respects, would readily adapt to utilizing the Council of India's experience. This feeling was best enunciated in *The Englishman*'s editorial note that "just as a wild elephant is made amenable by being run with a number of trained elephants, so, we doubt not, Mr. John Morley will run amicably with his Council at the India Office."[93] But this was not the case at all. Like many of his contemporaries in the post-Gladstonian Liberal elite, Morley was a firm believer in the ideal of "ministerial responsibility," and he was critical of what he perceived to be gross administrative incompetence.[94] The result was that he tended to take on much routine work himself—a task imposing enough for the entire office staff, let alone the Secretary of State for India. In a conversation with Dunlop Smith, Minto's Private Secretary, Godley assessed Morley's general office management:

He [Godley] then spoke freely about Lord Morley. He told me [Dunlop Smith, Private Secretary to Lord Minto] nothing that I did not know or guess, but it was most interesting as showing what is thought of their Chief by the India Office, and it gave me an insight into their mutual relations. Godley said that Lord Morley is at once the most autocratic *and* most vain person he has ever seen. In addition, he has a very quick sense of his responsibility for everything that is done by any official in India, whatever rank, and thinks he can supervise every small detail of the administration. Sir A[rthur] said he is quite as notorious a centralizer as Lord Curzon and is very impulsive. Frequently when a telegram reaches him at his home at Wimbledon he fires off a reply without consulting anyone or looking up the papers. He is perpetually on the look-out for any imaginary infringement of his rights and position, and is either blind to those of others or wilfully ignores them—as in the case of Lieutenant-Governorships. Even when anyone has a right of any kind and proves it up to the hilt, he declines to recognize it by saying he is "ultimately responsible" for everything that happens in India.[95]

Morley's intense dedication exacted its toll, and after a year in office he broached the subject of retirement with the Prime Minister. However, his growing interest in Indian reform, and the gentle persuasions of the Prime Minister and King, combined to convince Morley to remain at the India Office.[96]

Initially Morley's relations with his Council were amicable. Although he considered them not wholly possessing of "elasticity and spring and breadth," and few members were, in his words, "sagacious," Morley came to view the Council on the whole "assiduous and capable."[97] Morley too adopted the accepted procedures in dealing with the Council developed by his predecessors. He frequently discussed specific issues with individual Councillors whom he considered as having the requisite expertise, and he did not hesitate to tap valuable experts outside the India Office, such as Sir Alfred Lyall, recently retired from the Council of India, for aid in drafting his reforms.[98] Additionally, Morley, like previous Secretaries of State, recognized the value of the Council's committee system, and especially the usefulness of establishing special committees to consider difficult problems. The special committee "technique" could be used not only to counter the negativism of a particular Member of Council, but served also as the very best of "sounding-boards" for such difficult problems as Army Reorganization and the proposed legislative reforms.[99]

One of the first issues Morley faced was the complicated military administration question. In order to facilitate the new Secretary of State's understanding of the matter, Godley prepared a long memorandum on the subject for Morley.[100] Godley and the Council of India hoped to make the despatch on army reorganization, favoring Kitchener, stand. Morley, however, was concerned that it provided potential loopholes allowing for the assertion of military over civilian authority, and he established a special committee of Council to reconsider the situation one more time. The special committee did in fact reassess its position and agreed to limit the freedom of the Military Supply Member to bypass proper channels in the Calcutta Secretariat. The Council then helped Morley to "overrule" the combined opposition of the Commander-in-Chief (Kitchener) and Viceroy (Minto) in India. Morley was grateful for the Council's support in this first major piece of business, and declared he couldn't have had a "better tone" or "more conscientious attention" on the matter by his Councillors.[101]

The so-called Morley-Minto Reforms provided Morley another opportunity for utilizing special committees of Council. The Councillors' first chance to discuss the reforms came in the spring of 1907, when Morley brought Sir A. T. Arundel from India to London to discuss his committee's preliminary report on Indian reforms.[102] Despite his earlier success with the Council, Morley suspected they might not be "very helpful" in this issue because "certainly, with one or two exceptions, they are not exactly of the noble tribe of born reformers."[103] This skepticism, Morley confessed, was enhanced by such "trifles" as having to summon Arundel home, "only showing how frightfully stiff are the joints of the veteran steeds with which I have to do my share of our chariot-race."[104] Morley, however, accepted a great many of the committee's recommendations, and in September created yet another special committee to consider further reform proposals from the Government of India.[105] Despite some individual dissents, the Council of India adopted the special committee's report, and Morley, pleased that there had been fewer points of disagreement between the Council and Government of India than he had anticipated, elatedly called the Secretary of State and his Council one "happy family."[106]

Morley appointed a third special committee to deal with the question of Muslim representation. Here Morley encountered some stiff resistance from the Council's "Muslim bloc." In order to break the back of Council opposition, the Secretary of State initiated informal contacts with the Viceroy before taking his plan to the full Council; although he wound up breaking a tie-vote in Council himself, Morley was able to effect a compromise between the parties and avoid any extended debate.[107] Thus the Council of India played a primary role in the development of the Indian Councils Act of 1909, largely because of the Secretary of State's willingness to use it and his appreciation of their efforts. Equally important was the fact that the Cabinet was largely preoccupied with other matters, and Morley himself refrained from presenting them with any large amount of information until plans were largely completed.

Hence, a re-evaluation of Morley's relationship with the Council of India is required. The following assessment by Stanley Wolpert is perhaps closest to the truth:

Although many critics often accused Morley of doctrinaire disregard for his Councillors' advice, he was most sensitive to their criticism and opinions, trying always to sway them by reason of his position . . . rather than attempting to ride roughshod over the constitutional hurdle of their dissent.[108]

Godley's own interpretation of Morley's internal office relationships was tempered by his personal disagreements with the Secretary of State. He considered Morley "a very able, but very vain, impulsive, and ambitious Secretary of State, extremely anxious to leave his mark on the history of India and[,] nurtured in the principles of the French Revolution . . . [with] an exceptionally weak Council . . . [and] a ditto Viceroy—you know what to expect."[109] If Godley exaggerated Morley's relations with his Council and staff from his inside view, the press erred in the same manner outwardly, noting upon Godley's retirement how "the combination in recent years of two such powerful personalities as Lord Morley and his old friend Sir Arthur Godley at the India Office has tended, perhaps, to diminish the full measure of influence in the shaping of policy the India Council should possess."[110] Morley's Private Secretary, Arthur Hirtzel, discounted the mistaken impression of office relationships offered by *The Times* by noting the similar "autocratic" nature of the two men.[111]

Still, mistaken impressions of the internal relationships of the India Office during Morley's tenure persist. S. N. Singh contends that "from the moment Morley became the Secretary of State for India . . . he set himself to belittle and to counteract the functions which the Council was intended to exercise."[112] Such an erroneous assessment is based on observations by *The Times* which called Morley's tenure an "uncontrolled autocracy" that rendered his Councillors "mere ciphers,"[113] and the observation of one of Morley's former Secretaries that "no more autocratic Secretary of State for India ever reigned in Whitehall; none ever consulted his Council less."[114] Finally, Morley's own *Recollections*, according to Singh, clearly demonstrate that Morley "invariably had his own way."[115] Morley was, in fact, most cautious in dealing with his Council, and he was genuinely grateful for their aid in dealing with several difficult and complex problems. His success in obtaining their loyalty and aid was based upon his recognition and successful implementation of the formula developed by his predecessors in working with and utilizing the Council of India within the prescribed constitutional framework.

Nor can individual criticisms of Morley by a few Councillors be given too much credence. In 1910 Sir Steyning Edgerley accused the Secretary of State of bypassing the Council of India by using a Departmental Secretary as his final adviser in particular cases.[116] In fact, Edgerley had joined the Council in March 1909, and his criticism was hardly representative of the Council as a whole since he had missed virtually all of Morley's term. Besides, India Secretaries had long utilized the advice of experienced department secretaries in complementing Council deliberations or as a final authority in matters not requiring Council approval, with the Council's full knowledge and acquiescence. Another anonymous Member of Council allegedly complained, in an article in the *National Review*, of Morley's habit of using the Cabinet to override the Council after lengthy and careful consideration of a problem, always speaking of how important it was to agree on what would best "go down" in the House of Commons rather than the merits of a case. The Council vigorously denied the charge to Morley, and informed the author that such charges were "all moonshine." Morley, for his part, managed "innocently to survive, not a hair turned, and character unstained."[117] The Cabinet, however, was far too preoccupied to interfere actively in the Council of India's debates, and for the most part, Morley cautiously and deliberately fed information to them while legislation was in tentative form. Morley's "veiled threats" to the Council were largely designed to speed up their deliberations.[118]

It is safe to say that the Council of India in the late nineteenth century was more a consultative than a controlling body. It is also reasonable to suggest that its membership was comprised of men less captivated by the past, when the problems of consolidation and the legacy of the Mutiny dominated their thinking than the generation of Councillors who served in the sixties and even into the seventies.[119] Rather, the late nineteenth-century Councillors were men whose technical knowledge and diverse Indian experience had elevated them to the lofty heights of the Council and whose overall abilities were somehow recognized by each successive Secretary of State. Even if a Secretary of State with a strong personality was inclined to bypass or ride roughshod over his Council, there remained the legal obligation to conduct Indian business in Whitehall as a corporate entity, *the Secretary of State in Council*. So what evolved over time was an understanding about the manner in which business was conducted within the Office. This included not only the role of the Secretary of State and his permanent staff but also the relationship between the India Office departments and Council committees. It did not always work perfectly or smoothly—but it did work. This is not to say, however, that the various Secretaries of State could not and did not impress their own stamp on the *content* of policy; nor does it imply that individual styles did not affect the level of tension surrounding the policy-making process. But the remarkable feature of Indian policy-making from roughly 1880 to 1914 is how uniformly a series of highly individualistic Secretaries of State conformed to established conventions within the Office for the formulation of policy.

But the India Office, with all its component parts, was not alone in its responsibility for Indian policy. There were other important contributors to the decision-making process—Parliament, the Cabinet, and other departments of state, all with constitutional and quasi-constitutional obligations in the task of Indian governance. Understanding the office's external responsibilities and constitutional relationships is necessary in order to assess the formation of policy in the Home Government of India during the period after 1880.

NOTES

1. Donovan Williams, *The India Office, 1858–1869* (Hoshiarpur, Punjab: Vishveshvaranand Vedic Research Institute, 1983), *passim*, and S. N. Singh, *The Secretary of State for India and His Council, 1858–1919* (Delhi: Munshi Ram Monohar Lal, 1962), *passim*.

2. See John Lowe Duthie, "Pressure from Within: The 'Forward' Group in the India Office During Gladstone's First Ministry," *Journal of Asian History* 15 (1981), pp. 36–72.

3. See Singh, *The Secretary of State*, *passim*, and Edward C. Moulton, *Lord Northbrook's Indian Administration, 1872–1876* (Bombay: Asia Publishing House, 1968), *passim*.

4. Gladstone to Kimberley, 24 April 1880, Kimberley Papers [hereafter cited as KMP], private ownership, D/20.

5. Northbrook to Ripon, 8 June 1883, Ripon Papers, BL, Add. MSS. 43,598.

6. For an extended discussion of the Ilbert Bill and its ramifications, see Edwin Hirschmann, *White Mutiny: The Ilbert Bill Crisis in India and the Genesis of the Indian National Congress* (Columbia, Mo.: South Asia Books, 1980), *passim*. See also S. Gopal, *The Viceroyalty of Lord Ripon, 1880–1884* (London: Oxford University Press, 1953), *passim*.

7. Kimberley to Mallet, 3 March 1884, cited in Singh, *The Secretary of State*, p. 53.
8. Lord Kilbracken, *Reminiscences* (London: Macmillan and Co., 1931), p. 157.
9. Owen T. Burne, *Memories* (London: Edward Arnold, 1907), pp. 262–63.
10. Lyall's observations on Kimberley's assumption of office (1893) are quoted in Sir Mortimer Durand, *Life of the Hon. Sir Alfred Comyn Lyall* (Edinburgh: William Blackwood and Sons, 1913), p. 350. See also Kilbracken, *Reminiscences*, p. 158.
11. Extract from *The Hindu*, 2 May 1894, IOR, Public and Judicial, L/P&J/6/374/911.
12. During the cotton duties question, Kimberley confided to Elgin that "my Council disagreed with the views of the Cabinet, but they look, as is natural, at only one side of the question.... We are obliged to look all around and where there is nothing but a choice of evils to choose that which seems to us the least." (Kimberley to Elgin, 9 March 1894, Elgin Papers [hereafter cited as EP], IOL, MSS. Eur. F.84/12.)
13. R. F. Foster, *Lord Randolph Churchill: A Political Life* (Oxford: The Clarendon Press, 1981), p. 183.
14. Kilbracken, *Reminiscences*, p. 172.
15. Dufferin to Godley, 12 August 1885, Dufferin Papers [hereafter cited as DP], IOL, MSS. Eur. F.130/10.
16. Burne, *Memories*, pp. 262–63.
17. Quoted in R. R. James, *Lord Randolph Churchill* (London: Weidenfeld and Nicolson, 1959), p. 197. See also Winston S. Churchill, *Lord Randolph Churchill* (New York: The Macmillan Co., 1906), I, 476.
18. Churchill, *Lord Randolph Churchill*, p. 477. See also Gopal, *Lord Ripon*, *passim*.
19. Lord Dufferin, quoted in James, *Lord Randolph Churchill*, p. 197.
20. *Ibid*.
21. Foster, *Lord Randolph Churchill*, pp. 184–85.
22. Quoted in *ibid.*, p. 185.
23. Godley to Elgin, 25 January 1895, EP F.84/30b.
24. *The Indian Mirror*, 27 November 1885, cited in Foster, *Lord Randolph Churchill*, p. 205.
25. See Churchill, *Lord Randolph Churchill*, p. 308.
26. Quoted in Kenneth Rose, *Superior Person* (London: Weidenfeld and Nicolson, 1969), p. 242.
27. Kilbracken, *Reminiscences*, p. 174.
28. Godley to Mackenzie Wallace [postscript], 13 August 1886, DP F.130/24b.
29. Godley to Dufferin, 6 May, 1887, DP F.130/27a.
30. See draft correspondence regarding "Rules for the Conduct of Business [in the Council of India]," L/PO/Misc. 5.
31. Kilbracken, *Reminiscences*, p. 174.
32. H. W. Garrett Collection, IOL, MSS. Eur. D.515/1, p. 12.
33. For several assessments of Lansdowne's Viceroyalty, see J. P. Misra, *The Administration of India under Lord Lansdowne* (New Delhi: Sterling Publishers, 1975), and Marc J. Gilbert, "Lord Lansdowne in India: At the Climax of an Empire,

1888–1894, A Study in Late Nineteenth Century British Indian Policy and Proconsular Power," unpublished Ph.D. thesis, UCLA, 1978.

34. For an overview of the debates on the ICS, see R. K. Perti, *South Asia: Frontier Policies, Administrative Problems and Lord Lansdowne* (New Delhi: Oriental Publishers & Distributors, 1976), pp. 186–207. For a discussion of the India Office role in the Cantonment Acts crisis, see Arnold P. Kaminsky, "Morality Legislation and British Troops in Late Nineteenth Century India," *Military Affairs* 7:3 (June 1979), 249–64.

35. Godley to Elgin, 9 March 1894, EP F.84/23.

36. E. H. Fowler (née Hamilton), *The Life of Lord Wolverhampton* (London: Hutchinson and Co., 1912), p. 286.

37. Kilbracken, *Reminiscences*, p. 174.

38. See Lord Kilbracken's remarks in Fowler, *Wolverhampton*, p. 290.

39. For an overview of the cotton duties crisis, see Peter Harnetty, *Imperialism and Free Trade: Lancashire and India in the Mid-Nineteenth Century* (Vancouver, B.C.: University of British Columbia Press, 1972); Harnetty, "The Indian Cotton Duties Controversy, 1894–1896," *English Historical Review* 77:35 (October 1962), pp. 684–702; and P. L. Malhotra, *Administration of Lord Elgin in India, 1894–99* (New Delhi: Vikas Publishing House Pvt., 1979), pp. 33–67.

40. Fowler, *Wolverhampton*, pp. 289–90.

41. See Malhotra, *Elgin in India*, p. 37. For Indian criticism of Hamilton's handling of an investigation into the miscarriage of justice being carried out by the Government of India—in which the Secretary of State was charged with "playing to [a] Tory Gallery and cheers"—see *The Hindu*, 2 May 1894, L/P&J/6/374/911.

42. Elgin to Godley, 25 January 1895, EP F.84/13.

43. For a synopsis of the controversy, see R. V. Kubicek, *The Administration of Imperialism: Joseph Chamberlain at the Colonial Office* (Durham, N.C.: Duke University Press, 1969), pp. 154–73.

44. *India*, August 1895, p. 226.

45. See P. Bandyopadhyay, "British Famine and Agricultural Policies in India, with special reference to the Administration of Lord George Hamilton, 1895–1903," unpublished Ph.D. thesis, University of London, 1969, and Heather Coughlan, "The Role of the Council of India, 1898–1910," unpublished Ph.D. thesis, Duke University, 1971, pp. 68–144.

46. Hamilton to Curzon, 21 May 1902, Hamilton Papers [hereafter cited as HP], IOL, MSS. Eur. C.126/4. Coughlan, while providing a most useful account of Hamilton's position between his Council and Curzon, fails to point out the historic development of Hamilton's tactics (as regarded relations with his Council) as developed by his predecessors. Additionally, Coughlan has concentrated solely on private correspondence as a means of discerning the role of the India Council, including the functioning of Council Committees, to the total exclusion of draft minutes and despatches located in the India Office Records.

47. For contrasting views of the Elgin-Hamilton relationships, see Malhotra, *Elgin in India* and Bandyopadhyay, "Famine and Agricultural Policies," *passim*.

48. Hamilton to Curzon, 1 February 1900, HP C.126/2.

49. See Coughlan, "Role of the Council of India," pp. 75–76.

50. See memoranda, "Before Council," 23 March 1900; "Instructions as to the

Sending of Papers to the King," 20 June 1901; and "Method of appointing Members of Council, approved by the Secretary of State, 20th March 1905" (L/PO/Misc. 3).

51. Singh, *The Secretary of State*, p. 69.

52. Coughlan, "Role of the Council of India," p. 78.

53. Hamilton to Curzon, 13 March 1903, HP C.126/5.

54. Dawkins to Curzon, 24 May 1901, Curzon Papers [hereafter cited as CP], IOL, MSS. Eur. F.111/178.

55. This is particularly true in famine policy where Hamilton vacillated between support for and against the Government of India (Bandyopadhyay, "Famine and Agricultural Policies," pp. 24–89 and 90–154). Malhotra also places the blame for slow action on Hamilton (*Elgin in India*, pp. 106–86). Both, however, agree on the force of "Imperial" considerations operative on the Secretary of State in both his famine and plague policies.

56. Coughlan, "Role of the Council of India," pp. 119–44.

57. Lord George Hamilton, *Parliamentary Reminiscences & Reflections, 1886–1906* (London: John Murray, 1922), II, 26.

58. Bandyopadhyay, "Famine and Agricultural Policies," p. 365.

59. For an overview of the Curzon-Brodrick relationship, see David Dilks, *Curzon in India* (London: Rupert Hart-Davis, 1969), II, 30–50. For an account of Brodrick's War Office career, see Hamer, *The British Army: Civil-Military Relations, 1885–1915* (Oxford: Oxford University Press, 1971), *passim*.

60. Godley to Curzon, 3 January 1901, CP F.111/160.

61. Hamilton to Curzon, 14 August 1903, CP F.111/162.

62. See correspondence between Brodrick and Curzon, Midleton Papers, BL, Add. MSS. 50,073. This correspondence did, however, have some very delicate moments in 1902 (when Curzon threatened to resign over the issue of Coronation expenses) [Rose, *Superior Person*, p. 356].

63. Curzon to Godley, 23 September 1903, CP F.111/162.

64. Curzon to Hamilton, 23 September 1903, *ibid*.

65. Brodrick to Curzon, 15 October 1903, *ibid*.

66. The Earl of Midleton [St. John Brodrick], *Records and Reactions, 1856–1939* (London: John Murray, 1939), p. 209.

67. Kilbracken, *Reminiscences*, p. 183.

68. Brodrick to Godley, 14 October 1903, KP F.102/7.

69. Godley to Brodrick, 2 November 1903 and 8 August 1904, KP F.102/7. Coughlan ("Role of the Council of India," p. 148) has overestimated the "uniqueness" of these functions. Godley did in fact fulfill a similar function for *all* his previous chiefs. The assumption that this indicates a "weakness" on Brodrick's part is erroneous; for he was, in fact, shrewd enough not to alter the existing system by taking on too much work for himself as he had done previously at the War Office.

70. Again, Coughlan ("Role of the Council of India," p. 149) has taken Brodrick's relations with his Council out of context. Far from being an indication of inexperience or weakness on his part, Brodrick merely adapted to time-tested procedures. The fact that the Council occasionally rejected a proposal supported by both the SS and Viceroy (e.g., the proposal to move the Punjab Government from Simla in 1905) was neither unusual nor wholly distasteful to the Secretary of State for India.

71. Brodrick to Curzon, 10 February and 3 March 1905, CP F.111/164.
72. Brodrick to Curzon, 20 January 1905, *Ibid.*
73. Brodrick to Curzon, 17 December 1903, CP F.111/162.
74. Curzon to Brodrick, 8 June 1905, CP F.111/164. See also Curzon's assurances to Brodrick, 7 January 1904, CP F.111/163.
75. Brodrick to Curzon, 30 June 1905, CP F.111/164.
76. Curzon to Dawkins, 9 March 1904, CP F.111/162.
77. Curzon to Godley, 4 January 1904, KP F.102/60A.
78. Cf. Coughlan, "Role of the Council of India," pp. 169–70.
79. See Dilks, *Curzon in India*, II, *passim*. See also John E. Lydgate, "Curzon, Kitchener and the Problems of Indian Army Administration, 1899–1909," unpublished Ph.D. thesis, University of London, 1965; and Stephen P. Cohen, "Issue, Role, and Personality: The Curzon-Kitchener Dispute," *Comparative Studies in Society and History* 10:3 (April 1968), pp. 337–55.
80. The Committee consisted of Brodrick, Lord Salisbury (Lord Privy Seal), Lord Roberts, and Sir G. White (former Commanders-in-Chief of the Indian Army), J.J.H. Gordon and J. L. MacKay (Members of the India Council) and Sir E. Law (former Finance Minister, GOI). Godley himself was active in the resolution of this problem (file [by Sir G. White] on *Indian Army Administration*, KP F.102/61). A further summary is contained in *Diary of the Indian Military Administration Question*, Morley Papers [hereafter cited as MRP], IOL, MSS. Eur. D.573/41.
81. Curzon to Barnes, 14 September 1905, CP F.111/183.
82. Rose, *Superior Person*, p. 353.
83. Godley to Ampthill, 15 December 1905, Ampthill Papers, IOL, MSS. Eur. E.233/14.
84. Kilbracken to Sir Alexander Godley, 28 March 1925, cited in Eveline Godley (ed.), *Letters of Arthur, Lord Kilbracken and General Sir Alexander Godley* (Cheltenham: Privately Printed, 1949), p. 226.
85. S. A. Wolpert, *Morley and India, 1906–1910* (Berkeley and Los Angeles: University of California Press, 1967), pp. 27–28. See also Stephen Koss, *John Morley at the India Office 1905–1910* (New Haven, Conn.: Yale University Press, 1969), pp. 49–56.
86. In addition to Wolpert and Koss (*supra*), see M. N. Das, *India under Morley and Minto: Politics behind Revolution, Repression and Reforms* (London: George Allen and Unwin, 1964) and Syed Wasti, *Lord Minto and the Indian Nationalist Movement, 1905–1910* (Oxford: Oxford University Press, 1964).
87. Kilbracken, *Reminiscences*, pp. 224–28. Nevertheless, Godley did carry on correspondence and private consultations with Morley throughout the four-year period, giving Morley a "powerful and re-creating stimulus" in completing the formidable task (Morley to Godley, 15 July 1902, Kilbracken Papers, BL, Add. MSS. 44,902). Moreover, Godley was involved in dissuading Morley from destroying Gladstone's papers when he was completed with his work (F. E. Hamer [ed.], *The Personal Papers of Lord Rendel* [London: Ernest Benn, 1931], p. 180).
88. Kilbracken, *Reminiscences*, p. 183. Godley noted that he was delighted at the prospect of working with a man of such "quick and keen all-around intelligence" (Godley to H. E. Richards, 16 May 1906, Erle Richards Papers, IOL, MSS. Eur. F.122).
89. Kilbracken, *Reminiscences*, p. 183.

90. Ampthill to Godley, 30 January 1906, KP F.102/39.
91. 13 December 1907, Diary of Frederick Arthur Hirtzel [hereafter cited as HD], IOL, Home Miscellaneous Series, No. 864, II, 105.
92. 3 January 1908, HD III, 9.
93. Quoted in Biographical Notes by F. A. Hirst for his planned book, *Morley in 1906*, MRP D.573/1.
94. For an overall discussion of the philosophy and attitudes of the post-Gladstonian Liberal Party, see H.C.G. Matthew, *The Liberal Imperialists* (Oxford: Oxford University Press, 1973), pp. 257–64.
95. J. R. Dunlop Smith to Minto, 21 June 1908, cited in Martin Gilbert (ed.), *Servant of India* (London: Longmans, Green and Co., 1966), p. 158.
96. See Morley to Campbell-Bannerman, 22 and 30 December 1906, and 23 January 1907, Campbell-Bannerman Papers, BL, Add. MSS. 41,223. See also 25 February 1907, HD II, 22 and 7 March 1907, HD II, 25.
97. Morley to Minto, 21 May 1908, MRP D.573/3.
98. For a list of individual Councillors consulted in special areas, see Coughlan, "Role of the Council of India," pp. 201–22.
99. For an overview of special committees used in Morley's tenure, see Coughlan, "Role of the Council of India," pp. 207–58. See also Wolpert, *Morley*, pp. 75–79.
100. 12 December 1905, MRP D.573/41.
101. Morley to Minto, 9 February 1906, MRP D.573/1.
102. See Das, *Morley and Minto*, pp. 188–95, and Wolpert, *Morley*, pp. 129–66.
103. Morley to Minto, 28 March 1907, MRP D.573/2.
104. Morley to Minto, 17 April 1907, *ibid.*
105. Coughlan, "Role of the Council of India," p. 238.
106. Morley to Minto, 5 November 1908, MRP D.573/3.
107. Wolpert, *Morley*, p. 142.
108. For a discussion of the Muslim Bloc in the Council of India, see Wolpert, *Morley*, pp. 198-99.
109. Kilbracken to A. Chamberlain, 13 May 1917, Austen Chamberlain Papers, Birmingham, England, cited in Koss, *Morley at the India Office*, p. 95n.
110. *The Times*, 11 October 1909, p. 11.
111. 11 October 1909, HD IV, 82.
112. Singh, *The Secretary of State*, p. 61.
113. *The Times*, 29 June 1914, p. 9.
114. John H. Morgan, *John, Viscount Morley: An Appreciation and Some Reminiscences* (Boston: Houghton Mifflin Company, 1924), p. 32.
115. Singh, *The Secretary of State*, p. 61. Morley does not claim any "victory" over his Council or belittle their contribution in several difficult problems, as Singh might have us believe (footnote 3). Morley was "relieved at not having to overrule my Council" in the matter of the reform proposals (John Morley, *Recollections* [New York: The Macmillan Co., 1917], II, 317).
116. India Council Minute Book, 19 October 1910, pp. 277–78. Cf. Coughlan, "Role of the Council of India," pp. 203–4.
117. The article was by Sir Charles Roe, "India and the Democracy," *National*

Review 52:311 (January 1909), pp. 848–58. For the Secretary of State's evaluation of the happenstances, see Morley to Minto, 21 January 1909, MRP. D.573/4.

118. Morley described the stubbornness of some individual Councillors, and noted, "I am the least in the world of a Cromwellian, but I am beginning to understand in a way I never understood before, how impatience at the delays and cavillings and mistaking of very small points for big ones at last drove Oliver to send his councillors packing" (Morley, *Recollections*, II, 315).

119. See Chapter 2, *passim*.

4

External Responsibilities and Constitutional Relationships

The formation of policy in the India Office involved the consideration of external influences, including formal and informal relations with the Crown, Cabinet, Parliament, and other departments of state. Sir Arthur Godley outlined the scope and complexity of the Office's business:

> The constitution of the India Office is a peculiar one, and it is no easy matter to master either the letter of the law, or the way in which the law is practically worked; these two subjects being as is generally the case in English institutions, quite distinct and independent of each other.... The India Office ... differs from all the other public offices, with the exception of the Colonial Office, in having no special group of subjects allotted to it; it is concerned with all the affairs, great and small, of a gigantic Empire, and contains under one roof some eight or nine departments, corresponding respectively to the Treasury, the Board of Trade, the Foreign Office, and so on.[1]

India Office relations with the Crown in the late nineteenth century generally were cordial and especially well defined. While nominal deference was extended to the Crown in passing along necessary business, such as the formalization of certain Indian appointments and proposed alterations in the India Office establishment, Godley noted that "practically ... the whole of the patronage of the King, and of the Secretary of State in Council, is exercised by the Secretary of State."[2] Despite the strict control of information sent on to the King[3] and the virtual nullification of the Crown's constitutional rights as regarding Indian administration, both Victoria, who reigned for all but the last eight years of Godley's tenure, and Edward VII, who had visited India as the Prince of Wales in 1875–76, actively solicited information and maintained correspondence with the Governors-General in India.[4] Members of the Secretary of State's establishment, however, while conscious of their allegiance to the Crown, consistently took measures to counteract any palace interference in the administration of India. The relative absence of any major conflicts during the Godley era substantiates Sir Arthur's assessment that the Secretary of State by and large usurped the ability of the Crown to interfere in the internal affairs of the India Office. However, on several occasions between 1883 and 1909, the India Office had to reassert that principle.

The first notable clash between the India Office and Queen occurred in 1885, when Lord Randolph Churchill intended to appoint Sir Frederick Roberts Commander-in-Chief in India. The Queen disliked Roberts's wife, and the situation was further complicated by Victoria's desire to appoint the Duke of Connaught to the vacant Bombay command. At first Lord Randolph moved cautiously to circumvent this royal interference in the management of the India Office. In July 1885 the Secretary of State appealed to Salisbury, the Prime Minister, to use his good offices to communicate his support of Roberts to the Queen and explain his objection to conferring a post with enormous political and military responsibility upon a member of the royal household.[5] It was, of course, not just a question of Churchill's reluctance to give in to royal jobbery; the issue was compounded by the Secretary of State's disdain for the royal circle, particularly Connaught, and the Queen's Secretary, Henry Ponsonby. In fact, Churchill had referred the issue to the Queen only as a courtesy when the appointment of Sir D. M. Stewart to the Council of India, which did not require royal assent, created the vacancy.

The next phase of Lord Randolph Churchill's conflict with the Queen spotlighted a problem which would plague Secretaries of State throughout the late nineteenth and early twentieth centuries—private correspondence between Indian officials and the Crown. When Salisbury informed Lord Randolph that the Queen had privately solicited predictably "enthusiastic" responses from Roberts and Stewart on Connaught's appointment, and suggested that Churchill give way, the Secretary of State was furious and immediately threatened to resign. Churchill succinctly laid out the constitutional issue at hand: "A first-class question of Indian Administration has been taken out of my hands, and at any moment this action may recur, and it is clear to the Viceroy that I do not occupy towards himself the position which the Secretary of State ought and is supposed to occupy."[6] It was a "safe form of self-assertion," for Salisbury could not accept his resignation so soon after the formation of the Cabinet on such embarrassing grounds.[7] Not without some bitterness, Lord Randolph Churchill won the day, as Roberts became Commander-in-Chief and Connaught settled for the Bombay command in 1886, well after Churchill's India Secretaryship terminated.

The Secretary of State was not the only one concerned with private communications between India and England which bypassed the India

Office. The Viceroy at times also felt compelled to solicit his chief's help in curbing troublesome statements from the Queen. Elgin, in particular, was angered over the Queen's private correspondence with Indian Princes. Godley agreed with the Viceroy, and voiced strong objections to such communications, citing

1. the unsettling effect of any change;
2. the encouragement of the idea that communications with the Supreme power otherwise than through the Viceroy was permissible; and
3. the difficulty of deciding *which* of the Native Chiefs might be so honoured.[8]

The Queen's public telegrams after the Poona Plague riots in 1894 also created considerable difficulties for Elgin. Her references to the riots as "premeditated" and her citation of the Muslims as the "real friends of the British Government" were of grave political consequence.[9] Elgin again beseeched Godley to seek Fowler's help in curbing such royal excesses.

The Viceroy was also concerned with private communications between the Presidency Governors and both the India Office and Crown. Although the Governors had the legal right to carry on such correspondence, successive Viceroys complained that it only enhanced the tension between the Government of India and subordinate Governments. Curzon especially complained that as long as the two Governors alone had this right, "they would air their grievances to him [the Secretary of State] [and] regard themselves as petty Viceroys and India as a triumvirate."[10] The Secretary of State, Hamilton, eased the tension by continually reminding the Governors of their subordination to the Government of India and Governor-General. In fact the "aggressiveness" of the Governors was greatly exaggerated, although only a few, notably Sandhurst, Northcote, and Havelock, complained directly to the India Office and officials at Court. This line of communication, although carefully controlled by the Secretary of State, proved invaluable during the last months of Curzon's tenure when the Viceroy ceased writing to the India Office.[11]

Still, as much as the Governors were chastised for their private correspondence, the Viceroy was not above utilizing his own right of correspondence with the King as a foil to the Secretary of State and India Office. Curzon successfully solicited Edward VII's aid in the debate over Coronation expenses in 1902 when Lord George Hamilton and the Cabinet were presented with the threat of royal interference solely at the Viceroy's instigation.[12] The threat of such royal involvement, usually in the form of adverse publicity, often outweighed the real effects of any such action. In 1908 Morley agonized over Lord Minto's private correspondence with the King concerning negotiations with the Amir of Afghanistan for, as he informed Godley, he endorsed Lord Randolph Churchill's assessment of the legality of such correspondence rendered in 1885 on moral grounds:

"God forbid that I should allow myself for one moment to throw a shadow of a doubt upon the right of the Sovereign to communicate with the utmost freedom on any conceivable matter with any one of his subjects."[13] Godley, however, was quick to pose the question "would he [Churchill] have been prepared to give the same free hand to any one of the King's subjects who might happen to be his, Randolph's, subordinate? I am perfectly certain that if Lord Dufferin had done anything of this kind Randolph would have been as prompt to resent it as any of his predecessors or successors."[14] Although he believed in their legality, Morley remained unconvinced about the harmlessness of the Viceroy's conduct. But Godley assured Morley that Minto's correspondence would have little practical effect, and he could think of no other successful actions of this kind—even during Curzon's highly charged Viceroyalty—because

the fact is, I suppose, that one can generally rely upon the loyalty and good sense of the G[overnor] G[eneral], or, if by chance that should fail, upon his knowledge that the [Secretary of State] has the whip hand of him [and] will be displeased if he tried to press his views on the Government by means of his correspondence with the King.[15]

Godley called Minto's letters "pardonable indiscretions" and harmless, and succeeded in getting the Secretary of State to "deal with it with a light hand."[16] Thus circumvented, King Edward usually limited himself to questions of a personal nature, and rarely succeeded in forcing a decision upon the India Office in a matter of any substantive nature. Occasionally the Crown opted to exert its influence through another medium—the Cabinet.

The Secretary of State for India's relationship with the Cabinet was two-dimensional. As the head of the India Office and the "guardian" of Indian interests, the India Secretary was often at odds with the Cabinet regarding issues in which Indian and Imperial interests were opposed. Party considerations also weighed heavily in relations between the Secretary of State for India and the Cabinet. But the victories achieved by any Secretary of State were paltry indeed, compared to the number of times India had to conform to the absolute dictum that Imperial policies and needs had top priority. This situation created serious difficulties for the Indian Secretary. While conforming to Imperial policy on the one hand, simultaneously he had to reject many proposals by the Government of India on the other. The Secretary of State often hid behind the cloak of "Cabinet sanction" or "parliamentary legitimacy" in disallowing action by the Government of India. This produced an intriguing situation in which a number of Secretaries of State for India felt compelled to modulate the flow of detailed information to the Cabinet. In what manner then, did the relationship between the Cabinet and the Secretary of State manifest itself?

The Secretary of State for India was master in his own domain, the India

Office. However, he was also a member of the Cabinet and participated in policy-making for the Empire at large, and at times the tension created by these two loyalties strained even the most capable ministers. Lord Randolph Churchill's disagreements with Lord Salisbury over the appointment of the Duke of Connaught to an important Indian post (the Bombay military command) have already been mentioned. Salisbury's Cabinet could do little to salvage the deteriorating relations between the Queen and Churchill and, in fact, Lord Salisbury's opinion of Churchill decidedly worsened. The India Secretary caused the Prime Minister so much trouble that when a friend commiserated with Salisbury on the dual burden of the Premiership and Foreign Office, Salisbury quipped that "I could do very well with two departments, [but] in fact, I have four—the Premiership, the Foreign Office, the Queen, and Randolph Churchill—and the burden of them increases in that order."[17] The tension between the Prime Minister and Secretary of State for India was aggravated by an internal struggle within the "Ministry of Caretakers" over the Irish Home Rule question. This estrangement, however, did not preclude Churchill from pressing for and eventually securing Cabinet sanction for the annexation of Upper Burma (1885), ostensibly as a counterpoise to French intrigues in the area.[18]

Although the Conservatives held office during much of the late nineteenth century, they did not have a monopoly on disagreement between the India Office and Cabinet. The constant shifting of party politics in England was, as Godley noted, "very objectionable, [and] a real hinderance to business."[19] The Liberal victory in 1892 was decidedly unpopular with Victoria and relations, particularly between the Queen and Gladstone, were steadfastly proper in public but often strained in private.[20] Toward the end of Gladstone's fourth ministry, several significant disagreements occurred which highlighted the complex relationship among the Secretary of State for India, the Cabinet, and the Crown.

On occasion the head of the India Office could use the Cabinet to his advantage in admonishing the Government of India. In 1892 for example, Lord Roberts's term as Commander-in-Chief of the Indian Army was about to end, and the Viceroy, Lord Lansdowne, requested Roberts's reappointment. However, the Secretary of State, Lord Kimberley, confided to his Cabinet colleague Sir Henry Campbell-Bannerman, Secretary of State for War, that Roberts was the "powerful representative of a forward policy" which could involve India in "serious dangers." He suggested that Campbell-Bannerman find a sound *"military* reason" to remove Roberts from India, one to which the Indian government would be forced to accede.[21] This was a prelude to replacing the Viceroy. Privately Kimberley speculated that "if we are in Office when Lansdowne's term is over we can select a Viceroy, who is not a jingo [and who would be] strong enough to counteract" the advocates of a forward policy in Calcutta.[22] In the spring of 1893 the opportunity to remove Roberts arrived, and Sir George White was appointed Commander-in-Chief, shortly before Lansdowne himself was replaced by Lord Elgin, just as Kimberley had predicted.[23]

If Kimberley was ultimately successful in using the Cabinet to prevent Roberts's reappointment, the events surrounding the appointment of Lansdowne's successor clearly demonstrate the limited effectiveness of the Secretary of State in affairs closer to the Cabinet and Crown. While Lansdowne regretted Cross's resignation as a "most painful subject," he was nevertheless relieved to find Kimberley his new superior, since they had "always been on good terms."[24] Still, Lansdowne desired to return home, and privately communicated his desire to Godley. The Permanent Undersecretary of State quickly protested, pointing out that "no such idea has ever been mentioned here, and I can say at once that Mr. Gladstone has the most friendly disposition toward you, 'and hopes that you will fully reciprocate it.' "[25] At a Cabinet meeting in early August 1892, Kimberley brought up the subject of Lansdowne's successor. At that point the Queen actively involved herself in the deliberations by urging the appointment of Lord Rosebery, then Foreign Secretary. But neither Rosebery nor Lord Herschell, Chancellor of the Exchequer, could be spared.[26] Godley and Sir D. M. Stewart, former Commander-in-Chief in India and Member of the Council of India, recommended Sir Henry Norman, Governor of Queensland and a former Member of the India Council, for the Viceroyalty.[27] Rosebery countered with the name of the Scottish Liberal, the Ninth Earl of Elgin, although the impending debate on Irish Home Rule and the immediacy of reaching some agreement tempered his opposition to Norman. The next day Kimberley reported to the Prime Minister that the Foreign Secretary and Edward Majoribanks—once a candidate himself and the Party's Chief Whip—acceded to Norman's nomination.[28]

The Cabinet, however, was still divided on Norman, and in an attempt to avert continued internal dissention at a critical time, given the tenuous state of party politics, Kimberley approved of Elgin's nomination and Gladstone presented it to the Queen (whose technical approval was required).[29] Up to this point royal involvement had been minimal; now Victoria challenged Elgin's nomination, criticizing him as "very shy, and most painfully silent, [a man with] no presence [or] experience in administration . . . [who] would not command the respect which is necessary in that office."[30] Her new choice was Lord Carrington (later First Marquess of Lincolnshire and then Lord Chamberlain of the Household). After considerable argument the Queen finally agreed to offer Elgin the Viceroyalty on August 22, 1893. But Elgin refused, according to Kimberley basically "on account of his wife's health and his numerous children."[31] Again the lot fell to Norman. The events surrounding Norman's initial acceptance and subsequent withdrawal of the Viceroyalty were an acute public embarrassment to the Government.[32]

Queen Victoria suggested the possibility of extending Lansdowne's term, but neither Kimberley nor Gladstone would hear of it.[33] Meanwhile, more prominent names in the Government were bandied about: Lord Cromer, Lord Reay (formerly Governor of Bombay), Sir Henry Loch (High Commissioner to South Africa), and Lord Spencer. Finally, the Secretary of State for India and Prime Minister decided to offer Elgin another chance, failing which Kimberley was prepared to recommend Carrington.[34] The Queen, changing her mind for a third time, now pressed Kimberley to appoint Lord Spencer, asserting that he was "the only really fit person and India is well worth the sacrifice of sparing him from Home work."[35] The Queen's concerted efforts, however, were in vain; Lord Rosebery had already re-established informal contact with Elgin and received his assurance that if a second offer were made, he felt it his "duty to help."[36]

In the entire affair several important relationships are apparent. First, Kimberley, as head of the India Office, initiated Cabinet consideration of the viceregal appointment. As a responsible member of the Cabinet, he consulted his colleagues and utilized their good offices in order to present India with the best available candidate. The Secretary of State's voice in the matter was formidable—up to a point. Kimberley had to work within a frame of reference geared to political exigencies at home; only by remaining flexible, yet firm, was he able to persuade the Cabinet of the soundness of his choice of Elgin, and together with the other Government Ministers present a united front in opposition to the Queen. For Victoria's part, while her opinion elicited due respect from the Cabinet, her effectiveness was by and large neutralized by a strong-willed Prime Minister and a resolute Secretary of State for India. Perhaps the most maligned person in the selection of the Viceroy in 1893 was the victor, Elgin himself. Only recently has the historical record been corrected to reflect the true circumstances of his appointment and achievements in India.[37]

The selection process of a new Viceroy always contained considerable potential for conflict between a Secretary of State and the Cabinet. Kimberley was an able Secretary, actively concerned with Indian interests; nevertheless, he was susceptible to party considerations. In the end he was unhesitatingly faithful to the Prime Minister. Later, near the end of Morley's tenure, the Secretary of State actively opposed the Cabinet and Crown over Lord Kitchener's appointment as Viceroy of India.[38] King Edward VII and the Prime Minister, Asquith, strongly favored the retiring Commander-in-Chief's appointment in 1910, and when it failed to materialize, *Punch* caustically satirized Kitchener's "banishment" to the Mediterranean command as the work of jealous politicians at home.[39] Morley's ultimate weapon was the threat of resignation if Lord Hardinge was not appointed—a successful tactic because the Cabinet had become politically cautious when the King died during the previous month (May 1910).

The relationship between the Secretary of State and the Cabinet was flexible; yet the former could challenge the latter, even threaten it, only within the upper limits of the tolerance of the party leaders. The issues involved were always the prime factors in the conflict. In the struggle over Hardinge's appointment in 1910, Morley had to accept an important rebuff. According to one account, as early as September 1909, Morley had privately offered the Viceroyalty to Sir James Lyle Mackay, later First Earl Inchcape and Director of the P&O Steamship Lines. Godley, retired and elevated to the peerage as Lord Kilbracken, shared Morley's secret, and heartily approved of Morley's proposition. But the former Permanent Undersecretary of State issued an appropriate constitutional caveat that "we must... remember that the appointment lies with the Prime Minister."[40] Indeed, Morley had overstepped his authority, and Asquith and the Cabinet overruled the Secretary of State for India because they considered it unwise to appoint a man with so many commercial investments. Hence, a Secretary of State so often criticized for "running to the Cabinet" in order to bypass his Council, was anything but conciliatory in several vital issues.

Party politics inevitably affected relations between the India Office, Cabinet, and Crown, especially with regard to questions about honors. An especially difficult case concerned an honor for Lansdowne in 1894. Kimberley first broached the subject with Gladstone by noting that Lansdowne "on the whole served his term with credit and fully deserves such a mark of approval."[41] Kimberley proposed the Garter for Lansdowne, but Gladstone favored reserving such a high award for a local party supporter. Kimberley then pressed Lansdowne's "special case," and argued that Northbrook, Lytton, and Dufferin had all been advanced in peerage at the end of their time in India (Ripon already held the Garter). More important argued Kimberley, "if no mark of favour is bestowed upon him, it will give much offense... especially as he does not support us in politics."[42]

The Queen then entered the fray, and assuming Lansdowne would refuse a dukedom, she proposed the next vacant K.G. be reserved for Lansdowne (there was a precedent for this).[43] In January 1894 the Cabinet decided to make Lansdowne a Knight Grand Cross of the Order of the Bath (G.C.B.) first, and tentatively agreed to reserve for him the next vacant Garter if he turned it down. The Queen was surprised and dismayed that no announcement was made regarding Lansdowne's reward before he left for India, and complained to Kimberley that "politics never have had to do with such a thing before, and it would have the worse effect if this course were to be altered now."[44] Gladstone, who steadfastly opposed offering a dukedom to Lansdowne, considered that the reservation of the Garter was in itself an "extraordinary act."[45] Victoria repeated her denunciation of such gross political manipulations and was again "much surprised and grieved" to find that "party politics were allowed to interfere with the rewards of men who had so honourably and faithfully served their Sovereign and country abroad." She would be personally insulted to offer the G.C.B. to Lansdowne, and threatened to "leave him unnoticed" so that

1. Sir Arthur Godley reading newspaper, October 1893. Courtesy of the Godley family collection.

2. India Office interior: the Council Chamber. Courtesy of the India Office Library.

3. India Office interior: Durbar Court. Courtesy of the India Office Library.

4. India Office interior: two staircases. Courtesy of the India Office Library.

it would be "considered by the world as a *marked expression* of party hatred, which has never yet been expressed in this manner by any of her Prime Ministers." Besides, she argued, although the Cabinet might rightly discuss such matters, in the end, she, "as the fountain of honour," was solely responsible for them. It was a simple enough matter for the Queen— "the distribution of honours is not a question for the Cabinet."[46]

Gladstone set about clarifying the misunderstanding. He informed the Queen that the Cabinet had not formally discussed the matter, but as the people generally looked to the Cabinet as the seat of ultimate responsibility, he could not in good conscience "exclude from all concern in the honours bestowed upon a Viceroy those who have been and may be consulted upon his appointment, and who are absolutely responsible for his administrative acts."[47] The Prime Minister repeated his offer of the G.C.B. for Lansdowne. After further consultation between Lord Rosebery and the Queen, it was agreed that the first vacant Garter would be set aside for Lansdowne if he refused the G.C.B. Kimberley continued to press Gladstone to offer the Garter first.[48] Gladstone still resisted Kimberley's argument and called Lansdowne's career on the whole, "a very chequered one." On this basis, while he would allow for an honor for the returning Viceroy, he felt it the "special duty of my office . . . to be on the stingy side in order to keep up value."[49] To this statement Gladstone appended his explanation of events to the Queen.[50] On the same day (January 26, 1894) on which Lord Rosebery was being buttonholed on the subject by the Queen,[51] the Prime Minister secretly forwarded his concession to the Secretary of State for India, explaining that

my perspective would be this. The Garter is as a rule political. Some strong political claim might arise before there is a vacancy. Liberty as to such a claim should I think be reserved. Subject only to this reservation, I am quite ready to run the impression of willingness to offer Lansdowne should I be in office the first vacant Garter.[52]

Kimberley duly informed the Queen of the decision, adding his own assurances that "political exigency to which Mr. Gladstone refers does not seem . . . likely to arise."[53] The issue was thus resolved and later in the year, when Earl Grey died, Rosebery kept Gladstone's promise by formally recommending Lansdowne for the Garter. This episode clearly reflects the limitations of the Secretary of State in opposing the Prime Minister, even with substantive backing from the monarch. More than the Secretary of State's pressure the political necessity of having a united party in the face of difficult home legislation induced the Prime Minister to accede to the India Office requests.

The Government of India Act, 1858, failed to effect a fully operational system of checks and balances between Parliament, the Secretary of State,

Cabinet, and the Council of India. The ability of the Crown to influence the decision-making process of the India Office was severely limited and Indian affairs were generally ignored by the Cabinet except in instances of direct conflict with Imperial interests or of exceptional domestic political concern. Parliament, while theoretically the ultimate power in the governance of India, throughout most of the nineteenth century also surrendered its legal prerogatives to the Council of India and Secretary of State. Parliament, however, did reserve certain powers for itself which were an important consideration in the formation of policy in the India Office. What were the legal parameters of Parliament's jurisdiction over Indian affairs? Broken down into general categories, the powers reserved by Parliament under the Act of 1858 were:

1. The approval of all military expenditures beyond India's frontiers (except in certain sudden and urgent circumstances) [21 & 22 Vict., c. 106, s. 55];
2. The reporting of orders directing commencement of hostilities in India had to be communicated to Parliament within specific amounts of time (21 & 22 Vict., c. 106, s. 54);
3. The sole power to sanction loans raised in England based upon Indian revenues (9 & 10 Will. III, c. 44, s. 75);
4. The power to authorize additions to the staff and salaries of the India Office establishment (21 & 22 Vict., c. 106, s. 15);
5. The presentation to Parliament of additions to and alterations in regulations concerning the I.C.S. within 14 days (21 & 22 Vict., c. 106, s. 32);
6. The reservation of regulatory powers over superannuation and retirement allowances of members of the India Office establishment (21 & 22 Vict., c. 106, s. 18);
7. The right to determine the salary of the Secretary of State, two Undersecretaries of State, and Members of the Council of India (21 & 22 Vict., c. 106, ss. 6 and 13);
8. The right to approve Councillors' terms when either (a) reappointments were being considered or (b) candidates with special or peculiar qualifications were nominated to the Council (39 Vict., c. 7, s. 1);
9. The right to alter the numbers and conditions of office for Councillors, and the sole power to remove Members of Council upon an address by the Crown to both Houses of Parliament (21 & 22 Vict., c. 106, s. 11 and 32 & 33 Vict., c. 97, s. 7).[54]

By and large points 1 and 2 were of little consequence because virtually any military action in India was considered "defensive" or "urgent" by officials on the spot. Such a rationalization was almost always presented by the Indian Government or the India Office to Parliament as a fait accompli.[55] Parliament rarely gave any detailed consideration to proposals authorizing the raising of loans (3) or retirement benefits (6). Occasionally a specific issue requiring parliamentary approval, such as new I.C.S. regulations (5) was carefully reviewed by that body; however, the India Office and Civil Service Commission had usually worked out the details carefully enough so that any protracted debate was unnecessary.

Parliamentary concern over Indian affairs was greatest on specific issues dealing with the composition and functioning of the Council of India (8 and 9) and the source of the Secretary of State's salary (4 and 7). This latter issue especially created tension between the India Office and many Members of Parliament, who were under pressure from many segments of both the Indian and English press as well as the Indian National Congress. In this issue the crucial point was whether or not placing the Secretary of State's salary on the British rather than the Indian estimates would increase Parliament's control of Indian affairs. If effected, the House of Commons would then have an annual opportunity to discuss Indian affairs, aside from the pro forma presentation of the Indian budget, and it would be able to exert considerable "power of the purse" over the Indian Secretary and hence the Government of India.

Characterizing the unique relationship between Parliament and the Secretary of State in the 1880s, a knowledgeable observer commented that

for a Minister who loves an arbitrary and single-handed authority the India Office is the most attractive of all. The Secretary of State for India is (except in financial matters, where he is controlled by his Council) a pure despot. He has the Viceroy at the end of a telegraph-wire, and the Queen's three hundred millions of Indian subjects under his thumb. His salary is not voted by the House of Commons; very few M.P.'s care a rap about India and he is practically free from Parliamentary control.[56]

While Members of Parliament occasionally championed individual causes, as a body they usually had little concern or acquaintance with Indian affairs. Most Members of Parliament debated Indian questions aimlessly. John Morley described one old Anglo-Indian in the House of Commons, Sir George Campbell, who would preface his remarks with, "I am not well acquainted with this subject, but I should like to make a few remarks" and then "harangue . . . for an hour."[57] Shortly after Godley assumed the Undersecretaryship (1883), however, the India Office and particularly the independence of the Secretary of State in Council came under intense attack in Parliament. In 1885 John Slagg, senior Member for Manchester, vehemently attacked the India Office's independence of the House of Commons. He recounted the agonizing debate over the establishment of the India Council in 1858. "It must have been a weary affair," he noted. "The House, held fast in the thraldom of old East India traditions, struggling to make a new lamp of old worn-out materials" and eventually failing to reconcile the Council's responsibility with irresponsibility to Parliament.[58]

Slagg's assessment of the Council's independence from Parliament was fairly precise and accurate:

> According to Lord Palmerston the object of installing the India Council was to bring Indian affairs directly under Parliamentary control; but to what extent has it done this, or has it done it at all? The Council dislikes Parliament, and seeks on all occasions to stifle or ignore its influence, and Parliament may well return the sentiment. But the despotic power of the Council reaches far beyond Parliament: it can control every act of Government in India.[59]

This independence, claimed Slagg and his supporters, turned the Council into "a sort of *vehmgericht* or Secret Council," and "placed Parliament in dependence upon this body, so far its knowledge of Indian affairs was concerned."[60] While it was not the only such attack on the India Office, Slagg's assessment was the most incisive assault. In 1885–86 William Birkmyre, under the auspices of the Cobden Club, carried out a pamphlet campaign to stimulate the establishment of a Select Committee of both Houses of Parliament to inquire into the administration of Indian affairs.[61] Birkmyre repeated earlier accusations that the Council was really a secretive group of "ancient pensioners" who nearly brought the Empire to "ruin" thirty years earlier.[62] While specifically exposing alleged abuses in public works in India, Birkmyre charged that the Council and Secretary of State neglected to keep in touch with Indian "public opinion" and purposely ignored Parliament. The India Office felt compelled to reassess and clarify its constitutional relationship to Parliament in order to effect an acceptable response to these charges.

Within the India Office Godley was considered the resident expert on constitutional matters, especially with regard to the Office's responsibilities and obligations to Parliament. While he loyally deferred to Parliament's ultimate authority in Indian affairs, Godley fiercely resisted any attempts to involve either House in the daily management of India Office business. The Permanent Undersecretary particularly opposed placing the Secretary of State's salary on the British estimates. When he first went to the India Office, Godley favored such a move; after a short time, however, he realized such a fiscal relief would be purchased "very dearly." When the Welby Commission considered the idea in 1899, Godley privately scolded his former Treasury counterpart for such an "absurd" action.[63] Godley argued that the debate resulting from an annual discussion of the Secretary of State's salary would be serious:

> No one values more than I do the control of the House of Commons. Whenever they speak, they are our absolute masters: on the whole they are on the side of right [and] justice and of economy. We know this, [and] we try to govern ourselves accordingly. But it is a very different matter to bring India into the discussion of the estimate. It is playing into the hands of people like Wedderburn: men who do

not represent the general good sense [and] good feeling of the House of Commons; whose action in detail would, I believe, be disastrous to the cause of good government in India [and] would cost India, at a very moderate estimate, £100 for every £1 of the [Secretary] of State's salary.[64]

Godley's view of Parliament was admittedly one-sided, particularly with respect to Members of Parliament connected with various lobbies or special interests.[65] Certain parliamentary mavericks did not ease suspicions in the India Office about the mischief that an uninformed or partially informed member might play with India. The consequences of the independent travels of Curzon (before he assumed the Viceroyalty) and Keir Hardie were two glaring examples of such exasperation.[66] Oddly enough, Godley, who never visited the subcontinent himself, mistrusted the ability of M.P.'s to debate Indian matters expressly because they never visited India and therefore could not realize the substantial differences between England and the subcontinent. This, he proclaimed, was the "principal reason why most of us, who are concerned with the Government of India, have a wholesome dread of the interference of the House of Commons."[67] But even though he sympathized with the complaints about parliamentary interference emanating from India, Godley ultimately concluded that "it is vain to talk of 'English interference.' Nobody regrets the spasmodic interferences of the House of Commons more than I do, but when they *do* interfere we must accept it."[68]

The India Office successfully avoided the challenge of a Parliamentary Committee in 1885 after the sudden change of governments that spring. But the increased publicity about the functioning of the India Office, propagated by writers such as Slagg and Birkmyre, stimulated two Secretaries of State, Kimberley and Cross, to order internal investigations into the Council's routine and general office procedures.[69] The issue languished sub rosa until it was resurrected by the Welby Commission near the end of the nineteenth century. The revitalized proposal to place the Secretary of State's salary on the British estimates was sharply criticized by Curzon as Viceroy. He was "horrified" at the proposal, for while conceding the necessity of parliamentary control, the Viceroy reminded Godley that

Parliamentary interference, liable to be inspired by party spirit, and conducted by busybodies, would be a national danger.... I hope that whatever the Committee may recommend in this direction, the Government may think twice, thrice, and more before accepting it. "Keep India out of the House of Commons" is a motto that any well wisher of this country should always have before his eyes.[70]

Curzon's attitude changed markedly over the next few years. In order to curtail the Council of India's powers, in 1904 Curzon proposed amendments to the 1858 Act that would have increased parliamentary control. He attacked the composition and tenure of the Council membership and ironically echoing the sentiments of Birkmyre and Slagg, he revived charges about the "irresponsibility" of the Councillors, who were the only "irremovables" in public service with exception of Judges, the official Comptroller, and Auditors. The Secretary of State, responsible to the King and Parliament, could be forced to resign; the India Council, on the other hand, was responsible to no one, and "if a majority chose to insist upon their rights as against the Secretary of State, or the Prime Minister, or the Government, or Parliament, I am aware of no power short of a *coup d'état* that could deprive them of their prerogative."[71] While conceding the unlikelihood of such an "abuse of power," Curzon argued the mere existence of such provisions tended "to colour the relations between the Secretary of State and his Councillors, since both are conscious, the one of their power, the other of his impotence."[72] Godley generally sympathized with Curzon's proposal, but he recognized the inherent dangers of attempting to get any such bill through Parliament. The Permanent Undersecretary of State fully agreed with the Viceroy that the theory of irremovability of Councillors "puts them in an extraordinarily strong position as compared not only with slaves like myself, who can be removed by a stroke of the Secretary of State's pen, but also with Lords of the Admiralty and Members of the Army Council."[73] Still the dangers of this recommendation outweighed any advantages, and Godley recommended that the Secretary of State reject the measure.[74]

Curzon's complaints about the relationship between the India Office and Parliament were specifically related to his own troubles with the Council of India. Had Curzon extended his proposals, he might have acknowledged the soundness of Slagg's plan two decades earlier. In 1884 Slagg mooted the possibility that a really "responsible minister" would eventuate if a standing committee on Indian affairs—similar to the Foreign Affairs Committee of the U.S. Senate—were formed in the House of Commons. Additionally, he proposed that this committee should have the power to call for the production of all papers "without exception" and initiate debate on Indian policy, irrespective of any members holding a government post.[75] But the plan was rejected, and sporadic attempts to resurrect the old practice of East India days when Parliament held court to renew the Company's charter were also deflected easily. It was not until 1919, following the recommendations of the Montagu-Chelmsford Report, that Parliament formed such a committee. Godley was steadfast in his opposition to such a proposal, and he identified the basic reason for his lack of support by declaring confidently to Curzon that

you are wrong in thinking the authority of the H[ouse] of Commons over India has declined. Not a bit of it. When they are in earnest, they are the absolute masters of the situation. . . . True the [House] of Commons has not often interfered of late years, but why? *Mainly because pains have been taken to keep a finger on their pulse, and to avoid doing anything that could excite them. On this subject I claim to speak with some knowledge.* [Italics added.][76]

Godley's statement reveals an important aspect of the India Office attitude towards Parliament. In 1899 Godley redefined the responsibilities of the Parliamentary Branch of the Records Department (previously responsible for collating and collecting parliamentary materials) to include the mechanical preparation and editing of Parliamentary Returns. This Branch was also required to screen all parliamentary questions to make sure nothing on Indian affairs was missed. For the greater part of his service, Godley prepared the answers to key parliamentary questions and superintended the preparation of Parliamentary Returns himself.[77] This practice, plus the great care exercised by the India Office in editing sensitive materials from Parliamentary Blue Books, made it easier to control the flow of information to the House of Commons and avoid controversial issues.[78]

Thus it can be surmised that Parliament, with few exceptions, was not inclined to interfere with Indian administration "as long as all went well and Indian affairs hardly touched British politics."[79] In great measure the mere threat of parliamentary discussion was sufficient to stimulate the India Office to fulfill its legal obligations to the Commons. While this matter is discussed more fully in a later chapter, one should be aware that Parliament was also the political arena within which various lobbies and special interest groups, both in and out of Parliament, concentrated their efforts to affect Indian policy. In assessing the tension between Parliament and the India Office, one should not view attempts by the India Office bureaucracy to monitor discussions, control the flow of information, or even work around that body as contempt for Parliament or even disputation of its ultimate authority over Indian affairs. Virtually all agreed that the overriding goal was to sustain British political and economic preeminence in India. Nor was the India Office filled with career-seeking individuals jealous of Members of Parliament and determined to undermine their authority. Rather there was a well-defined feeling within the India Office that *they* were best suited to attend to the daily management of Indian affairs. So while there was recognition by the India Office that Parliament was the source of authority with regard to British India, there was also a deep conviction that the India Office was the heart of the Indian Empire and was best equipped—both departmentally and with the experience of the Council of India—to deal with the diverse and urgent business of India on a daily basis. Hence, because special procedural and political efforts were required to keep Parliament at a distance, it was indeed an important factor in the formation of policy within the India Office but in a manner different from that perceived by contemporary opinion and even more recent interpretation.

Within the working of the Imperial machine, the India Office was unique. In modern parlance, the India Office stood on the sidelines in the flowchart of governmental responsibility. Lord George Hamilton's following characterization of the nature of India Office activity bears repetition:

> The India Office is a miniature Government in itself. There is not a branch of administrative or executive work connected with the big Government which is not represented inside the Office, and the great bulk of questions that come from the Government of India are not trivial or prosaic details of administration, but questions either of importance, or matters upon which there is difference of opinion or controversy, or connected with change or reforms.[80]

The India Office, however, was not and could not be totally isolated from communications and consultations with other great departments of state. While administrative studies have achieved popularity in recent years, it is a testament to the anomaly of the India Office that no scholars have ventured to disentangle the intricate web of the Office's role within the Imperial framework.[81] This, of course, requires a complete and detailed study in itself and beyond the scope of the present work; however, some general remarks as to the Office's external relations with other Imperial Departments are germane.

The India Office was not subject to the usual Treasury "suggestions" on finance and budgetary review as were other departments—that was reserved for Parliament, which rarely involved itself in the accounts of Office expenditure. The annual India budget debate in the House of Commons was considered a somewhat "somnolent affair."[82] Indeed, India sustained such an exempted status that the voluminous five-year Royal Commission on Civil Establishments (Ridley Commission) at the end of the nineteenth century included only a few sparse communiqués on points of information from the India Office. Representatives of every major department of state were examined except the permanent subordinates of the India Office.[83] India Office disputes with the Treasury generally fell within two categories—policies governing promotion, and salaries and status of India Office clerks. Some of these conflicts over internal India Office staffing and management have been mentioned earlier. (See Chapter 1.) The India Office, largely because of Godley's expert leadership, successfully withstood any challenge by the Treasury to involve itself in what the Permanent Undersecretary considered internal office management. Sir Reginald Welby, Permanent Undersecretary at the Treasury, bitterly resented the independence of Godley and the India Office in the late nineteenth century. Welby complained that

> an office like the India Office will accept our rules as long as it suits their conscience; but [if] it does not do so, they will laugh at us and our rules—we in fact have no control over theirs, and I think it would be best that their arrangements [for staff]

should be independent of us. You, however, have a very strong wish to have the conveniences and may I add none of the inconveniences of the Treasury system.[84]

The Treasury did not establish control such as Welby described until 1937, although progressive inroads were made after 1920. But in the matter of the two Exchequers, Imperial and Indian, India Office-Treasury relations were often strained. Two noteworthy examples of the whimsical nature of this relationship were the considerations of an Imperial Famine Grant to India both in 1896–97 and again 1899–1900.[85] With the Government of India's resources severely strained in 1896, Lord Elgin's administration proposed cutting back railway expenditures in order to finance famine relief. When this plan was rejected by the Council of India, the Imperial Exchequer offered to help. There was little need for an elaborate justification for assisting India since it had just contributed Rs. 380 lakhs toward frontier policy; in reply to a "request" from the Secretary of State, Hamilton, the Exchequer offered a gift £2 million for India's recent war contribution. But Elgin and his Council wanted no part of the expected parliamentary criticism if they accepted the grant, and the Exchequer was rebuffed. Despite Hamilton's pleas, the Exchequer refused to discuss the matter unless the Government of India made a formal request for a loan.

In the famine of 1899–1900, Curzon initiated a request for an Imperial grant-in-aid, and this time Hamilton, who had earlier pleaded for such a contribution, rejected it. Curzon based his solicitation on the massive Indian contributions to the Transvaal War Fund. Hamilton reversed his earlier logic and argued that a grant would destroy the independence of the Indian Exchequer and lead to increased parliamentary interference in Indian affairs. It would, concluded the Secretary of State, set a "mischievous precedent."[86] The logic was, of course, indefensible, and Curzon was particularly disturbed because the Government of India expected not an Imperial *loan*, but an Imperial *gift*. Hamilton had implied otherwise in Parliament. The House of Commons defeated a motion for a free grant because of the strain of recent Imperial wars on the British Exchequer.[87] Such instances of capriciousness and callousness for India only reinforced the determination of the India Office to remain separate from and out of reach of Treasury control.

In normal times India Office relations with the Foreign Office were carried on with great formality and some jealousy. It was essential that the two offices communicate about India's relations with its neighbors, the treatment of British Indian subjects by foreign powers, and the effects of European diplomacy on India. Additionally, the India and Foreign Offices jointly subsidized certain consuls and embassies in the Persian Gulf, where they shared some areas of joint jurisdiction.[88] This relationship was so discouraging at times that General Sir O'Moore Creagh, Commander-in-Chief of the Indian Army from 1909 to 1914 and a former Military Secretary at the India Office, mused: "one wonders whether the Foreign Office and India Office ever exchange confidences, or whether these two Departments of State keep each other at arm's-length...."[89] The Foreign Office operated on the premise that a military confrontation was usually a real possibility in a disagreement with a European foe. As a result of this perspective, the Foreign Office tended to be conciliatory and lacked the determination to disturb any "balance of power." The Government of India, on the other hand, emphasized the long-range policies and consequences of actions by foreign governments, and in many cases this prompted the Indian Government to advocate early action to forestall a potentially dangerous situation. The tension between the India Office and Foreign Office reached its zenith during Curzon's Viceroyalty when the Persian Gulf became the center of attention.[90] The complex questions of jurisdiction and overlapping interests meant that progress on questions of external policy was inevitably slow and cumbrous, and when all the necessary consultations had been concluded, the resultant policy was often reduced either to the lowest common denominator or emasculated beyond recognition. Lord Selborne once summed it up by exclaiming, "What an intolerable method of doing business! Indian Government, India Office, Minister at Teheran, Foreign Office, Cabinet Committee, Treasury, Cabinet! Bah! The Russians ought to walk round us each time."[91]

Relations between the India Office and War Office were intimately involved with the conduct of foreign affairs. As Britain's international obligations and commitments increased in the second half of the nineteenth century, the strain on the British Army enlarged proportionately. The Indian Army, as distinct from the British Army in India, had been used in the China Wars (1840–42 and 1857–60) and in the Abyssinian campaign of 1867. In 1878, 7,000 Sepoys were dispatched to Malta, and Indian troops were used in Egypt in 1882, in the Sudan (Suakim) in 1896, and in China during the Boxer Rebellion in 1900–1901. Additionally, Indian soldiers served on garrison duty in Ceylon, Mauritius, Singapore, Aden, Weihaiwei, and in the 1890s in parts of Africa.[92] Such widespread involvement gave rise to a feeling on the part of the British public that Indian troops were always at their beck and call. A popular jingle reflecting this attitude read:

> We don't want to fight
> But, by jingo, if we do,
> We'll stay at home and sing our songs
> And send the mild Hindoo.[93]

British Indian forces also contributed heavily to the Boer War at the end of the nineteenth century. The advantages of the Indian Army—which was paid for by the Indian taxpayer and whose size was not mandated by Parliament—was a convenient instrument of military policy. The sole legal objection, that Indian troops required parliamentary authorization to be deployed outside India, was usually circumvented by an escape clause wherein troops could be used without prior Cabinet approval "in urgent necessity or to repel invasion." The rapid deployment of Indian troops was often rationalized in this manner. When the Empire went to war in 1914, few questioned the urgency (and thus the legitimacy) of sending Indian troops to Europe. At that time the relations between the India Office and War Office could hardly be expected to be cordial, especially since India was rarely compensated for the use of its manpower and resources.[94]

The seemingly continuous state of flux and turmoil at the War Office did nothing to ease tension with the India Office. St. John Brodrick's career at the end of the nineteenth century was badly tarnished by the confusion reigning there before, ironically, he moved over to the India Office. Even Curzon, who had hoped to return to a prestigious home appointment, was alarmed by rumors that he was to go to the War Office to replace Brodrick:

No consideration in the world would induce me to take part in the administration of the War Office . . . [for] there is no reason in the world why one should sacrifice the whole of the best of one's life for work for which you get no gratitude and are, on the contrary, overwhelmed with ignorant calumny and malignant scorn.[95]

Consistent with its grudging submission to "greater Imperial considerations," the India Office could do little else but render assistance when the War and Foreign Offices requested it. This frustrated India Office officials, who maintained a running feud over troop movements and reimbursements with those departments. Uncharacteristically, Godley informed Lord Elgin in 1896 that

we were startled yesterday by a demand from the Foreign Office for the loan of an Indian regiment for the East Coast of Africa. . . . It seems to me an unfortunate move, in the present sensitive condition of European politics. Of course we could only act as post office, and pass on their request.[96]

Several months later Godley informed the Viceroy that India was to provide troops to Suakim (a Sudanese port). "I need not say how much I regret this: but you will understand, of course, that *it has been decided without any consultation of the India Office*." (Italics added.) Lord George Hamilton had been sounding out members of the India Council on the possibility of such a move but, as Godley reported, they were also helpless. He reported that the Councillors did not like the proposals "at all, but will of course agree, and in fact they cannot help doing so."[97] Godley felt that it was "another bad precedent," but proponents could easily argue that India had a far greater stake in the security of Egypt than the proportionately small requests then being made.[98] The Permanent Undersecretary strongly believed that Egypt should have been charged, and that the Council of India's hope for future "reciprocity" in the use of English troops in India was a hopeless and naive position.[99] The Suakim expedition is a prime example of the vulnerability of the India Office and the Government of India when confronted by other departments pleading "Imperial" causes. While conceding Indian interests in Egyptian affairs, Elgin protested vainly the Egyptian Government's attitude that "any policy... [they] choose to pursue in England entitles them to draw upon India in this manner."[100] The Government of India had little choice, and revised their Suakim despatch, which had come to Elgin in very "official [and] bald" language, strengthening arguments as to India's costs so that the India Office might challenge the Treasury.[101]

Again Godley's ultimate allegiance to Imperial policies forced him to urge the Viceroy to join him in pushing their personal disagreement with the policy aside, for "surely that does not affect the question: India, like the rest of the Empire, must bear the result of the mistakes of the Cabinet, and must take their share in carrying out their policy."[102] The entire episode resulted in bitter feelings not only in England, between the India Office and the War and Foreign Offices, but also between the governments of Egypt and India.[103] The incident further reduced the Government of India's inclination to aid the regular army, and when the prospect of a war with Abyssinia over the Somaliland Protectorate became imminent six months later, Elgin wanted the Government of India to "wash its hands of the whole thing."[104]

The "bad precedent" which Godley had envisioned came to fruition as great demands on Indian resources during Curzon's Viceroyalty. The Viceroy was completely frustrated and angered over requests for troops for South Africa, the West Coast of Africa, Uganda, Somaliland, Egypt, China, and Siam. Moreover, the Gold Coast and Persian Gulf wanted surgeons and guards from the Government of India. India was straining to sustain prisoner-of-war camps in South Africa and absorb Boer internees in India—for all of which the War Office wanted India to pay. Thus Curzon protested to the Secretary of State for India:

There is no time in history when India has been so indented upon and drained before: and though you will never have a Viceroy more willing to subordinate local to Imperial interests, I say advisedly that you may not again have a Viceroy who can afford to assume these risks; and you have to be very careful that you are not starting a precedent which will break down in future hands, and land you in very serious trouble. I feel compelled to utter this note of emphatic warning, because it is my duty, and because I think that undue trespass is being made upon our goodwill.[105]

The Secretary of State, Hamilton, strained the Government of India's nerves even more when, in 1903, he forwarded and generally supported a plan to garrison Indian troops in South Africa which would be "on call" for quick despatch to India in case of trouble there. Both Kitchener, freshly arrived from South Africa, and Curzon protested vociferously. The Viceroy cited a special India Office-War Office joint committee (1902) which recommended against such a deployment of troops; if trouble broke out on the Indian frontier, the troops simply could not be rushed to India quickly enough. Besides, India was again being asked to foot the bill. To Hamilton, Curzon enunciated the Government of India position when he wrote:

For years we have kept in India what is neither more nor less than a reserve for the wars of the Empire. There is scarcely a request that you address to us with which we do not uncomplainingly comply. We drain our forces, we deplete our establishments, we run all sorts of risks, for the sake of the Empire. If we did not place our troops and resources at your disposal, you could not fight these wars, or could not fight them with credit. I have never heard so much as a suggestion that England should pay anything to us for the almost priceless advantage she thus enjoys.[106]

On this occasion the combined displeasure of the Viceroy and Commander-in-Chief convinced Hamilton to withdraw the plan.

As a rule, the India and Colonial Offices steered clear of each other. Their mutual interests were basically in the area of the treatment of Indian subjects in the colonies. Interoffice communication remained poor throughout the Godley era, perhaps the legacy of earlier confusions over events surrounding the transfer of Malayan interests from the India Office to the Colonial Office in 1867. The shift had in fact been proposed as early as 1858 but the Colonial Office malingered so long that eventually the War Office and Treasury entered the fray and more than an eight-year delay occurred as a result of the confusion.[107] A source of friction was the treatment of Indians in the colonies. The issue was especially exasperating to Indian officials because the Cabinet, at Colonial Office prompting, was reluctant to dictate policy to supposedly self-governing areas. Even Curzon, severely criticized for his Anglo-Saxon ethnocentrism in India, doggedly waged a battle for the better treatment of Indians in Africa. As Viceroy he refused a request for Indian labor in German East Africa when he learned that Indians were treated "more or less on the level of aborigines with whom they have nothing in common but colour," and were subjected to treatment "degrading and injurous to their self-respect."[108] Moreover, in the face of Brodrick's threat to veto the Government of India's policy, Curzon refused to cooperate with the Governor of Natal in relaxing Indian emigration restrictions to that colony.

The problem of immigration was an especially sensitive one in the self-governing colonies such as Australia and New Zealand, which were quick to accuse the Colonial Office of interference in internal affairs. India Office protests in those cases fell on deaf ears, because again alleged "greater Imperial considerations" were at stake. A Colonial Office legal expert at the turn of the century went right to the heart of the matter. He stated that by amending such laws by Imperial legislation it would be impossible to keep Australia in the Empire. Elgin, ex-Viceroy of India and then Colonial Secretary, agreed and reluctantly informed the India Office of the official position.[109] On this issue the Liberals especially had a difficult time in maintaining some semblance of a balance between their promises to India and the Transvaal. With Ripon and Elgin in the Cabinet in 1905, the sincerity of the Liberal grant of self-government to the Transvaal was pitted against sympathy for Indian interests. Gandhi himself led a deputation to Elgin. But Elgin was opposed to intervention; he believed it was impossible to do anything officially for Indians against a self-governing Colony's determination to restrict their rights. Still, Elgin succeeded in mitigating the worst features of the Transvaal Registration Bill, which required fingerprinting of Indians in most instances, and felt some flush of victory inasmuch as India had in some small way received a reciprocal "Imperial consideration" by a colony.[110] Overall, however, there was little the India Office could do to help Indians abroad. In part, this was due to the lack of an effective system of departmental liaison with other departments of state. But the India Office also made a conscious choice not to cooperate too closely with the Colonial Office, and this tended to mute their protestations when problems did arise.

In its daily work the India Office interacted with almost every other British administrative department. For example, India Office relations with the Civil Service Commissioners essentially involved the testing and selection of Indian Civil Servants and Indian Police. Certain other home appointments and salaries also required the Commissioners' approval. Among other more specialized interests, the India Office was involved with the Board of Trade (on commercial matters and the interests of Lascar seamen), the Admiralty (with interests in Indian waters), the Judicial Committee of the Privy Council (which heard appeals from Indian courts), and the General Post Office (responsible for transporting Indian mail). Each of these relationships was a cog in the overall functioning of the India Office and hence a consideration, however major or minor, in the formation of Indian policy.

In retrospect, the India Office in the late nineteenth century exhibited considerable independence of its external constitutional partners in the governance of India. Interference by the Crown was a highly personalized activity with minimal impact except in select areas. In spite of its specific constitutional obligations to oversee Indian policy, Parliament's ability to influence the India Office in the critical stages of policy formation was negligible. The Cabinet was more successful in influencing Indian policy, but this too tended to be issue-oriented rather than reflecting any broadly based interest in the specifics of Indian administration. The India Office had to alert itself constantly to the sensitivities of other Imperial departments whose attitudes and policies could intimately affect the efficacious despatch of Indian business. By and large, the India Office performed creditably in the late nineteenth century and successfully avoided any major imbroglio with its administrative counterparts. One partner in Empire, however, caused the India Office to defend its policy-making process with some regularity and proved its most formidable contestant for the seat of decision making regarding Indian affairs—the Government of India.

NOTES

1. Lord Kilbracken, *Reminiscences* (London: Macmillan and Co., 1931), pp. 160–61.

2. Sir Arthur Godley, *Memorandum on the Home Government of India* (India Office, 1901 [first published, 1887]), p. 7. The Crown could make specific appointments to India on the recommendation of the Prime Minister (the Governor-General) or the Secretary of State for India (the Governors of Madras and Bombay, members of the Viceroy's Council and Governors' Councils). Additionally, the Monarch could, on such advice, legally appoint certain Judges of the higher courts, the Auditor of Accounts (with the countersignature of the Chancellor of the Exchequer), the Bishops of Calcutta, Madras, and Bombay, the Advocate-General, and members to the Indian Service not otherwise expressly provided for in the Act of 1858 (21 & 22 Vic., c. 106, s. 29).

3. See confidential memorandum, "Instructions As to Sending of Papers to the King" 20 June 1901, IOR, Private Office [Miscellaneous Home Establishment Papers], L/PO/Misc. 3.

4. Curzon noted that Queen Victoria wrote to the Governors-General every two or three weeks with her own hand. Viceregal letters to Victoria were written in the third person (except by Lytton). King Edward VII wrote less frequently than Queen Victoria, according to Curzon, "but followed Indian affairs with a not inferior interest, reinforced by a personal experience which he never ceased to quote with pleasure" (G. N. Curzon, *British Government in India* [London: Cassell and Co., 1925], II, 129).

5. See Lord Randolph Churchill to Salisbury, 25 July 1885, cited in R. R. James, *Lord Randolph Churchill* (London: Weidenfeld and Nicolson, 1959), p. 200. See also Churchill to Salisbury, 5 August 1885, cited in Winston S. Churchill, *Lord Randolph Churchill* (New York: The Macmillan Co., 1906), I, 509.

6. Quoted in James, *Lord Randolph Churchill*, p. 201. Churchill was especially distrustful of the Queen's private secretary, Sir Henry Ponsonby, who he considered was always intriguing against the India Office. See also R. F. Foster, *Lord Randolph Churchill: A Political Life* (Oxford: The Clarendon Press, 1981), pp. 191–93.

7. Foster, *Lord Randolph Churchill*, p. 193.

8. Godley to Elgin, 3 August 1894, Elgin Papers (9th Earl of Elgin) [hereafter cited as EP], IOL, MSS. Eur. F.84/24. See also Elgin to Godley, 14 September 1898, Kilbracken Papers [hereafter cited as KP], IOL, MSS. Eur. F.102/16; and Curzon to Godley, 12 July 1899, KP F.102/17.

9. Elgin to Godley, 19 September 1894, KP F.102/12.

10. David Dilks, *Curzon in India* (London: Rupert Hart-Davis, 1969), I, 79. See also Curzon to Hamilton, 31 May and 14 June 1899, Curzon Papers [hereafter cited as CP], IOL, MSS. Eur. F.111/158.

11. For an overview of this problem, see Dilks, *Curzon in India*, I, 71–96. Sometimes the India Office tightened the rein on this correspondence in a peculiar manner. In 1905 Lord Ampthill (Governor of Madras) was astonished when the Office refused to forward his birthday telegram to the King (via the Secretary of State for India) without his first sending it to the Viceroy (Ampthill to Godley, 1 November 1905, KP F.102/39).

12. The King's private secretary wrote to Hamilton saying that it was "a scandal on the part of the India Office to endeavour that the Indian Government should pay for the entertaining of our India Visitors for the Coronation" (Knollys to Hamilton, 5 September 1902, Hamilton Papers [hereafter cited as HP], IOL, MSS. Eur. C.123/57). For an elaboration of this debate, see Heather Coughlan, "The Role of the Council of India, 1898–1910," unpublished Ph.D. thesis, Duke University, 1971, pp. 119–44; and Dilks, *Curzon in India*, I, 249–66.

13. Morley to Godley, 14 September 1908, KP F.102/8.

14. Godley to Morley, 15 September 1908, *ibid.*

15. *Ibid.*

16. *Ibid.*

17. Quoted in James, *Lord Randolph Churchill*, p. 203.

18. For an overview of the Burmese problem, see D. P. Singhal, *The Annexation of Upper Burma* (Singapore: Eastern Universities Press, 1960), *passim.*

19. Godley to Elgin, 3 May 1894, EP F.84/23.

20. For a recent treatment of this relationship, see P. Stansky, *Ambitions and Strategies. The Struggle for Leadership of the Liberal Party in the 1890's* (Oxford: Oxford University Press, 1964). See also R. R. James, *Rosebery* (London: Weidenfeld and Nicolson, 1963).

21. Kimberley to Campbell-Bannerman, 7 October 1892, Campbell-Bannerman Papers, BL, Add. MSS. 41,221.

22. Kimberley to Campbell-Bannerman, n.d. (c. December 1892), *ibid.*

23. Godley favored White's appointment, and felt that the promotion of an officer of comparatively low rank (albeit the most qualified man) "will surely do good, [and] not harm, to let it be seen that these high appointments are really given by merit [and] not by seniority" (Godley to Kimberley, 12 October 1892, Kimberley Papers [hereafter cited as KMP]), private ownership, E/5.

24. Lansdowne to Cross, 16 August 1892, Cross Papers, IOL, MSS. Eur. E.243/32.

25. Godley to Lansdowne, 12 August 1892, Lansdowne Papers [hereafter cited as LP], IOL, MSS. Eur. D.558/14.

26. Godley had in fact, been shortlisted as a candidate for the Viceroyalty at a very early stage (Gladstone Papers [Cabinet Notes], BL, Add. MSS. 44,648, f. 112).

27. Kimberley to Gladstone, 9 August 1893, KMP E/10. Kimberley, however, also indicated that both men would have "preferred an eminent home politician, if one had been available."

28. See Rosebery to Gladstone, 10 August 1893, Gladstone Papers, BL, Add. MSS. 44,290; and Kimberley to Gladstone, 11 August 1893, KMP E/10.

29. Gladstone to Queen, 11 August 1893, cited in G. E. Buckle (ed.), *Letters of Queen Victoria* [hereafter cited as LQV] (London: Longmans, Green and Co., 1932), ser. 3, vol. 2, p. 300.

30. For a detailed account of the Queen's involvement, see J. Chandran, "Queen Victoria, Gladstone and the Viceroyalty of India 1893–1894," *New Zealand Journal of History* 3:2 (October 1969), pp. 175–89. Ripon considered Elgin a *"safer"* man" than Lord Carrington (Ripon to Kimberley, 18 August 1893, KMP E/10); but Kimberley noted that in a pinch, Carrington (if appointed) would "obey orders [and] if warned against imprudent speeches, I believe has sense enough to avoid [trouble]" (Kimberley to Gladstone, 10 August 1893, KMP E/10).

31. Kimberley to Rosebery, 24 August 1893, quoted in Chandran, "Viceroyalty 1893–1894," p. 180.

32. Chandran, "Viceroyalty 1893–1894," *passim*. Norman's basic reason for reversing his position was his reassessment of his physical well-being and age (sixty-seven).

33. Queen to Lansdowne, 21 September 1893, LP D.558/1. See also Kimberley to Lansdowne, 21 September 1893, LP D.558/6.

34. Kimberley to Gladstone, 26 September 1893, Gladstone Papers, BL, Add. MSS. 44,229.

35. Queen to Kimberley, cypher telegram, 28 September 1893, Royal Archives (Windsor) N.49/19, quoted in Chandran, "Viceroyalty 1893–1894," p. 183.

36. Elgin to Rosebery, 27 September 1893, quoted in Chandran, "Viceroyalty 1893–1894," p. 183. In a bold suggestion Norman had wired Ripon that he wanted to reconsider his withdrawal; but Kimberley informed the Prime Minister that such public vacillation would imply a weakness in the Government (Kimberley to Gladstone, 8 October 1893, Gladstone Papers, BL, Add. MSS. 44,229).

37. Rosebery himself did not malign Elgin's appointment, as has been commonly suggested. A note from Rosebery to Queen Victoria (4 September 1893) is quoted in James, *Rosebery*, p. 290, indicating that Rosebery found it "positively sad ... that more fit and aspiring men should not be found for this splendid position." This reference is actually to Sir Henry Norman, not Elgin, for James's footnote failed to include the previous sentence in which Rosebery said that he "knows nothing of the new Viceroy who is obviously too old to undertake the post." This view (and that of several recent writers who have compounded the historical error) has been corrected by Ronald Hyam, *Elgin and Churchill at the Colonial Office, 1905–1908* (London: Macmillan and Co., 1968), p. 18.

38. See Phillip Magnus, *Kitchener, Portrait of an Imperialist*(New York: E.P. Dutton & Co., 1968), pp. 239–51. See also John Morley, *Recollections* (New York: The Macmillan Co., 1917), II, 330–31.

39. *Punch*, 27 April 1910, vol. 138, p. 299.

40. Hector Bolitho, *James Lyle Mackay, First Earl Inchcape* (London: John Murray, 1936), p. 112.

41. Kimberley to Gladstone, 18 October 1893, Gladstone Papers, BL, Add. MSS. 44,229.

42. Kimberley to Gladstone, 25 October 1893, *ibid*.

43. Queen to Gladstone, 2 January 1894, LQV, p. 340. The existing Garter was awarded to Lord Breadalbane.

44. Queen to Kimberley, telegram, 11 January 1894, LQV, p. 343. However, a slightly different version of this "official" communiqué was forwarded by the Queen to the Indian Secretary pivately and further indicated the Queen's displeasure (Queen to Kimberley, telegram, 11 January 1894, KMP E/17).

45. See Chandran, "Viceroyalty 1893–1894," p. 186.

46. Queen to Gladstone, 14 January 1894, LQV, p. 346. The original letter, with the Queen's alterations, is located in the Royal Archives (Windsor), RA N.49/73, cited in Chandran, "Viceroyalty 1893–1894," p. 186. At the same time the Queen's private secretary informed Kimberley that Victoria could not agree to offering Lansdowne the G.C.B., and "will offer nothing and leave the world to know that party hatred has prevented any reward being given to the Viceroy. Her Majesty also strongly objects to the matter being discussed in the Cabinet most of whom know nothing about honours and rewards" (Ponsonby to Kimberley, 14 January 1894, KMP E/17).

47. Gladstone to Queen, 17 January 1894, LQV, pp. 348–50. See also Chandran, "Viceroyalty 1893–1894," pp. 187–88.

48. Kimberley to Gladstone, 20 January 1894, Gladstone Papers, BL, Add. MSS. 44,229. See also, Kimberley to Gladstone, 21 January 1894, KMP E/6b.

49. Gladstone to Kimberley, 18 January 1894, KMP E/6b.

50. Gladstone to Queen, 17 January 1894, LQV, pp. 348–51.

51. Rosebery to Gladstone, 26 January 1894, Gladstone Papers, BL, Add. MSS. 44,290.

52. Gladstone to Kimberley, 26 January 1894, KMP E/6b.

53. Kimberley to Queen, 3 February 1894, quoted in Chandran, "Viceroyalty 1893–1894," p. 189.

54. Godley, *Home Government*, pp. 14–15.

55. See John S. Galbraith, "The 'Turbulent Frontier' as a Factor in British Expansion," *Comparative Studies in Society and History* 2:2 (January 1960), pp. 150–68.

56. G. W. E. Russell, *Collections and Recollections* (New York: Harper & Brothers, 1899), p. 346. Russell served as Parliamentary Undersecretary for India, 1892–1894.

57. Morley to Minto, 11 January 1906, Morley Papers [hereafter cited as MRP], IOL, MSS. Eur. D.573/1.

58. John Slagg, "Parliament and the Government of India," *Contemporary Review* 45 (February 1884), p. 216.

59. *Ibid.*, p. 217.

60. *Ibid.*, p. 219.

61. William Birkmyre, *The Secretary of State for India in Council* (London: Cassell and Co., 2nd ed., 1886).

62. *Ibid.*, p. 8.

63. Godley to Welby, 20 July 1899, KP F.102/1.

64. *Ibid.*

65. In the general election of 1895, Godley informed the Viceroy (Elgin) that "there were not a few 'ejections' over which I heartily rejoiced; and not only those which affected the India Office, such as Naoroji, Seymour Keay &c.; Conybeare

and Keir Hardie thoroughly deserved their fate and others of the same class" (Godley to Elgin, 22 August 1895, EP F.84/30b).

66. For an example of such frustrations within the India Office, see Morley to Campbell-Bannerman, 2 October 1907, Campbell-Bannerman Papers, BL, Add. MSS. 41,223. For a similar outburst by a Viceroy, see Elgin's remarks on Curzon's journey to the Pamirs in 1894 (Elgin to Godley, 7 August 1894, KP F.102/12).

67. Godley to Sir Henry Erle Richards, 1 July 1904, Richards Papers, IOL, MSS. Eur. F.122/3a. Richards was Legal Member of the Viceroy's Council at the time.

68. Godley to Elgin, 23 December 1894, EP F.84/24.

69. "First Report of the Special Committee on India Office Procedure" [hereafter cited as "First Report"] 9 February 1886, L/PO/Misc. 5. See also draft correspondence on proposed "Rules for the Conduct of Business" drawn up in 1887 by Godley for Lord Cross (L/PO/Misc. 5).

70. Curzon to Godley, 9 August 1899, CP F.111/158.

71. Memorandum by Lord Curzon on a Proposed Amendment of the Government of India Acts, 1 December 1904, CP F.111/440, ff. 41–44.

72. *Ibid.*

73. Godley to Curzon, 26 June 1904, CP F.111/440.

74. Godley to Brodrick, 8 August 1904, KP F.102/2.

75. Slagg, "Parliament and the Government of India," p. 222.

76. Godley to Curzon, 26 February 1904, KP F.102/60.

77. Memorandum dated 6 February 1899, IOR, Political and Secret Department Memoranda Book, p. 378.

78. An example of India Office censorship was the Cotton Duties Blue Book (C. 7602, 1895), which did not include an important memorandum from Sir James Westland, Finance Member of the Indian Government. See P. L. Malhotra, *Administration of Lord Elgin in India 1894–99* (New Delhi: Vikas Publishing House, 1979), pp. 52–58.

79. H. H. Dodwell (ed.), *Cambridge History of India* [hereafter cited as CHI] (Cambridge: Cambridge University Press, 1932), VI, 216.

80. Lord George Hamilton, *Parliamentary Reminiscences and Recollections, 1868–1885* (London: John Murray, 1917), I, 68.

81. Most notably, Henry Roseveare, *The Treasury* (London: Allan Lane, The Penguin Press, 1969); Zara Steiner, *The Foreign Office and Foreign Policy, 1898–1914* (Cambridge: Cambridge University Press, 1969); and Ray Jones, *The Nineteenth-Century Foreign Office: A Study in Administrative History* (London: Weidenfeld and Nicolson, 1971) virtually ignore the India Office. Sir Malcolm Seton, *The India Office* (London: G. P. Putnam's Sons, 1926), pp. 5–7, gives only a brief mention to the mutual interests between the India Office and other departments of state. Williams throws some light on the first decade, *The India Office, passim*.

82. "Sir Arthur Godley at the India Office," by J. E. Shuckburgh, November 1945, Findlater Stewart Papers, IOL, MSS. Eur. D.890/12.

83. See G.B., Parliament, *Report of the Royal Commission on Civil Establishments*: C. 5226 (1887), XIX; C. 5545 (1888), XXVII; C. 5748 (1889), XXI; C. 5748-1 (1889), XXI; C. 6172 (1890), XXVII; C. 6172-1 (1890), XXVII.

84. Welby to Godley, 18 September 1887, KP F.102/53.

85. For an overview of both famine situations, see P. Bandyopadhyay, "British

Famine and Agricultural Policies in India, with special reference to the Administration of Lord George Hamilton, 1895–1903," unpublished Ph.D. thesis, University of London, 1969, pp. 24–89 (1896–1897) and pp. 90–154 (1899–1900).

86. Hamilton to Curzon, 5 April 1900, HP C.126/2.

87. The policy was most clearly enunciated by the Chancellor of the Exchequer, Sir Richard Hicks-Beach, and supported by Hamilton in the House of Commons, G.B., *Parliamentary Debates*, 4th ser., vol. 86, cols. 1383–435.

88. "Her Britannic Majesty's Political Resident in the Persian Gulf and Consul-General for Fars and Khuzistan" was usually appointed from the ranks of the Indian Political Service. However, these men, "picked men, picked from picked men" (Phillip Woodruff, *The Men Who Ruled India: The Guardians*[London: Jonathan Cape, 1965], II, 270) were responsible as well to the Minister in Teheran who was appointed by the Foreign Office. India paid half the bill for the Persian legation, and staffed as many as nine of fourteen posts in Persia (c. 1906), but did not have any representation on the Minister's staff (Briton Cooper Busch, *Britain and the Persian Gulf, 1894–1914* [Berkeley and Los Angeles: University of California Press, 1967], pp. 6–7 and 350–52).

89. G. E. Callwell (ed.), *The Autobiography of General Sir O'Moore Creagh* (London: Hutchinson and Co., n.d. [c. 1924], p. 257.

90. See Dilks, *Curzon in India*, I, *passim*. For additional examples of Indian interests being affected by European diplomacy, note remarks concerning the Ango-Japanese Treaty of 1905 (Lord Newton, *Lord Lansdowne* [London: Macmillan and Co., 1929], pp. 327–28) and the Anglo-Russian accord of 1907 (S. A. Wolpert, *Morley and India, 1906–1910* [Berkeley and Los Angeles: University of California Press, 1967], pp. 80–81).

91. Selborne to Curzon, 24 April 1903, quoted in Dilks, *Curzon in India*, I, 111.

92. See W. S. Hamer, *The British Army: Civil-Military Relations 1885–1905* (Oxford: Oxford University Press, 1971), pp. 89–90; and Sir Charles Lucas, *The Empire at War* (London: Oxford University Press, 1921), I, pp. 45–47, 54–55, and 121.

93. Sir Henry Lucy, *A Diary of Two Parliaments* (London, 1885–86), cited in Donald B. Gordon, *The Dominion Partnership in Imperial Defence, 1870–1914* (Baltimore: The Johns Hopkins Press, 1965), p. 61.

94. Creagh noted that the India Office, not the War Office, was to blame, "because things used to be done which would not stand the criticism of the Army Council" (Caldwell, *Creagh*, p. 254). The India Office, of course, was hardly interested in that body's opinion, but placed much more emphasis on Indian public opinion and the strain on India Government revenues.

95. Curzon to Hamilton, 12 March 1903, CP F.111/162.

96. Godley to Elgin, 21 February 1896, EP F.84/31a.

97. Godley to Elgin, 1 May 1896, *ibid.*

98. Godley to Elgin, 8 May 1896, *ibid.*

99. Godley to Elgin, 15 May 1896, *ibid.*

100. Elgin to Godley, 19 May 1896, KP F.102/14.

101. Elgin to Godley, 2 June 1896, *ibid.* Elgin, however, did believe the India Office could have better luck in the matter than did Cross in 1887.

102. Godley to Elgin, 25 June 1896, EP F.84/31a.

103. Cromer was surprised at what he considered to be the excessive amount of troop support sent by India—which in fact included their own postal department (Cromer to Elgin, 9 June 1896, EP F.84/31a). Elgin acknowledged Egypt's great difficulties, and was certain that more "cordiality" on Egypt's part would have helped the situation greatly (Elgin to Brackenbury, 27 July 1896, EP F.84/31a).

104. Elgin to Godley, 13 January 1897, KP F.102/15.

105. Curzon to Hamilton, 23 January 1902, CP F.111/161.

106. Curzon to Hamilton, 29 July 1903, CP F.111/162. See also Dilks, *Curzon in India*, I, 126–30 and 201–10.

107. R. B. Pugh, "The Colonial Office, 1801–1925," in E. A. Benians, et al. (eds.), *Cambridge History of the British Empire* (Cambridge: Cambridge University Press, 1959), III, 734.

108. Curzon to Col. S. H. E. McCallum, 5 June 1902, CP F.11/280, cited in Dilks, *Curzon in India*, I, 111.

109. Hyam, *Elgin and Churchill*, p. 315.

110. See Elgin to Hamilton, 1 June 1897, EP F.84/15. For an overview of the problem, see Hyam, *Elgin and Churchill*, pp. 262–74. Ironically, Curzon, considered Britain's most Imperialist Viceroy, followed the movement by Gandhi in South Africa very closely, and when Gandhi returned to India for a visit, a meeting of the two great figures was scheduled, and then cancelled because of sensitivity in the Anglo-Indian press.

5

The India Office and the Government of India

The establishment of the India Office in 1858 did not materially change the working relationship between the Home Government and the Government of India. In its first decade the Viceroyalty of India remained the most glamorous posting in the British Empire, and the occupant of the *gadi* was perceived as the absolute ruler of British India's millions and as a *burra sahib* to Native Princes. The history books are full of accounts of larger-than-life proconsuls ruling India autocratically, with little regard for or constraint by the Home Government. But such independence was found largely in the pre-1858 period when India's Governors-General, unfettered by the imperative of instant communications, were not intimidated by the Company's legal powers, which lapsed into obscurity because of their progressive disuse.

After 1870, however, improved communications with the subcontinent—including the opening of the Suez Canal, better steam transportation, and the completion of telegraphic lines between London and India—brought the Indian Government increasingly within Whitehall's reach. The actual number of the Governor-General's references home increased steadily in the 1870s and 1880s. The number of referrals home in Mayo's time (1869–72) is estimated to be four times that in Canning's tenure (1858–62);[1] it doubled again in Ripon's Viceroyalty (1880–84); and the 1890s Elgin, facing an ususual number of major crises, wired the India Office as often as twice a day. Although the India Office moved slowly in its first ten years to define the parameters of independent action by its representatives in India, as early as 1873 Sir Charles Treveylan told a Select Committee of Parliament that while there was "no doubt the primary function of the Secretary of State [for India] is revision and control, . . . I conceive that a practice has grown up, since the transfer of the Government, of more frequently originating... works in India [by the India Office]."² Sir John Strachey, writing with long and intimate knowledge of the Indian Government both in India and London, also acknowledged that "the increased facilities of communication, the establishment of telegraphs... etc. have made the relations between the two countries far more intimate than was formerly necessary or possible, and have made more frequent the cases in which final orders cannot be passed in India...."³ And Lord Ripon—the only Secretary of State for India to go out to that country as Viceroy—complained in 1881 that

there has been a marked change in the relations between the India Office and the Government of India since I knew the former in days gone by. In those times it was considered a great mistake to attempt to govern India from London. It was held the business of the Secretary of State to lay down general principles upon which India was to be administered and then so long as those principles were observed to leave a large freedom to the Governor-General and to accord him a cordial support. Now-a-days owing to a variety of causes... a different system to a great extent prevails, and the interference of the India Office has largely increased....⁴

While the India Office usually refrained from interference in the ordinary work of Indian administration, Whitehall unquestionably exercised greater and more efficient control over significant policy questions. The increased attention by the India Office to policy-making in India, and the subsequent efforts by various Indian Secretaries to curb independent action by the Government of India were in part related to the development and presence of the Council of India in London. It was also related to the greater efficiency of the permanent officials in the India Office in handling the large amount of material now flowing back to London, especially after Arthur Godley's assumption of the Permanent Undersecretaryship in 1883. The widespread and unchecked internal powers of the Governor-General in Council, the splendor attached to his office, and the inevitable misunderstandings over policy due to distance and time, especially in exchanging private letters, further stimulated the India Office to action. Following a series of conflicts between the two centers of Indian governance concerning who controlled the formulation of Indian policy, a rather inflexible administrative framework emerged at the supreme level in which the India Office consistently asserted its constitutional prerogatives over Calcutta and Simla. The hardening of the technical situation reached its height during Elgin's tenure (1894-98) and was vigorously reinforced during the Viceroyalties of Curzon and Minto.

During the period 1858-80, the India Office and the Government of India were in conflict over constitutional issues involving the Civil Procedure Bill (1864), the question of "previous sanction" (1874), and Indian tariff legislation (1875-76).⁵ In each case the issue was to what extent

Whitehall could dictate policies to the government in India. The India Office and Government of India debated the role of the Governor-General's Executive Council vis-à-vis the Home Government and legislative prerogatives reserved by the Secretary of State over the Indian Government. There was also substantial tension between Whitehall and India over questions related to the doctrines of "leaving acts to operation," the constitutional position of the Viceroy (as viewed by the India Office), and the relationship of the Council of India to the Government of India in Calcutta.

The significance of this tension and constitutional haggling between the centers of Indian governance has usually been underestimated. One recent study asserts that after 1870

> periodic assertions of the "great principle" that the home government retained "final control and direction" over Indian affairs then became fashionable. To the hour of Curzon's fall, Salisbury served perhaps as the one Indian secretary whose clear dominance over his Viceroy, Lytton, may be cited as the exception to the rule of ever-increasing viceregal pretentions to independent action. Among the more obvious reasons for the continuing relative autonomy enjoyed by the Government of India were its complete freedom from Treasury supervision and remoteness from the average Englishman's political consciousness.[6]

Surely, as Donovan Williams asserts, "no stroke of the pen in 1858 could extinguish the capacity of India for making proconsuls."[7] But in the late nineteenth century this generalization about the relationship between the India Office and Government of India is no longer valid. In the resolution of these conflicts, Whitehall progressively built up and consistently maintained its dominance over the Government of India not only in matters of Imperial importance but also in matters of significant internal policy. Sometimes these disputes were settled amicably, often with the judicious mediation of Sir Arthur Godley, who retained the confidence of both his India Office superiors and a succession of Viceroys in India. On other occasions, however, personalities in India and London made the discussions acrimonious and occasionally downright hostile. In the end, however, it is clear that the Viceroy's administrative flexibility was steadfastly reduced as the century came to a close and continued to be until the end of World War I when the Government of India Act, 1919, introduced significant changes in the composition of the official majority of the Viceroy's Executive Council and in some ways loosened the grip of the Home Government.

The legislation governing the composition and function of the Government of India has been adequately chronicled elsewhere.[8] However, in order to clarify the relationship between the Home and Indian governments, some general remarks about the structure of the Government of India are in order. The Government of India was a corporate body whose business was always conducted in the name of the Governor-General in

Council. The distinction between the terms "Viceroy," first used in the Royal Proclamation of 1858, and "Governor-General" is constantly blurred; in fact, the former title had no statutory basis and only emphasized the ceremonial aspect of the office. The designation "Viceroy," then, was really an indication of status. Thus, while the head of the Indian Government frequently sent messages to the Indian Legislature signed "Viceroy and Governor-General," all official acts were in the name of the Governor-General in Council, commonly called the Government of India.[9] Technically the Governor-General was appointed by the Crown on the recommendation of the Prime Minister, although the Secretary of State for India, acting on behalf of the Crown, signed the Warrant of Appointment.

The Governor-General in the late nineteenth century was assisted by an Executive Council of six members and the Commander-in-Chief of the Indian Army, who sat as an extraordinary Member of Council. To insure that the Viceroy had experienced advisers, at least three members of his Executive Council had to have ten years' experience in India and one, usually the Law Member, had to have five years' service as an English or Irish barrister or a Scottish Advocate. During the weekly Executive Council meetings the Governor-General retained both a regular and a casting vote. In normal practice the Viceroy abstained from voting; he did, however, retain the power to overrule his Council if necessary. For the normal execution of business, the Governor-General was empowered to act on behalf of the entire Council in the presence of a single Member of Council. From 1861 the executive work of the Government of India was carried out under a portfolio system, with up to nine departments conducting business at various times.[10] The Governor-General invariably maintained the Foreign and Political portfolios himself.

Appointments to the Governor-General's Executive Council were the prerogative of the Secretary of State, and it was through these appointments that the India Office could exert control. The Executive Council was expanded into a Legislative Council by the addition of between ten and sixteen additional Members, at least one-half of whom had to come from outside the Civil Service or Military. An official majority was maintained in the Legislative Council until 1919. This ensured the final veto of the India Office through the official Members over provincial councils, which became increasingly "Indianized" as the century progressed. At the same time the Executive Council was in no way responsible to the Imperial *or* Provincial Legislative Councils.

The role played by the Secretary in each department is of special interest in the organization of the Government of India. Appointed by the Governor-General from the Civil Service, the Secretary was technically a Government Secretary and was not specifically assigned to any one department. Practically, however, the Secretary had direct access to one Member of the Viceroy's Executive Council, with whom he worked, and in fact to the

Governor-General, to whom he reported once a week. Moreover, the Secretaries usually attended meetings of the Executive Council and fulfilled a role much like that of a Parliamentary Undersecretary at home by sitting in one of the chambers of the Legislature. Although the Secretary was an integral part of the Government of India's policy-making processes, the Member was officially in charge of the department and the one answerable to the Home Government. The Secretary of a given department, although he retained the right of appeal to the Governor-General himself, usually refrained from openly challenging Members of the Executive Council publicly or privately.

The first important controversy between the Secretary of State and the Government of India over the superiority of the Home Government in legislative matters occurred in 1864. The Secretary of State, Sir Charles Wood, suggested that the Indian Government postpone considerations of a bill amending the Civil Procedure laws in India. The Government of India vehemently objected, arguing that even though the Indian Councils Act, 1861, had spelled out the Secretary of State's power to veto Indian legislation, it did not allow for interference in *preliminary* stages of consideration by the Indian Legislature. Wood responded that the Secretary of State's control extended to *all* acts of the Government of India, whether in draft or final form, and was definitely intended to influence the Executive's decision when forthcoming.[11] After all, Wood argued, as regarded the power of disallowance by the Secretary of State, it was certainly

more and more calculated to maintain the character and dignity of the [Executive] Council, that the Secretary of State should suggest to the Executive Government to suspend, and even withdraw, a Bill, than leaving them to proceed without any intimation of his opinion that he should ultimately disallow it.[12]

A few years later the Duke of Argyll as Secretary of State for India forcefully asserted those practices hinted at by Wood. Argyll informed the Government of India that it was duty bound to introduce legislation (in this case the Indian Contract and Evidence bills) sent to it by the Home Government. The Viceroy, Mayo, protested this attempt to deprive the Legislative Council of "all real power in the discussion of the Bills in question."[13] The Government of India based its case on the sections 21 and 22 of the Act of 1861, which invested in the Government of India the duty of legislation in India. The Governor-General and his Council maintained that "any other view would invest the Secretary of State with the character of the legislator for British India, and would convert the Legislative Council into a mere instrument to be used by him for that purpose."[14] Argyll rejected the argument outright, stating categorically that "the final control and direction of the affairs of India rest with the Home Government, and not with the authorities appointed and established by the Crown, under Parliamentary enactment, in India itself." Furthermore, Argyll continued

> the Government established in India is (from the nature of the case) subordinate to the Imperial Government at home. And no Government can be subordinate unless it is within the power of the superior Government to order what is to be done or left undone, and to enforce on its officers, through the ordinary and constitutional means, obedience to its directions... finally decided upon by the advisers of the Crown.

He concluded by adding that the Home Government "must hold in its hands the ultimate power of requiring the Governor-General to introduce a measure, *and of requiring also all the Members of his Government to vote for it.*" [Italics added.][15]

Argyll's successor, Salisbury, showed little patience with the Government of India on the question of "previous sanction." Salisbury was incensed that the Government of India had not consulted him before passing several important legislative acts. He publicly chastised the Government of India in Parliament, proclaiming that since Argyll's time, "the Indian Legislative Council was left in a state which practically amounted to entire independence of England."[16] With the aid of Sir Henry Maine, the Council of India's premier jurist, Salisbury laid down the ground rules for his future relations with the Government of India: he expected a full explanation and details of any proposed legislation to be forwarded home (including any legislation substantially amended during debate), with the only exceptions being measures of "slight importance" or those "urgently requiring speedy enactment."[17] Salisbury conceded that the Governor-General should determine the extent of "urgency." Northbrook's Government echoed Mayo's earlier apprehensions, stating that the rules "might lead to an interposition on the part of the Governor-General in Council, which would be contrary to former practice and in itself inexpedient."[18] However, the Secretary of State avoided open conflict with the Viceroy by presenting his demands as a request for "official consultation" as had been done in the 1860s, thus reassuring the Viceroy that his discretionary powers (i.e., declaring legislation "urgent") remained intact and a safeguard against total conciliation.

The respite was a temporary one. Salisbury, without formally notifying the Indian Government, introduced legislation into Parliament designed to amend the Act of 1861 by adding a Public Works Member to the Viceroy's Executive Council.[19] The Secretary of State's failure to consult the Government of India further distressed Northbrook, who requested his Law Member (Arthur Hobhouse) to write to the Chancellor of the Exchequer and former Secretary for India, Sir Stafford Northcote, complaining of the "sudden and peremptory modes of doing business that are now in vogue."[20] Salisbury, for his part, was merely extending his opinion of his own Council to the Viceroy's Executive body; that is, he considered it more of a consultative than decision-making body which should not be allowed to become too independent. Northbrook argued that the Viceroy almost always acted in conjunction with his Council and retained the legal power to overrule them if necessary: "It would in my opinion be a dangerous thing if India comes to be governed by a Secretary of State at home acting on his own views without consulting his Council in private communication with the Governor General here doing the same."[21]

The constitutional issue of "previous sanction" intensified in 1875 when Northbrook's Government enacted tariff legislation which was partly unacceptable to the Home Government. The Governor-General had informed Salisbury by telegram of the bill's approval, and the Secretary of State immediately noted it exceeded the definition of "urgent" legislation. The India Office reaffirmed its requirement that the Government of India inform the home authorities of any changes in legislation incurred after its initial reference back to India. The Government of India issued a long response, carefully citing arguments by Wood and Argyll that while no one disputed the Secretary of State's superior powers of control, "they must indeed be used with great deliberation, and on the rarest occasions."[22] Salisbury responded by re-emphasizing the unpalatable fact that the disallowance of an act gave "the greatest publicity and the strongest emphasis ... to the divergence of opinion between the Home and Indian Governments." Furthermore, he argued that the Governor-General was still free "to act at once, in any way which a public emergency may seem to him to demand."[23] Having articulated their respective postures, the tension subsided and although the pace of Indian legislation in the 1880s was spectacular and the exchanges between London and Calcutta often spirited, the specific debate over the constitutional question of the extent of India Office control over the Government of India did not emerge again until the 1890s.

The most acute battles over the constitutional relationship between the Home and India governments were waged during Elgin's troubled Viceroyalty. Elgin was bedeviled by tariff problems, currency crises, persistent and costly frontier wars, famine and plague, and sedition—all of which marked momentous changes in the condition of British India. Within this context Elgin seemed a very unlikely candidate to contest Whitehall over the question of administrative independence. Indeed, as mentioned earlier, his appointment to the Viceroyalty had come in the wake of a fiasco during which Sir Henry Norman now accepted and rejected the position several times. In the selection process Elgin's credibility and reputation were damaged even before he began his work in India. It was not a good beginning;

later, the public estimate of his handling of these problems was remarkably biased, as reflected in the following statement in the *Dictionary of National Biography*:

[Elgin's] recognition of his own limitation was so far justified that he cannot be reckoned among the outstanding governors-general of India. His personal influence was weakened by a retiring disposition and a self-distrust from which there sprang a subservience to Whitehall that has, perhaps, no parallel in viceregal records.[24]

Further emphasizing the circumstances under which Elgin accepted the Indian post, the author of the sketch stated that

Elgin, apart from his public spirit, his chivalry, and his high sense of duty, had little to counteract the handicaps of reserve of manner, his habitual silence, a retiring disposition, a certain homeliness in his aspect and bearing, a curious dislike of riding and a general ineptitude for social leadership. He neither looked the part which he had accepted so reluctantly, nor trusted himself in it.[25]

The historical record shows otherwise. In private Elgin displayed great confidence not only in arguing his position on various complicated issues to his superiors at home but also in tactfully handling an openly rebellious Executive Council and hostile native press in India. Elgin had been assigned full responsibility for the behavior of his associates in India and virtually ordered to follow specific policy guidelines presented by the Home Government. However, the Supreme Government in India still carried on much of the business of administering the subcontinent without reference to London. Additionally, the Viceroy's ability to respond to spontaneous crises or "urgent" matters was not seriously eroded. But in the formulation and execution of major long-range policy decisions, the Viceroys of late nineteenth-century India by and large had their minds made up for them by authorities in Whitehall. The whole series of events in the 1890s has been misrepresented, and Elgin has been unjustifiably characterized as a "weak and unimaginative administrator" whose career in India was notable only for his espousal of and capitulation to the Secretary of State's "mandate."[26] Elgin has been much maligned for confirming a trend which, as indicated above, had been evolving for two decades before his arrival in India. Moreover, historians, failing to identify the multiplicity of issues leading up to Elgin's struggle with the India Office, overemphasize the cotton duties dispute of 1894–96 as the most important issue involved.

The Indian cotton duties controversy arose in the 1870s when Manchester industrialists and Lancashire mill owners became alarmed at the rapid expansion of the Indian cotton industry.[27] Their fear intensified as the Indian cotton mills grew by some 700 percent between 1873 and 1893.[28] The divergent pulls of Indian versus British interests brought intense pressure on the India Office. They also created great tension between the Home and Indian governments whose perspectives differed dramatically on the issue. As each side felt compelled to argue its case more and more forcefully, the constitutional issue emerged once again. Throughout the dispute various Secretaries of State asserted India Office authority over the Viceroy and his Executive Council. The earlier Salisbury-Northbrook estrangement, which occurred in part over the cotton duties issue, was in retrospect only a mild precursor to the constitutional struggle played out in full during Elgin's term.

Soon after his arrival in India, Elgin assessed the Government's financial position and wasted no time in recommending the imposition of wide-ranging import duties to offset declining revenues.[29] He included cotton in the proposed tariff package. At home the Secretary of State, Kimberley, was subjected to pressure to reject the plan from Lancashire manufacturers, who were looking to curtail Indian competition, and by the Cabinet, which feared that the inclusion of cotton in the new tariff legislation might actually bring down the Government.[30] Godley also wrote to Elgin explaining that any extended public debate over cotton in the House of Commons would have potentially disastrous effects on India and might result in concerted attacks on all of the other badly needed tariff proposals as well as the delicate matter of Indian currency policy.[31] Kimberley conceded to the pressures at home, and in the process of rejecting the unanimous request of the Supreme Government in Calcutta, he also overruled the unanimous opinion of the Council of India, which favored the inclusion of cotton goods on the list of import duties.[32]

At this point Elgin privately informed his confidant at the India Office, Godley, that trouble was brewing in his Executive Council. Despite the Viceroy's assurances to his Council that the Cabinet and India Office had overruled them only after giving the fullest consideration to their arguments, Elgin warned the Permanent Undersecretary that it was

a dangerous position—not only by the British opinion out of door combining with the Native [against] the [Government] which is bad enough, but by an increase of friction between those in the [Home Government] here [and] the Home authorities—which there is plenty of already I fear.[33]

Elgin's worst fears materialized when Sir James Westland, the Finance Member of his Executive Council, introduced the Tariff Bill to the Supreme Legislative Council on March 1, 1894. In introducing the legislation, Westland clearly pointed the finger at London for the exclusion of cotton goods and yarn from import duties.[34] The hue and cry over India's sacrifices to Lancashire was led by Sir Charles Pritchard, Public Works Member of Council, and Patrick Playfair, a nonofficial, representing the European mercantile community of Calcutta. The Indian nonofficial Members of the

Legislative Council also bitterly criticized the Government.[35] The Government of India, by virtue of its official majority, voted down proposed amendments for inclusion of cotton. But the Viceroy's Councillors made it clear that they really favored the inclusion of cotton goods in the tariff and strongly implied that they voted it down under orders from home.[36]

The initial phase of the controversy was a rude awakening for the Government of India. The Indian press vehemently condemned the action, labeling the Legislative Members as "pure non entities" and "veritable puppets" of the Home Government.[37] Others questioned the need for "a mock Viceroy" and maintenance of a "sham" Legislative Council.[38] Furthermore, the weak financial position of the Government of India was publicly revealed. It is from an uncritical acceptance of this rhetoric and lack of information as to how the situation subsequently evolved that the charge of Elgin's alleged "subservience" to Whitehall (e.g., *The Dictionary of National Biography*) is derived. The Viceroy was uniquely "caught between his conscience and his politics; between positive action and expediency; between independence of action and obedience to superior authority."[39] On his own initiative Elgin forwarded to London his Councillors' objections to the exclusion of cotton in the tariff legislation. The Cabinet did not, as suggested by S. Gopal, have to help Elgin overrule his Council.[40] After considerable negotiating on Elgin's part, the Home Government finally agreed to allow cotton duties with a comparable excise duty on Indian goods. The size and limits of the excise duty were not particularly to Elgin's liking, but he accepted them. His Councillors, however, had other thoughts, and it is from this second phase of the crisis especially that Elgin's reputation suffered the most.

At the time that the Tariff Bill (sans cotton duties) passed in 1894, another controversial issue strained constitutional relations between the Home and Indian governments—the Cantonment Act Amendment Bill. The resistance of the Executive Council to this bill, which was debated concurrently with the cotton duties, prompted the new Secretary of State, Sir H. H. Fowler, to reaffirm the India Office's dominance over its official members in India. This issue, which was completely overshadowed by the cotton duties crisis, elicited much of the correspondence regarding the constitutional relationship of the Home and Indian governments that is often misrepresented as being related to the tariff issue.

In brief, the cantonment controversy involved the Government of India's licensing and compulsory examination of prostitutes in order to control the incidence of venereal disease in military cantonments.[41] Under the system in India before 1888, prostitutes were in fact licensed by the Indian Government and forcibly examined for venereal disease. In 1888 the House of Commons (under pressure from several lobbies in and out of Parliament) passed a resolution demanding the cessation of such practices in India. Cross, Secretary of State in 1889, ordered the Government of India to draft new legislation along the lines of the House of Commons resolution. In the process he overruled the Council of India, which strongly favored the cantonment rules and regulations because they regarded the incredibly high incidence of venereal disease in the British Indian Army as an issue of military efficiency more than morals. Nevertheless, in 1889 the Indian Government drafted a new Cantonment Act which was brought into operation in 1890. It was not long, however, before various social purity and religious groups charged that the old system of government registration and compulsory examination remained in effect essentially because the new rules still allowed the Medical Officer to detain anyone *suspected* of venereal disease in the cantonment hospital. This forced Kimberley, back for his third term as Secretary of State, to convene a special joint India Office-parliamentary committee on the matter (1893). The committee recommended (1894) that yet another round of regulations be drafted—but this time specifically prohibiting the classification of venereal disorders as contagious diseases requiring compulsory detainment. The directive also contained a section (clause 3) which imposed severe penalties on any public servant caught carrying out compulsory examinations—to which the official members of the Viceroy's Council unanimously objected. The issue came to the forefront just as the cotton duties crisis reached a momentary lull, from March to November 1894, and upset relations between Elgin and the new Indian Secretary, Henry Fowler.[42]

The Cantonment Bill legislation caused further dissatisfaction among the Members of the Viceroy's Executive Council and especially Sir Arthur Miller, the Legal Member of the Government of India. When Miller introduced the new bill into the Legislative Assembly, he made his remarks in negative terms, and he compared the position of a Member of Council in India to that of a Minister at home who had the right to oppose proposed legislation. Miller also strongly intimated that the bill was put forward under orders from Whitehall and against the opinion of the government of India.[43] On receiving the *Proceedings* of the Legislative Assembly, Fowler reminded Elgin of the constitutional position of Members of the Viceroy's Council:

He [Sir Arthur Miller] has the option of either accepting loyally the decision of the Cabinet, without any intimation, direct or indirect, of any dissent from that decision, or resigning his office. The position of a Member of the Viceroy's Council is this respect analogus [sic]. If, therefore, any Member of the Government of India feels that he cannot conscientiously support the proposals which you have directed to be submitted to the Council, it *is his duty to resign* his appointment. Sir A. Miller appears to have adopted the course of openly disassociating himself from the policy of the measure which it was his duty to introduce.[44]

Elgin again tried to protect his Councillors from the Secretary of State. He was prepared to carry out his orders—but he confessed that the "health of the Army is a very serious matter too, and I hope something may be devised to meet our difficulties."[45] Elgin also tried to mollify Miller. He likened the position of a member in India not to a Cabinet Minister (as Miller had done), but to a Minister outside the Government; the former, the Viceroy argued, had already had his say before the introduction of legislation into Parliament.[46] Miller vehemently denied that he was in the position "in any sense, of a Minister, in or out of the Cabinet." He insisted that he was

simply a subordinate official.... I do not question the right of the Secretary of State to dismiss me from Office... but the Government of India is not "Government by party," and no one is bound by the class of ties which so often vitiate the action of Members of the House of Commons.[47]

Miller eventually accepted Elgin's argument that he should not vote against the Government. But Elgin warned Fowler that "it does not altogether smooth the difficulties in a Viceroy's path ... if he has too often to say to his colleagues 'you must submit or resign.' "[48] Elgin emphasized that this was the second occasion (the Tariff Bill was the first) on which he had confronted this problem since his arrival in India. Fowler's patience had worn thin by continuous haggling over the new excise and cotton duties, as well as the outright rebellion over the Cantonment Bill, and he sent a strongly worded letter to Elgin on October 12, 1894. The Secretary of State compared the position of a Member in India to an M.P. in the Government at home, who, if he could not agree with a Government decision, had to resign because

a Government, whether in Downing Street, or Calcutta, must act as a homogeneous body, not representing certain political opinions, but as representing an executive authority which cannot act, whether in administration or legislation, efficiently unless they act unitedly.[49]

Fowler regretted Miller's objections to the legislation, but so long as the Secretary of State remained responsible to Parliament and the Queen for Indian affairs, the Members of the Executive Council in India had to support Government policy. To support his case, Fowler cited an 1868 despatch in which Lord Northcote had argued that it was inconsistent to speak of "imposed" voting in a legislature such as India's. If members of the Government opposed or abstained from Government programs, it would seriously detract from the authority and efficiency of the Executive. Moreover, Northcote had pointed out that the importance of upholding authority should be sufficient reason to induce Members of the Indian Government to support it. Finally, Fowler underscored the importance of Northcote's last observation that Members who could not conscientiously vote for Government proposals had no alternative but to resign. All of these propositions applied to Members of the Home Government, and from this Fowler concluded that

so long as any matter of administration, or policy is undecided, every Member of the Government of India is at liberty to express his own opinion; but when a certain line of policy has been adopted under the directions of the Cabinet, it is the clear duty of every Member of the Government of India to consider, not what the policy ought to be, but how effect may best be given to the policy which has been decided upon; and, if any Member of that Government is unable to do this, there is only one alternative [resignation] open to him.[50]

The Viceroy's Executive Council, after lengthy debate, decided to accept the relationship outlined in Northcote's despatch, rather than attempt any collective negative representation to the Secretary of State.[51] Internally, however, the Council continued to dispute the implications of the despatch. Henry Brackenbury, the Military Member, took one extreme position and said that he felt obligated to vote as directed; Miller, on the other hand, refused to concede this point and maintained that he could be dismissed if the home authorities so desired. Most of the others claimed the right to abstain, which, they pointed out, was not prohibited in Northcote's communiqué.[52] Elgin refuted Miller's pretensions to challenge the Secretary of State and his Council, arguing that

it surely cannot be denied that India is governed under the authority of Parliament by a Minister of the Government responsible to Parliament. He, with the consent of his Council, is the ruler—the Viceroy and his Council are the Representatives of that authority necessary for actual Executive work, but they have no right to go against any orders that issue from the Secretary of State.... It is my duty to the Queen to carry out loyally the orders that issue in her name.[53]

When advised of the debate in India, Fowler again carefully stated his position that Brackenbury's was the "proper constitutional view" and submitted that if Miller persisted in his course, he would be dismissed "promptly." He also informed Elgin: "I do not want you to be embarrassed with either resignations or dismissals... but the whole principle of the relation between a Government and its individual Members is at stake."[54] In response to Elgin's earlier request, Fowler issued a despatch explicitly detailing the amendments which the Government of India could and could not consider on the Cantonment Bill.[55] Elgin, for his part, accepted the decision by the Imperial Parliament, but he added that he could not shut his eyes to the fact "that if I act strongly on that argument [publicly] I may stir up considerable resentment."[56]

The Viceroy, however, had no respite. The long-awaited legislation on the cotton duties and countervailing excise taxes was introduced in the

Legislative Council on December 17, 1894. Westland apologetically made the proposals and grudgingly admitted conformity to the Home Government's wishes. Opposition came immediately from Indian and nonofficial Members, and the official Members again found themselves in a quandary—duty or conscience.[57] Elgin reported the new uneasiness in his Council to Fowler, who personally resented the phrase used by some Members that they had been "ordered" to vote for the bill or resign. Miller was still the main culprit; exasperated by the Cantonment Bill issue, his vexation was shared by C. B. Pritchard and several nominated official Members still troubled over the cotton duties question which remained unresolved. Fowler again conveyed the Home Government's position.

I do not like the phrase which some Members of your Council appear to employ, *viz.* that they are "ordered" to vote or resign. I think that the Lord Chancellor, the Cabinet and myself are quite as competent to form an opinion as to the "constitutional" position of the Executive Council as Sir A. Miller. At all events, as the responsibility rests with us, he *must* accept our decision as final. The Cabinet have decided that the position of the Executive Council in the Legislative Council corresponds to the position of the Members of the Government in Parliament; and as the unquestioned and unquestionable rule is that *all* Members of the Government are bound to support the legislative proposals of the Government, or to resign, the same course must be followed in India. There is no question of "ordering." The constitutional duty is clear and no honourable man could require an "order." If any of your Council decline to recognise this principle, I shall be compelled to take the extreme course.[58]

Godley commiserated with the Viceroy, and he was "painfully conscious how it is easy for us here, sitting in armchairs, to lay down principles which you have to put into force." The fact remained, however, that the Government of India, under the Act of 1858, had to conform, and the Viceroy, said Godley

is in fact, in the position in which every servant of the Crown is, from the Prime Minister downwards: our common Master being the Cabinet, or rather, the House of Commons which is behind the Cabinet. In this respect we are all of us in the same boat: when H.M. [Government] have adopted a policy, we must do our best to carry it out, or resign. I see no reason why members of your Council should be exempt from this universal rule. But, again I say, I wish the principle had been settled by one of your predecessors.[59]

The pressure on Elgin intensified, and on December 27, 1894, the Viceroy had to exercise his casting vote to ensure a Government victory in the new tariff legislation, and finally put on record the Secretary of State's "mandate" in the following statement:

In every legislative body a man must sit... by what in modern parlance is called a mandate, and that mandate must be given by some authority.... Here we have no election, and I am glad to say no party, but everyman who sits by the authority and sanction of Parliament, and to say that he can refuse to obey the decisions of Parliament would be absurd. But that is not all. Parliament has provided for the Government of the Indian empire. The British Raj can be provided for in no other way.[60]

The next day Elgin explained his position again, specifically on the Cantonment Bill issue. He also asked Pritchard not to resign over the constitutional issue,[61] for the Viceroy anticipated considerable public debate on his constitutional stand if it leaked to the press.[62] Indeed, a short time later the issue burst out in India in both the vernacular and the English-language press. The *Times of India* accused the Legislative Council of being a "group of automats worked by wires directed in London," and advocated the abolition of that body.[63] Indian-owned papers in particular reminded the Councillors that even if the cotton duties issue was lost, there still remained a chance for the Council to redeem itself over the Cantonment Bill. The *Hindoo Patriot*, for example, urged the Legislative Council to act independently and not to play the role of some automatic organization which existed merely to carry out the so-called mandates of the Secretary of State. Such unquestioning obedience, the paper argued, could only lead to a quick succession of fresh surrenders. The article in this influential native paper concluded by pointing out that

the Bill raises a grave constitutional danger, and makes the Government of India a subordinate to a clique represented by three Members of a Commission which can in no sense be regarded as representing the public, either in this country or in England.... It seems to us that of all the evils which may befall this unfortunate country of ours the worst is the evil of a weak Ministry which depends for its tenure of office upon the votes of every clique, however, insignificant, and never hesitates to sacrifice the interests of India to prolong by a few weeks its tenure of office.[64]

Elgin was extremely sensitive to criticism of his role in the crisis. He sought to clarify his position to Fowler and denied that he had argued for the so-called mandate theory asserting:

I assert the supremacy of Parliament and allege that the Secretary of State is the only proper exponent of what Parliament means, [but] I reserve absolutely the right of voting to men who act under a due sense of their responsibility. I only mention these points because it is generally assumed that I argued for your "mandate" overriding everything. Even as regards the Members of the Executive that is not what I said or intended.[65]

Unfortunately Elgin's private denials were of little use in responding to his public critics. Fowler, however, felt compelled to do something to alleviate the pressure on Elgin. The Secretary of State informed Elgin that he would give the House of Commons all previous correspondence on the issue of constitutional relations among the Government of India, the India Office, and Parliament, and that he would also direct a despatch to him on the matter. Furthermore, Fowler noted that he would state unequivocally that anyone who did not adjust to the Government position must resign.[66] The agitation over the Cantonment Bill subsided with the modification of clause 3; but the controversy over the Indian import duties and excise taxes continued through 1896, although the constitutional issue did not emerge again during that time.[67]

In his promised despatch of June 26, 1895, Fowler sealed the constitutional question by repeating categorically the Executive Council's obligation to vote the Government line or resign.[68] Years later John Morley observed that this despatch, which had been drafted by Godley, contained some of the "most edifying and nutritious doctrine on the position of Parliament in regard to India" which he had encountered.[69] Although it seemed a "settled" fact, Elgin mildly complained at the end of his term about being overruled by the India Office in plague and pilgrimage administration. Wearily Elgin lamented: "[S]urely the [Government] of India is the proper body to exercise all executive function *in India* [and] not the [Secretary of State] or his Council."[70] But the supremacy of Whitehall had been reaffirmed, and the Montagu-Chelmsford Report in 1918 noted a steadfast adherence to the policy of "previous sanction." It did, however, recommend some relaxation of the copious references to London because the Secretary of State's power of veto was sufficient to hold the Government of India in check.[71]

Because he felt obligated to articulate an already existing policy, Elgin gained his reputation as "subservient to Whitehall." While the highly volatile issues of his administration spotlighted the problem, he was neither more nor less "subservient" than his predecessors or successors as Viceroy during the Godley era (1883–1909). Curzon and Minto succumbed to the pressures. Even Curzon, who shortly after his arrival in India said that Elgin, "never, by one single word or deed, touched the imagination either of Indian or English society,"[72] acknowledged several decades later, just before his own death, that Elgin was a "much more sagacious administrator than the world knew or allowed."[73]

The tension over the constitutional relationship between the Home and Indian governments continued during Curzon's Viceroyalty and was increased by Curzon's personal vexations with the Council of India. Viceroys in India, regardless of political philosophy, had always been especially sensitive to the whims of the India Council. Lytton was "inexpressibly disgusted by the cackling of the Council at him," and Ripon, frustrated in his attempts to introduce progressive legislation in India, chaffed at the "set of old gentlemen, whose energies are relaxed by age, and who, having excellent salaries and no responsibility, amuse themselves by criticizing the proposals and obstructing the plans of those who have the most recent knowledge of India."[74] Curzon also recoiled at the notion of toadying to Councillors "who, having trembled at the nod of the Viceroy for the greater parts of their lives," should "with impunity dance a hornpipe on his prostrate frame."[75] He went so far as to send the Secretary of State, Hamilton, a detailed list of twenty-two instances in which he felt the Council of India had unjustly overruled him.[76] Curzon sought to remedy the "problem" by introducing parliamentary legislation to emasculate the powers of the Council.

Curzon's quarrels with the Council of India were in large part due to his opinion that his own Executive Council was in a state of "lamentable inefficiency and dislocation."[77] That Curzon was irritated at the constant cries of ex-Governors and retired Civil Servants on the Council of India about overcentralization in India is evident when he wrote to Hamilton:

When therefore, your greybeards crowd round you and whisper warnings in your ear about centralisation and so on, I wish you to take their protestations with a very considerable grain of salt, and politely to remind them that we are dealing with a state of affairs in which "superfluous lags the veteran on the stage."[78]

Godley warned Curzon early in the game not to persist in his attacks upon the India Council:

The fact that the Viceroy is personally or specially interested in a proposal is a card which sometimes may be played with effect, but it is to be played cautiously, and by no means too often.... I can assure you that it is very undesirable to make the Viceroy's personal wishes a common argument. You may rely on my doing my best to get your proposals agreed to, but you will, I hope, also believe that, being on the spot, and having now a good deal of experience, I know pretty well what forms of pressure it is advisable to use.[79]

Hamilton was annoyed that Curzon's superior abilities were being "warped by his growing sense of self-importance," and regretted that it was "not easy to get through his very rough pachyderm."[80] His predecessors had appropriately addressed the Secretary of State in Council as their "opponent" in the constitutional battle, but Curzon chose to isolate the Council of India as his "enemy." When the Council complained in 1902 that the Government of India was bypassing it on railway legislation, Curzon stated his position in the constitutional issue in the following terms:

I cannot recollect in official communications ever intentionally giving the [Council of India] the go-by, or seeming to appeal over their heads to His Majesty's Government, or to the House of Commons, or to anybody else.... The fact is that if the Council at home regard themselves as the Government of India—a view which

I do not share, seeing that I regard them as advisers (endowed with excessive powers) of the Secretary of State—they must be a little disturbed at the spectacle of so vigorous an initiative being taken in India, whereas, according to their theory, all impulse ought to spring from them.[81]

Hamilton, like his predecessors, was well aware of the Council's usefulness, and told Curzon that the Council of India was not "a pugnacious, fussy or aggressive body." They only wanted to be kept informed, Hamilton explained, and the Secretary of State had to be impartial in his relations between the two governments.[82] Curzon rejected the idea of official neutrality; while Godley said the Secretary of State was the "natural ally of the Viceroy," Curzon felt he ought to be his "official protector."[83] Curzon also rejected Hamilton's claims of Cabinet superiority and he asserted that

it is not against the exercise of superior authority that I have any complaint to make. It is against the assertion of an interference greater than has been exercised before, and conducted in a spirit, not of confidence or helpfulness, but of distrust and suspicion.[84]

Curzon urged Hamilton to control his Council, and added that "it would not be a bad thing if over the door of the room of every Member of Council at the India Office were inscribed the words spoken by Sir Bartle Frere on his death-bed: 'o that England would only trust her sons whom she sends forth to do her business.' "[85] Godley tried to calm Curzon's fears. He offered no judgment as to who was right or wrong; it was a poor consolation, the Permanent Undersecretary said, but "this sense of being thwarted by persons whose ignorance and stupidity is (to put it modestly), greater than one's own is common to every official in this country, from the Prime Minister . . . down to the humble 'permanent,' such as he who has the honour of addressing you."[86]

The conflict escalated when the Government of India disagreed with the Cabinet on Persian and Tibetan policy in 1903. Curzon grew increasingly rebellious, and declared outright: "[Y]ou cannot treat the Government of 300,000,000 of people as though it was a subordinate department."[87] Finally, Godley laid down the law; drawing upon the doctrines enunciated in Elgin's time, he wrote to Curzon on his relations with the Cabinet and India Office:

[A]fter all is said, this fact remains, and cannot be got over—the fact that the responsibility for every one of your acts, great and small, lies with the Secretary of State, the Prime Minister, and the Cabinet, and that where the responsibility is absolute and unshared, there must be a corresponding right of control, absolute and unshared. I say this fact cannot be got over, and it is quite certain that when Elgin defined his position in the way to which you take exception, he spoke the exact truth, neither more or less.[88]

Curzon was delighted at receiving "so rollicking and wholehearted a statement of the finest old crusted doctrines of the royal prerogative (as embodied in the Secretary of State in Council)—'right of control, absolute and unshared,' and so on."[89] He argued that the Viceroy, because he had immediate responsibility for administering India, should have a corresponding freedom to respond to exigencies and plan policy in that country without interference or constant reference home. Besides, Curzon pointed out, the Viceroy was always condemned before the Secretary of State when things went wrong. The India Office response was again tendered by Godley in the following despatch:

I think we must all agree that the real government of India is in the House of Commons; that the Cabinet speaks with the authority of the House of Commons, and must decide everything with reference to the question—"Can we defend this in the House?"; and that a Viceroy who cannot conscientiously acquiesce in and carry out the policy of the Cabinet has no choice but to resign.

Let me assure you that I say this without implying in the smallest degree that the Cabinet is more likely to be right on any given question than the Viceroy is: on the contrary, my instinct always impels me to believe in the man on the spot. But the Cabinet has to take into account matters as to which the Government of India cannot be thoroughly informed: and, right or wrong, so long as the law and practice of the Constitution remain what they are, they are entitled, not only to the last word, but the co-operation of the Viceroy.[90]

The Permanent Undersecretary indulged Curzon by noting that "our Acts of Parliament and official traditions are based upon the average Viceroy, and not the exceptional one 'who must live with the constitutional checks.' "[91]

The circumstances surrounding Curzon's resignation are varied and complex. But on the constitutional issue, Curzon was never really on firm ground. By personalizing his attacks on the Council of India, he not only merited their anger, but annoyed the Secretaries of State, Hamilton and Brodrick, and Godley to the point where an official restatement of the India Office's supremacy over the Government of India was necessary. Godley delivered that message, privately and on behalf of successive India Secretaries, and his correspondence repeated the official position so often that finally, in the spring of 1905, Curzon complained that the Permanent Undersecretary had written to him without provocation "a letter which the meanest of mankind could not have read without a feeling of deep pain and regret." After defending himself against specific charges, Curzon said, "I have torn up your letter and I hope to forget that I ever read it."[92] Eventually correspondence between the India Office and Curzon ceased altogether; but the principle of the Home Government's superiority over the Government of India had once again been firmly established.

The principle of Whitehall's supremacy over the Indian Government did not change during Minto's Viceroyalty. In fact, "Whitehall versus Simla" or the "war against the bureaucrats" has been a favorite theme among scholars of the Morley era.[93] Morley's intense dissatisfaction over the handling of the partition of Bengal contributed to a natural tension between the Secretary of State and Viceroy whose political philosophies differed tremendously. Morley and Minto also differed early in the latter's term over the Secretary of State's right to enter into private correspondence with Indian officials. Morley rejected the warnings of both Godley and his confidant and Private Secretary, Arthur Hirtzel, about the Viceroy's growing resentment over the Secretary of State's independent lines of communication with India. He insisted that he had been "kept in the dark all the time," and that communication was necessary to keep him informed about events in the subcontinent.[94] The Secretary of State also pointed out that the Viceroy himself privately corresponded with the royal family, and although this was not unusual, Morley called it "an illegitimate influence" which might lead to unwanted royal meddling in Indian affairs.[95] Godley tried to calm both parties in the dispute—but Minto rejected the Permanent Undersecretary's suggestions that he allow himself to "be guided" by Morley's policy and he scrawled "infernal ass" over the top of Godley's letter.[96]

The two heads of the Indian Government also differed over the appointment of Lieutenants-Governor, legally the sole responsibility of the Secretary of State for India. Minto's attempts to claim the right of selection of Indian officers prompted a concise constitutional ruling from Morley: "To put it plainly and in a single sentence, the responsibility of recommending a Lieutenant-Governor to the Sovereign is a compound thing, to which the Governor-General and the Secretary of State contribute, but the Secretary of State cannot help having the last word."[97] Minto's persistent protestations irritated Morley, who replied that "the Viceroy can no more 'submit' anything to the King than Godley can. Any Whig ghost, or living lawyer, will convince you of this."[98]

The India Office imposed its will on the Government of India as needed. This dominance extended to administrative questions, such as the distribution of work between departments and creation of new offices. The most glaring cases of such direction of internal matters by the Government in London were in the military administration question; the Curzon-Kitchener dispute is a good example. Matters relating to foreign policy were almost always directed by the India Office. This was because the Secretary of State was a member of the Cabinet and therefore the overriding consideration in India policy was the security of the Empire. For example, when the time came for negotiations for the Anglo-Russian entente, Morley rejected the Government of India's pleas for consultations. The Secretary of State noted that "the plain truth is and you would not mind me saying it frankly because you will agree—that this country cannot have two foreign policies," one for his Majesty's Government and the other by the Government of India.[99]

The Secretary of State's control also extended to legislative action by the Government of India. The doctrine, firmly entrenched by Minto's time, of obligatory voting by official Members of the Viceroy's Council to instructions from home, was reinforced by Morley. During the crisis over the Government of India's deportation of "seditious" Indians, Morley reminded the Government of India of the doctrine of "previous sanction" and reprimanded Minto's government for ignoring his direct (telegraphic) instructions that any steps about seditious speeches, meetings or writings "should only be taken after reference to Home Government, unless of course [in] sudden emergency."[100] When the Government of India used the loophole (of "sudden emergency") in the sedition case of Lala Lajpat Rai, Morley was incensed, and asserted that "the [Government of India] is no absolute or independent branch of Imperial Government. It is in every respect answerable to the Cabinet as any other department is."[101] Godley endorsed Morley's stand, explaining to Members of the India Council that "whatever is done in India, the [Secretary of State] must, if challenged, be prepared either to defend . . . or to condemn . . . [it] publicly."[102]

During the Reforms debate Minto's council balked at accepting an Indian Member, and Morley reached back to an already well-established set of dicta to bring the Viceroy's Council into line.[103] Referring to the Fowler-Elgin correspondence, Morley informed Minto:

I trust the occasion may never arise during your term, but if it should, it would much refresh me to think of your addressing your men as Elgin addressed his Council on December 27, 1894. There is also a dispatch of Fowler's, June 26 . . . which contains some most edifying and nutritious doctrine on the position of Parliament in regard to India, from the Duke of Argyll and Lord Salisbury.[104]

A year later, when the Viceroy's Council—against instructions from home—refused to give in on the question of the deportees, Morley reminded Minto that: "I earnestly hope that I am not to understand that you reject the unanimous suggestion of the Cabinet. Such a result would be most grave, and I am sure you will consider the situation with a full sense of responsibility, as I sincerely try to do."[105]

Minto retorted that his Council had twice expressed opposition to releasing the deportees, and "if His Majesty's Government decides upon the opposite course the Viceroy and Government of India must accept their instructions, but they could not be held responsible for the results [e.g., increased sedition]."[106] The tension between the India Office and the Indian Government increased substantially as a series of despatches dictating the prior submission of a wide variety of financial matters to the Home Government went out to India at that same time.[107]

This most single-minded Secretary of State, oddly enough, was almost responsible for eliminating one of the India Office's most efficient means of controlling the actions of the Government of India. Early drafts of the proposed Reforms legislation show that Morley originally favored an end to official majorities on all levels of government, provincial and Imperial. However, he finally agreed—for the sake of political expediency—to retain the official majority at the supreme level in Calcutta.[108] In a long address to the House of Lords, Morley assured the Peers that he was *not* moving too fast in restructuring the Indian Government:

> There is one proviso in this matter of the official majority in which your Lordships may, perhaps, find a surprise. We are not prepared to divest the Governor-General in his Council of an official majority. In the Provincial Councils we propose to dispense with it, but in the Viceroy's Legislative Council we propose to adhere to it, though let me say that here we may seem to lag a stage behind the Government of India themselves—so little violent are we—because the Government say, in their despatch—on all ordinary occasions we are ready to dispense with an official majority in the Imperial Legislative Council, and to rely on the public spirit of non-official members to enable us to carry on the ordinary work of legislation. My Lords, that is what we propose to do in the Provincial Councils. But in the Imperial Council we consider an official majority essential. It may be said that is a most tremendous logical inconsistency. So it would be on one condition. If I were attempting to set up a Parliamentary system in India, or if it could be said that this chapter of reforms led directly or necessarily up to the establishment of a Parliamentary system in India, I, for one, would have nothing at all to do with it.[109]

The assertion of the Secretary of State's superiority over the Government of India was summed up by Edwin Montagu, Parliamentary Undersecretary of State, in introducing the Indian budget in 1910. Montagu reminded the House of Commons that the Secretary of State in Council was responsible to "conduct" Indian business, and that the "Secretary of State is separated from this task by the sea, hampered by delays of communication, often checkmated by the lapse of time.... The most liberal-minded, hard-working Secretary of State is helpless without a loyal, conscientious and statesmanlike Viceroy." Montagu sealed the restatement of Whitehall's domination by noting that "Lord Morley and his Council, working through the agency of and with the help of Lord Minto, have accomplished much."[110] *The Times* reacted spontaneously, vigorously protesting that "the Viceroy and Government of India, though possibly exceedingly unobtrusive, still exist."[111] Lovat Fraser, a Curzonian and old Anglo-Indian journalist, protested "Lord Morley's growing tendency to usurp the functions of the Government of India."[112]

When he received the speech by mail, Minto fumed that he "had not realised that the Viceroy was merely an *agent*, and the Government of India apparently only a *registry office!*"[113] He referred Morley to John Strachey's book *India: Its Administration and Progress*, citing Chapter 5 on the danger of excessive home interference. Lady Minto considered that "the hand of

Morley, who has never quite forgiven Rolly for having stated publicly that he was the author of reforms," was really behind the speech.[114] Sir J.R. Dunlop Smith, Minto's former Private Secretary who had recently shifted to the India Office as an Aide-de-Camp, alleged that Montagu "had nothing to do with the speech except deliver it. The hands were those of Montagu, but the voice was the voice of Morley."[115] In Simla, Minto and his Council drafted minutes "regarding the powers of the Secretary of State and of the Government of India." While vigorously denouncing Montagu's statement of the constitutional relationship, the Councillors agreed with Minto

that such action on our part would afford an opportunity to the Secretary of State for a definite pronouncement as to his interpretation of his constitutional authority and the powers of the Government of India. There would be grave risk . . . of the conversion of his "pretentions" into "useage."[116]

Privately Minto confided to a colleague that "it seems better to continue as we have done to assert our rights in answer to any dictatorial despatch as we have done, but not to raise the main question of the Secretary of State's control."[117] While shying away from a direct confrontation with Morley and the India Office, Minto added his contention that

the present Secretary of State does not read Acts of Parliament in this way [i.e., leaving direct administration of affairs in India to the Government of India], and claims his right to interfere with and command every individual in India—direct—irrespective of their being the servants of the Government of India. Of course such claims must be ruin to all discipline! Legally his position may be sound, but constitutionally it is impossible.[118]

Minto firmly believed that "we here have continued quietly to rule."[119] Morley, however, persisted in informing Minto privately that the Governor-General was subject to orders from home,[120] and publicly spelled out the Cabinet's ultimate authority over its Indian servants (through the Secretary of State) in an essay written shortly after leaving office: "British Democracy and Indian Government."[121]

By Minto's time the "agency" theory of the constitutional prerogatives of the India Office was well defined. It was merely another way of expressing Elgin's "mandate theory," which in itself was a definition of the technical situation as dictated by the Home Government. Sir Arthur Godley was the prime advocate and keeper of the doctrine for successive Secretaries of State in the late nineteenth century. Early in his Undersecretaryship Godley advised Cross of his right to correspond with individuals in India despite the Viceroy's protestations of the "disloyalty" of such correspondence.[122] Godley, however, advocated moderation in the application of this right throughout his tenure, including the crisis precipitated by Kitchener's private correspondence with the India Office during his dispute with Curzon.¹²³ Godley also zealously guarded the Secretary of State's rights to review Indian honors and appoint members of the Viceroy's Council.¹²⁴ As issues increased in intensity and number during Elgin's administration, Godley's pronouncements over the subordinate role of the Viceroy to the India Office sharpened. The Permanent Undersecretary compared the relationship with Sir Alfred Lyall's idea of an "administrative understanding" between the Secretary of State and the Government of India: "When after a full hearing, the [Secretary] of State has given his decision, it ought to be recognized by the Departments in India that the thing must be done, and cannot be waded by delays [and] pretexts."¹²⁵ Put in this light, Morley's assertiveness over Minto and his Government is not an isolated instance of "autocracy" by the Secretary of State, but a logical extension of a debate which had been developing throughout the late nineteenth century. The confrontation was not wholly Minto's fault, nor of Morley's design. Minto may have been right in noting the limited depth to which the India Office could extend its control in India; but in the existing system, the Secretary of State could not help but subordinate the Government of India in matters of "greater Imperial importance." What distinguished the controversy between 1906 and 1910 was the intensity with which the constitutional conflict was played out, rather than the substance of the battle.

The issue of subordination was not limited to legal questions. Fundamental to the assertion of India Office dominance was its perception of the role and function of the Viceroy himself. The India Office's image of the Viceroy's constitutional position was most succinctly expressed during Curzon's Viceroyalty when the Viceroy took a leave of absence to England in 1904. Prior to his leave, Curzon had criticized the Governor of Madras, Lord Ampthill, who incurred the Viceroy's wrath by forwarding private correspondence between them to the Secretary of State in London. Curzon attributed it to "some impatience when a grown man behaves like a petulant school-boy."¹²⁶ The Viceroy concluded that Ampthill's early appointment to high office had given him a "sense of self-importance and . . . [a] touch of the pompous."¹²⁷ After the Delhi Durbar Curzon again cited Ampthill's "tendency to pompousness and self-importance" and said the "only person who made an ass of himself at Delhi was Ampthill."¹²⁸

After considerable lobbying for his leave of absence, Curzon was suddenly unnerved when he realized that Ampthill as the senior presidency Governor in India would become Acting Viceroy when Northcote unexpectedly left for Australia. Although the Secretary of State, Hamilton, sincerely respected Ampthill's "seriousness and industry and purpose," Curzon said his age (thirty-four) and the fact that he was not an "exceptional personage" made Ampthill's appointment comparable to "putting in a curate to act for the Archbishop of Canterbury."¹²⁹ Both Hamilton and Godley assured the Viceroy that Ampthill was competent, and reminded him that an Acting Viceroy, hemmed in by the Viceroy's Council on one side and the Secretary of State on the other, would have little chance of interfering with Curzon's Indian policies.[130]

But Ampthill's appointment, however, could not and did not interrupt the normal correspondence between the India Office and Government of India. Godley carefully explained the position of the Viceroy to the surrogate Governor-General in terms which are strikingly similar to those used by Montagu years later in describing the "agency" theory of the relationship between the two governments:

You ask why the Secretary of State asked you (in an official telegram) for your opinion on the Persian scheme of financial reform when you had been only two days in office? In the reply to this question a point of some constitutional importance is involved. What he wanted, or must be assumed to have wanted, was the opinion of Your Excellency's Government, and this opinion he has a right to ask for and to expect, full-blown, at any stage in your Viceroyalty and at any hour of the day or night. Of course, if the matter admits of delay (as it did in this case), the Viceroy may for personal reasons postpone his reply until he, individually, has had time to think the matter over; but to the Secretary of State, for official purposes, the Viceroy never dies and never changes: he is simply the figurehead of the Government of India to whom telegrams and despatches are addressed, and from whom telegrams (though not despatches) issue.[131]

As Acting Viceroy Ampthill became accustomed to his new position, took Godley's advice about doing things his own way, and strongly denied any implication that he acted cautiously because he regarded Lord Curzon as some kind of "Pope." Ampthill informed Godley that "since I am merely keeping his place warm for him, I feel bound in honour and loyalty to do as he would have done or would wish to be done." He would, however, not let that sense of loyalty prohibit his acting independently if called upon to do so.[132] Godley emphasized that the Viceroy, while in many respects an "independent sovereign," was in fact "the representative of H.M. [Government] in India, [and] the channel by means of which the views of that Government—and through them those of the House of Commons, who are our real masters—find their expression in the administration of India."[133] Godley reassured Ampthill that the India Office would not add pressure to his position by taking advantage of Curzon's leave. The Permanent Undersecretary proceeded to give a most specific definition of the India Office position: "*you must remember that . . . the Government of India is immortal, and incapable of 'suspended animation,' and that we cannot officially recognize the absence of any individual as a sufficient reason for postponing business or modifying decisions.*"[134] [Italics added.] In England Curzon complained of being "left out" and "kept so much in the dark" about events in India.[135] This compelled the Secretary of State, St. John Brodrick, to clarify Curzon's position while he was in England: he was not

Viceroy, and therefore could not see Ampthill's private correspondence. The India Office would, however, attempt to keep him informed.[136] Curzon accused Brodrick of personal weakness in the face of his Council and created havoc by publicly challenging the Cabinet and Council of India over Afghan policy while in London. Godley was alarmed, and he wrote to Ampthill:

[Curzon] seems almost to have lost sight of the merits of the various questions, in which he has differed from the Cabinet or from our Council (or they from him), and to be absorbed in a struggle for prerogative, control, independence. In any of these disputed matters, the thought that seems to rise in his mind is not "I will prove to the Cabinet, or to the Council of India, that they are wrong about this and that I am right," but "I have given my opinion, I have even reiterated it in two or more despatches, I am the Viceroy of India, and, confound you, how do you dare to set your opinion against mine? . . . " It is lucky for him that the Secretary of State is an intimate friend, who is most anxious to meet him at every point and to humour him as much as he can; for, constitutionally speaking, he has not a leg to stand upon, and an unfriendly person, in Mr. Brodrick's position, might make things very unpleasant for him.[137]

Shortly after he returned to India, Curzon entered the fray with Kitchener which would eventually lead to his resignation. By spring 1905 Godley pressed the Secretary of State to let Ampthill relieve the embattled Viceroy, but Brodrick was reluctant, for it almost assuredly meant Ampthill would have to be appointed permanently.[138] Curzon finally stopped all correspondence with the India Office, and the Governors of Bombay and Madras filled the breech.

On the constitutional issue outlined above, there is little doubt that Whitehall dominated the struggle. It was an intense debate at times, but it never brought the government of the Indian Empire to a halt. This was in great measure due to Godley's perception of himself as an intermediary between the India Office and the Government of India, and his success in gaining the confidence of a number of diverse personalities occupying the Viceroyalty. For example, Godley has been characterized as Minto's "foremost agent" in Whitehall, acting as a foil on the Viceroy's behalf against the vexations of the Secretary of State.[139] This is not surprising, for throughout his career Godley acted as the "agent" and "informed source" for all Viceroys with whom he communicated. This role facilitated the expeditious despatch of complex business both in India and England and allowed both parties to sound out each other on sensitive issues through informal channels of communication. It also allowed the Permanent Undersecretary a private channel through which he could enunciate constitutional positions candidly.

Godley's personal influence with the various Viceroys was substantial. When Dufferin became concerned at reports that the India Office and

Council of India were unhappy with his government's performance, he wrote to Godley, calling him "almost the only friend... that I have at the India Office," questioning the rumors behind the Secretary of State's back.[140] Dufferin appealed to Godley to clarify the situation, proclaiming

> it is well that there should be at the India Office some sensible calmjudging intermediary to whom a person in my situation can communicate his opinions and feelings without reserve, and in a more unrestricted language than it would be fitting for him to use to his Chief.[141]

Dufferin's successors followed his example, and indeed, Lansdowne established a "private" link to Godley even before departing Canada for India.[142] When Elgin arrived in India, Godley advised the Viceroy's Private Secretary (Babington-Smith) to "remember that it is sometimes distinctly advantageous that I should be well posted privately as to your views [and] wishes."[143] This independent line of communication proved invaluable when the problems which beset Lord Elgin and his government threatened to bring some members of the Government of India to open rebellion. The private Elgin-Godley correspondence certainly eased that tension and in fact solved some of the difficulties. Elgin had tremendous respect for Godley, and while writing openly to the Secretary of State, he informed Godley that he would "keep back anything that might be productive of mischief— [and] you will judge if these things need to be mentioned as from me."[144] Elgin deeply appreciated Godley's advice, acknowledging wholeheartedly that it was "very useful to know a little behind the scenes."[145] He was grateful to the Permanent Undersecretary for the "little glimpses behind the scenes" that enabled him to sort out often unintelligible impulses from home sent via official means.[146] On his part, Godley considered Elgin one of the best correspondents among the Viceroys he had known.[147] Before he left India, Elgin "spoke strongly" to Curzon about the advantages of a full and free correspondence with Sir Arthur Godley, and the new Viceroy immediately adopted the plan.[148]

The candor and frankness of the Godley-Curzon correspondence are reflected in Godley's constitutional dicta to Curzon, and the eventual cessation of correspondence between the two was in large part related to Godley's candid assessment of Curzon's behavior. During Curzon's leave, Ampthill relied heavily on Godley's advice. By the time he assumed full control, Ampthill informed Godley that while he was being guarded in his correspondence with the Secretary of State, he was "nevertheless... trying to form a habit of writing to you every week so as to 'preserve the right of way' and to elicit the letters from yourself which form such a refreshing part of my weekly mail."[149]

After returning to Madras, Ampthill continued his close correspondence with Godley, whom he considered his "lightning-conductor" in the India

Office.¹⁵⁰ By Minto's Viceroyalty then, it is easy to understand the Viceroy's gratitude for Godley's actions on his behalf.¹⁵¹ Minto considered the Permanent Undersecretary part of a special "family circle who must keep each other posted."¹⁵²

Godley's role as an intermediary between the London and Indian governments not only allowed him the advantage of advance information on important matters but enabled him to promote compromises between the Secretary of State and the Viceroy on policy matters as well. To do that effectively, Godley had to be discreet, and Godley's discretion was rarely doubted by his correspondents.¹⁵³ Godley's high sense of morality paralleled his discretion. Conscientiously he refrained from informing Elgin of Curzon's appointment until it was finally settled; he later referred to his restraint as somewhat silly, and admitted that it tended to "cramp my style."¹⁵⁴ The only real attack on Godley's prudence came from Curzon toward the end of his Viceroyalty. Curzon complained bitterly that the Prime Minister, Arthur Balfour, had cited a phrase, which criticized the Government's Russian policy, in a letter to him which Curzon had originally written privately to Godley. The Viceroy was indignant, and claimed that for years he had corresponded with Godley in a totally free and honest manner; "it certainly never occurred to me that expressions from such a correspondence could be handed to you as the basis of a charge against me."¹⁵⁵ Soon after that, Curzon ceased his correspondence with the India Office. In actual fact the letter quoted had been written to Godley, but was excerpted and sent to the Prime Minister by the Secretary of State, Brodrick.¹⁵⁶

The incident is an important example of the power Godley wielded as an intermediary between the constituent parts of the Indian Government. After Hamilton's resignation in 1903, Curzon welcomed Brodrick to the India Office and advised him that "usually, indeed I think invariably, [Hamilton] showed my letters to Godley, who is a very wise and experienced councillor, and I have little doubt that you will do the same."¹⁵⁷ Brodrick agreed to treat Curzon's letters with care, adding that he certainly would show them to Godley, "who is in all respects a great 'stand-by.' "¹⁵⁸ Although he encouraged Brodrick to show his letters to the Undersecretary, the Viceroy was upset when Godley revealed portions of a letter criticizing the India Office's Russian policy to his chief. Godley hurried off a note to Curzon reminding him that

> whether I was right or wrong, you may be sure that I did it quite deliberately, and in the belief that its perusal would do not only no harm, but positive good. I *never* show your letters to me without carefully considering whether it is or is not advisable to do so.¹⁵⁹

Godley restated his selective methods and his relationship to the Secretary of State for Lord Ampthill:

Mr. Brodrick, like his predecessors for many years back, always shows me his letters from India (there may be exception, but they must be very few): on the other hand, I *generally* show him mine; but as to this I exercise my discretion, [and] if there is the slightest reason for not doing so, I refrain—*on this you may rely absolutely.*[160]

But the Permanent Undersecretary of State also knew his limitations. As the Curzon-Kitchener imbroglio climaxed, Curzon angrily protested the "invidious and derogatory" letters from the India Office. Godley said that he could not do anything about it, for the conflict had reached a stage beyond his influence or purview. As for the content of mail from London, Godley told the Viceroy that he had neither been consulted nor overruled and that he saw no harm in it.[161]

Were India's Viceroys in the late nineteenth century autocrats or agents? There is no doubt that the Indian proconsuls had tremendous influence in the decision-making process. Therefore, they cannot be regarded as mere agents. On the other hand, there is a clearly identifiable pattern of the exercise of authority by the Home Government of India in long-range planning and implementation of policy. This trend is discernible from the 1870s on, but was most clearly enunciated in Elgin's time as a result of the unusual number of crises that enveloped his administration. It continued to be reinforced in the Viceroyalties of Curzon and Minto. So it is apparent that the Viceroys in the latter part of the century were not as independent or autocratic as many contemporary critics or subsequent accounts have assumed. The truth is, perhaps, that, by regularly conceding to the dictates of the Home Government, viceregal pretentions to independence were severely circumscribed.

If the myriad of constitutional obligations both in England and India were not enough to complicate policy-making for the India Office, there were also several important nonofficial groups which influenced or attempted to influence the decision-making processes in Whitehall. These groups represented a rather ill-defined "public opinion" both in England and India, and the India Office closely monitored their activities. Their ultimate success in influencing the course of Indian policy was marginal; however, the efforts expended by the India Office to keep this pressure at the periphery of the policy-making process were considerable.

NOTES

1. R. S. Jain, *The Growth and Development of [the] Governor-General's Executive Council (1858–1919)* [Delhi: S. Chand and Co., 1962], p. 181.

2. G.B., Parliament, *East India Accounts and Papers (Legislation)*, [1876], LVI, pp. 112–14.

3. Sir John Strachey, *India: Its Administration and Progress* (London: Macmillan and Co., 4th ed., 1911), p. 52.

4. Ripon to Lord Aberdale, 24 May 1881, quoted in Lucian Wolf, *Life of Ripon* (London: John Murray, 1921), II, 68.

5. Brief summations of these controversies are found in A. B. Rudra, *The Viceroy and Governor-General of India* (Oxford: Oxford University Press, 1940), pp. 150–59.

6. S. A. Wolpert, *Morley and India, 1906–1910* (Berkeley and Los Angeles: University of California Press, 1967), p. 42.

7. Donovan Williams, "The Formation of Policy in the India Office, 1858–66, with special reference to the Political, Judicial, Revenue, Public and Public Works Departments," unpublished thesis, Oxford, 1962, p. 56. Williams disagrees with Rudra's observation (*Viceroy and Governor-General*, pp. 146–47) that the Secretary of State commanded increased respect over the Court of Directors, and this then, meant increased home control. The constant divisiveness and bickering of the India Council retarded the development of that control for the first two decades of the India Office. See also Donovan Williams, *The India Office 1858–1869* (Hoshiarpur, Punjab: Vishveshvaranard Vedic Research Institute, 1983), *passim*.

8. See Rudra, *Viceroy and Governor-General*, *passim*; and Sir Courtney Ilbert, *The Government of India* (Oxford: The Clarendon Press, 3rd rev. ed., 1915), *passim*.

9. Legislative sanction for describing the action by the Governor-General as "the Government of India" was extended by the Indian General Clauses Act (X of 1897, s. 3 [22]) [Ilbert, *Government of India*, p. 112].

10. For an outline of the departments and their roles, see Rudra, *Viceroy and Governor-General*, p. 70. Some special departments worked in conjunction with the Secretariat departments. The Directors-General of the Post Office and Telegraph Departments, Surgeon-General's Department, and Railway Board were centrally administered. On the other hand, the Inspectors-General of Forests and Agriculture and Directors-General of Education and the Indian Medical Service represented departments administered by local governments but supervised by the Government of India (Ilbert, *Government of India*, p. 113).

11. G.B., Parliament, *East India, Accounts and Papers (Legislation)*, [1876], LVI, (Legislative No. 12, 31 March 1865), No. 102, col. 1515, p. 20.

12. *Ibid.*, p. 21.

13. SS to GOI (Legislative No. 8, 18 March 1869), *ibid.*, p. 22; and GOI to SS (Legislative No. 1, 22 March 1870), *ibid.*, pp. 23–24.

14. *Ibid.*

15. SS to GOI (Legislative No. 47, 24 November 1870), *ibid.*, p. 26.

16. G.B., *Hansard's Parliamentary Debates*, ser. 3, vol. 227 (1876), col. 1972. See also columns 1960–75.

17. G.B., Parliament, *East India, Accounts and Papers (Legislation)*, [1876], LVI, No. 102, p. 20.

18. GOI to SS, 17 March 1876, *ibid.*

19. See Edward C. Moulton, *Lord Northbrook's Indian Administration, 1872–76* (Bombay: Asia Publishing House, 1968), pp. 264–65.

20. Hobhouse to Northbrook, 27 September 1874, quoted in Moulton, *Northbrook*, p. 266.

21. Northbrook to Grey, 20 September 1874, *ibid.*, p. 267.

22. See Jain, *Development of Executive Council*, pp. 187–93. Excerpts from this despatch (GOI to SS, Home Department No. 9, 17 March 1876) are provided therein. For an overview of the tariff controversy, see Moulton, *Northbrook*, pp. 174–214.

23. G.B., Parliament, *East India, Accounts and Papers (Legislation)*, [1876], LVI, pp. 596 ff.

24. "Bruce, Victor Alexander, 9th Earl of Elgin," *Dictionary of National Biography 1912–1921*, p. 72.

25. *Ibid.*, p. 73.

26. Sir Richard Jebb, *The Imperial Conference* (London, 1911), quoted in R. B. Pugh, "The Colonial Office, 1801–1925," in E. A. Benians, et al. (eds.), *Cambridge History of the British Empire* (London: Cambridge University Press, 1959), III, 737.

27. See P. L. Malhotra, *Administration of Lord Elgin in India 1894–99* (New Delhi: Vikas Publishing House Pvt., 1979), pp. 33–67. For a detailed discussion of the controversy, see Peter Harnetty, "The Indian Cotton Duties Controversy, 1894–1896," *English Historical Review* 77:35 (October 1962), pp. 684–702.

28. See Malhotra, *Elgin in India*, p. 33–34.

1854	1 mill
1873	20 mills
1876	47 mills
1882	62 mills
1894	142 mills

29. Elgin to Kimberley, 31 January 1894, Elgin Papers (9th Earl of Elgin) [hereafter cited as EP], IOL, MSS. Eur. F.84/12.

30. Godley privately informed Elgin of Kimberley's problems and asked the Viceroy to "consider the difficulty of *his* position" (Godley to Elgin, 16 February 1894, EP F.84/23).

31. Godley to Elgin, 22 February 1894, EP F.84/23; see also Arnold P. Kaminsky, " 'Lombard Street' and India: Currency Problems in the Late Nineteenth Century," *The Indian Economic and Social History Review* 17:3 (July-September 1980), pp. 307–27.

32. All eleven members dissented from the exemption of cotton from the tariff lists (IOR, Minutes of the Council of India, C/72, pp. 98–99). See also "Copies of Minutes of Dissent by Members of the Council of India (1894–1913)," IOR, C/129.

33. Elgin to Godley, 7 March 1894, Kilbracken Papers [hereafter cited as KP], IOL, MSS. Eur. F.102/12.

34. *Proceedings of the Legislative Council [of the Governor-General in India]*, Vol. 33, p. 119.

35. Malhotra, *Elgin in India*, pp. 43–45.

36. Elgin to Kimberley, private telegram, 10 March 1894, EP F.84/17.

37. *Bhangavasi*, 15 March 1894, cited in Malhotra, *Elgin in India*, p. 37.

38. *Sulabah Dainik*, 7 April 1894, *ibid.*

39. *Ibid.*, p. 38.

40. See S. Gopal, *British Policy in India, 1858–1905* (Cambridge: Cambridge University Press, 1965), pp. 180–81.

41. A survey of the events leading up to the controversy over cantonments legislation is found in PRO, Cabinet Papers, CAB/37/38/4/7340.

42. See Arnold P. Kaminsky, "Morality Legislation and British Troops in Late Nineteenth Century India," *Military Affairs* 43:2 (April 1979), pp. 78–83.

43. Elgin to Fowler, 17 July 1894, Wolverhampton (Fowler) Papers [hereafter cited as FP], IOL, MSS. Eur. C.145/1.

44. Fowler to Elgin, 20 July 1894, EP F.84/12.

45. Elgin to Fowler, 7 August 1894, FP C.145/1.

46. Elgin to Miller, 9 August 1894, EP F.84/65.

47. Miller to Elgin, 9 August 1894, *ibid*.

48. Elgin to Fowler, 14 August 1894, EP F.84/12.

49. Fowler to Elgin, 12 October 1894, *ibid*. Malhotra (*Elgin in India*, p. 44) erringly includes this as part of the correspondence relating to the cotton duties question. Fowler's daughter (and biographer) quotes the letter, too, but cited it as an example of her father's "toughness" aside from the cotton duties issue (E. H. Fowler [née Hamilton], *The Life of Lord Wolverhampton* [London: Hutchinson and Co., 1912], pp. 315–17.

50. Fowler to Elgin, 12 October 1894, EP F.84/12.

51. Elgin to Fowler, 16 October 1894, *ibid*.

52. Elgin to Fowler, 30 October 1894, *ibid*. Miller, in fact, proclaimed that "so long as I was acting in accordance with the views of the Government of India, [I] should never hesitate to 'get round' his [the Secretary of State's] order if I could" (Miller to Elgin, 30 October 1894, EP F.84/65).

53. Elgin to Miller, 7 November 1894, EP F.84/65.

54. Fowler to Elgin, 23 November 1894, EP F.84/12. Elgin had reported these threats earlier (Elgin to Fowler, 30 November 1894, *ibid*.).

55. Elgin to Fowler, 28 November 1894 *ibid*. See also SS to GOI (Mil. No. 13), 29 November 1894 (CAB/37/38/4/7340, Appendix D).

56. Elgin to Fowler, 30 October 1894, FP C.145/1.

57. See *Proc. of the Legislative Council*, vol. 33 (1894), pp. 384–92 and 402–46.

58. Fowler to Elgin, 21 December 1894, EP F.84/12.

59. Godley to Elgin, 23 December 1894, EP F.84/23.

60. *Proc. of the Legislative Council*, vol. 33 (1894), p. 447.

61. Elgin to Sir C. B. Pritchard, 28 December 1894, EP F.84/65.

62. Elgin to Godley, 19 December 1894, KP F.102/12.

63. *Times of India*, 7 January 1895, quoted in *The Times* (London), 8 January 1895, p. 5. *The Times* was chastised by Manchester merchants as "the organisation of the protectionists of India," and its Calcutta correspondent was especially criticized (*The Times*, 9 January 1895, p. 10).

64. *The Times*, 10 January 1895, p. 5; and 15 January 1895, p. 5.

65. Elgin to Fowler, 9 January 1895, EP F.84/13.

66. Fowler to Elgin, 29 March 1895, *ibid*. See also G.B., Parliament, C. 7731 (1895), vol. LXXII.

67. For a discussion on the resolution of the cotton duties crisis of 1894–1896, see Harnetty, "Cotton Duties Controversy," pp. 690–704; and Malhotra, *Elgin in India*, pp. 45–67.

68. SS to GOI (Legislative No. 21), 26 June 1895.

69. John Morley, *Recollections* (New York: The Macmillan Co., 1917), II, 244.
70. Elgin to Godley, 18 May 1898, KP F.102/16. See also Godley to Elgin, 18 February 1897 and 10 June 1898, EP F.84/136.
71. G.B., Parliament, *Report on Indian Constitutional Reforms*, Cd. 9109 (1918), pp. 217-18.
72. Curzon to Hamilton, 17 May 1899, Curzon Papers [hereafter cited as CP], IOL, MSS. Eur. F.111/158.
73. Lord Curzon, *British Government in India* (London: Cassell and Co., 1925), II, 250.
74. Lytton to John Strachey, 24 October 1877, quoted in S. N. Singh, *The Secretary of State for India and His Council (1858-1919)* [Delhi: Munshi Ram Monohar Lal, 1962], p. 36; Ripon to Hartington, 14 September 1882, *ibid.*, p. 47.
75. Curzon to Hamilton, 7 March 1901, Hamilton Papers [hereafter cited as HP], IOL, MSS. Eur. D.510/8.
76. Curzon to Hamilton, 28 May 1902, CP F.111/161. Hamilton dismissed the complaints in detail, proving to Curzon that in reality only two of the twenty-two examples he had listed could be considered valid objections to the Council's action. The Council, Hamilton concluded, was fulfilling its constitutional role to review in detail long-range planning that would affect India long after Curzon left it (Hamilton to Curzon, 19 June 1902, CP F.111/161).
77. Curzon to Hamilton, 4 June 1903, cited in David Dilks, *Curzon in India* (London: Rupert Hart-Davis, 1969), I, 92.
78. *Ibid.*
79. Godley to Curzon, 14 February 1901, CP F.111/160.
80. Hamilton to Godley, 4 April 1901, KP F.102/6.
81. Curzon to Godley, 13 March 1902, CP F.111/161.
82. Hamilton to Curzon, 25 June 1902, *ibid.*
83. Curzon to Godley, 8 July 1902, *ibid.*
84. Curzon to Hamilton, 9 July 1902, *ibid.*
85. Curzon to Hamilton, 16 July 1902, *ibid.*
86. Godley to Curzon, 27 November 1903, CP F.111/162.
87. Curzon to Northbrook, 12 August 1903, quoted in Dilks, *Curzon in India*, I, 113.
88. Godley to Curzon, 1 January 1904, CP F.111/163.
89. Curzon to Godley, 27 January 1904, *ibid.*
90. Godley to Curzon, 8 January 1904, quoted in Kenneth Rose, *Superior Person* (London: Weidenfeld and Nicolson, 1969), p. 360.
91. Godley to Curzon, 3 March 1904, CP F.111/163.
92. Curzon to Godley, 20 April 1905, CP F.111/164.
93. See Wolpert, *Morley*, p. 43. For an overview of this argument, see Wolpert, *Morley*, pp. 41-74, and Stephen Koss, *John Morley at the India Office 1905-1910* (New Haven, Conn.: Yale University Press, 1969), pp. 95-110.
94. 30 January 1909, Diary of Frederick Arthur Hirtzel [hereafter cited as HD], IOL, Home Miscellaneous Series, No. 864, IV, 9.
95. Morley to Godley, 14 September 1908, KP F.102/8.
96. Godley to Minto, 29 June 1906, Minto Papers, [hereafter cited as MTP], National Library of Scotland, MS. 12729. See also Godley's warning to Minto

about the "phraseology" of his letters to Morley, Godley to Minto, 3 August 1906, MTP 12736.

97. Morley to Minto, 7 May 1908, Morley Papers [hereafter cited as MRP], IOL, MSS. Eur. D.573/3.

98. Morley to Minto, 17 June 1908, *ibid.* See also Minto to Morley, 27 May 1908, MRP D.573/14.

99. Morley to Minto, 6 July 1907, quoted in John Buchan, *Lord Minto: A Memoir* (London: Thomas Nelson and Sons, 1924), pp. 227–28. For discussion of this idea in the earlier period, see Williams, *The India Office*, p. 188.

100. SS to GG, 6 May 1907, private telegram, MRP D.573/27.

101. Morley to Minto, 14 May 1909, MRP D.573/4.

102. Godley to Wm. Lee-Warner, 4 October 1907, Lee-Warner Collection, IOL, MSS. Eur. F.92/2.

103. For an overview of the racial problems and the Viceroy's Council, see Wolpert, *Morley*, pp. 167–84.

104. Morley to Minto, 14 February 1908, quoted in Morley, *Recollections*, II, 244.

105. Morley to Minto, 31 October 1909, telegram, quoted in Buchan, *Lord Minto*, p. 292.

106. Minto to Morley, 2 November 1909, telegram, *ibid.*

107. See Jain, *Development of Executive Council*, pp. 204–7.

108. For an assessment of the evolution of Morley's position on the role of official members of the GOI, see Wolpert, *Morley*, pp. 146–54. In fact, the Council of India in this case convinced Morley that the provincial majorities could be dispensed with contrary to the GOI's despatch (October 1, 1908) on the matter.

109. G.B., *Parliamentary Debates* (House of Lords), Vol. 198 (1908), cols. 1983–1987, cited in C. H. Philips et al., *The Evolution of India and Pakistan 1858–1947: Select Documents* (London: Oxford University Press, 1962), p. 85.

110. Montagu's Budget Speech, G.B., *Parliamentary Debates* (House of Commons), 5th ser., vol. 19 [6th of session 1910], cols. 1950 ff.

111. *The Times* (London), 27 July 1910, p. 11.

112. Lovat Fraser to Lee-Warner, 31 July 1910, Lee-Warner Collection, F.92/2.

113. Minto to Morley, 18 August 1910, quoted in Mary, Countess of Minto, *India, Minto and Morley, 1905–1910* (London: Macmillan and Co., 1934), p. 408.

114. Lady Minto's *Indian Journal*, 9 August 1910, II, 271–72, quoted in Koss, *Morley at the India Office*, p. 109.

115. Dunlop Smith to Lady Minto, 23 August 1910, quoted in Martin Gilbert (ed.), *Servant of India* (London: Longmans, Green and Co., 1966), pp. 244–46. Minto's former private secretary likened Montagu's speech to the "lecturing of a set of schoolboys by a pedagogue of the most priggish type." (Dunlop Smith to Minto, 29 July 1910, MTP 12777).

116. Minutes by Minto, 2 September 1910; by H. W. Woodman, 19 August 1910; by A. Earle, 20 August 1910; by J. L. Jenkins, 22 August 1910; and by Guy Fleetwood Wilson, 9 September 1910. These are preserved in the Fleetwood Wilson Papers, IOL, MSS. Eur. E.224/4. See also correspondence between Minto and Sir George Clarke (Governor of Bombay), July 23 and 29, 1910, MTP 12773; and Minto to Sir Arthur Elliot, 31 August 1910, MTP 12777.

117. Minto to A. Elliot, 31 August 1910, MTP 12777. See also M. N. Das, *India under Morley and Minto: Politics behind Revolution, Repression and Reforms* (London: George Allen and Unwin, 1964), pp. 57–61.
118. *Ibid.*
119. *Ibid.*
120. Morley to Minto, 28 July 1910, MRP D.573/5.
121. John Morley, "British Democracy and Indian Government," *Nineteenth Century and After* 69 (February 1911), p. 193.
122. Godley to Cross, 17 April 1888, Cross Papers, BL, Add. MSS. 51,277.
123. As early as 1903, Curzon warned Kitchener not to correspond with the SS and to send his proposals via the Viceroy (Curzon to Kitchener, 13 May 1903, Kitchener Papers, PRO, 30/57/26/z12). Two years later Curzon was still complaining about the Commander-in-Chief's private correspondence; but Godley called the letter harmless, and informed Curzon not to read too much into the correspondence. It was easy enough to construe such writing as "being behind someone's back," and even as regarded his own writing, Godley noted "it would be easy enough... to assume an objectionable form, if either party to it were disposed not to play the game" (Godley to Curzon, 24 February 1905, CP F.111/164).
124. See extract of letter Godley to Curzon, 26 May 1905, filed with Midleton Papers, BL, Add. MSS. 50,572, ff. 230–231; and regarding Curzon's request to add a Sanitary Member to his Council, Brodrick to Knollys, dated September, 1905, Midleton Papers, PRO 30/67/22/ff. 1183–94.
125. Godley to Elgin, 22 February 1894, EP F.84/23.
126. Curzon to Hamilton, 29 November 1901, CP F.111/160.
127. Curzon to Hamilton, 9 January 1902, CP F.111/161.
128. Curzon to Hamilton, 13 January 1903, CP F.111/162.
129. Curzon to Hamilton, 22 July 1903, *ibid.* Curzon later wrote across the printed page in his own holograph, "I was wrong in this. For Ampthill made an excellent loyal and trustworthy substitute."
130. Hamilton to Curzon, 14 August 1903, *ibid.* See also Godley to Curzon, 14 August, 1903, *ibid.*
131. Godley to Ampthill, 27 May 1904, Ampthill Papers [hereafter cited as AP], IOL, MSS, Eur. E.233/37.
132. See Godley to Ampthill, 19 May 1904, *ibid.*, and Ampthill to Godley, 9 June 1904, KP F.102/23.
133. Godley to Ampthill, 29 March 1904, AP E.233/14.
134. Godley to Ampthill, 1 July 1904, AP E.233/37.
135. Curzon to Brodrick, 30 October 1904, Midleton Papers, BL, Add. MSS. 50,076.
136. Brodrick to Curzon, 1 November 1904, *ibid.*
137. Godley to Ampthill, 17 June 1904, quoted in Rose, *Superior Person*, p. 359. See also Curzon to Brodrick, 3 November 1904, and Brodrick to Curzon, 4 November and 6 November 1904, Midleton Papers, BL, Add. MSS. 50,076. Frustrated, Brodrick added to his last note (November 6) the thought: "I sometimes wonder if you realise that other people have feelings besides yourself."
138. Brodrick to Balfour, 14 August 1905, Balfour Papers, BL, Add. MSS. 49,721.

139. Wolpert, *Morley*, p. 53. See also Godley to Minto, 12 October 1906, MTP 12730.
140. Dufferin to Godley, 10 April 1887, KP F.102/10.
141. Dufferin to Godley, 25 August 1887, *ibid*.
142. Lansdowne to Godley, 26 February 1888, KP F.102/11.
143. Godley to Babington-Smith, 16 February 1894, EP F.84/23.
144. Elgin to Godley, 9 May 1894, KP F.102/12.
145. Elgin to Godley, 14 April 1897, KP F.102/15.
146. Elgin to Godley, 25 August 1897, *ibid*.
147. Godley to Elgin, 19 November 1897, EP F.84/136.
148. Elgin to Godley, 5 January 1899, KP F.102/16.
149. Ampthill to Godley, 31 May 1904, AP E.233/37. Ironically, Curzon had advised Ampthill about Godley's sound advice and the value of private correspondence with him, even showing the Acting Viceroy samples of such (Ampthill to Godley, 27 April 1904, KP F.102/23). Curzon, of course, later complained at being left out of that correspondence.
150. Ampthill to Godley, 1 November 1905, KP F.102/39.
151. Minto to Godley, 25 April 1906, KP F.102/25.
152. Minto to Godley, 16 January 1908, *ibid*.
153. See Elgin to Godley, 27 January 1898, KP F.102/16; Ampthill to Godley, 12 May 1904, KP F.102/23; Minto to Godley, 25 April 1906, KP F.102/25.
154. Godley to Elgin, 5 August and 12 August, 1898, EP F.84/136.
155. Curzon to Balfour, 21 September 1905, CP F.111/162.
156. Note entitled "extracts relating to Afghanistan from letters received from Lord Curzon by last mail," Brodrick to Balfour, n.d., BL, Add. MSS. 49,731.
157. Curzon to Brodrick, 2 October 1903, CP F.111/162.
158. Brodrick to Curzon, 29 October 1903, *ibid*.
159. Godley to Curzon, 20 November 1903, *ibid*.
160. Godley to Ampthill, 29 March 1904, AP E.233/14.
161. Godley to Curzon, 7 July 1905, KP F.102/60.

6

Pressure on the Periphery: Public Opinion, Special Interests, and Lobbies

As the final arbiter on Indian questions, the India Office was intimately involved in the initiation and evaluation of Indian policy of all kinds; this included allocations of resources, both human and material. The India Office worked within a complex constitutional and legal framework both inside and outside Whitehall. Formal and informal relations with the Crown, Parliament, Cabinet, other departments of state, political parties, all affected the course of policy-making by the London Government and the Government of India in Calcutta and Simla.

Several important nonofficial special interest groups commanded the attention of the India Office. These groups represented rather ill-defined aspects of public opinion in both England and India; nevertheless, their activities were carefully monitored by the India Office between 1880 and 1910. Prominent among these groups were the British Committee of the Indian National Congress and the Indian Parliamentary Committee. As both groups identified London as the arena within which to seek reforms in India, the India Office was deeply concerned with their public and private efforts. The fact that these groups aimed their lobbying activities at Parliament—*technically* the ultimate authority on Indian questions—created some anxiety in Whitehall as well as in the viceregal chambers in Calcutta.

The bureaucratic response to actual or perceived public challenges to the India Office and its conduct of Indian affairs is indicative of the relationship between policy and paperwork in the late nineteenth century. Although there were critical organizational and ideological weaknesses which ultimately limited the effectiveness of these groups as advocates of Indian reform in London, the India Office was sensitive to their attempts to publicize India in Parliament regardless of the prospects of success.[1] Ironically, while the Congress, its London agency, and other special interest groups in and out of Parliament often miscalculated the de facto control of Parliament over Indian policy, the India Office—even though it understood the limitations of parliamentary control—exerted extraordinary efforts to neutralize such activities. Another medium through which various lobbyists hoped to influence Parliament and thence the India Office was the English press. Advocates of various causes concentrated on cultivating British public opinion by disseminating information on India to newspapers and journals in Britain, and in the process they hoped to influence the formulation of Indian policy in Whitehall. The net effect, however, was to further stimulate public discussion in India; recognizing this, the India Office responded by managing the news at home and in India. How was this done?

Indian resolve to influence the decision-making processes of the Home Government predates the transfer of authority from the East India Company to the Crown. Early associations in London, such as the India Reform Society (1853) and the London Indian Society (1858) petitioned individual M.P.s to raise specific questions in the House of Commons. These usually related to educational or I.C.S. admission policies and generally reflected the goals of the East India Association (1866) to supply Parliament and the British public with information on India. The East India Association was dedicated to the "independent and disinterested advocacy of the interests of India and promotion by all legitimate means of her welfare."[2] Increased parliamentary interest in Indian affairs resumed less than two decades after the imposition of Crown rule. Florence Nightingale, for example, noted that "there is ... so powerful an interest awakening in England for the affairs of India as I never expected to live to see. The Houses of Parliament now discuss India as if it were a *home* question, a vital and moral question, *as* it *is*."[3] Her description was exaggerated. Surely India had attracted the attention of Parliament, especially because of the Second Afghan War and persistent questioning by M.P.s sympathetic to India (e.g., John Bright and Henry Fawcett [the "Member for India"]). But a far more critical *home* question engulfed Parliament and the nation—Home Rule for Ireland. From 1874 Irish grievances and Indian problems were wedded in a "marriage of convenience"; ultimately, however, this liaison deflected parliamentary interest from India.[4]

What the young Indian nationalists needed, said William Wedderburn, M.P., former Indian Civil Servant and a founding father of the British Committee of the Indian National Congress, was some kind of "flanking movement"—an appeal to the British electorate which would more effectively illuminate Indian problems in Parliament.[5] The "flanking movement" that ultimately emerged in the form of the British Committee of Congress and the Indian Parliamentary Committee was the logical extension of earlier lobbying efforts in England. It reflected the limited goals of early Indian nationalists who held a "highly optimistic, and even naive faith in the idealism and goodwill of the British public.'"[6] There was a flurry of activity between 1883 and 1885, including intense public criticism of Indian policy from individuals in and out of Parliament. In 1883 John Bright, along with fifty other M.P.s, created an informal Indian Committee within Parliament devoted to securing "just and sympathetic" action on Indian questions in the House of Commons. John Slagg, Member for Manchester, almost carried a motion for a full-scale parliamentary inquiry into the Government of India Act, 1858, while William Birkmyre and the Cobden Club launched an intense pamphlet campaign criticizing the India Office and Government of India on a number of charges. Although these challenges were successfully met, the increased publicity about the functioning of the India Office served notice to the members of that establishment that they, as well as India's public image, were under attack.

A concerted effort by Indian nationalists to influence the 1885 general election in Great Britain, in which "India's Appeal to the British Voter" went so far as to list "friends" and "false friends" of India among the candidates, further alerted the India Office that India's public image—and indeed the policy-making process in general— was under attack in the most serious quarters, Parliament, and the press. Not one of the endorsed "friends" of India was successful in his election bid—a thorough defeat that visibly delighted members of the India Office establishment.[7] It was, however, only a momentary setback to the rising tide of Indian propaganda efforts in England. As early as 1879, S.N. Banerjea, editor of the *Bengalee*, advocated establishment of a *permanent* Indian agency to propagate Indian interests in Whitehall by trying to influence party platforms in Britain.[8] After the special deputation of the Bombay Presidency Association failed in its 1885 lobbying efforts, Dadabhai Naoroji, Congress President in 1886, recognized the validity of Banerjea's plea, and in 1887 went to England to serve unofficially as an "agent" for Indian interests. He was joined the next year by W.C. Bonnerjee, Eardley Norton, and William Digby, and the small band established the Indian Political Agency.

The fledgling group determined that their first priority was to give some structure to their lobbying efforts. Naoroji himself set about systematizing propaganda resources in England by collecting volumes of Hansard as well as other reports, returns, and public documents concerning Indian affairs. This provided the group with more information on Indian issues before addressing Parliament. Next the Indian Political Agency solicited the advice of sympathetic M.P.s, among them Charles Bradlaugh and R.P. Reid (later Lord Loreburn) on the "best means of getting a hearing" from Parliament and the British public.[9] The advice included trying to get M.P.s to commit themselves privately to pay attention to Indian affairs and then publishing their answers in the press, thus effecting a subtle blackmail of sorts. Reid also suggested to A.O. Hume, a former civil servant instrumental in the organization of the Congress and its British Committee in London, that he seek "coadjutors" in and out of Parliament, who, like Hume himself, were "high-class men" who could "coach and inform members" on Indian questions.[10]

The Indian Political Agency carried out these assignments in part. The Agency circulated reports of the third Indian National Congress meeting, which included a preface citing "Some of England's Pledges to India" that continued in use until 1908, when it was replaced by the Congress constitution.[11] Hume continued to impress on the young Congress the value of having an organized propaganda unit in England, and finally in 1889 the British Committee of the Indian National Congress was constituted with Sir William Wedderburn as chairman, and Naoroji, W.S. Caine and W.S.B. McLaren as important members.[12] Later that year, Wedderburn presided over the Congress and again pointed out that the Congress's success depended heavily on its ability to influence Parliament and English public opinion on Indian questions. The Congress confirmed the constitution of the Committee in England and voted it an annual sum each December (c. Rs. 45,000).[13]

A critical question remains—why engage the India Office in battle rather than concentrate on political agitation in India? As already alluded to, this is related in great measure to the limited goals of early, moderate nationalists and their faith in British fair play. It is also related to the disillusionment of several key dissentient former Indian Civil Servants—A.O. Hume, William Wedderburn, Henry Cotton among them—who acted as the Congress's agents in England, and who were, by and large, disenchanted with what Wedderburn called the "Simla Clique" of aloof and pretentious Indian officials, each of whom viewed himself as *the burra sahib* in the subcontinent.[14] Furthermore, the public perception of parliamentary control over the India Office and hence the formulation of Indian policy influenced the choice of tactics. In actual fact the Act for the Better Government of India in 1858 failed to effect a fully operational system of checks and balances between Parliament, the Secretary of State (as representing the Cabinet), and the Council of India. Parliament, while *theoretically* the ultimate authority in the governance of India, throughout most of the nineteenth century surrendered its legal prerogatives to the Secretary of State in Council. Parliament, however, retained certain powers for itself (see Chapter 4), which gave the outward appearance of control over Indian affairs.

The new British Committee of the Indian National Congress soon absorbed the Indian Political Agency and in 1890 started its own journal, *India*, edited by William Digby, in order to provide "a continuous summary of political events" and inform the British public of Indian "economic, administrative and personal" grievances.[15] Publication was irregular at first, but in 1892 *India* became a monthly (appearing the second Friday of the month) and in 1898 the newsletter appeared as a weekly publication. The burst of activity by the British Committee was paralleled by the re-establishment of the Indian Parliamentary Committee (disbanded in 1883) between 1889 and 1893 along the very lines suggested by Reid and others. By the end of the 1894 session, India's parliamentary "friends" numbered roughly 154. The defeat of many "Indian Members" in 1895 dropped the Committee's rolls to eighty-five, although it rose to 125 the next year. It was not until the Liberal victory of 1905 that the Indian Parliamentary Committee's membership reached its early membership again.

Parliamentary debate and concern over Indian affairs loomed greatest on general issues dealing with the composition and functioning of the Council of India, the source of the Secretary of State's salary, and other Home Charges.[16] There were also likely to be numerous questions about Indian currency, trade, and frontier policies at anytime. But significantly, members of the Indian Parliamentary Committee, whose leadership reflected that of the British Committee of Congress, never realized the power implied by their numbers. M.P.s occasionally championed their own individual causes which had some Indian connection and in the process gave the *appearance* of commanding support from the numbers officially on the Indian Parliamentary Committee's rolls. In point of fact these diverse interests—temperance groups, anti-opium activists, social purity advocates, etc.—only *seemed* to be asking sensitive questions about Indian policy.[17] In general, as a knowledgeable contemporary pointed out, "very few M.P.'s care a rap about India" and aimlessly debated Indian questions when the opportunity arose.[18] Perhaps even more important is the fact that many English supporters of India were in private philosophically opposed to the overriding goal of the Indian National Congress to relax British rule in India; they supported specific Indian reforms in part on humanitarian principles but also because they perceived them as the best means of strengthening British control on the subcontinent.[19] The discrepancy between the vocal advocacy of Indian reforms and substantive action in the late nineteenth century did not go unnoticed in India.

The Indian National Congress and its London organization were elated when two of its leading members, Naoroji and Wedderburn, were elected to Parliament in 1892. Expectations were high, but it was not long before Congressmen in India began questioning privately the seemingly small return on their large financial investment in English lobbying. This concern became public after the Government demonstrated its ability to circumvent Parliament on a matter of great importance to the Congress, the issue of simultaneous examinations for the ICS. Remarkably enough, when Herbert Paul, M.P. and the Secretary of the British Committee of Congress, succeeded in securing parliamentary approval in a rump session, 84–78 for simultaneous examinations in India and England, the Secretary of State for India, Lord Kimberley, simply called it a "fatal mistake" and took measures to prevent its implementation. On the surface, nonetheless, Kimberley appeared to comply with the wishes of Parliament, even to the extent of overruling the India Council and forwarding the House of Commons resolution—with appropriate caveats of course—to India.[20] Several leading vernacular papers pressed Congress to scrap their illusions about the extent of parliamentary control over Indian affairs, noting that if a supposedly sympathetic Liberal government had disappointed them, what chance would they have when the Conservatives came to power?[21]

It was an awkward situation for the leadership of the British Committee and for its moderate supporters in India. Hume attributed the rebuff to "practical politics," and Banerjea persuaded the tenth Congress at Madras to petition Parliament dutifully about the Government's abuse and circumvention of a parliamentary resolution.[22] In his presidential address of 1895, Banerjea proclaimed that "our voice would be that of one crying in the wilderness but for our organization in London, the British Committee. The money that we spend in England is worth its weight in gold."[23] Thus, while it netted only meager results, the Congress maintained its official position that propagandizing in England was its best chance for reform in India. This position, however, became increasingly untenable.

By 1894 the Congress had disassociated itself from several of its leading English supporters, notably Digby and Norton.[24] The poor fortunes of the British Committee in the elections of 1895 further added to the dreary state of things. The gloom lifted momentarily when the Welby Commission on Indian financial affairs included among its membership Wedderburn, Caine, and Naoroji, all executives with the British Committee. The Commission also examined a number of prominent Congressmen called from India at public expense; these included S. Banerjea, G.S. Iyer, D.E. Wacha and G.K. Gokhale.[25] But the final report, apart from suggesting some slight alterations in Indian finance and government, was bitterly disappointing to Congress, and further proof for many Indians of the ineffectiveness of English lobbying efforts. All the Indian supporters could do was issue a Minority Report, which itself gained partial acceptance two decades later in the Montagu-Chelmsford Report.[26]

The fortunes of the British Committee of Congress declined markedly at the turn of the century as lagging Congress financial and moral support reflected steady disenchantment with lobbying efforts in England. In 1903 Wedderburn and his colleagues Banerjea, Naoroji, and Hume published a series of articles entitled "A Call to Arms," warning Indians of the dangers of apathy and calling upon supporters to secure funds to sustain the Congress movement in England.[27] But by 1905 Indian nationalist attention had shifted elsewhere, and the Congress was consumed by the events surrounding the partition of Bengal and the Svadeshi movement. There was a brief upsurge in the rhetoric about the essential nature of organized lobbying by Congress in England following the Liberal victory of 1905; but the die was irretrievably cast. The direction of Indian nationalism was dramatically altered by the Surat split between Moderates and Extremists in 1907, and the redirection of energies and disparate goals of the two groups marked the end of overt Congress lobbying in England. It was thus a short-lived experiment with few successes. But it is no coincidence that in addition to whatever internal weaknesses the British and Indian Parliamentary Committees had, the India Office increasingly took measures to circumscribe such activities from the early 1890s.

The India Office possessed the technical wherewithal to deal with its critics both in London and India. The Office successfully deflected attempts to place its establishment costs on the British estimates, and thus, in effect, denying the Treasury "power of the purse." The India Office also controlled the flow of information to Parliament by editing Parliamentary Returns and Questions and thus avoiding controversial issues. Furthermore, the India Office tightened the rules for submitting memorials and petitions to the Secretary of State in London, making it difficult for advocates of Indian reform to gain access to the titular head of Indian Government.[28] It also undermined the British Committee's efforts at lobbying by manipulating the composition of royal and parliamentary commissions. The India Office had no difficulty in defining the scope of the investigation, the membership, and witness lists for several key commissions in the late nineteenth century, whether directly, by such appointments as Welby, or indirectly, in currency, opium, temperance, and social purity questions related to India.[29]

Such tactics by the India Office did not go unnoticed. From a very early stage some lobbyists recognized that speeches asking for parliamentary inquiries, challenging Home Charges, or seeking ICS reform were doomed to failure because all essential information emanated only from the India Office—reviled by critics as "that great manufactory of falsehood."[30] Because it provided all answers to parliamentary questions, Hume and the British Committee of Congress proclaimed that the India Office was "an organisation perpetually employed in popularising the official view of all Indian questions"; if Indian grievances were ever to be remedied, it would have to be in Parliament, in the press, and by "an organisation [i.e., the British Committee of Congress] equally persistent and strenuous in disseminating the people's view of these same questions."[31] The India Office, and Sir Arthur Godley in particular, remained acutely aware of this attitude and the attempts—successful or otherwise—to influence Indian policy-making through parliamentary agitation and in the press. But it was not only a question of *what* was being asked, but of *who* did the asking, among other things, that irritated the India Office establishment.

The early Indian National Congress and its supporters in England were largely unaware of the limitations of parliamentary influence on Indian affairs. On the other hand, officials in Whitehall and India never took potential parliamentary interference lightly. If officials needed any additional stimulus to work toward subverting the activities of the British Committee and its parliamentary allies, it was found in the personal animosity many of them felt toward Englishmen dedicated to lobbying in Britain. Almost from the start, with the emergence of the Indian Political Agency in 1888 and the British Committee of Congress a year later, the India Office determined to scrutinize and where possible circumscribe lobbying efforts in England, not only because they threatened to bring pressure on the Office and Government of India in Parliament and the English press but also because of a rather deep-seated personal dislike of the key individuals involved. William Digby, William Wedderburn, Henry Cotton, A.O. Hume, all evoked a kind of personal animosity that occasionally overshadowed the alleged threats themselves.

Although William Digby's link with the Congress lobbyists ended in 1892, his early association with the Indian Political Agency and British Committee was somewhat destructive to the lobbyists' case beyond that time—at least from the India Office perspective. As early as 1885, Digby called the India Office that "Palace of Obstruction and Routine" which worked to India's detriment at a "killing slow" rate. A few years later, he accused the British of having "outdone Irish absentee landlordism in India."[32] Digby's personal behavior incensed British officials at home and in India. His role with the Indian Political Agency and the British Committee of Congress also scandalized Indian leaders and provided ample fodder to critics within the India Office bureaucracy. At various times he was accused of stealing official documents, of misrepresenting himself as having India Office authorization to act as agent for Indian princes, and of conspiring to defraud his clients.[33] Even though Digby eventually parted ways with the British Committee, he persisted in nettling the India Office, and as a result the British Committee of Congress suffered further guilt by association.

As he prepared to stand for Parliament in 1892, Digby proudly advertised his links with the Indian press—he was London correspondent for the *Hindu* (Madras) and *Amrita Bazar Patrika* (Calcutta), papers which were considered antigovernment in India and England.[34] Indeed, Motilal Ghose, editor of the *Amrita Bazar Patrika*, had long supported Digby financially and "prayed" for him to enter Parliament, adding that any Indian in Britain who did not support Digby "deserved to be drowned in the Bay of Bengal."[35] The India Office often intercepted Digby's mail and it was not above unofficially encouraging unkind stories about him in the Indian and English press.[36] Although Digby failed to win a seat in Parliament, he continued to irritate the India Office. Thus the frontispiece of his book *"Prosperous" British India* (1901) began:[37]

> This Book is Dedicated
> (Without permission)
> to

The Right Honourable Lord George Hamilton
      to
His Excellency Lord Curzon of Kedleston
      to
The Right Honourable Sir Henry H. Fowler
      and to
Every Man or Woman of British India.

Hamilton, Secretary of State for India, was furious, and said, "Digby repeats and reiterates for nearly 600 pages that same series of falsehoods, supported by crooked calculation."[38] He assaulted Digby for "statistical frauds of the most barefaced character."[39]

William Wedderburn's case is another instance where personality dominated the India Office view of things. When his advocacy of Indian political reform while he was a member of the Indian Civil Service shortened his career in India, he returned home and became the guiding force behind the British Committee of Congress for over a quarter-century. He also sat in the House of Commons between 1893 and 1900.[40] Wedderburn championed political and bureaucratic reform and spoke eloquently in support of Indian civil liberties. On occasion he even went so far as to keep the India Office posted on his correspondence with Indian leaders, especially G.K. Gokhale.[41] But Wedderburn irritated the India Office by continually raising Indian questions in Parliament. As if that were not "crime" enough, his persistent touring of English political clubs and numerous speeches and writings made him persona non grata in official eyes. Wedderburn went about the banquet circuit castigating the former Indian Civil Servants on the Council of India, and the English press for listening to them.[42] What the India Office establishment found particularly grating was Wedderburn's repetitiveness. He used the same critical phraseology, and indeed whole sections of speeches, over and over again—some speech material used in 1899 was still being employed in 1905.[43]

The India Office could not—or more to the point, would not—differentiate between those Radicals and British Committee members who might be classed as "moderate" and those whose tactics and rhetoric were overtly aggressive.[44] The India Office had very little appreciation of the British Committee's financial woes or of its increasingly precarious ideological divergence from the course of events in India. And while they understood the essential weakness of the Indian Parliamentary Committee—the inability of its leaders to command constituent pressures—they always felt it was something illusory that could vanish in a moment. Incredibly, as late as 1906 the India Office still questioned the Viceroy of India about the "alarmist" reports reaching the Office concerning the spread of Congress ideas, although Godley admitted that the "Members of Council here are inclined to pooh-pooh" such information![45] The bureaucrats in England were singularly unaware of the raging debate in India over the efficacy of any Congress agency in Britain at all or of the significance of the desperate pleas for money that appeared in the columns of the British Committee's paper in England, *India* and, of course, in intercepted private letters.[46]

The India Office only saw Wedderburn, unrepentant Indian Civil Servant, conspiring with Radicals of all sorts at home, stirring up trouble in the House of Commons and the press, encouraging alleged Indian "experts" to come lobby in England. Wedderburn, of course, saw his own role as an intermediary between the India Office and the forces of moderation in India. How could he know that as late as 1909, the Indian leader with whom he was most closely identified, Gokhale, was being called the "most dangerous man in India" by the Government's Criminal Investigation Department.[47] (Gokhale, of course, was equally unaware of precisely how much the bureaucrats in the India Office mistrusted him.[48]) It did not matter that Wedderburn counselled against violence and agitation in India; his mail, like Digby's, was routinely intercepted by officials in India.[49] It did not matter that Wedderburn offered to go to India on John Morley's behalf after the Surat split in 1907;[50] he was seen as an influential member of that small group who had the *potential* to wreak havoc in Parliament.

As the fortunes of the Congress in England suffered generally under the Conservative Party rule between 1895 and 1905, and as the financial woes of the British Committee of Congress deepened, Wedderburn's personal credibility suffered along with that of the British Committee in Parliament and at the India Office. The Office was overjoyed at the poor electoral fortunes of the Indian Parliamentary Committee in 1895. The weak condition of the Indian advocates in England evoked considerable sarcasm from the Permanent Undersecretary. There were rousing condemnations of Wedderburn and company in the House of Commons by M.M. Bhavnagri,[51] a Parsi opposed to Congress, and during the severe Indian famine of 1896–97, Godley wrote to Elgin that

> you will see a report in today's Times [sic] of a question asked in the H[ouse] of Commons by Mr. Schwann, on behalf of Sir W. Wedderburn, in which it was suggested that the S[ecretary] of State should order all the workers on Relief Works to be weighed on beginning work and periodically afterwards, so as to see whether they get enough to eat. Such is the wisdom of the Congress party in this country: if the brains of Sir W. Wedderburn [and] his friends could be periodically weighed [and] reported on it would be much more to the point.[52]

Wedderburn and his colleagues persisted in claiming that while the parliamentary groups' contribution did not seem overwhelming, its usefulness in keeping Indian questions in the public eye should not be underestimated.[53] But Wedderburn was banned from the India Office, while the

British Committee's large financial demands and minimal results had reached the breaking point for many Indian supporters, and from 1901 the Committee's relations with the Congress steadily worsened. The situation for the Congress in England, although certainly bleak, was not entirely hopeless—there was still *India*, the British Committee's journal which consumed the lion's share of its expenditures, and which Wedderburn himself had undertaken to support financially.[54]

When *India* became a weekly in 1896, it created new concern within the India Office. Anxiety within the Office, however, stemmed not from the journal's possible influence on British "public opinion," but its potential effects *in India*. This perspective, of course, was diametrically opposed to areas of impact to which the British Committee itself directed attention. Roughly one thousand copies of the newsletter went free of charge to the Indian Parliamentary Committee, sympathetic M.P.s who did not belong to the group, newspapers, and other political and business leaders. The India Office's concern over Indian (as opposed to British) press opinion was clear. In 1899 Lord George Hamilton asked Curzon to determine which Indian princes subscribed to Congress: "I note that *India* frequently starts lies here that are reproduced in detail by the Congress paper, in fact nearly all information about India is derived from this poisonous little rag."[55] C.S. Bayley, Superintendent for the Suppression of Thuggee and Dacoity, confirmed the influential position of *India* to the native press.[56] Furthermore, the Chief Secretary to the Government of Bengal, C.W. Bolton, reported to the Secretary of State that of 6,000 copies of *India* printed in England, 1,500 (one-fourth) went to Bengal alone, and many other papers received it in exchange.[57] Once again Hamilton attributed much of the trouble in the Indian press to that "pernicious little rag *India*," and refuted Curzon's suggestion that he was overestimating its influence by pointing out to the Viceroy that one Indian paper had "an exact reproduction of the wretched little paper at home (*India*)."[58] Not coincidentally, at about this time Godley took firm control of the India Office Parliamentary Branch and reorganized its operation. The correlation between increased activity in Parliament and the Indian and English press, and the need to keep ahead of inquisitive M.P.s, was abundantly clear.

The Government of India and India Office became increasingly suspicious of the Indian National Congress and its agents in England at the turn of the century, although neither the British Committee nor the Indian Parliamentary Committee enjoyed very much success. Their low profile reflected lack of funds, ideological differences among members in England, and increasing tension with the Congress itself. Many members opted to distance themselves from Indian questions, concentrating instead on other causes such as opium, temperance, famine, etc.[59] The reduced numbers and weakened state of the British Committee and Indian Parliamentary Committee, whose actual enrollments always exaggerated the real support of its membership for Indian questions, dictated a cautious interlude for lobbyists in Britain.[60]

At the end of 1904, the India Office received reports that the Congress extremists were gaining control and were "flagrantly disloyal" to the Indian Government.[61] In May 1905 Curzon warned the India Office that a Congress deputation would soon arrive in England. The proposed delegation was to include Pherozeshah Mehta, S. Nair, Lala Lajpat Rai, M.M. Malaviya, and S.N. Banerjea; however, only two, Gokhale and Lajpat Rai, were actually appointed to the delegation.[62] Curzon was relieved, for he had earlier described Banerjea as a "vitriolic windbag." Thus Curzon warned the India Office about the delegation:

They will seek to pose as representatives of the Indian people, coming to plead for justice at the hands of the justice-loving British public and appealing impartially to the sympathies of parties. I should not be surprised if they were to solicit an interview with the Prime Minister. I need not tell you because you already know it, that they come as the nominees of an organization which is exclusively in extreme Radical hands, which is engineered by men like Wedderburn and Cotton, whose real views are represented weekly in the lying sheet called *India*, and which exists for the purpose of attacking the Government and vilifying and insulting British rule. Their object in proceeding to England now is purely electoral. They want to secure pledges from the Radical party to give them a Viceroy like Lord Ripon and a Secretary of State of the type of Sir H. Cotton. They will coo like suckling doves in London. But on provincial platforms their roars will awake an echo in Hades, and, amid such secure surroundings, to no meaner or cooler destiny will they assign.[63]

Plans to publicize the British Committee and Congress suffered a severe reverse when Lala Lajpat Rai arrived before Gokhale and spurned the Committee in favor of the Socialists, led by Henry Hyndman, and then set off to tour America. Lajpat Rai further alienated the Committee's supporters by publicly criticizing Liberal politicians for their timidity in Indian affairs and by appealing to the rising Labour groups for support.[64] The British Committee, even in India Office eyes, seemed to have spent its force. Attention now focused on the "Indians" in Parliament.

The Liberal victory of 1905 signified the revival of the Indian parliamentary forces and a renewed boldness on the part of the British Committee of Congress. The new Indian Parliamentary Committee boasted at least 150 M.P.s in the new House, "at least five who will be likely to raise Indian questions" at any time, especially Sir Henry Cotton.[65] (Of the many Radicals in Parliament, Morley liked Cotton least, referring to him, at various times, as a "fine fleur," and a "vain peacock of a man." Once, while musing to Lord Minto on W.S. Blunt's public misfortune in a savage divorce case, Morley hoped for "an equally disastrous action against ... Sir Henry Cotton!!"[66]) Morley at once capitalized on this new force in

Parliament for his own personal administrative advantage. He "wasted no time in using the leverage of so impressive a popular mandate to pry an autocratic Government of India from its Olympian isolation, determined as he was to bring it effectively within the responsible orbit of Her [*sic*] Majesty's Liberal government."[67] Morley's desire to achieve this goal is unquestionable; however, there are serious reservations about whether or not the India Office had ever lost control of the Government of India in the first place. Moreover, despite the obvious benefit of such vocal support in Parliament, the situation was fraught with danger, and Morley, no doubt counselled by Godley (with twenty years experience) and the permanent staff at the India Office, continued the existing policy of controlling the British Committee's efforts in Parliament and moderating the enthusiasm of the Indian Parliamentary Committee.

Morley recognized at once that the diverse political mixture of the "Indian Members" was an advantage to the India Office; even Sir Charles Dilke admitted "they [the Indian Parliamentary Committee] don't agree about anything, and have no leading mind among them." This reassured Morley who felt that with "moderate common sense on my part, I have no serious difficulties to fear."[68] The test of Morley's assessments came quickly. In February 1906, after only a few months in office, the "Indians in the House of Commons" assailed the new Secretary of State on the partition of Bengal question. The challenge failed, however, and Morley reported to the Viceroy that "they began to show their teeth," which was "very foolish of them, for I have fairly good tusks of my own."[69] This was quickly followed by a second, more serious challenge when Keir Hardie solicited Radical and Liberal votes in a move to put the Secretary of State's salary on the estimates during the annual Indian budget speech.[70] It also failed, but the near defeat for the Government was sobering to Morley, who by then was convinced of the necessity for much "management" of Keir Hardie and the other "mischief-makers" in the House of Commons.[71] His attitude hardened further after Hardie's tempestuous visit to India in 1907—where he was under surveillance by the Indian Criminal Investigation Department and castigated in the conservative English press[72]—in spite of Morley's assertion that Hardie's rhetoric and impact were mere "claptrap."[73] At times it seemed that well-informed critics of Government policy in India had a mole in the India Office itself, and indeed there are several likely candidates within the Office establishment who might have been responsible for occasional leaks.[74]

Within the India Office concerned officials warned Morley about potential dangerous intercourse between Congresswallahs, especially Gokhale, and the "Indians" in Parliament.[75] Morley summarily dismissed these warnings, as well as the charges of the Viceroy who believed Gokhale was influenced by "wirepullers and . . . affected of mercenary consideration," because he gave great weight to his own abilities to capitalize on personal relationships to counter the influence of the lobbyists.⁷⁶ Early in his term Morley's Private Secretary, Arthur Hirtzel, recorded that the Secretary of State "saw Gokhale [and] determined to make use of him to influence [the] Indian Parliamentary Committee, as Gokhale was advising them to ask as few questions as possible."⁷⁷ While Morley's estimate of Gokhale's ability to influence his fellow nationalists was low, he felt it remained a distinct possibility that "among the Indophile Radicals in the House of Commons . . . Gokhale may, voluntarily or involuntarily, be of some possible service."⁷⁸

Congress activists in England suffered greatly in the wake of the Surat split in Congress, 1907. Writing to Minto, Morley cited a letter from Gokhale to William Wedderburn in which the moderate leader acknowledged that the crisis in India was "bound to affect the work of the English Committee and of *India* (the newspaper)." He informed the Viceroy about Gokhale's dismay that "even Sir P. Mehta . . . has lost heart, and the only thing consistent with self-respect is to stop all agitation in England and India for a time, and let the officials do as they please."⁷⁹ Morley, although angry that Gokhale had privately criticized his first two budget speeches, concluded that Gokhale was merely inept as a leader rather than perfidious.⁸⁰ The Secretary of State concluded that Gokhale "as [a] party manager is a baby," and for a politician aspiring to be a leader he "should never whine."⁸¹

Like Lord George Hamilton, Morley was more concerned with the effect of propaganda in India than in Great Britain. Morley did not ordinarily accept accusations based upon rumors, but he was so concerned over the increase of public questions on Indian matters and their potentially explosive nature in *India* that he carefully "documented" the stories circulating in the India Office that a "regular tariff of bribes" (said to be £25 per question) was paid to Congress sympathizers who raised questions in Parliament. The journal *India* was also implicated as receiving an appropriate percentage when grievances were ventilated.⁸² Morley utilized this information to reinforce Godley's rules drafted in 1893 for memorializing the India Office within a strict constitutional framework.⁸³ The Secretary of State proclaimed his victory in 1908 when he wrote to Minto:

If I have been able to do any real service during the difficulties of the last eighteen months, it has been this, that I have succeeded in keeping back the information of any serious group at Westminster whose utterances and tactics in our public life would have provided powder and shot for revolutionaries in India.⁸⁴

Morley successfully disguised his connivance in the manipulation of Congress lobbyists in Britain. When a deputation of the British Committee of Congress visited Morley in 1908 to thank him for his interest in and efforts for Indian reform, the Secretary of State observed to Minto: "even if I have to stay in Purgatory for my many misdemeanors, I shall claim a corner of Paradise for this particular performance."[85] The 1909 session of Congress also voted a resolution of thanks to Morley for his help—completely unaware of his carefully charted program to subvert Congress lobbying efforts in England.

The British and Indian Parliamentary Committees retreated into a low profile between 1909 and 1917 as Moderates and Extremists struggled fiercely for control of the Congress in India. The conflict between these groups sharply affected the number of Indian subscriptions to *India*, as did increased production costs when World War I broke out. Amidst the titanic ideological struggle the British Committee's arguments as to its unique contribution to the Congress cause fell on deaf ears.[86] Moreover, reeling from the precarious financial situation and the death of a number of long-time supporters, notably Gokhale, Keir Hardie, Henry Cotton, and P. Mehta, the Committee issued a last, desperate call for support in 1918, repeating its conviction that *India* was a "vital" necessity which alone among Indian appeals reached "highly influential circles."[87] But as the Congress steadily came under Extremist control, more and more Indian politicians suspected that *India* was too moderate and ineffective in influencing the British electorate.[88] Despite efforts to remain neutral, the British Committee was doomed once Congress leadership passed to Bal Gangadhar Tilak in 1919. Tilak, somewhat mellowed from his early political Extremism, led a deputation to England to discuss the impending reforms, and reported adversely on the British Committee's attitudes and activities.[89] The Congress's British allies had no choice but to submit to demands to change the editorial staff of *India* and to adopt a new constitution giving Congress more direct control over them.[90] Gandhi's ascendancy to the leadership of Congress marked the Committee's end. In December 1920 the British Committee of Congress submitted a new request for funding at the annual Congress session, again emphasizing the importance of organized lobbying in England. The Committee argued that it was *not* co-operating with the British Government nor soft in its publications.[91] The decision to end the London organization was, however, irrevocable, and the Nagpur Congress discontinued both the British Committee of Congress and *India* a few weeks later.[92]

The Committee's usefulness seemed obvious—it provided a convenient source of opinion gleaned from the Indian press for M.P.s and party leaders who would use this information to press for Indian reform in Parliament. This was predicated, of course, on their understanding of the constitutional link between Parliament and the India Office, which in fact was considerably weaker than it looked on paper. Throughout its existence the journal *India*, the petitioning of the British Committee of Congress, and the activities of the Indian Parliamentary Committee produced few tangible results in England. The Committee's influence on the India Office, however, was certainly out of all proportion to its effectiveness as a lobby which might possibly influence Parliament. At first the India Office was content to view the Committee's activities as a kind of barometer of India newspaper reports and native opinion. As long as the flow of information was one way, to England, the Office gave moderate attention to the Committee's efforts because it understood the limitations of parliamentary influence. When it became obvious that the flow of distorted news back *to* India threatened the security of the subcontinent, the India Office acted to counteract *India* and other lobbyists' efforts by throwing up several technical impediments in their path. India Office actions were inspired by personal animosity to British supporters of Indian reform.

India published its final issue on its thirtieth anniversary, recalling its past glories and proclaiming its vital role in obtaining Indian reform legislation over the years.[93] Congress eventually recognized the need for some sort of foreign propaganda. In 1921, hardly a year after the British Committee of Congress was liquidated, £3000 was authorized for such efforts, under strict supervision of the All-India Congress Committee,[94] and in 1925 Congress established a "foreign department" to look after Indian interests abroad and carry out "educative propaganda" in foreign countries about Indian affairs.[95] But the dissolution of the Congress agency in England in 1920 no doubt pleased the India Office, which recognized all along that its disruptive potential lay in exciting Indians rather than Englishmen.

The relative ineffectiveness of Congress propaganda in England to influence policy in the India Office was in great measure the consequence of inadequate funds and poor circulation in England itself. But the India Office, and Godley in particular, identified a far more basic reason for the failure of these propaganda efforts. Indian politicians and their sympathizers in England sought to inform the *British public* who, hopefully, would then pressure Parliament and ultimately the India Office into being "fair" to India. But the general public was as apathetic toward Indian affairs as the House of Commons. Thus Congress moderates and their allies in Britain misconceived the power of public opinion. From his post in Whitehall Godley carefully analyzed the situation. When a large tidal wave ravaged the Chittagong area in 1897, Godley commiserated with the Viceroy, Elgin, wryly noting that "in this country, the news has not attracted the smallest notice: one wounded Highlander is an object of far greater compassion than 5000 drowned natives."[96] The situation, as the Permanent Undersecretary viewed it, was tragic:

What a time we are having here, with burning questions in every part of the world: Egypt, Crete, West Africa, South Africa, East Africa, China and the Indian frontier. These things interest Parliament [and] the Public Offices: but the man in the street cares more about the Australian cricket matches.[97]

Godley was equally aware that when speaking of the man in the street's ignorance and lack of interest of Indian affairs, he did not by any means exclude the editors of newspapers.[98] The India Office traditionally disregarded the English press; the only paper which generated much concern within the Office was *The Times*, whose long history of reporting Indian affairs was basically conservative.[99] Despite a limited circulation, its readers included all Parliamentarians who might well ask questions in the House on the basis of its reports. However, the India Office, through the Government of India, did not lack the means to influence the flow of information to *The Times* or other English papers because the source of all news lay in the subcontinent.

In general, the Government of India was the main provider of news and information in India. Efforts to influence the press in India, aside from coercive or preventive legislation, began shortly after the Crown assumed control over Indian affairs. Between 1864 and 1870 the Indian Government maintained an editors' room in Calcutta, where news releases and certain correspondence were made available to "friendly" press representatives.[100] In 1876 Robert Knight, editor of the *Statesman*, succeeded in persuading the Indian Government to establish a Press Bureau and to appoint a sympathetic liaison officer to provide the Indian press with official news.[101] That Press Commissionship lasted only three years (1877–80), largely because it had become, as Knight had feared, a "moniteur" and check on the press.[102] Indian editors in particular became wary of the system, and although the Indian Government continued to disseminate official reports, the Indian press attacked the news as stale and old since it was usually issued two or three days after its appearance in the *Civil and Military Gazette*. One journal said that its editors simply threw "the official news in the wastepaper basket" as soon as it was received.[103] Although Lord Lansdowne, Viceroy, 1888–94, pondered the idea of re-establishing the Press Officer, he could not find any "suitable" candidate to deal with an increasingly hostile vernacular press. Reflecting his own self-assuredness with regard to Indian "public opinion," Curzon early in his Viceroyalty re-established the press facilities at Calcutta and Simla.

This partly explains the Government of India's attempts to control the release of information in India; but these efforts were specifically directed toward the native press. The treatment of the English press in India and the reason for the India Office's lack of concern about their reports to England are most revealing. As early as 1870, O.T. Burne urged the cultivation of the English press in India, because "the only formidable Public Opinion—which is the more formidable from being distant from India, is the heart of the British Parliament, and liable to real or intended error— is *at Home*."[104] Burne urged an elaborate, secretive scheme of managing the news sources of correspondents of the English press, as well as of certain native papers in India. Burne carried his convictions back to the

India Office when he became head of the Political and Secret Department. The success of Burne's suggestions is apparent in the way in which the India Office and Government of India's relationship with *The Times* was cultivated. When Dufferin's Private Secretary (D. Mackenzie Wallace) returned from India to head the Foreign Department of *The Times*, Sir A. Mackenzie, Chief Commissioner of Burma, on leave in England, reported to the new Viceroy, Lansdowne, that he hoped to meet with Wallace to discuss India. Mackenzie noted that "this may prove useful," and "at any rate, I am free to coach him up on any question and shall be glad to do so if at any time your Excellency thinks this desirable."[105] Lansdowne found Wallace's strategic placement "very satisfactory" since it afforded him an opportunity of "guiding" him in important questions.[106] Other English papers were also "coached" in this way.[107]

It is also clear that the Government of India sustained a policy of feeding selected information to English reporters in India. Shortly after Elgin's arrival in 1894, J.C. Macgregor, correspondent of *The Times*, thanked Colonel John Ardagh, Lansdowne's Private Secretary, for an advance copy of the Government's financial statement, and promised to keep it confidential.[108] Feeding information to *The Times* served the Government's purposes, for delivery of the paper usually took between two and three weeks. There was also a quid pro quo attached. In return for advance information, Elgin's Private Secretary, Babington-Smith, requested copies of all Macgregor's telegrams to England. Macgregor complied confidentially, stipulating that they should be burned "after perusal." The private secretary, however, carefully catalogued them and retained them in his own files.[109] Babington-Smith continued the policy with Macgregor's successor, J.V. Woodman, who also received extracts from official papers in advance and reciprocated with his telegraphic correspondence.[110]

Although Curzon had serious difficulties with the press in India, he supported the policy of tampering with the flow of information supplied to the English reporters. Soon after his arrival, Minto privately reported to Godley that he had found that

Secret Service money . . . was partly used by the last regime to subsidize Reuter's Agent in respect to messages sent home! I will leave you to read between the lines as to this, and as to the possible effects in public opinion such a policy may have produced.[111]

In a rather spectacular memorandum to Minto's private secretary, G.S. Buck, of Reuter's, admitted that for seven to eight years during the tenure of Elgin and Curzon "I received a private subsidy through the P.S.V. [Private Secretary to the Viceroy] for extending Reuter's service on certain important occasions."[112] He urged J.R. Dunlop Smith, Minto's Private Secretary, to continue to favor his "useful friend" and pledged his "absolute readiness" to assist the Viceroy "in every possible manner."[113] Minto at first resisted Morley's suggestions that such connections might be useful in the long run. However, it was not long before Minto confessed that while it was "a proceeding very distasteful to me . . . on exceptional occasions it may be advisable."[114]

The India Office, for its part, kept a watchful eye on *The Times*'s reporters at home. The paper often employed former Anglo-Indians, which somewhat facilitated the Office's efforts to neutralize various lobbying efforts. Following in the footsteps of Donald Mackenzie Wallace, Sir Walter Lawrence, Curzon's Private Secretary, joined *The Times*'s staff and, during his short tenure at Printing House Square, Lawrence recorded several attempts by the India Office to influence him.[115] In 1907 Lawrence joined the Council of India. Likewise Valentine Chirol, Director of the Foreign Department of *The Times* between 1899 and 1912 and author of several books on India, whose Indian reports influenced the paper more than any other correspondent, was subject to surveillance. Chirol enjoyed excellent sources of information within Curzon's administration,[116] with one result being that Minto, very early in his tenure, accepted a distinct "Curzonian influence in *The Times*."[117] Minto complained that Chirol's reportage encouraged papers in India, particularly Lovat Fraser's *Times of India*, to criticize his administration. The Viceroy feared that Chirol's "hostile Curzonian undercurrent will be brought to bear against us whenever opportunity offers."[118]

It is significant that Minto's overriding concern was with the influence of *The Times* in India, not in England. Even Morley, who felt strongly that the paper was the "only journal read by the very limited class of folk who take a real interest in India,"[119] and as such the only paper "which really matters," agreed that the impact of the newspaper in England was marginal compared with the potential mischief adverse reports might cause in the subcontinent.[120] The Secretary of State was particularly keen on refuting reports of the Government of India's inability to halt unrest in India.[121] Basically *The Times*'s reports, as well as those from other English papers, were reported in India in *India*, and, for a short time, in an anthology of English press reports, *English Opinion on India*, published in Poona.[122] From the beginning of their association Morley perceived Minto's "apparent nervousness" at newspaper criticism in India.[123] Four years later Minto still admitted that the "attitude of *The Times*, and other publications, is . . . a constant source of anxiety" because of their readiness to convert any riot or minor incident into the cry of weak government in Calcutta.[124] Morley explained his efforts to ease the situation, but the Viceroy continued to complain that agitation at home, in the press and in Parliament, were a great danger to British rule in the excitement they generated in India.[125]

As Indian nationalism became increasingly violent after 1907, the India Office was more aggressive in its efforts to prevent inflammatory material from reaching India. The office worked closely with Scotland Yard to contain Indian radical activity in England and the continent. This involved increased surveillance of Indians in the United Kingdom and various schemes to proscribe "seditious" pamphlets and even some private letters bound for India. As terrorism in India was instituted in 1908 and 1909, a new generation of press controls was initiated in India after 1910.[126]

The India Office could exert considerable influence on the press if it had to. Earlier, during the Curzon-Kitchener dispute, even Chirol's decidedly pro-Curzon posture could not alter the refusal of the *Times*'s editor-in-chief, G.E. Buckle, who was pro-Kitchener, to attack the India Office. The decision had less to do with who supported whom than the fact that the Secretary of State, St. John Brodrick, effectively threatened to cut off all official information to *The Times*, a ploy that Chirol bitterly resented.[127] When Curzon's resignation was imminent, and lobbying at Printing House Square was intense, Godley himself went to Buckle with telegraphic correspondence in hand to demonstrate the India Office case.[128]

Chirol reached an uneasy truce with the Government of India toward the end of Minto's term. Both the correspondent and the Viceroy agreed that the prestige and authority of the Government of India were badly eroded by the circumstances surrounding Curzon's downfall and the *"appearance"* of the transfer of power from Simla to Whitehall.[129] Still, Chirol was the harbinger of exaggerated accounts (or so it seemed to Minto) of sedition and unrest in India.[130] The fact is that Chirol only scratched the surface in recognizing the limits within which the Government of India could act independently in so vital an Indian policy. As an epilogue to Chirol's relations with the India Office, it should be noted that during World War I he approached the India Office with an offer to write a series of articles in *The Times* on India specifically to counter German propaganda. The Foreign Office concurred, and Chirol's articles aimed at neutralizing *Khilafat* criticisms and assuring the Indian Muslims of Britain's good intentions toward the Ottomans. The Government of India, however, was less than enthusiastic, and when Chirol went to India in 1915 as a correspondent, the "informal pipeline" of reports and confidential intelligence material he had been receiving abruptly ended.[131]

While public opinion in England was diffuse and elusive, and a factor to which the India Office accorded only passing concern, the rise of a much more readily identifiable Indian public opinion, essentially reflected in the Indian press, was very real to the bureaucrats in Whitehall. It was the growth of such public criticism in India, combined with the increasing imperative to maintain law and order in that country, which precipitated calculated action by the India Office and Government of India to monitor and manipulate the public image of India. Although officials in India and England responded to this new challenge at the end of the nineteenth century, they had indeed been forewarned. As early as 1832, Mountstuart

Elphinstone, Governor of Bombay, had predicted that a free Indian press would put the British in India "in such a predicament as no state has ever yet experienced."[132] Yet until the 1880s the Government of India generally refrained from executing preventive or punitive press legislation (the exceptions being short-lived restrictive measures enacted during Canning's and Lytton's Viceroyalties).[133]

It is noteworthy that during the 1880s there was continuous intercourse between Calcutta and London regarding the increase of public criticism by the press in India. Successive Viceroys were suspicious of leaks to the native press, which they implied came from London—while the India Office suggested that perhaps the culprits were part of the Government of India's confidential printing office. They were also increasingly uneasy about public criticism of the Indian Government that seemed to go hand in hand with a perceptible increase in violence and "sedition."[134] Such reservations were sometimes dismissed lightly by Secretaries of State who implied that Indian editors were "so far removed from the illiterate dumb masses of Indians" that the Government worried needlessly.[135] By the time Curzon became Viceroy such perceptions about the nature of Indian public opinion were dangerously *passé*.

As his tenure progressed, Curzon became less and less tolerant of the Indian press, especially in Bengal. He believed that the Bengalis criticized his proposed extension not because of his failures, but because of his success in solidifying British rule.[136] In the India Office, Godley needed more convincing. On New Year's Day 1904 he noted that

we hear a good deal more now-a-days than we used to hear (say) 8 or 10 years ago about "outcries" and public opinion; but, for all that, I cannot say that I see any reason why what is called public opinion in India should have any more overwhelming weight either with Your Excellency's Government or with the Secretary of State than it had 10 or 15 years ago.[137]

Curzon reacted vehemently to Godley's assessment, and delivered a clear and precise statement of the India Office's confused perception of events in India:

Ah! There is a world of meaning behind that simple reflection. To you in England, it seems so clear that there is no difference between the end of Lord Dufferin's *regime* and the end of mine. To me in India (and having been here in Lord Dufferin's time) it is transparent that there is all the difference in the world. What is the great difference at this end? It is that public opinion has been growing all the while, is articulate, is daily becoming more powerful, [and] cannot be ignored. What is the origin of mistakes sometimes made at the other end? It is that men are standing still with their eyes shut, and do not see the movements here.[138]

The India Office was slow to acknowledge the validity of Curzon's statements. Nevertheless, Godley's view of the fluid political climate in India was beginning to change. While others speculated that the Japanese victory over Russia (1904–05) would lead to unrest in India, Godley remained calm and discounted the impact of such outside influences.[139] More important, he began to take notice of Curzon's complaints about the internal unrest caused by the Indian press. Curzon continued to attack the Bengali press, whose "best wirepullers and most frothy orators" manipulated public opinion from Calcutta.[140] In India English papers and officials scoffed at the agitation. But Curzon warned that

> one could afford to laugh were it not that constant repetition of this sort of invective tends sooner or later to sway the minds of the educated classes, and I doubt not in my own case that the impression exists among them, which men like Cotton and Wedderburn have done their best to propagate, that I, who am regarded in England as ultra-Indian, am in India ultra-English, and am inspired by the most dangerous and reactionary designs.[141]

Slowly the India Office position began to shift toward firm support of the Government of India in its efforts to curtail "abuses" in the press. Momentous events like the agitation over the partition of Bengal still only indirectly affected the policy-making in the India Office. Morley, for example, noted how much "sillier" Indian public opinion was if it thought it could force the Secretary of State to reverse the partition decision.[142] However, a change was in the air. The year 1907 earmarked a definitive move by the India Office and Government of India to check growing Indian opposition reflected in the press. The new activism in India, spearheaded by the extremists, was accompanied by the emergence of a grand and complicated system of press controls imposed on all levels of government.[143]

In terms of external pressures upon the India Office, the Secretary of State and permanent staff were reasonably free from outside interference. The peculiar constitutional relationship of the India Office to other departments of state insured it a high degree of independence of action. Royal interference was a highly personalized activity with minimal effects, and Parliament's practical ability to influence the India Office was severely circumscribed.[144] Efforts to influence the India Office by the Indian National Congress through lobbying Parliament and the press were rarely successful. The diffuse political nature of M.P.s interested in India and the potentially explosive linkage of Indian and Irish politics when combined with a largely disinterested and preoccupied British public, also militated against any such successes.

For the greater part of the nineteenth century, public opinion in India was a distant threat which blossomed into a full-blown pressure only after 1900. At least this was the perception in London. Before 1900 the India Office was not complacent in dealing with efforts to influence the policy-making process either in England or India; it was cautious and highly circumspect. After the turn of the century, however, the India Office was more sensitive to the pressures facing the Government of India and became more vocal in its public support of it. The India Office believed strongly that persistent public debate at home would ultimately create problems in India; thus it sought to neutralize Indian National Congress and Parliamentary lobbying in England. This imperative fostered a policy of official pressure on key English and Indian newspapers. Thus for most of the late nineteenth and early twentieth centuries, the bureaucrats kept lobbying and special interest pressure on the periphery of the policy-making process.

NOTES

1. For an analysis of the origins, composition, and motivations of the British Committee of Congress and the Indian Parliamentary Committee, see Margot Morrow, "The Origins and Early Years of the British Committee of the Indian National Congress," Ph.D. thesis, University of London, 1977.

2. R.P. Masani, *Dadabhai Naoroji* (London: George Allen & Unwin, 1930), p. 101; see especially Mary Cumpston, "Some Early Indian Nationalists and their Allies in the British Parliament, 1851–1906," *The English Historical Review* 76:299 (April 1961), pp. 279–97.

3. Florence Nightingale to P.K. Sen, quoted in P.K. Sen (ed.), *Florence Nightingale's Indian Letters* (Calcutta, 1937), pp. 16–17, cited in Cumpston, "Early Nationalists and Allies," p. 281.

4. Cumpston, "Early Nationalists and Allies," p. 286. The way in which Irish support sometimes worked against Indian interests is reflected in Lansdowne being warned by party leaders at Home to delay proposals for the Indian Councils Act until Irish politics had disentangled themselves from the Indian question (Northbrook to Lansdowne, 1 March 1889, Lansdowne Papers [hereafter cited as LP], IOL, MSS. Eur. D.558/11). See also Margot Morrow, "The Limits of Radical Anti-Imperial Ideology: The Case of the British Committee of the Indian National Congress and the Parliamentary Committee, 1889–1906," unpublished paper presented to the Southern Conference on British Studies, Louisville, Ky., 1981.

5. Sir William Wedderburn, *Allan Octavian Hume* (London: T.F. Unwin and Co., 1913), p. 86.

6. Morrow, "Origins and Early Years of the British Committee," p. 25.

7. For details on the formation of India's Appeal to the British electorate, and its results, see Briton Martin, Jr., *New India, 1885* (Berkeley and Los Angeles: University of California Press, 1969), pp. 197–272.

8. See "Deputation in England," 3 September 1879, in R.C. Palit and R.S. Mitter (eds.), *Speeches by Surendranath Banerjea* (Calcutta, 1894–1908), I, 166, cited in Daniel Argov, *Moderates and Extremists in the Indian Nationalist Movement, 1883–1920* (Bombay: Asia Publishing House, 1967), p. 38.

9. Wedderburn, *Hume*, p. 54. Hume also established extensive newspaper contacts and arranged for Indian intelligence to be printed therein. For a list of participating English papers, see Martin, *New India*, p. 195.

10. Wedderburn, *Hume*, p. 56.

11. The pledges included citations from the Act of 1833, Queen Victoria's

proclamation of 1858, and excerpts of speeches by Lords Northbrook, Lytton, Ripon, and Dufferin. For an example of this preface page, see Argov, *Moderates and Extremists*, p. 39.

12. Wedderburn, *Hume*, p. 85.

13. *Report of the Fifth INC Bombay 1889*, p. 5. See also S.K. Ratcliffe, *Sir William Wedderburn and the Indian Reform Movement* (London: George Allen and Unwin, 1923), pp. 63–65. For information on Charles Bradlaugh, who was present at the session of Congress, see J.M. Robertson, *Charles Bradlaugh: A Record of His Life and Work* (London: T. Fisher Unwin, 1898).

14. The phrase "Simla Clique" was used often by Wedderburn in his criticism of Indian officialdom. See William Wedderburn, *Speeches and Writings of Sir William Wedderburn* (Madras: G.A. Natesan and Co., 1918), pp. 199–200. See also Edward C. Moulton, "Indian Nationalism and British Radicals: William Wedderburn and the Indian National Congress, 1885–1917," unpublished paper presented to the Western Conference of the Association for Asian Studies, Boise, Idaho, 1979.

15. Ratcliffe, *Wedderburn*, p. 106.

16. See Chapter 4, *supra*. Home Charges included, among other things, interest on debts to England incurred by the Raj, pensions for former ICS and British Army officials, payments to the War Office for upkeep of the Indian Army, shared costs with the Foreign Office for various Middle East outposts, purchase of material stores for India in London, and the upkeep and salaries of the India Office establishment.

17. See Morrow, "Origins and Early Years of the British Committee," *passim*.

18. G.W.E. Russell, *Collections and Recollections* (New York: Harper & Brothers, 1899), p. 346. Russell served as Parliamentary Undersecretary for India, 1892–1894. See also, Morley to Minto, 11 January 1906, Morley Papers [hereafter cited as MRP], IOL, MSS, Eur. D.573/1.

19. See Morrow, "The Limits of Radical Anti-Imperialism Ideology," *passim*.

20. H.L. Singh, *Problems and Policies of the British in India, 1885–1898* (Bombay: Asia Publishing House, 1963), pp. 64–68.

21. For the response of the India Press, see *Bhangavasi*, 1 September 1894, cited in Argov, *Moderates and Extremists*, p. 55.

22. Argov, *Moderates and Extremists*, p. 56.

23. *Report of the Eleventh INC Poona 1895*, p. 51.

24. John R. McLane, *Indian Nationalism and the Early Congress* (Princeton, N.J.: Princeton University Press, 1977), pp. 123–29. McLane includes Hume in this "Discredited" group, but Hume remained an active participant and supporter of the British Committee and Congress until he died in 1912.

25. See P.C. Ghosh, *The Development of the Indian National Congress, 1892–1909* (Calcutta: Firma K.L. Mukhopadyay, 1960), pp. 55–56.

26. G. B., Parliament, *Final Report of the Royal Commission on the Administration of the Expenditure of India*. C.131 (1900), XXIX. A number of points from the *Minority Report* found their way into the Indian Councils Act, 1909, and the Government of India Act, 1919.

27. Ghosh, *Congress Development*, pp. 93–94. See also McLane, *Early Congress* p. 139.

28. E.g., *The Cotton Duties Blue Book* (c. 7602, 1885) purposely omitted several

key minutes; memorials, the India Office said, had to be routed through various provincial governments and the Imperial Government in India (Godley to Kimberley, 13 June 1893, Kimberley Papers [private ownership], E/29.).

29. See Morrow, "Origins and Early Years of the British Committee," pp. 152–93; see also Arnold P. Kaminsky, "Morality Legislation and British Troops in Late Nineteenth Century India," *Military Affairs* 43:2 (April 1979), pp. 78–83; and *idem*, " 'Lombard Street' and India: Currency Problems in the Late Nineteenth Century," *The Indian Economic and Social History Review* 17:3 (July–September 1980), pp. 307–27.

30. R.D. Osborne, *Statesman and Friend of India*, 11 September 1885, quoted in S.R. Mehrotra, *The Emergence of the Indian National Congress* (Delhi: Vikas Publ., 1971), p. 336.

31. Wedderburn, *Hume*, p. 89.

32. William Digby, *The General Election of 1885: India's Interest in the British Ballot Box* (London: Indian Political Agency, 1888), p. 8. See also *idem*, *British Rule in India: Has It Been, Is It Still, a Good Rule for the Indian People?* (London: Indian Political Agency, 1891), p. 15 (located in BL, Political tracts, Etc., 1854–93, No. 6).

33. See Morrow, "Origins and Early Years of the British Committee, " pp. 38–41. See also IOR, Political and Secret Department Demi-Official Correspondence, L/P&S/8/3/f. 165 (September 1889); L/P&S/8/12 (25 October 1889); L/P&S/8/13/ff. 79–135 (July 1893).

34. William Digby, speech to electors, *The General Election of 1892: Mr. Digby's Record* (London: Indian Political Agency, 1892). (BL, Political Tracts, 1868–94).

35. Motilal Ghose to William Digby, 30 March 1892, William Digby Papers, IOL, MSS. Eur. D.767/9. See also L/P&S/8/3/f. 735, for a copy of Ghose's pledge of money (18 February 1890) to "Digabhai" that had been intercepted by the GOI/CID.

36. For charges that INC and Digby were supported by Russian gold see *India in England, Vol. II, Being a Collection of Speeches Delivered and Articles Written on the Indian National Congress in England in 1889* (Lucknow: G.P. Varma & Brothers, 1889), pp. 15–18.

37. William Digby, *"Prosperous" British India: A Revelation from Official Records* (London: T. Fisher Unwin, 1901).

38. Hamilton to Curzon, 23 January 1902, Hamilton Papers [hereafter cited as HP], IOL, Eur. MSS. C. 126/4.

39. Hamilton to Curzon, 6 February 1902, *ibid*. As late as 1907 Digby was being blamed for the increasing popularity of the "drain theory" among Indian critics (Dunlop Smith to J.D. Rees, 20 November 1907), Minto Papers (hereafter cited as MTP), National Library of Scotland, MS. 12776.

40. The only current biography of Wedderburn is S.K. Ratcliffe, *Sir William Wedderburn and the Indian Reform Movement* (London: G. Allen and Unwin, 1923). Ed Moulton is currently working on a new biography of Wedderburn and other "Indian " Radicals. See Moulton, "British Radicals and India in Early Twentieth Century," in A.J.A. Morris (ed.), *Edwardian Radicalism, 1900–1914* (London: Routledge & Kegan Paul, 1974), pp. 26–46; see also footnote 14, *supra*.

41. For valuable insight into the Wedderburn-Gokhale relationship, see B.R.

Nanda, *Gokhale: The Indian Moderates and the British Raj* (London: Oxford University Press, 1977), pp. 89–117.

42. For example, see Wedderburn, *Speeches*, pp. 50–51; 58–59; 170–80.

43. *Ibid.*, pp. 140–48 (1899); 199–200 (1903).

44. Morrow has used the terms "diplomatic" and "militant" in "Origins and Early Years of the British Committee," p. 304.

45. Godley to Minto, 23 March 1906, MTP 12735.

46. Throughout its operation *India*'s columns frequently appealed for money to support it. The Gokhale Papers ("India"), IOL, Microfilm Reel 2221, contain frequent requests for money and support from individuals in England.

47. Arthur Crawford to Richmond Ritchie (IO), Demi-Official Correspondence, 28 August 1909, L/P&S/8/9/f. 96.

48. Gokhale believed that his interviews with officials at the India Office went well; however, Godley and Hirtzel urged Morley to beware of INC representatives, and if he needed any hint of the distrust officials felt for him, Gokhale was treated quite rudely while visiting the India Office in 1913, and had a terse correspondence with T.W. Holderness on the subject (Gokhale to Holderness, 22 July 1913, and Holderness to Gokhale, 23 July 1913, Gokhale Papers, Reel 2220).

49. See Wedderburn to Gokhale, 5 September 1907, Gokhale Papers ("Wedderburn") and 2 Sept., 1907, Diary of Frederick Arthur Hirtzel [hereafter HD], IOL, Home Misc. Sales, No. 864, II.

50. 30 October 1907, HD II.

51. Morrow, "Origins and Early Years of the British Committee," pp. 201–222. See also M.N. Das, *Indian National Congress versus the British, 1885–1918* (Delhi: Ajanta Publications, 1978), pp. 160–61. In the elections of 1895, Godley informed the Viceroy (Elgin) that "there were not a few 'ejections' over which I heartily rejoiced; and not only those which affected the India Office, such as Naoroji, Seymour Keay &c.; Conybeare and Keir Hardie thoroughly deserved their fate and others of the same class" (Godley to Elgin, 22 August 1895, Elgin Papers (9th Earl) [hereafter cited as EP], IOL, MSS., Eur. F.84/30b).

52. Godley to Elgin, 26 March 1897, F.84/136.

53. "India's National Appeal," *India* (October 1894), pp. 305–306.

54. See documentation on the "India Newspaper Co., Ltd." formed in 1903, in Gokhale Papers ("India"), Reel 2221, and Morrow, "Origins and Early Years of the British Committee," pp. 265–67.

55. Hamilton to Curzon, 18 May 1899, HP D.510/2.

56. C.S. Bayley to Hamilton, 18 June 1899, HP D.510/2.

57. C.W. Bolton to Hamilton, 18 July 1899, HP D.510/2. This letter is also printed in C.H. Philips et al. (eds), *The Evolution of India and Pakistan 1858–1947: Select Documents* (London: Oxford University Press, 1962), pp. 149–50. Hamilton's suspicions that Indians received the greatest portion of *India*'s press run are corroborated by the Congress "Scheme for Distribution" authorized by the seventeenth session of Congress, Calcutta, 1901 (cited in D. Chakrabarti and C. Bhattacharya, *Congress in Evolution Being a Collection of Congress Resolutions (from 1885 to 1934), and Other Important Documents* [Calcutta, The Book Company, 1935], p. 157).

Bengal	1500
Madras	700

N-W Provinces	200
Oudh	50
Punjab	100
Berar and Central Provinces	450
Bombay	1000
	4000

Statistics in the Gokhale Papers (Reel 2228/1905), however, show a considerable drop in circulation in India.

58. Hamilton to Curzon, 6 July 1899, cited in Prem Narain, *Press and Politics in India 1885–1905* (Delhi: Manoharlal, 1970), p. 263. Hamilton's estimates on *India*'s impact do not reflect reality. More accurately, Henry Cotton noted that *India* "retailed stale news to India" in a style most Indians could not understand (Cotton to Wedderburn, 5 March 1905, Gokhale Papers, Reel 2228).

59. For an overview of this individualized lobbying and its relation to India, see Morrow, "Origins and Early Years of the British Committee," pp. 280–342. See also P. Bandyopadhyay, "British Famine and Agricultural Policies in India, with special reference to the Administration of Lord George Hamilton, 1895–1903," Ph.D. thesis, University of London, 1969, pp. 207–73.

60. Morrow, "Origins and Early Years of the British Committee," includes various statistical appendices of BCC and IPC questioning patterns. They clearly reveal that the bulk of parliamentary questioning (c. 75 percent by eleven men) originated with the Executive Committee of the British Committee of Congress.

61. Ampthill to Lamington, 29 November 1904, Lamington Papers, IOL, MSS. Eur. B.159/1.

62. *Report of the Twentieth INC Bombay 1904*, p. 151.

63. Curzon to Godley, 11 May 1905, Curzon Papers [hereafter cited as CP], IOL, MSS. Eur. F.111/164.

64. D. Argov, *Moderates and Extremists*, pp. 105–8. See also Nanda, *Gokhale*, pp. 187–201.

65. Morley to Minto, 25 January 1906, Morley Papers [hereafter cited as MRP], IOL, MSS. Eur. D.573/1; see also Morley to Minto, 23 June 1906, *ibid*.

66. See Morley to Minto, 2 April 1908, MTP 12738; 21 February 1907; HD II; Morley to Minto, 2 November 1906, MTP 12736.

67. S.A. Wolpert, *Morley and India, 1906–1910* (Berkeley and Los Angeles: University of California Press, 1967), p. 42.

68. Morley to Minto, 23 June 1906, MRP D.573/1.

69. Morley to Minto, 2 March 1906, *ibid*. For an overview of "Politics in England" during the preparation of the 1909 reforms, see M.N. Das, *India under Morley and Minto: Politics behind Revolution, Repression and Reforms* (London: George Allen and Unwin, 1964), pp. 62–87.

70. Das, *Morley and Minto*, p. 68.

71. Morley to Minto, 8 October 1907, MRP D.573/2.

72. See Kenneth O. Morgan, *Keir Hardie: Radical and Socialist* (London: Weidenfeld and Nicolson, 1975), pp. 191–95; see also "Diary of Events, 1907–1910," MTP 12609.

73. Morley to Minto, 8 October 1907, cited in Countess of Minto, *India, Minto and Morley, 1905–1910* (London: Macmillan and Co., 1934), pp. 158–59.

74. G.W.E. Russell (Parliamentary Undersecretary, 1892–94) had close ties with morality crusaders and British Committee members H.J. Wilson and James Stansfeld, and also knew Wedderburn. J.E. Ellis (Parliamentary Undersecretary, 1905–06) had been a member of the British Committee from 1889 to 1895. George Birdwood, a lifelong Conservative but a friend of Naoroji and Wedderburn, often wrote on Indian affairs under the pseudonym "John Indigo" and served in the Geographical Department of the India Office from 1879–1902. Guy Fleetwood Wilson, Member of the Viceroy's Executive Council, 1908–1912, offered to show Gokhale secret testimony from Islington Commission (Wilson to Gokhale, 29 February 1912, Gokhale Papers, 883–2). Thomas Charles Fenton, 2nd Class Clerk in the Record and Registry Department of the India Office, 1873–1912, had a brother who was secretary to the Holborn Division of the Liberal Association and once wrote Naoroji about his "warmest sympathy" for the Congress movement and later exchanged information on India Council reform with him and Digby (Fenton to Digby, 28 November 1889, Digby Papers, D.765/5). None of these individuals, however, was ever formally charged or suspected of leaking information, and in all likelihood none had access to critical enough information to affect the course of events.

75. Wolpert, *Morley*, p. 132.
76. Morley to Minto, 29 November 1907, MRP D.573/2.
77. 9 May 1906, HD I, 42.
78. Morley to Minto, 29 November 1907, cited in Stephen Koss, *John Morley at the India Office, 1905–1910* (New Haven, Conn.: Yale University Press, 1969), p. 188.
79. Morley to Minto, 21 October 1907, cited in Philips, *Select Documents*, p. 164. For background information on the Surat split in Congress, see S.A. Wolpert, *Tilak and Gokhale: Revolution and Reform in the Making of Modern India* (Berkeley, Calif.: University of California Press, 1962), pp. 157–212; and Das, *Morley and Minto*, pp. 88–146.
80. Das, *Morley and Minto*, pp. 96–97.
81. Morley to Minto, 31 October 1907, MRP D.573/2.
82. 12 July 1907, HD II, 61; see also Martin, *New India*, p. 224.
83. 13 July 1907, HD II, 61.
84. Morley to Minto, 28 May 1908, MRP D.573/3.
85. *Ibid*.
86. "Report of the Activities of the British Committee of the Indian National Congress," *India* [1910–11], 8 December 1911, p. 277; [1911–12], 13 December 1912, p. 291; [1912–13], 5 December 1913, p. 271; [1913–14], 23 October 1914, p. 170.
87. *India*, 8 November 1918, p. 158.
88. The British Committee argued that such postal propaganda was useless, and noted that of 1,500 election circulars sent to notables, only 50 replied (*India*, 7 March 1919, p. 74). One example of the disquiet about the British Committee's moderation regarding the Montford Reforms is found in "Weekly Report of Director of Central Intelligence," 7 December 1918 and an unsigned report by Tilak ("How We Get On II") enclosed in a letter from Tilak to G.S. Khaparde, 20 March 1919 (cited in Judith M. Brown, *Gandhi's Rise to Power, Indian Politics 1915–1922* [Cambridge: Cambridge University Press] note 3, p. 298).

89. Tilak to Khaparde, 28 November 1919, cited in Wolpert, *Tilak and Gokhale*, p. 289. See also *India*, 8 November 1918, p. 158; and 8 August 1919, pp. 59–60.

90. *India*, 8 August 1919, pp. 59–60.

91. See *India*, 7 November 1919 (p. 179); 12 January 1920 (pp. 2–3); 9 January 1920 (p.14); 20 February 1920 (p. 77); 27 February 1920 (pp. 85–86); and 3 December 1920 (pp. 188–91).

92. Diary of G.S. Khaparde, 29 December 1920, cited in Brown, *Gandhi's Rise to Power*, note 1, p. 298. Early in 1920 Motilal Nehru wrote that even a deputation to England of Gandhi, Malaviya, and Das multiplied four times over, would only be "as so many drops in the ocean.... Our destiny lies in our own hands and we must work it out in our own country. If we can only quicken our own nation to life the rest will follow as surely as day follows night" (Nehru to G. Lal, 11 March 1920, *ibid.*, note 3, p. 298).

93. J.M. Parikah (Vice Chairman, British Committee), "The British Committee: A Retrospect," *India*, 14 January 1921, p. 13; and W.E. Imeson, "The British Committee and 'India': Thirty Years After," *ibid.*, p. 16.

94. All-India Congress Committee Meeting, Nagpur, 1921, cited in Chakrabarti and Bhattacharya, *Congress in Evolution*, p. 161.

95. *Report of the Forty-First INC Cawnpore 1925*, cited in *ibid.*, p. 163.

96. Godley to Elgin, 4 November 1897, EP F.84/136.

97. Godley to Elgin, 9 February 1898, *ibid.*

98. Godley to Elgin, 3 February 1897, *ibid.*

99. Memorandum, 20 May 1870, O.T. Burne Papers [hereafter OTB], IOL, MSS. Eur. D.951/27.

100. A survey of nonlegislative attempts to influence the distribution of the news may be found in Government of India Home Political Proceedings, May 1911 [150] and S.P. Sen (ed.), *The Indian Press* (Calcutta, 1967), cited in N.Gerald Barrier, *Banned: Controversial Literature and Political Control in British India 1907–1947* (Columbia, Mo.: University of Missouri Press, 1974), p. 7. For the Government of India's breakdown of "friendly" and "unfriendly" papers see in S.N. Paul, *Public Opinion on British Rule: A Study of the Influence of Indian Public Opinion on British Administration and Bureaucracy, 1899–1914* (New Delhi: Metropolitan Book Co., 1979), pp. 6–14.

101. Robert Knight to O.T. Burne, 31 July 1876, quoted in S.C. Sanial's article on the "History of Indian Press," *Calcutta Review* (July 1908), pp. 366–74 (cited in Narain, *Press and Politics*, p. 265).

102. *Ibid.*

103. *Delhi Punch*, 30 August 1882, cited in Narain, *Press and Politics*, note 37, p. 265.

104. See fn. 99, *supra*.

105. A. Mackenzie to Lansdowne, 9 November 1892, Lansdowne Papers, IOL, MSS, Eur. D.558/14.

106. Lansdowne to Mackenzie, 12 December 1892, *ibid.*

107. Dunlop Smith to Minto, 20 April 1910, Dunlop Smith Papers [hereafter cited as DSP], IOL, MSS. Eur. F.166/9. Dunlop Smith had "coached" the *Daily Mail*, as well as *The Times*.

108. J.C. Macgregor to Col. John Ardagh, 20 March 1894, EP F.84/92/#32.

109. See copies of telegrams in EP F.84/92/#76 [1894]; and EP F. 84/94/#291 [1895].

110. J.V. Woodman to Babington-Smith, 3 July 1895, EP. F.84/96.

111. Minto to Godley, 17 January 1906, Kilbracken Papers, [hereafter cited as KP], IOL, MSS. Eur. F.102/25.

112. G.S. Buck to Dunlop Smith, 20 December 1907, DSP F.166/13. See also Graham Storey, *Reuter's Century, 1851–1951* (London: Max Parrish & Co., 1951), pp. 123–26.

113. *Ibid*. However, even Buck had problems. The Calcutta correspondent of Reuter's was an unscrupulous man who irritated Buck and the GOI (G.S. Buck to Dunlop Smith, extract, n.d. (January 1910), MTP 12854; and Minto to Morley, 17 December 1908, MTP 12738; and Morley to Minto, 15 April 1908, MTP 12738).

114. Minto to Godley, 9 May 1906, KP F.102/25. See also, Morley to Minto, 16 February 1908, MTP 12738; Brodrick to Minto, 2 November 1905, MTP 12729; Dunlop Smith, 25 May 1908, DSP F.166. The Reuter's connection was also invaluable in helping the Government co-opt the activities of the Indian-owned Central News Agency as a source of information. This group was allegedly a Congress "front" (Lee-Warner to C.S. Bayley, 30 August 1897, L/P&S/8/13, ff. 195–96). See also K.C. Roy to Gokhale, 5 June 1910, Gokhale Papers, Reel 12225 and Minto to Morley, 28 July 1910, MTP 12740.

115. Walter R. Lawrence, *The India We Served* (Boston: Houghton Mifflin Company, 1929), pp. 254–55.

116. David Dilks, *Curzon in India* (London: Rupert Hart-Davis, 1969), II, 99.

117. Minto to Morley, 15 August 1906, quoted in Minto, *India, Minto and Morley*, p. 309.

118. Minto to Morley, 3 September 1906, *ibid.*, p. 310.

119. Morley to Minto, 13 January 1909, MRP D.573/3.

120. Morley to Minto, 4 February 1909, *ibid*.

121. Morley to Minto, 11 July and 3 October 1907, MRP D.573/2; and 24 December 1908, *ibid*.

122. The journal was founded in 1886 to provide information to Indian papers which could not afford to subscribe to English papers. At first it was published bimonthly, and in 1892 it became a fortnightly publication. See Narain, *Press and Politics*, p. 281.

123. 3 September 1906, HD I, 76.

124. Minto to Morley, 26 August 1909, MRP D.573/20.

125. Reviewing the state of the British press and attitudes toward the Congress, the British Committee noted that it was "not likely to escape the careful reader . . . that the stupid and abusive articles always appear in Tory newspapers, and the thoughtful and well-informed articles usually appear in the Liberal papers" (*India*, 6 January 1905, p. 3).

126. See Barrier, *Banned*, pp. 26–45.

127. Dilks, *Curzon in India*, II, 173 and 211. Chirol accused Brodrick of falsifying the reports and misleading *The Times* regarding the origin of the military minutes published on 23 August 1905, which the paper had used in critically editorializing Curzon (Chirol to Moberly Bell, 10 November 1905, Chirol Papers, *The Times* Archives, Printing House Square, 28).

128. Dilks, *Curzon in India*, II, 239.

129. Chirol to Lady Minto, 4 May 1910 [forwarded to Dunlop Smith], cited in Martin Gilbert (ed.), *Servant of India* (London: Longmans, Green and Co., 1966), p. 236.

130. Minto to Chirol, 18 May 1910, *ibid.*, p. 238. Dunlop Smith noted to the Viceroy that Chirol allegedly was concerned about the "erroneous impression" going about that there was no longer a Government of India; Dunlop Smith explained that "in plain English this means that had *The Times* been squared, all would have been well" (Dunlop Smith to Minto, 23 June 1910, *ibid.*, p. 240).

131. Barrier, *Banned*, p. 73.

132. 5 August 1832, before a Select Committee of the House of Commons, cited in H.H. Dodwell (ed.), *Cambridge History of India* (Cambridge: Cambridge University Press, 1932), VI, 548.

133. For an overview of nineteenth-century press legislation in India, see J. Natarajan, *History of Indian Journalism* (New Delhi: Government of India, 1955), pp. 1–21; and Barrier, *Banned*, pp. 1–16.

134. See Arnold P. Kaminsky, "Pressure on the Periphery: Lobbys, Special Interests and the Home Government of India, 1880–1910," *Journal of Indian History* 58 (April–December 1980), parts 1–3, pp. 168–70.

135. Hamilton to Curzon, 3 August 1899, CP F.111/158.

136. Curzon to Hamilton, 9 July 1904, CP F.111/162.

137. Godley to Curzon, 1 January 1904, CP F.111/163.

138. Curzon to Godley, 27 January 1904, *ibid*.

139. Godley to Ampthill, 11 May 1904, cited in Das, *Morley and Minto*, p. 19.

140. Curzon to Brodrick, 2 February 1905, CP F.111/164. Ampthill (Governor of Madras) beseeched Godley to listen to Curzon's pleas, and noted that "once let the Congresswallah see that seditious agitation can succeed and he will never drop it. The imitative faculties of the Native of India will then very soon produce on a vast scale the same conditions of unrest, terrorism and tyrannical political influence as prevail in Ireland. The Congresswallah will play the part of the Irish M.P. and the Brahmin behind the scenes will do what the Roman Catholic Priest does in Ireland" (Ampthill to Godley, 21 December 1905, KP F.102/39).

141. Curzon to Brodrick, 23 March 1905, CP F.111/164.

142. Morley to Godley, 21 September 1906, KP F.102/2.

143. For an overview of the emergence of press controls between 1907 and 1913, see Barrier, *Banned*, pp. 16–65.

144. See Chapter 4 *supra*.

7

Conclusion

From the late 1860s through the 1890s a number of changes in the working relationships of the India Office departments and the committees of the Council of India greatly enhanced the role of the India Office in the formation of Indian policy. Many of these changes were effected by the astute Sir Arthur Godley, who served as Permanent Undersecretary for much of this period. The technical changes in the way the Office dealt with Indian business were in great measure linked to improved communications with and transportation to India. In the latter part of the nineteenth century, more and more business was conducted on a short-term basis without the inordinate delays which had characterized the operation of the East India Company, and to some extent, the India Office in the first decade of its existence. The advent of the telegraph, and a corresponding increase in the number of written despatches and letters home that "fleshed out" the steadily increasing cable traffic, made adjustments in the cataloguing and distribution of materials within the Office inevitable.

In many ways this was a further "rationalization" of the India Office bureaucracy along Weberian lines, an adaptation to new conditions.[1] Weber argued that administrative modernization occurred as the modern bureaucratic department evolved in the nineteenth century. In his "ideal type" he identified an office staffed by appointed officials responsible for the discharge of their duties; organized in such a way that spheres of competence and hierarchy of responsibility are clearly defined; and filled with men whose salaries are usually fixed and whose appointments are generally based on seniority. Moreover, members of the modern bureaucracy tend to think of their official duties as a "career," albeit one in which they are subject to discipline and control from above. In the despatch of business, administration is carried out "rationally" and in an orderly manner—that is, all action is directed toward a given end. According to Weber, the modern administrative unit tends to operate impersonally, usually within the context of a given set of written rules and precedents.

From its inception in 1858, the India Office outwardly conformed to the Weberian model. In spite of inheriting both the structure and personnel of the defunct East India Company, complete with their peculiarities and anomalies, the India Office comprised identifiable departments with specific areas of competence, a clearly identifiable permanent hierarchy headed by a Permanent Undersecretary of State, and a reconstituted committee system for the Council of India, with its clearly demarcated lines of authority. The duties and functions of the Undersecretaries, the department heads, and the committees of the India Council were progressively delineated as the office matured in its first decade.[2] By 1870 most reorganization within the India Office was complete; therefore it should be possible to categorize adjustments in handling paperwork in the 1880s and 1890s as technical innovations—routine adaptations to new circumstances rather than indicative of any "revolution" in government.[3] But there are strong indications that this was not the case; there were dramatic changes in the India Office in the late nineteenth century that might legitimately be defined as "revolutionary"—changes that affected not only the manner in which Indian business was processed but also its configuration and direction between 1880 and World War I.

In his study of the Colonial Office in mid-nineteenth century,[4] John Cell suggests that in evaluating the changes that took place in that office into the 1870s

the term "revolution in government" seems inappropriate. The word "revolution" must pertain to rapid changes *in kind*, what social scientists call "systemic change." In the Colonial Office there were primarily changes of degree . . . a grudging and in most cases a belated adaptation of outmoded machinery and procedures to new functions demanded by changing circumstances.[5]

In the India Office, however, there were "systemic changes" that could not help but affect the formulation of Indian policy. These included further reorganization of the flow of paper, which intimately affected policy-making by determining which officials would contribute to the process; modifications in the relationship between the Secretary of State and his Council, bearing in mind that unlike his colleagues in the Cabinet, the India Secretary acted as a corporate entity with the Council of India; a redefinition of departmental and committee prerogatives in the policy-making process; and the evolution of new (although arguably old) constitutional relationships with Parliament and the Government of India. All this enhanced the role of Whitehall in the formation, assessment, and implementation of Indian policy. Once again, a comparison with recent assessments of the

Colonial Office is instructive. Cell concluded that well into the 1870s the Colonial Office system

was modified but not replaced. Officials continued to preserve their primary loyalty, as [Sir James] Stephen had done, not for the empire they administered but for the prestige of the office of which they were members. In the Weberian sense their office did not necessarily get "better." But it did become more modern.[6]

In the case of the India Office, it is apparent that in many ways it modernized and became "better." It was more efficient, and its staff was less emotionally tied to the past. The shadow of the East India Company was gone as the 1880s unfolded—both in terms of office procedure and to a large extent in its personnel. This was particularly significant with regard to the Council of India, a group which possessed enormous theoretical power in its charge to "conduct" Indian business at home, and by virtue of its "financial veto." Council membership itself varied between ten and fifteen between 1883 and 1909. It continued, following the original design of the Act of 1858, to provide the permanent officials of the India Office with a special brand of advice gained from first-hand experience on the subcontinent. But in the 1880s and 1890s the Council of India was wholly different from its predecessors.

The committee system remained vital, processing huge quantities of paper. The Council committees continued to be arranged according to the Indian experience of Councillors, who were appointed to the rarefied air of Whitehall by virtue of outstanding performance in India. But the Councillors of the late nineteenth century had not, for the most part, participated in the conquest and consolidation of the Raj. They had not personally experienced the trauma of the so-called Sepoy Mutiny and did not debate in despatches as their predecessors had done, the reasons for the near collapse of British rule in India. In other words the personalities who served on the Council of India in the late nineteenth century were not victims of the "tyranny of the past."[7] This had a tremendous effect on the conduct of business within the office. This meant that the protracted discussions which had characterized the earlier period no longer hindered the policymakers in the India Office. There was no longer a tendency to temporize in the matter of critical despatches or produce "half-and-half" letters which encouraged the Government of India to act independently of Whitehall. While regional experience in India remained a factor in appointments to the India Council, the persistent regional loyalties of Councillors, which had produced divisiveness and pettiness in committee deliberations and hampered the formation of policy, had by and large disappeared. Often, because they were less flamboyant and categorical in their deliberations than Councillors in the 1860s and 1870s, members of the India Council in the latter nineteenth century were caricatured as deficient in "reputation and intellect" and as somewhat passive participants in the decision-making process.[8] But it is difficult to characterize the likes of John and Richard Strachey, Alfred Lyall, J.L. Mackay, and other Councillors of this period as anything less than distinguished and capable men. They represented the increased specialization on the Council, and as a result of reforms in the conduct of Office business the work of the Council of India aligned itself more closely with that of the India Office departments. If an occasional Secretary of State for India was less than enamoured with the character of the Council, Godley, for one, recognized that "for the practical working of the office, we have a far better team now than we had in the old days."[9]

Certain myths persist about the Council of India. For example, some modern Indian historians have used Lord George Hamilton's critical remarks to create a negative image of the Council as a "reactionary body"[10] operating solely at the beck and call of the Secretary of State.[11] Others have criticized the Council's obstruction to the development of representative institutions in India as proof of its essentially defensive and retrogressive nature. These generalizations tend to distort the role of the Council of India in the governance of British India. There is no question that the Council of India, and indeed the India Office staff itself, were deeply committed to the preservation of British rule in India. Within this framework their resistance to change was predictable. Hence they were quite different from administrators in the Colonial or Foreign Offices. They had an identifiable "empire" to which they could attach their loyalties, and this superseded any desire to enhance the prestige of the India Office. The health and well-being of Britain's Indian Empire—which in this period paid for the India Office establishment—was primary among Councillors and permanent staff. But it is also important to remember that with the institutionalization of and upsurge in Indian nationalist activity from the mid-1880s, the India Office agreed with the Government of India on expanding Indian representation at various levels and on adding two Indian members to the India Council itself in 1909. In the consideration of major Indian reforms, several Secretaries of State utilized the advice of Special Committees of Council and encouraged individual consultations to solve difficult problems.

The Council of India did *not* initiate policy. It discussed only those matters presented to it by the Secretary of State, including specific Indian expenditures. By the 1880s the Council no longer had the power to impose its views in the formation of policy. Individual consultation between the committees of Council and India Office departments was a routine occurrence; it is wrong to describe policy-making in the India Office in this period as "government by committee" as was the case in the first decades.[12] But it is also wrong to blame the Council for not making certain policy decisions which it was precluded by statute from making. Legislation eventually reduced the number of Councillors, shortened their term of service to five-year appointments, and reduced the permissible length of absence from India from ten to five years. The Council, however, retained the unique characteristic of having its members "nonremovable" by the Secretary of State, Prime Minister, or Cabinet. This "irresponsibility" of Councillors was protested by Viceroys and Indian nationalists alike.[13] What often goes unnoticed is the fact that this unique position of Councillors allowed them a certain freedom from the gyrations of domestic politics and provided the India Council with some continuity of experience while India Secretaries rotated through the office.

The Council suffered from two basic disadvantages in the policy-making process: first, it slowed up work by its meticulous and lengthy examination of new proposals, and second, Councillors were out of touch with Indian opinion. Notwithstanding, the Council of India played an important role in the administration of the vast Indian Empire in the late nineteenth and early twentieth centuries. The Council provided a variety of Indian experience in a system where the Secretary of State was constantly changing. In many instances hastily conceived legislation received deliberate consideration and modification by the India Council. And the Council was especially attentive to Indian expenditures, according to its constitutional duty. Indeed, given the volume and complexity of Indian correspondence between 1880 and 1910—and the legal obligation of the Council to review large portions of it—it is astonishing that paperwork in the India Office was handled with any kind of efficiency at all.

Sir Arthur Godley had a high regard for the Council of India. He staunchly defended the Council from outside attacks; but he was equally diligent in seeing that the proper constitutional relationship between the Secretary of State and his Council was maintained. When Lord Crewe introduced legislation to reduce the power of the Council in 1914, Lord Kilbracken expressed his opinion that the members' knowledge of Indian matters was "simply priceless, and any measure which tends to diminish its influence, however slightly, is very strongly to be deprecated." The former Permanent Undersecretary, who had served for a quarter century, added, "a Captain of a ship may be an excellent navigator, but for local knowledge he depends, nay, he is compelled by law to depend, upon a pilot. Compulsory pilotage has been found necessary at sea; it is no less necessary at the India Office."[14]

The India Office departments also played a key role in the formation of Indian policy. While lacking extensive initiatory powers—even after adjustments in their relationship with the India Council in the first decade of the Office—departmental Secretaries were generally efficient men, and a harmonious relationship was established between them and the Council committees in handling the large amounts of paper. The duties of the India Office departments were carefully delineated in the 1880s, largely under Godley's direction. India Office clerks and secretaries effectively catalogued and processed an extraordinary volume of paperwork essential to the formation of policy. Department Secretaries and Assistant Secretaries had some leeway in the area of demiofficial correspondence with Indian officials, usually to gather additional information on a subject, but most other policy despatches were carefully scrutinized by the Undersecretaries before being presented for further consultation to the Council of India. A crucial difference between the India Office departments of the late nineteenth century and those of its early years is the diminution in the number of department heads who had served in India. This was in large part due to Arthur Godley's conviction that the Council of India provided the necessary Indian experience and his belief that the promotion of "insiders" (i.e., those without Indian experience) to key departmental positions provided an incentive to junior staff and balance in the decision-making process.

Relations between the India Office and the external bodies in Indian administration—Parliament, the Cabinet, and the Government of India—were greatly influenced by consideration of Imperial matters. There is no evidence, however, that there was any lengthy debate over whether or not India should be the bastion of Britain's late nineteenth-century Empire—this was the underlying assumption of administrators both in India and London. However, there was considerable discussion on the means by which this was to be accomplished. The bureaucrats in the India Office remained convinced that the most effective way to sustain British power in India was for them to continue to direct India policy. There were corollaries to this basic assumption, viz., that the independence of the Government of India had to be curbed; the notion that while they often had to subordinate Indian questions to "Imperial" issues, they could work assiduously behind the scenes to neutralize the impact of royal, parliamentary and Cabinet interference in the daily management of the Indian Empire; and, finally, that lobbying by both British and Indian advocates of reform should be kept on the periphery of the policy-making process.

For over a quarter of a century Sir Arthur Godley was the linchpin of the India Office and the man who shaped its approach to the formation policy. In twenty-six years Godley served seven ministers in ten successive administrations and accumulated an unrivaled command of the "guild secrets" of the India Office which afforded him ample opportunities to influence Indian policy. However, although he was clearly one of those nineteenth-century "permanent secretaries [who] were notoriously self-possessed and wielded considerable power,"[15] and although he appeared to some knowledgeable politicians outside the Office as the man who actually "ruled India,"[16] he was generally unknown to the public until after his retirement in 1909.[17] He scrupulously avoided political involvements while he held the Undersecretaryship. Instead, he concentrated on keeping the office running smoothly. He minimized external involvement in office routine by keeping the Treasury at a distance and by such devices as regulating the flow of information to the Crown and Parliament, manipulating committees, etc. If there was very little understanding of Godley's role—and indeed, of the entire functioning of the India Office bureaucracy—at the time, modern scholars have similar misunderstandings. For example, David Dilks, in his work on George Curzon, believes that Godley, by "virtue of his long tenure and dispassionate judgment... acted as a catalyst in many disputes [and] neither he nor any Secretary of State seems to have attempted any reform of the somewhat Gilbertian organisation."[18] The inaccuracy of this charge is amply demonstrated in the preceding chapters. Nevertheless, it is representative of the general lack of understanding about the India Office and its role in the policy-making process.

The strain on the India Office of handling the increasing complexity and volume of India business was considerable indeed. This by no means implies that the India Office staff and the Council of India regarded themselves as the sole, or even the best, judges of India policies. However, there was a clearly identifiable belief among the paladins of the India Office that unless they acted as a clearing house or buffer for India policy, the centrifugal forces of party politics in England and nationalist politics on the subcontinent would shake the very foundations of British rule in India. Hence, while there were no attempts to deny the importance of the views of officials on the spot in India or to deny the ultimate powers of Parliament to control Indian affairs, there is a pattern of subversion or co-option in India Office behavior in the late nineteenth century. A brief look at two issues reveals the character of India Office attitudes and behavior in the 1880s and 1890s.

India and the India Office were deeply involved in the world monetary crisis of the late nineteenth century.[19] In its efforts to develop a currency for India, the India Office was subjected to a variety of internal and external pressures. The tremendous fluctuations in gold and silver prices in the last quarter of the nineteenth century played havoc with India's silver rupee. This in turn affected all aspects of India's political and military posture, as well as the "home charges," including the financing of the India Office establishment itself. The way in which the India Office handled the extended monetary crisis is a microcosm of its philosophical and administrative outlook during the 1880s and 1890s. The Office had to deal with an anxious and nervous Government of India, aggressive lobbying in Parliament and the press (both English and Indian), its sister departments, and the Cabinet while trying to reconcile India's needs with Great Britain's domestic and international monetary requirements.

Beginning in 1892, a number of significant forces came into play in the formation of Indian currency policy. First, several English and Indian lobbies came into existence, intimately affecting policy-making inside the India Office. This was so because two of the main lobbies—the Indian Currency Association and the Gold Standard Defence Association—were represented directly on the Viceroy's Council and the Council of India. There were also attempts by the Indian National Congress to influence the deliberations of two Royal Commissions on the subject (the Herschell and Fowler Committees). Moreover, the India Office played a key role in filtering information provided to the press and Parliament and in acting as a go-between for the Cabinet and Government of India. In negotiating these dangerous waters, the India Office manipulated and cajoled, pressured and dictated events in order to keep the decision-making process under control.

The India Office closely monitored international monetary negotiations, such as the Brussels Conference (1892) to which it sent two of its own people, Richard Strachey and Bertram Currie—both members of the India Council—to give India separate representation.[20] The India Office even restricted the statistical information provided to the British delegates to this conference.[21] To monitor closely the deliberations of the Herschell Committee on Indian Finance (1893), Godley himself participated as a panelist, and the Office entered tough negotiations with the Treasury to skew the Committee's composition its way.[22] In India and England the India Office sought to minimize public debate on currency matters and to neutralize lobbying efforts by tightening memorializing procedures, preventing the release of certain information, and clandestinely fostering animosity between groups like the British Committee of Congress and the Indian National Congress, whose members had divergent views on the cause of and solution for India's monetary ills. The disposition of the currency crisis was of first-rank importance to the India Office, for exchange remained "sick" into the 1890s and threatened to engulf Elgin's government when it faced additional crises in frontier wars, famine, and plague.[23] All of those problems cost much money, and were linked directly to tax revenues, import duties, etc.—issues which in and of themselves were potentially explosive politically.

As the India Office tried to assess international forces, such as the impact of American silver mines on Indian currency, the attitude of Lombard Street (symbolic of England's gold interests) and the Treasury's position in all this, it also faced a revolt from the Government of India when it favored a gold standard for the subcontinent, which was in opposition of prevailing attitudes at home and abroad. In 1898, when the Fowler Commission was formed to investigate again Indian finance and currency, the India Office was well served by a former Secretary of State in the chair and two Members of the Council of India's Finance Committee, J.L. Mackay and Charles Croswaithe, on the Commission.[24] Godley used private lines of communication to the Gold Standard Defence Association to inform them of India Office plans and urge them to reduce their intense pamphlet campaign, which threatened to keep India in front of the Commons.[25] The Office also worked behind the scenes to discredit some critics of its Indian policy, such as Sir Robert Giffen, assistant editor of *The Economist*,[26] and again tried to manipulate the witness list for the Fowler Committee.[27]

Eventually, between 1898 and 1913, India evolved a Gold Exchange Standard.[28] But in the assessment of the whole currency question, certain conclusions are apparent. The India Office successfully negotiated the trends of English and Indian interests in the currency crisis. Imperial and Indian interests could not be divorced in Whitehall, and in steadying the ship amid the flood of discontent, the India Office had to withstand the vexations of various lobbies at home and in India if it was to stabilize the Indian Government and thus perpetuate British rule in India. The Office was meticulous in answering all correspondence from these groups, and they were imbued with pabulum as required. The India Office Finance Department and the Finance Committee of Council worked long and hard to sort out difficult statistical analyses so that the India Office could direct the flow of debate in Parliament and contain critics at home and in India. Internally, the Secretary of State and his Council agreed generally on a modus operandi which allowed the India Office to present a united front to other departments of state on this important issue. While there was scope for philosophical debate on the efficacy of the gold standard, the major concern for the India Office establishment was the stability of India currency, and all administrative efforts were channeled into that effort.

The success of the India Office in controlling the means by which the currency crisis was settled and in minimizing any deep divisions within the Office itself, or between it and other departments of state, was not matched by its performance in the Cantonment Acts crises in the late nineteenth century. The means were similar—control of various lobbies in and out of Parliament, neutralizing the Indian and English press, manipulating Blue Books and Parliamentary Commissions—all in an effort to control information and make the issue less volatile in the public eye. From the India Office perspective this was consistent with its attempt to keep pressure on the periphery and retain control over the policy-making process. However, the resolution of this crisis, either in or out of the Office, was nowhere near as smooth as one might suspect. The agitation over this emotionally charged issue in England and India had weighty consequences for the India Office and Government of India, for it was largely the concurrence of this issue with the Cotton Duties crisis in the 1890s that precipitated an assertion of India Office control over the official members of the Viceroy's Council.

The details of the Cantonment crisis are outlined elsewhere.[29] Essentially, it centered about the extension to India of the social purity campaign in England to end government licensing of prostitutes and compulsory examination of women suspected of venereal disease. The resolution of the conflict in the late nineteenth century illuminates the mechanism of Indian governance during that time since it involved the India Office relationship with the House of Commons, Cabinet, and Government of India. The constitutional relationship between the Secretary of State and his Council, and the Secretary of State *in* Council and the Viceroy's Executive Council was also strained considerably over this issue.

Throughout the 1860s and 1870s a series of Contagious Disease Acts were passed in Britain, actually to control the widespread incidence of venereal disease in and about military posts and naval stations, but with a veneer of social morality as the movement progressed. A protracted struggle saw Parliament first enact and later rescind the legislation. The extensive public debate ended only in the mid-1880s when Parliament finally repealed the Contagious Disease Acts. However, the anti-CD Acts "crusade" then spilled over into India. Several members of the British Committee of Congress pressed the India Office for information regarding official procurement and regulation of prostitutes for the British Indian Army.[30] These inquiries were supported by a widespread agitation for investigation of the "iniquitous and God-defying system of licenced sin in India"[31] by certain religious groups in England and India—who especially concentrated on various rules and regulations which seemed, on the surface, to encourage legalized prostitution.[32]

This issue was so emotionally charged, and of such domestic political concern, that the India Office was pressured by the Cabinet and Parliament to amend the existing rules regulating Indian military cantonments. Several Secretaries of State, including Cross, Kimberley, and Fowler, were sensitive to the demands of their Cabinet colleagues to conform at least outwardly to Parliament's wishes. Ironically, the Council of India almost unanimously opposed any restrictions on Indian military authorities to control venereal diseases in India because statistics clearly indicated that military effectiveness was already severely diminished by the extraordinarily high incidence among British soldiers in India (reaching as high as 500 admissions per thousand in the late 1890s). Any attempts to control the freedom of Medical Officers to police their own actions was also calculated to effect discontent among civil servants in India.

In resolving this issue, the Secretary of State for India overruled his Council several times in ordering the Government of India to frame new, less obvious rules for controlling their cantonments.[33] The India Office also faced considerable protest in the English and Indian press when it was discovered that local military authorities in India often contravened these directions from home. This in turn gave rise to a heated exchange between Indian officials on the spot and the India Office over who was better positioned to assess the military requirements of India. Although the India Office concluded the debate in its favor, the Office also faced considerable pressure in Parliament. Not only was it an emotionally charged issue on which certain well-known lobbyists such as James Stansfeld and James Stuart assailed the office, but there was also a decisive defection by the

Parliamentary Undersecretary of State for India, G.W.E. Russell.[34] Again the India Office managed to control the situation by deflecting a full parliamentary investigation with its own in-house committee, which included Stansfeld, Stuart, and Russell, and authorized the Government of India to conduct its own investigation too.[35]

There was bitter debate in the India Office on how much pressure it should exert on the Indian Government to conform at least outwardly to Parliament's desire to end state regulation of vice. With the currency crisis, cotton duties, plague, sedition, and reform troubling India, as well as imperial crises throughout the world in the 1890s, the overriding concern of the various Secretaries of State and Godley was to end parliamentary debate and agitation over this issue. Ironically, when public opinion, such as it was, suddenly veered in the direction of the India Office at the turn of the century after it was amply demonstrated that comparable venereal disease rates for foreign armies were considerably lower, the India Office finally acknowledged the soundness of some form of cantonment control for British troops in India.[36]

The India Office expended much time and money in the resolution of the Cantonment Act crises—energies that might otherwise have been channeled into more pressing issues of the day. Above all, the interaction between the constituent parts of Indian Government proved to be highly reactive to the ebb and flow of "Imperial" needs. What did not change, however, was the conviction that it was the India Office that should determine the character and timing of any changes in the governance of British India. If it was politic to give the public appearance of conforming to Parliament—even when steps were being taken to subvert full implementation of directions from home in India—then the India Office establishment was willing to do it. It was a question of tactics. The necessity to remain in control of the policy-making process dominated the thinking of the hierarchy in the India Office. On this the Council of India and the permanent establishment agreed. Even if the Military Committee of Council was correct in its assessments of India's military needs vis-à-vis cantonment regulation, the Secretary of State and the Permanent Undersecretary believed that tactically it would be better to allow slippage in India and overrule the Council at home rather than risk sustained agitation and adverse publicity on Indian administration in Parliament and the press. Ultimately, when it was determined that public opinion would neutralize the efforts of lobbyists to stir up the hornet's nest in the House of Commons, the leadership in the India Office reversed its position and adopted the India Council's position.

The India Office between 1880 and 1910 had freed itself from the shackles of the past. Both operationally and in terms of its personnel, it was much better equipped to handle the increasing volume and complexity of Indian business. It would be unfair to suggest that the India Office was filled with technocrats—for the continued existence of the Council of India prevented the India Office from being totally detached from the Indian Empire in the way that the Colonial Office was from the colonies and dependencies. The India Office increasingly involved itself in all manner of Indian business because it was attuned to the shifting tides of British domestic politics which from the bureaucratic standpoint threatened to complicate the management of the Indian Empire. In all of its work, the India Office was guided by the premise that its function was to sustain British rule in India.

It is easy to attack the India Office as a retrogressive institution because it opposed Indian participation in government and impeded reforms. It is undoubtedly true that few members of the India Office establishment in the late nineteenth century favored Indian nationalists. But this is perhaps a value judgment on the role of the India Office establishment beyond its assigned functions within the framework of Indian Government. As the twentieth century unfolded, the India Office did not oppose the idea of expanded Indian participation in government because this development was seen as the further insurance of British domination. The India Office played a formidable role in the formation of Indian policy in the nineteenth and twentieth centuries, and understanding its operation and personnel helps place the history of this period in better perspective.

NOTES

1. For an overview of Weberian models, see Max Weber, *Theory of Social and Economic Organization*, ed. Talcott Parsons (New York: Oxford University Press, 1947), pp. 329–41. See also R. Merton et al. (eds.), *Reader in Bureaucracy* (Glencoe, Ill.: Free Press, 1952).

2. See Donovan Williams, *The India Office, 1858–1869* (Hoshiarpur, Punjab: Vishveshvaranand Vedic Research Institute, 1983), pp. 1–107.

3. See O. MacDonagh, "The Nineteenth-Century Revolution in Government: A Reappraisal," *Historical Journal* 1 (1958), pp. 52–57; H. Parris, "The Nineteenth-Century Revolution in Government: A Reappraisal Reappraised," *ibid.* 3 (1960), pp. 17–37; J. Hart, "Nineteenth-Century Social Reform: A Tory Interpretation of History," *Past and Present* 31 (1965), pp. 39–61; and V. Cromwell, "Interpretations of Nineteenth-Century Administration: An Analysis," *Victorian Studies* 9 (1966), pp. 245–55.

4. John W. Cell, *British Colonial Administration in the Mid-Nineteenth Century: The Policy-Making Process* (New Haven, Conn.: Yale University Press, 1970).

5. *Ibid.*, p. 40.

6. *Ibid.*, p. 39.

7. See Williams, *The India Office*, pp. 453–81.

8. Lord George Hamilton, *Parliamentary Reminiscences and Reflections, 1886–1906* (London: John Murray, 1922), II, 261.

9. Godley to Curzon, 11 March 1904, Curzon Papers [hereafter cited as CP], IOL, MSS. Eur. F.111/163.

10. R. S. Jain, *The Growth and Development of Governor-General's Executive Council (1858–1919)* [Delhi: S. Chand & Co., 1962], p. 174.

11. Singh, *The Secretary of State for India and His Council (1858–1919)* [Delhi: Munshi Ram Manohar Lal, 1962], p. 69.

12. Williams, *The India Office*, p. 456.

13. See Memorandum by Lord Curzon on a Proposed Amendment of the Government of India Acts, 1 December 1904, CP F.111/440. See also Godley to Curzon, 26 June 1904, *ibid*. For the Indian viewpoint on this issue, see M.A. Jinnah, "Reorganization of the India Council," *Fortnightly Review* (October 1914), pp. 612–20.

14. Letter by Lord Kilbracken to the House of Lords (read by Viscount Midleton [Brodrick], G.B., *Parliamentary Debates* (Lords), vol. 16, ser. 5, col. 824.

15. Roy M. MacLeod, "Statesmen Undisguised," *American Historical Review* 78:5 (December 1973), p. 1405.

16. Lord Asquith, quoted in Diary of Frederick Arthur Hirtzel, IOL, Home Miscellaneous Series, No. 864, III, 50.

17. See *The Times* (London), 11 October 1909, p. 11.

18. David Dilks, *Curzon in India* (London: Rupert Hart-Davis, 1969), I, 106.

19. See Arnold P. Kaminsky, " 'Lombard Street' and India: Currency Problems in the Late Nineteenth Century," *The Indian Economic and Social History Review* 17:3 (July–September 1980), pp. 307–27.

20. Bertram Currie, a leading banker, Member of the India Council, and active member of the Gold Standard Defence Association was considered by the Treasury England's leading spokesman and defender of the gold standard. See Welby to Sir W. V. Harcourt, 16 November 1892, Welby Papers, London School of Economics (British Library of Political and Economic Science), R (S.R.) 1017/5/#92.

21. See various enclosures, Finance Department, IOR, file L/F/6/538/#3824; see also draft instructions to delegates, 18 October 1892, L/F/6/547/#4711; and Treasury to India Office, 12 November 1892, L/F/6/550/#5068.

22. See Bertram Currie to Kimberley, 19 September and 11 October 1892, Kimberley Papers, private ownership, E/11; see also Currie to Kimberley, 20 October 1892, *ibid*.

23. H. Babington-Smith to Godley, 9 May 1894, Elgin Papers (Ninth Earl) [hereafter cited as EP], IOL, MSS, Eur. F.84/29. See also Godley to Elgin, 1 June 1894; Lord Reay to Elgin, 29 August 1894, *Ibid*. Moreover, see Elgin to Fowler, 1 May 1894, EP F.84/12.

24. Hamilton to Elgin, 25 March 1898, EP F.84/16.

25. See Godley to Farrer, 14 July 1898, Farrer Papers, London School of Economics (British Library of Political and Economic Science), R (S.R.) 1018/1/#68. See also G. Peel to Farrer, 8 July 1898, Farrer Papers, R (S.R.) 1018/3/#30.

26. Barbour to Farrer, 7 September 1897, Farrer Papers, R (S.R.) 1018/1/#14; see also Wm. Carlie to Farrer, 24 May 1898, Farrer Papers, R (S.R.) 1018/1/#6.

27. Godley to Elgin, 22 July 1898, EP F.84/136.

28. For an explanation of the Gold Exchange Standard, see John Maynard Keynes, *Indian Currency and Finance* (London: Macmillan and Co., reprint, 1971), p. 71.

29. See Arnold P. Kaminsky, "Morality Legislation and British Troops in Late Nineteenth Century India," *Military Affairs* 43:2 (April 1979), pp. 78–83. See also

Kenneth Ballhatchet, *Race, Sex and Class Under the Raj: Imperial Attitudes and Policies and Their Critics, 1793–1905* (New York: St. Martin's Press, 1980).

30. See W.J. Moore (Surgeon-General), "Memorandum on the Contagious Disease Act," October 1886, Reay Papers, School of Oriental and African Studies (London), MS. 254,560/4 [Loose Papers on PWD and Health and Sanitation matters]; see also Parliamentary Return (61), 1887, p. 903, filed with IOR, Military Department, L/MIL/7/13811.

31. Originally datelined Bombay, 30 March 1888, and later reported in the *Sentinel*, May 1888, L/MIL/7/13817.

32. G.B., Parliament, *Report of the Committee Appointed by the Secretary of State for India to Inquire into the Rules, Regulations and Practice in the Indian Cantonments and Elsewhere in India with Regard to Prostitution and the Treatment of Venereal Disease*, C.7148 (1893), copy filed with L/MIL/7/13850.

33. See GOI (Mil) No. 123, 17 May 1888, copy in PRO, Cabinet Papers, CAB/37/38/4/7340.

34. GOI (Mil) No. 134, 6 Sept. 1892, L/MIL/7/13837.

35. See IO (MIL) No. 50, 20 April 1893, L/MIL/7/13839. A complete copy of the report (C.7148) is also located in IOR, Parliamentary Branch, L/PARL/233.

36. See Kaminsky, "Moral Legislation and British Troops," pp. 82–83.

Bibliography

PRIMARY SOURCES

Manuscripts

India Office Library

Ampthill Collection	MSS. Eur. E.233
Barnes Letters	Reel 603 (Film)
Burne Papers	MSS. Eur. D.951
Butler Collection	MSS. Eur. F.116
Cotton Papers	Reels 1619–1620 (Film)
Cross Collection	MSS. Eur. E.243
Curzon Papers	MSS. Eur. F.111
Curzon-Kitchener Conflict	MSS. Eur. D.555
Digby Collection	MSS. Eur. D.767
Dunlop Smith Papers	MSS. Eur. F.166
Dufferin Papers	MSS. Eur. F.130
Elgin (Ninth Earl) Papers	MSS. Eur. F.84
Fleetwood Wilson Papers	MSS. Eur. E.224
Foster Correspondence	MSS. Eur. E.242
Garrett Collection	MSS. Eur. D.515
Gokhale Papers	Reels 2217–2230 (Film)
Hamilton Papers	MSS. Eur. C.125; C.126; D.508-510
The Diary of Frederick Arthur Hirtzel	Home Miscellaneous Series No. 864

Hirtzel Papers	MSS. Eur. D.713
Kilbracken Collection	MSS. Eur. F.102
Lamington Papers	MSS. Eur. B.159
Lansdowne Papers	MSS. Eur. D.558
Lawrence Collection	MSS. Eur. F.143
Lee-Warner Collection	MSS. Eur. F.92
Lyall Collection	MSS. Eur. F.132
McNally Manuscript	MSS. Eur. D.801
Morley Papers	MSS. Eur. D.573
Private Secretaries of the Governors-General and Viceroys, 1774–1908	Reel 990 (Film)
Reed Memorandum	MSS. Eur. B.229
Richards Papers	MSS. Eur. F.122
Richmond Ritchie Papers	MSS. Eur. C.343
Tej Bahadur Sapru Collection	Reels 4986–5020 (Film)
Sladen Collection	MSS. Eur. E.290
Sir (Samuel) Findlater Stewart Collection	MSS. Eur. D.890
Richard Strachey Papers	MSS. Eur. F.127
Walpole Collection	MSS. Eur. D.781
White Collection	MSS. Eur. F.108
Wolverhampton Papers	MSS. Eur. C.145

British Library

Balfour Papers	Add. MSS. 49,721
Campbell-Bannerman Papers	Add. MSS. 41,206–41; 41,252; 52,512–21
Cross Papers	Add. MSS. 51,263–51,289
Gladstone Papers	Add. MSS. 44,223; 44,227–29; 44,643–48
Gladstone (Viscount) Papers	Add. MSS. 46,044–67; 46,084–85
Kilbracken Correspondence	Add. MSS. 44,900–44,902
Kitchener-Marker Papers	Add. MSS. 52,276–52,278
Macmillan Archives	Add. MSS. 55,245
Midleton Papers	Add. MSS. 50,072–50,077
Nightingale Papers	Add. MSS. 44,778; 44,781–85
Ripon Papers	Add. MSS. 43,515–18; 43,523–27; 43,541; 43,569; 43,573; 43,633; 43,639

Bibliography 207

Public Records Office

Admiralty Papers	ADMIRALTY 116/26/file 206
Ardagh Papers	PRO 30/40
Kitchener Collection	PRO 30/57
Midleton Papers	PRO 30/67

Other Libraries and Collections

Chirol Papers	Printing House Square Archives, London
Farrer Collection	British Library of Political and Economic Science, R (S.R.) 1018
Giffen Collection	British Library of Political and Economic Science, R (S.R.) 1016
Private Library, Paintings and Photographs of Lord Kilbracken (Part)	Brede, Sussex, England, Private Ownership, The Rt. Hon. W.A.H. Godley
Private Library, Paintings and Photographs of Lord Kilbracken (Part)	Shute Barton, Axminster, England, Private Ownership, Mr. Patrick A. Rice
Private Library, Translations in Greek and Latin Verse by Lord Kilbracken	London, England, Private Ownership, Mr. Arthur Coleridge
Kimberley Papers	West Hall, Sherbourne, England, Private Ownership, The Earl of Kimberley
Minto (Fourth Earl) Papers	National Library of Scotland (Edinburgh), MSS. 12588–803
Reay Papers	School of Oriental and African Studies (London), MS. 254,560
Welby Papers	British Library of Political and Economic Science, R (S.R.) 1017

RECORDS

India Office Records

Accountant-General's Department Papers, 1884–1910	L/AG/30
Council of India, Minutes 1858–1910	C/1–105
Council of India, Minutes of Dissent by Members of Council (originals), 1881–1900	C/125–29

Council of India, Minutes of Dissent by Members of Council (copies), 1881–1900	C/131–32
Minutes on Orders or Communications made under the Urgency Clause (C.26) of the GOI Act 1858, 1875–1920	C/133–34
Council of India Order Book, 1858–1917	C/143
Revenue, Statistics and Commerce Departmental Papers, 1885–1906	L/E/7
Finance Department Letter Books, Home Letters out, 1857–1903	L/F/2
Financial Despatches to India, 1880–1909	L/F/3
Finance Department, Compilations and Miscellaneous letters, 1881–1911	L/F.5
Finance Departmental Papers, 1892–1900	L/F/6
Reports of Committees on Home Charges, 1879–1894	L/F/9
Sir John Kaye's Confidential Letter Book	Unclassified
Military Department, Papers referred to Military Committee of Council of India, 1885–1925	L/MIL/1
Military Department, Military Papers to/from India, 1880–86	L/MIL/3
Military Departmental Papers	L/MIL/6
Military Department, Collections, 1885–1910	L/MIL/7
Parliamentary Questions and Addresses, 1881–1911	L/P&S/17
Political and Secret Department, Home Correspondence, 1885–1906	L/P&S/3
Political and Secret Department, Correspondence with India, 1875–1930	L/P&S/7
Political and Secret Department, Demi-Official Correspondence, 1862–1912	L/P&S/8
Political and Secret Subject Files, c. 1880–1920	L/P&S/10

Political and Secret Department Memoranda, *passim*.	L/P&S/18
Political and Secret Department Memoranda Book	Unclassified
Private Office, Miscellaneous Papers	L/PO/Misc.
Public and Judicial Departmental Papers, 1885–1906	L/P&J/6
Public Works Departmental Papers, 1885–1906	L/PWD/6
Papers and Orders relating to the Re-Department	L/R/5
Proceedings (1899–1936)	L/P
Records and Registry Departmental Papers, 1884–1920	L/R/6
Surveyor's Departmental Papers, 1885–1892	L/SUR/7
Surveyor's Department, Miscellaneous Papers	Unclassified

Public Records Office

Cabinet Papers, Currency, 1892	CAB/37/31/5; 12; 15
———, Cantonments Bill, 1895	CAB/37/38/4
———, Cotton Duties, 1895	CAB/37/40/69
———, Currency, 1897	CAB/37/45/35–38
———, Army Administration, 1905	CAB/37/77/95–96

OFFICIAL AND SEMIOFFICIAL PUBLICATIONS

The Dictionary of National Biography, 1900–1940, *passim*.
Godley, Arthur. *Memorandum on the Home Government of India*. London: India Office, 1901.
Great Britain, Parliament. *Cantonments Acts*. C.7148 (1893), LXIV.
———, ———. *Cantonments Acts and Regulations*. C.8919 (1898), LXI.
———, ———. *Correspondence Relating to the Government of India*. C.7731 (1895), LXXII.
———, ———. *East India, Accounts and Papers (Legislation)*. (1876), LVI.
———, ———. *Report of the Committee appointed by the Secretary of State for*

India to enquire into the Home Administration of Indian Affairs. Cmd. 207 (1919), XX.
——, ——. *Report on Indian Constitutional Reforms*, C.9109 (1918), VIII.
——, ——. *Report of the Indian Currency Committee, 1893–94*. C.7060 (1894), LXV.
——, ——. *Report of the Indian Currency Committee, 1899*. C.9390 (1899), XXXI.
——, ——. *Report of the Select Committee on East India Finance*. (1873), XII.
——, ——. *Royal Commission on the Administration of the Expenditure of India*. C.131 (1900), XXIX.
——, ——. *Royal Commission on Civil Establishments*, C.5226 (1887), XIX; C.5545 (1888), XXVII; C.5748 (1889), XXI; C.6172 (1890), XXVII.
——, ——. *Royal Commission on Indian Finance and Currency*, Cd. 7238 (1914), XX.
Hansard's Parliamentary Debates. House of Commons and House of Lords, 1858–1915, *passim*.
India Office Lists, 1858–1920. London: H.M.S.O., *passim*.
The India Office and Burma Office List, 1947 (With Supplement). London: H.M.S.O., 1947.
Proceedings of the Legislative Council [of the Governor-General of India], 1894–99, *passim*.
Reports of the Indian National Congress, 1885–1920, *passim*.

SECONDARY SOURCES

Books

Abbott, E., and Campbell, L. (eds.). *Life and Letters of Benjamin Jowett*. London: John Murray, 1897. 2 vols.
—— (eds.). *Letters of Benjamin Jowett*. London: John Murray, 1899.
Alder, G. J. *British India's Northern Frontier 1865–95*. London: Longmans, Green and Co., 1963.
Ali, Parveen Shaukat. *Pillars of British Imperialism: A Case Study of the Political Ideas of Sir Alfred Lyall, 1813–1903*. Lahore: Aziz Publishers, 1976.
Arbuthnot, Sir Alexander J. *Memories of Rugby and India*. London: Leipsic, T. F. Unwin, 1910.
Argov, Daniel. *Moderates and Extremists in the Indian Nationalist Movement, 1883–1920*. Bombay: Asia Publishing House, 1967.
Armstrong, John A. *The European Administrative Elite*. Princeton, N.J.: Princeton University Press, 1973.
Arnstein, Walter L. *The Bradlaugh Case: A Study in Late Victorian Opinion and Politics*. Oxford: Oxford University Press, 1965.
Arthur, Sir George. *Life of Lord Kitchener*. London: Macmillan and Co., 1920. 3 vols.
Asquith, H. H. [Earl of Oxford and Asquith]. *Memories and Reflections, 1852–1927*. Boston: Little, Brown and Company, 1928. 2 vols.

Bahlman, D.W.R. (ed.). *The Diary of Sir Edward Hamilton, 1880–1885*. Oxford: Oxford University Press, 1972. 2 vols.

Ballhatchet, Kenneth. *Race, Sex and Class Under the Raj: Imperial Attitudes and Policies and Their Critics, 1793–1905*. New York: St. Martin's Press, 1980.

Banerjea, Surendranath. *A Nation in the Making*. London: Oxford University Press, 1925.

Barbour, David. *The Theory of Bimetallism and the Effects of the Partial Demonetisation of Silver of England and India*. London: Cassell and Co., 1885.

Barnard, Chester I. *The Functions of the Executive*. Cambridge, Mass.: Harvard University Press, 1953.

Barrier, N. Gerald. *Banned: Controversial Literature and Political Control in British India 1907–1947*. Columbia, Mo.: University of Missouri Press, 1974.

Bassett, Arthur Tilney. *The Life of the Rt. Hon. John Edward Ellis, M.P.* London: Macmillan and Co., 1914.

Bence-Jones, Mark. *Viceroys of India*. London: Constable, 1982.

Benians, E. A; Butler, J. R. M.; Mansergh, P. N. S.; and Walter, E. A. (eds.). *Cambridge History of the British Empire*. Volume III. Cambridge: Cambridge University Press, 1959.

Benson, A. C., and Esher, Viscount (eds.). *The Letters of Queen Victoria*. Volume III (1854–1861). New York: Longmans, Green and Co., 1907.

Bhatia, B. M. *Famines in India (1860–1965)*. 2nd edition. Bombay: Asia Publishing House, 1967.

Bhattacharya, S. *A Dictionary of Indian History*. New York: George Braziller, 1967.

Birkmyre, William. *The India Council*. London: Cassell and Co., 1885.

———. *The Secretary of State for India in Council*. 2nd edition. London: Cassell and Co., 1886.

———. *The Wealth of India and the Hindrances to Its Increase*. Glasgow: M'Naughtan & Sinclair, 1890.

Blunt, Wilfred S. *My Diaries, Being a Personal Narrative of Events 1888–1914*. New York: Alfred A. Knopf, 1932.

Bolitho, Hector. *James Lyle Mackay, First Earl of Inchcape*. London: John Murray, 1936.

Bonner, H. B. *Charles Bradlaugh. A Record of His Life and Work*. London: T. Fisher Unwin, 1898. 2 vols.

Bose, Nemai Sadhan. *Racism, Struggle for Equality and Indian Nationalism*. Calcutta: Firma KLM Pvt., 1981.

Braybrooke, D., and Lindbloom, Charles. *A Strategy of Decision*. New York: The Free Press, 1963.

Buchan, John. *Lord Minto, A Memoir*. London: Thomas Nelson and Sons, 1924.

Buckle, George E. (ed.). *The Letters of Queen Victoria*. Volumes II, III. New York: Longmans, Green and Co., 1931–1932.

Burne, Owen T. *Memories*. London: Edward Arnold, 1907.

Busch, Briton Cooper. *Britain and the Persian Gulf, 1894–1914*. Berkeley, Calif.: University of California Press, 1967.

Cairncross, A. K. *Home and Foreign Investment, 1870–1913*. Cambridge: University Press, 1953.

Callwell, Sir G. E. (ed.). *The Autobiography of General Sir O'Moore Creagh, V. C., G. C. B., G. C. S. I.* London: Hutchinson & Co., n.d. [1924?].

Carnduff, H. W. C. *Practice & Procedure of the Government of India (Confidential)*. Calcutta: Office of the Superintendent of Government Printing, India, 1906.

Cecil, Lady Gwendolen. *Life of Robert, Marquis of Salisbury*. Volume II. London: Hodder & Stoughton, 1922.

———. *Life of Robert, Marquis of Salisbury*. Volume IV. London: Hodder & Stoughton, 1932.

Chailley, Joseph. *Administrative Problems of British India* Translated by Sir William Meyer. London: Macmillan and Co., 1910.

Chakrabarti, D., and Bhattacharya, C. *Congress in Evolution. A Collection of Congress Resolutions from 1885–1934 and Other Important Documents*. Calcutta: The Book Company, 1935.

Chesney, George. *Indian Polity: A View of the System of Administration in India*. 3rd edition. London: Longmans, Green and Co., 1894.

Chamberlain, M. E. *Britain and India: The Interaction of Two Peoples*. Devon, U. K.: David & Charles, 1974.

Chatterji, P. K. *The Making of India Policy, 1853–65*. New Delhi: Orient Longman, 1975.

Chirol, Valentine. *Indian Unrest*. London: Macmillan and Co., 1910.

Churchill, Winston S. *Lord Randolph Churchill*. Volume I. New York: The Macmillan Co., 1906.

Coyajee, Sir. J. C. *The Indian Currency System (1835–1926)*. Madras: University of Madras, 1930.

Crane, Robert I., and Barrier, N. Gerald (eds.). *British Imperial Policy in India and Sri Lanka, 1858–1912: A Reassessment*. Columbia, Mo.: South Asia Books, 1981.

Crapol, Edward P. *America for Americans. Economic Nationalism and Anglophobia in the Late Nineteenth Century*. Westport, Conn.: Greenwood Press, 1973.

Currie, B. W. *Recollections, Letters and Journals*. London: Roehampton, 1901. 2 vols.

Curzon, G. N. *British Government in India. The Story of the Viceroys and Government House*. London: Cassell and Co., 1925.

———. *Indian Administrative System*. London: Privately Printed by R. Clay & Sons, 1906.

———. *Leaves from a Viceroy's Note-Book and Other Papers*. London: Macmillan and Co., 1926.

Curzon of Kedleston, Marchioness. *Reminiscences*. London: Hutchinson & Co., 1925.

Dadachanji, B. E. *History of Indian Currency and Exchange*. 2nd rev. edition. Bombay: D. B. Taraporevala Sons & Co., 1931.

———. *The Monetary System of India*. 2nd edition. Bombay: D. B. Taraporevala Sons & Co., 1952.

Das, M. N. *India Under Morley and Minto: Politics behind Revolution, Repression and Reforms*. London: George Allen and Unwin, 1964.

Bibliography 213

———. *Indian National Congress Versus the British, 1885–1918*. Delhi: Ajanta Publications, 1978.

Dasgupta, Uma. *Rise of An Indian Public: Impact of Official Policy, 1870–1880*. Calcutta: Riddhi Press, 1977.

Digby, William. *British Rule in India: Has It Been, Is It Still, a Good Rule for the Indian People?* London: Indian Political Agency, 1891.

———. *1857: A Friend in Need; 1887, Friendship Forgotten: An Episode in Indian Foreign Office Administration*. London: Indian Political Agency, 1890.

———. *The General Election of 1885: India's Interest in the British Ballot Box*. London: Indian Political Agency, 1888.

———. *The General Election of 1892: Mr. Digby's Record* (Indian Political Agency Tracts, 1868–94). London: A. Boner Publishers, 1892.

———. *"Prosperous" British India: A Revelation from Official Records*. London: T. Fisher Unwin, 1901.

Dilks, David. *Curzon in India*. London: Rupert Hart-Davis, 1969. 2 vols.

Dodwell, H. H. (ed.). *Cambridge History of India*. The Indian Empire, Volume VI. Cambridge: University Press, 1932.

Duff, Sir M. E. Grant. *Sir Henry Maine. A Brief Memoir of His Life*. New York: Henry Holt & Co., 1892.

Durand, Sir Mortimer. *Life of the Right Hon. Sir Alfred Comyn Lyall*. Edinburgh: William Blackwood and Sons, 1913.

Dutt, Romesh C. *The Economic History of India*. New Delhi: Ministry of Information and Broadcasting, Government of India, 1960. 2 vols.

Edgcumbe, Sir Robert P. *Popular Fallacies Regarding Bimetallism*. London: Macmillan and Co., 1896.

Elsmie, G. R. *Field-Marshall Sir Donald Stewart: An Account of His Life, Mainly in His Own Words*. London: John Murray, 1903.

Faber, Geoffrey. *Jowett. A Portrait with Background*. London: Faber & Faber, 1957.

Feis, Herbert. *Europe, the World's Banker, 1870–1914*. Rev. edition. New York: W. W. Norton & Company, 1965.

Fieldhouse, D. K. *The Colonial Empires. A Comparative Survey from the Eighteenth Century*. New York: Delacorte Press, Dell Publishing Co., 1971.

———. *Economics and Empire, 1830–1914*. Ithaca, N.Y.: Cornell University Press, 1973.

Forrest, G. W. *The Administration of the Marquess of Lansdowne as Viceroy and Governor-General of India, 1888–1894*. Calcutta: Superintendent of Government Printing, India, 1894.

Foster, R. F. *Lord Randolph Churchill: A Political Life*. Oxford: The Clarendon Press, 1981.

Foster, William. *A Descriptive Catalogue of the Paintings, Statues, & c., in the India Office*. London: H. M. S. O., 1924.

———. *The East India House. Its History and Associations*. London: John Lane, The Bodley Head, 1924.

Fowler, E. H. [née Hamilton]. *The Life of Henry Hartley Fowler, First Viscount Wolverhampton, G. C. S. I*. London: Hutchinson and Co., 1912.

Fraser, Lovat. *India Under Curzon & After*. London: W. Heineman, 1911.

Furber, Holden. *John Co. at Work*. Rev. edition. New York: Octagon Press, 1970.

Ghosh, P. C. *The Development of the Indian National Congress, 1892–1909.* Calcutta: Firma K. L. Mukhopadyay, 1960.
Gilbert, Martin (ed.). *Servant of India. A Study of Imperial Rule from 1905–1910 as Told Through the Correspondence and Diaries of Sir James (Robert) Dunlop Smith.* London: Longmans, Green and Co., 1966.
Godley, Eveline (ed.). *Letters of Arthur, Lord Kilbracken and General Sir Alexander Godley.* Cheltenham, Eng.: Privately Printed, 1949.
Godley, John [3rd Lord Kilbracken]. *Living Like a Lord.* London: Victor Gollanz, 1956.
Godley, John Arthur. *D. E. G. [Denis E. Godley] 1890–1896.* London: Roehampton, 1898.
Gopal, S. *British Policy in India, 1858–1905.* Cambridge: Cambridge University Press, 1965.
———. *The Viceroyalty of Lord Ripon, 1880–1884.* London: Oxford University Press, 1953.
Gordon, Donald C. *The Dominion Partnership in Imperial Defence, 1870–1914.* Baltimore: The Johns Hopkins Press, 1965.
Gorst, Harold. *The Fourth Party.* London: Smith, Edler, 1906.
Greaves, Rose Louise. *Persia and the Defence of India, 1884–1892.* London: The Athlone Press, 1959.
Griffiths, Sir Percival. *To Guard My People. The History of the Indian Police.* London: Ernest Benn, 1971.
Hardie, Frank. *The Political Influence of Queen Victoria, 1861–1901.* London: Frank Cass and Co., 1963.
Hamer, F. E. (ed.). *The Personal Papers of Lord Rendel.* London: Ernest Benn, 1931.
Hamer, W. S. *The British Army. Civil-Military Relations, 1885–1905.* Oxford: Oxford University Press, 1970.
Hamilton, Lord George. *Parliamentary Reminiscences and Reflections.* Volume I. London: John Murray, 1917.
———. *Parliamentary Reminiscences and Reflections.* Volume II. London: John Murray, 1922.
Hammond, J. L., and Hammond, Barbara. *James Stansfeld: A Victorian Champion of Sex Equality.* London: Longmans, Green and Co., 1932.
Hardie, Keir J. *India: Impressions and Suggestions.* New York: Huebsch, 1909.
Harnetty, Peter. *Imperialism and Free Trade: Lancashire and India in the Mid-Nineteenth Century.* Vancouver: University of British Columbia Press, 1972.
Hirschmann, Edwin. *"White Mutiny": The Ilbert Bill Crisis in India and Genesis of the Indian National Congress.* Columbia, Mo.: South Asia Books, 1980.
Holderness, Sir T. W. *Peoples and Problems of India.* New York: Henry Holt and Company, 1911.
Holland, Bernard. *The Life of Spencer Compton, Eighth Duke of Devonshire.* Volume I. London: Longmans, Green and Co., 1911.
Hutchinson, Horace G. (ed.). *Private Diaries of the Rt. Hon. Sir Algernon West, G. C. B.* London: John Murray, 1922.
Hyam, Ronald. *Elgin and Churchill at the Colonial Office 1905–1908: The Watershed of the Empire-Commonwealth.* London: Macmillan and Co., 1968.

Ilbert, C. *The Government of India*. 3rd rev. edition. Oxford: The Clarendon Press, 1915.
Imlah, Albert. *Economic Elements in the Pax Britannica*. Cambridge: Cambridge University Press, 1958.
Indian National Congress. Madras: C. A. Nateson & Co., 1909.
Jain, Ranbir Singh. *The Growth & Development of [the] Governor-General's Executive Council (1858–1919)*. Delhi: S. Chand & Co., 1962.
James, Robert Rhodes. *Lord Randolph Churchill*. London: Weidenfeld and Nicolson, 1959.
———. *Rosebery: A Biography of Archibald Philip, Fifth Earl of Rosebery*. London: Weidenfeld and Nicolson, 1963.
Johnson, Gordon. *Provincial Politics and Indian Nationalism: Bombay and the Indian National Congress, 1880–1915*. Cambridge: Cambridge University Press, 1973.
Jones, Ray. *The Nineteenth-Century Foreign Office: An Administrative History*. London: Weidenfeld and Nicolson, 1971.
Kazemzadeh, Firuz. *Russia and Britain in Persia, 1864–1914. A Study in Imperialism*. New Haven, Conn.: Yale University Press, 1968.
Kaushik, Harish P. *The Indian National Congress in England (1885–1920)*. Delhi: Research, 1973.
Keith, A. Berriedale. *A Constitutional History of India, 1600–1935*. 2nd rev. edition. London: Metheun & Co., 1937.
Keynes, John Maynard. *Indian Currency and Finance*. Reprint. London: Macmillan and Co., 1971.
———. *The Collected Writings of John Maynard Keynes. Activities 1906–1914: India and Cambridge, Volume XV*. London: Macmillan and Co., 1971.
Kilbracken, Lord. *Reminiscences of Lord Kilbracken*. London: Macmillan and Co., 1931.
———. *S. K. [Sarah Kilbracken] 1871–1921*. London: Privately Printed, 1921.
Knaplund, Paul. *The British Empire, 1815–1939*. New York: Harper & Brothers, 1941.
———. *James Stephen and the British Colonial System, 1813–1847*. Madison, Wis.: University of Wisconsin Press, 1953.
Koss, Stephen. *John Morley at the India Office, 1905–1910*. New Haven, Conn.: Yale University Press, 1969.
Kubicek, Robert V. *The Administration of Imperialism: Joseph Chamberlain at the Colonial Office*. Durham, N.C.: Duke University Press, 1969.
Langer, William. *The Diplomacy of Imperialism, 1890–1902*. 2nd edition. New York: Alfred A. Knopf, 1965.
Laurie, Col. W. F. B. *Sketches of Some Distinguished Anglo-Indians, with an Account of Anglo-Indian Periodical Literature*. Rev. edition. London: W. H. Allen & Co., 1887.
Lawrence, Walter R. *The India We Served*. Boston: Houghton Mifflin Company, 1929.
Leigh-Smith, Phillip. *Record of an Ascent: A Memoir of Sir Richmond Thackeray Ritchie*. Cambridge: Dillon's University Bookshop, 1961.
Lindbloom, C. E. *The Policy-Making Process*. Englewood-Cliffs, N.J.: Prentice-Hall, 1968.

———. *A Strategy of Decision: Policy Evaluation as a Social Science*. New York: The Free Press of Glencoe, 1963.
Lloyd, T. *Bimetallism Examined*. London: "Statist" Press, 1894.
Lord Curzon in India, Being a Selection from His Speeches as Viceroy and Governor-General of India 1898–1905 with an Introduction by Sir Thomas Raleigh. London: Macmillan and Co., 1906.
Lucas, Sir Charles Prestwood. *The Empire at War*. London: Oxford University Press, 1921–1926. 5 vols.
Lucy, Sir Henry William. *A Diary of Two Parliaments*. 2nd edition. London: Cassell and Company, 1885–1886.
Lyall, A. C. *The Life of the Marquis of Dufferin and Ava*. London: John Murray, 1905. 2 vols.
———. *The Rise and Expansion of the British Dominion in India*. London: John Murray, 1920.
Macgregor, Sir Charles. *The Defence of India: A Strategical Study*. Simla: Government Central Branch Press, 1884.
MacLeod, H. D. *Bimetallism*. 2nd edition. London: Longmans, Green and Co., 1894.
———. *Indian Currency*. London: Longmans, Green and Co., 1898.
Magnus, Phillip. *Gladstone*. New York: E. P. Dutton & Co., 1964.
———. *Kitchener: Portrait of an Imperialist*. New York: E. P. Dutton & Co., 1968.
Malhotra, D. K. *History and Problems of Indian Currency, 1835–1949*. 5th edition. Simla: Minerva Book Shop, 1949.
Malhotra, P. L. *Administration of Lord Elgin in India, 1894–99*. New Delhi: Vikas Publishing House Pvt., 1979.
Mallet, Bernard. *Sir Louis Mallet. A Record of Public Service and Political Ideals*. London: James Nisbet & Co., 1905.
Martin, Briton, Jr. *New India: 1885*. Berkeley, Calif.: University of California Press, 1969.
Martin, Ralph G. *Jennie: The Life of Lady Randolph Churchill*. New York: Signet, 1969. 2 vols.
Masani, R. P. *Dadbhai Naoroji*. London: G. Allen & Unwin, 1939.
Matthew, H. C. G. *The Liberal Imperialists. The Ideas and Politics of a Post-Gladstonian Elite*. London: Oxford University Press, 1973.
Mehrotra, S. R. *The Emergence of the Indian National Congress*. Delhi: Vikas Publications, 1971.
———. *India and the Commonwealth 1885–1929*. London: G. Allen & Unwin, 1965.
Mersey, Viscount. *The Viceroys and Governors-General of India, 1757–1947*. London: John Murray, 1949.
Metcalf, Thomas R. *The Aftermath of Revolt, India 1857–1870*. Princeton, N.J.: Princeton University Press, 1965.
Midleton, Earl of. *Records and Reactions, 1856–1939*. London: John Murray, 1939.
Minto, Mary, Countess of. *India, Minto and Morley: India 1905–1910, Compiled from . . . Correspondence [and] from . . . Her Indian Journal*. London: Macmillan and Co., 1934.
Misra, B. B. *The Bureaucracy in India: An Historical Analysis of Development up to 1947*. Delhi: Oxford University Press, 1977.

———. *The Central Administration of the East India Company, 1773–1834*. Manchester: Manchester University Press, 1959.
Misra, J. P. *The Administration of India Under Lord Lansdowne (1885–1894)*. New Delhi: Sterling Publishers, 1975.
Mody, H. P. *Sir Pherozeshah Mehta: A Political Biography*. Bombay: The Times Press, 1921. 2 vols.
Moore, R. J. *Sir Charles Wood's Indian Policy, 1853–66*. Manchester: Manchester University Press, 1966.
———. *Liberalism and Indian Politics, 1872–1922*. London: Edward Arnold, 1966.
Morgan, John H. *John, Viscount Morley: An Appreciation and Some Reminiscences*. Boston: Houghton Mifflin Company, 1924.
Morgan, Kenneth O. *Keir Hardie, Radical and Socialist*. London: Weidenfeld and Nicolson, 1975.
Morley, John. *The Life of William Ewart Gladstone*. London: Macmillan and Co., 1903. 3 vols.
———. *Recollections*. New York: The Macmillan Co., 1917.
———. *Speeches on Indian Affairs*. Madras: G. A. Natesan & Co., n.d. [1910?].
Morris, A. J. A. (ed.). *Edwardian Radicalism 1900–1914*. London: Routledge & Kegan Paul, 1974.
Mosley, Leonard. *Curzon: The End of an Epoch*. London: Longmans, Green and Co., 1960.
Moulton, Edward C. *Lord Northbrook's Indian Administration, 1872–1876*. Bombay: Asia Publishing House, 1968.
Nanda, B. R. *Gokhale: The Indian Moderates and the British Raj*. Delhi and London: Oxford University Press, 1977.
Naoroji, Dadabhai. *Poverty and UnBritish Rule in India*. London: S. Sonnenschein & Co., 1901.
Narain, Prem. *Press and Politics in India, 1885–1905*. Delhi: Munshiram Manoharlal, 1970.
Natarajan, J. *History of Indian Journalism*. Delhi: Government of India Press, 1954.
Newton, Lord. *Lord Lansdowne. A Biography*. London: Macmillan and Co., 1929.
O'Donnell, C. J. *The Causes of Present Discontent in India*. London: T. Fisher Unwin, 1908.
O'Malley, L. S. S. *The Indian Civil Service, 1801–1930*. Rev. edition. London: Frank Cass & Co., 1963.
Owen, E. R. J., and Sutcliff, R. B. (eds.). *Studies in the Theory of Imperialism*. London: Longmans, Green and Co., 1972.
Pandey, B. N. (ed.). *The Indian Nationalist Movement, 1885–1947: Select Documents*. London: Macmillan and Co., 1979.
Parris, Henry. *Constitutional Bureaucracy. The Development of British Central Administration since the Eighteenth Century*. London: George Allen & Unwin, 1969.
Patwardhan, R. P., and Ambekar, D. V. (eds.). *Speeches and Writings of Gopal Krishna Gokhale*. Volume I. Bombay: Asia Publishing House, 1962.
Patwardhan, R. P. (ed.). *Dadabhai Naoroji Correspondence*. Bombay: Allied Publishers, 1977. 2 vols.
Paul, S. N. *Public Opinion and British Rule: A Study of the Influence of Indian*

Public Opinion on British Administration and Bureaucracy, 1899-1914. New Delhi: Metropolitan Book Co., 1979.

Peel, George (ed.). *The Gold Standard Papers, 1895.* London: Cassell and Co., 1895.

———. *The Gold Standard: A Selection from the Papers Issued by the Gold Standard Defence Association in 1895-1898.* London: Cassell and Co., 1898.

Pellew, Jill. *The Home Office, 1848-1914: From Clerks to Bureaucrats.* London: W. Heinemann, 1982.

Philips, C. H. *The East India Company, 1784-1834.* 2nd edition. Manchester: Manchester University Press, 1961.

———, (ed.). *The Evolution of India and Pakistan 1858-1947: Select Documents.* London: Oxford University Press, 1962.

———, (ed.). *Historians of India, Pakistan and Ceylon.* London: Oxford University Press, 1961.

Probyn, L. C. *Indian Coinage and Currency.* London: Effingham Wilson, 1897.

Pope-Hennessey, James. *Lord Crewe, 1858-1945: The Likeness of a Liberal.* London: Constable & Co., 1955.

Ratcliffe, S. K. *Sir William Wedderburn and the Indian Reform Movement.* London: G. Allen and Unwin, 1923.

Reid, Fred. *Keir Hardie: The Making of a Socialist.* London: Croom Helm, 1978.

Robb, Peter G. *The Government of India and Reform: Policies towards Politics and the Constitution, 1916-1921.* Oxford: Oxford University Press, 1976.

Robertson, J. M. *Charles Bradlaugh. A Record of His Life and Work.* London: T. F. Unwin, 1898.

Rose, Kenneth. *Superior Person: A Portrait of Curzon and His Circle in Late Victorian England.* London: Weidenfeld and Nicolson, 1969.

Roseveare, Henry. *The Treasury.* London: Allen Lane, The Penguin Press, 1969.

Ronaldshay, Earl of. *The Life of Lord Curzon.* London: E. Benn, 1928. 3 vols.

Rudra, A. B. *The Viceroy and Governor-General of India.* London: Oxford University Press, 1940.

Russell, G. W. E. *Collections and Recollections.* New York: Harper & Brothers, 1899.

Seton, Sir Malcolm. *The India Office.* London: G. P. Putnam's Sons, 1926.

Sharma, Parmatma. *The Imperial Legislative Council of India (from 1861 to 1920).* Delhi: S. Chand & Co., 1961.

Shirras, G. Findlay. *Indian Finance and Banking.* London: Macmillan and Co., 1919.

Simon, Herbert A. *Administrative Behavior.* New York: The Macmillan Co., 1957.

Singh, H. L. *Problems and Policies of the British in India, 1885-1898.* Bombay: Asia Publishing House, 1963.

Singh, S. N. *The Secretary of State for India and His Council (1858-1919).* Delhi: Munshi Manohar Lal, 1962.

Sitaramayya, B. Pattabhi. *The History of the Indian National Congress (1885-1935).* Madras: The Working Committee of the Congress, 1935.

Spangenberg, Bradford. *British Bureaucracy in India: Status, Policy and the I. C. S., in the Late 19th Century.* Columbia, Mo.: South Asia Books, 1976.

Spear, Percival (ed.). *The Oxford History of India.* 3rd edition. Oxford: The Clarendon Press, 1967.

Speeches by Lord Curzon of Kedleston, 1898–1900. Calcutta: Office of the Superintendent of Government Printing, India, 1900.
Srivastava, Hari Shanker. *The History of Indian Famines and the Development of Famine Policy, 1858–1918*. Agra: Sri Ram Mehra, 1968.
Staebler, W. *The Liberal Mind of John Morley*. Princeton, N.J.: Princeton University Press, 1943.
Stansky, P. *Ambitions and Strategies. The Struggle for Leadership of the Liberal Party in the 1890's*. Oxford: The Clarendon Press, 1964.
Steiner, Zara S. *The Foreign Office and Foreign Policy, 1898–1914*. Cambridge: Cambridge University Press, 1969.
Stokes, Whitley (ed.). *Sir Henry Maine... Speeches and Minutes, by Sir M. E. Grant-Duff*. New York: Henry Holt and Co., 1892.
Strachey, Sir John. *India: Its Administration and Progress*. 4th edition. London: Macmillan and Co., 1911.
Sturges, James L. *John Bright and the Empire*. London: The Athlone Press, 1969.
Sutherland, Lucy S. *The East India Company in Eighteenth Century Politics*. Oxford: The Clarendon Press, 1952.
Sutherland, Gillian (ed.). *Studies in the Growth of Nineteenth-Century Government*. London: Routledge & Kegan Paul, 1972.
Temple, Sir Richard. *Letters & Character Sketches from the House of Commons*. London: John Murray, 1912.
Thorner, Daniel. *Investment in Empire: British Railway and Steam-Shipping Enterprise in India, 1825–1849*. Philadelphia: University of Pennsylvania Press, 1950.
Tollemache, Lionel A. *Benjamin Jowett: Master of Balliol*. London: Edward Arnold, 1895.
Tullock, Gordon. *The Politics of Bureaucracy*. Washington, D.C.: Public Affairs Press, 1965.
Vakil, C. N. and Muranjan, S. K. *Currency and Prices in India*. Bombay: P. S. King & Son, 1927.
Wasti, Syed Razi. *Lord Minto and the Indian Nationalist Movement, 1905–1910*. Oxford: The Clarendon Press, 1964.
Wedderburn, Sir William. *Allan Octavian Hume, C. B., "Father of the Indian National Congress," 1829 to 1912*. London: T. Fisher Unwin, 1913.
———. *Speeches and Writings of Sir William Wedderburn*. Madras: G. A. Natesan & Co., 1918.
West, Algernon. *Contemporary Portraits. Men of My Day in Public Life*. London: T. Fisher Unwin, 1920.
———. *Sir Charles Wood's Administration of Indian Affairs from 1859 to 1866*. London: Smith, Elder and Co., 1867.
Williams, Donovan. *The India Office, 1858–1869*. Hoshiarpur, Punjab: Vishveshvaranand Vedic Research Institute, 1983.
Williams, Donovan and Potts, E. Daniel (eds.). *Essays in Indian History in Honour of C. C. Davies*. Delhi: Asia Publishing House, 1974.
Wilson, John. *CB: A Life of Sir Henry Campbell-Bannerman*. London: Constable and Co., 1973.
Wolf, Lucien. *Life of the First Marquess of Ripon*. London: John Murray, 1921. 2 vols.

Wolpert, S. A. *Morley and India, 1906–1910*. Berkeley and Los Angeles: University of California Press, 1967.
———. *Tilak and Gokhale: Revolution and Reform in the Making of Modern India*. Berkeley, Calif.: University of California Press, 1962.
Woodruff, Phillip. *The Men Who Ruled India*. London: Jonathan Cape, 1965.
Wright, Maurice. *Treasury Control of the Civil Service, 1854–1874*. Oxford: The Clarendon Press, 1969.
Yasin, Madhvi. *Indian Administration: A Study of Indian Polity towards the End of the Nineteenth Century*. New Delhi: Light & Life Publishers, 1979.
Zaidi, A. Moin and Shaheda (eds.). *The Encyclopedia of the Indian National Congress*. New Delhi: S. Chand & Co., 1976–81. 8 vols.

Articles

Anonymous. "The House That Scott Built," *Cornhill Magazine* 16 (1867), 356–69.
———. "An Indian Correspondent: Why We Went to Chitral," *Blackwood's Magazine*, 158 (September 1895), 402–419.
———. "Lord Curzon, Lord Kitchener, and Mr. Brodrick," *Blackwood's Magazine* 178 (September 1905), 427–44.
———. "Sir Charles Wood's Administration of Indian Affairs," *Blackwood's Magazine* 102 (December 1867), 686–701.
Aylmer, G. E. "Problems of Method in the Study of Administrative History," *Annali della Fondazione Italiana per la Storia Amministrativa* 1 (1964), 20–26.
Bhattacharya, Sukumar. "The Men Who Ruled India, 1899–1901," *Modern Review* 102 (August 1957), 114–19.
Cell, John W. "The Colonial Office in the 1850's," *Historical Journal* 12:48 (October 1965), 43–56.
Chandran, J. "Queen Victoria, Gladstone and the Viceroyalty of India, 1893–1894," *New Zealand Journal of History* 3:2 (October 1969), 175–89.
Clark, G. Kitson. " 'Statesmen in Disguise': Reflections on the History of the Neutrality of the Civil Service," *Historical Journal* 2:1 (1959), 19–39.
Cohen, Stephen P. "Issue, Role and Personality: The Kitchener-Curzon Dispute," *Comparative Studies in Society and History* 10:3 (April 1968), 337–55.
Compton, J. M. "Open Competition and the ICS, 1854–76," *English Historical Review* 83:327 (1968), 261–84.
Cotton, Henry. "Civil Service in India," *Contemporary Review* 104 (October 1913), 477–86.
Cromwell, Valerie. "Interpretations of Nineteenth-Century Administration: An Analysis," *Victorian Studies* 9:3 (March 1966), 245–54.
Cumpston, M. "Some Early Indian Nationalists and Their Allies in the British Parliament, 1851–1906," *English Historical Review* 76 (1961), 279–97.
Curtin, Phillip. "The British Empire and Commonwealth in Recent Historiography," *American Historical Review* 65:1 (October 1959), 72–91.
Davies, C. C. "India and Queen Victoria," *Journal of the East India Association* 28 (1937), 200–215.
Duthie, John Lowe. "Pressure From Within: The 'Forward' Group in the India

Office During Gladstone's First Ministry," *Journal of Asian History* 15 (1981), 36–72.
Forrest, Sir George. "Sir Alfred Lyall," *Blackwood's Magazine* 193 (May 1913), 698–715.
———. "Plague in India," *Blackwood's Magazine* 182 (October 1895), 413–22.
Galbraith, John S. "The 'Turbulent Frontier' as a Factor in British Expansion," *Comparative Studies in Society and History* 2:2 (January 1960), 150–68.
Ghose, A. S. "India's Case for Silver," *North American Review* 165:491 (1897), 477–86.
Gokhale, B. G. "John Bright and India (1848–1861)," *Journal of Indian History* 41 (April 1963), 57–67.
Gunn, Lewis. "Politicians and Officials: Who Is Answerable?" *Political Quarterly* 43 (1972), 253–60.
Harnetty, Peter. "British and Indian Attitudes to the Indian Problem at the End of the Nineteenth Century," *Report, 1959, of the Annual Meeting of the Canadian Historical Association*, pp. 48–62.
———. "The Indian Cotton Duties Controversy, 1894–1896," *English Historical Review* 77:35 (October 1962), 684–702.
———. "Nationalism and Imperialism in India (The Viceroyalty of Lord Curzon, 1899–1905)," *Journal of Indian History* 41:2 (August 1963), 391–403.
Hart, Jenifer. "Nineteenth-Century Social Reform: A Tory Interpretation of History," *Past and Present* 31 (July 1965), 39–61.
Hazlewood, Arthur. "The Origin of the State Telephone Service in Britain," *Oxford Economic Papers*, Ser. 2, 5:1 (March 1953), 13–25.
Husain, S. A. "The Secretary of State for India and His Council: An Analysis of Organisation and Procedure, 1858–1919," *Bangladesh Historical Studies* 4 (1979), 64–76.
———. "The Administrative Departments of the India Office, 1858–1919," *Indian Journal of Public Administration* 27 (1981), 430–43.
Jacobson, Peter D. "Rosebery and Liberal Imperialism, 1899–1903," *Journal of British Studies* 13:1 (November 1973), 83–107.
Jinnah, M. A. "Reorganizing the India Council," *Fortnightly Review*, Old Series 102 (October 1914), 612–20.
Kaminsky, Arnold P. "Morality Legislation and British Troops in Late Nineteenth Century India," *Military Affairs* 43:2, (1979), 78–83.
———. " 'Lombard Street' and India: Currency Problems in the Late Nineteenth Century," *The Indian Economic and Social History Review* 17:3 (July-September 1980), 307–27.
Kennedy, P. M. "Imperial Cable Communication and Strategy, 1870–1914," *English Historical Review* 86:341 (October 1971), 728–52.
Khera, P. N. "Role of the Indian Army, 1900–1939," *Royal United Service Institution of India Journal* 94 (July 1964), 277–89.
———. "Impact of India's Foreign Policy on Her Military Policy and the Role of the Army in India, 1899–1921," *Quarterly Review of Historical Studies* (Calcutta) 4:4 (1964–65), 195–202.
Koss, Stephen. "John Morley and the Communal Question," *Indo-British Review* (Madras) 1:3 (January-March 1969), 59–63.

———. "Morley and Kitchener," *Indo-British Review* (Madras) 2:3 (October-December 1969), 49–54.
Kurian, G. B. T. "Early British Viceroys and the Indian National Congress," *Indo-British Review* (Madras) 1:4 and 2:1 (1969), 71–86.
Lancaster, Joan C. "The India Office Records," *Archives* 9:43 (April 1970), 130–41.
Lee-Warner, William. "Civil Service of India," *Nineteenth-Century* 74 (August 1913), 233–43.
MacDonagh, O. "The Nineteenth-Century Revolution in Government: A Reappraisal," *The Historical Journal* 1:1 (1958), 52–67.
McLane, J. R. "The Decision to Partition Bengal," *The Indian Economic and Social History Review* 2 (July 1965), 221–37.
MacLeod, Roy M. "Statesmen Undisguised," *American Historical Review* 78:5 (December 1973), 1386–1406.
Majumdar, R. C. "The Manipur Rebellion of 1891," *Bengal Past and Present* 78 (January-June 1959), 1–29.
———. "Rebellion in Manipur, 1891," *Indian Historical Records Commission, Proceedings* 35 (February 1960), 140–50.
Malleson, Wilfred. "Curzon and Kitchener: Some Personal Reminiscences," *Fortnightly Review* 130 (August 1928), 145–50.
Misra, J. P. "Lansdowne and the Indian National Congress," *Indo-British Review* (Madras) 1:3 (January-March 1969), 22–28.
Moore, R. J. "The Composition of 'Wood's Education Despatch,' " *English Historical Review* 80:314 (1965), 70–85.
Morley, John. "British Democracy and Indian Government," *NineteenthCentury and After* 69 (February 1911), 189–209.
Oddie, G. "Some British Attitudes Towards Reform and Repression in India, 1917–1920," *Australian Journal of Political History* 19 (August 1973), 224–40.
Parris, Henry. "The Nineteenth-Century Revolution in Government: A Reappraisal Reappraised," *The Historical Journal* 3:1 (1960), 17–37.
Patwardhan, Dileep. "British India and Imperial Defence: Aspects of Military Organization and Defence Expenditure, 1858–1900," *India* 17 (1980), 61–71.
Penner, Peter. "Haileybury: School for Anglo-Indian Statesmanship," *Bengal Past and Present* 93 (January-April 1974), 39–58.
Platt, D. C. M. "The National Economy and British Imperial Expansion before 1914," *Journal of Imperial and Commonwealth History* 2:1 (October 1973), 3–14.
Pugh, R. B. "The Colonial Office, 1801–1925," in E. A. Benians, *et al.* (eds.), *Cambridge History of the British Empire*. Volume III. London: Cambridge University Press, 1959, pp. 711–68.
Rai, Lala Lajput. "The Debate on the India Councils Bill in the House of Lords," *Modern Review* (Calcutta) 16 (September 1914), 299–303.
Rothermund, Dietmar. "India's Silver Currency, 1876–1893," in Dietmar Rothermund, *Phases of Indian Nationalism and other Essays*. Bombay: Nachiketa Publications, 1970, pp. 249–65.
Schwartz, Anne Jacobson. "Monetary Trends in the United States and the United

Kingdom, 1878–1970: Selected Findings," *Journal of Economic History* 35 (March 1975), 138–59.
Slagg, John. "The National Indian Congress," *Nineteenth Century* 19 (May 1866), 710–21.
———. "Parliament and the Government of India," *Contemporary Review* 45 (February 1884), 210–23.
Smith, Brian. "Sir Henry Maine," *Indo-British Review* (Madras) 1:1 (June-August 1968), 75–79.
———. "Sir Henry Maine and the Government of India (1862–87)," *Journal of Indian History* 41 (December 1963), 565–75.
Spangenberg, Bradford. "The Problems of Recruitment for the Indian Civil Service During the Late Nineteenth Century," *The Journal of Asian Studies* 30:2 (February 1971), 341–60.
Steiner, Zara and Dockrill, M. L. "The Foreign Office Reforms, 1919–21," *The Historical Journal* 17:1 (March 1974), 131–56.
Stokes, Eric T. "The Administrators and Historical Writing on India," in C. H. Philips (ed.), *Historians of India, Pakistan and Ceylon*. London: Oxford University Press, 1961, 385–403.
Sutherland, Gillian. "Recent Trends in Administrative History," *Victorian Studies* 13:4 (June 1970), 408–11.
———. "Reform of the English Civil Service 1780–1914: A Project for a Colloquium," *Past and Present* 42 (1969), 163–65.
Temple, Richard. "The Manipur Blue-Book," *Contemporary Review* 59 (June 1891), 917–24.
Thorner, Daniel. "Great Britain and the Development of India's Railways," *Journal of Economic History* 11 (1951), 389–402.
Tripathi, A. "India Office on the Indian National Congress," *Indian Historical Records Commission, Proceedings* 35:2 (February 1960), 203–7.
Tripathi, Dwijendra. "The Silver Question: India and America," *Journal of Indian History* 44:3 (December 1966), 789–93.
Vakil, C. N. "Employment of Indian Troops out of India," *Modern Review* (Allahabad) 32 (September 1922), 301–7.
Warman, Roberta. "The Erosion of Foreign Office of Influence in the Making of Foreign Policy, 1916–18," *The Historical Journal* 15:1 (1972), 150–57.
Williams, Donovan. "Clements Robert Markham and the Introduction of the Chinchona Tree into British India, 1861," *The Geographical Journal* 128:4 (December 1962), 431–42.
———. "Clements Robert Markham and the Geographical Department of the India Office, 1867–77," *The Geographical Journal* 134:3 (September 1968), 343–52.
———. "The Council of India and the Relationship between the Home and Supreme Governments, 1858–1870," *English Historical Review* 81:318 (January 1966), 70–85.
———. "The Formation of Policy in the India Office, (1858–1869): A Study in the Tyranny of the Past," *Journal of Indian History* (Golden Jubilee Volume)(1973), 873–92.
Wood, John. "Henry Fawcett and the British Empire," *The Indian Economic and Social History Review* 41:4 (1979), 395–414.

Unpublished Theses and Papers

Bandyopadhyay, Premansukumar. "British Famine and Agricultural Policies in India, with special reference to the Administration of Lord George Hamilton, 1895–1903," Ph.D. dissertation, University of London, 1969.

Chandra, Bipan. "Economic Policies of Indian National Leadership, 1880–1905," Ph.D. dissertation, Delhi, 1963.

Coughlan, Heather T. "The Role of the Council of India, 1898–1910," Ph.D. dissertation, Duke University, 1971.

———. "The Royal Commission upon Decentralization: The British *Raj* and Indian Opinion, 1907–1909," M.A. thesis, Duke University, 1965.

Gilbert, Marc Jason. "Lord Lansdowne in India: At the Climax of an Empire, 1888–1894, a study in Late Nineteenth Century British Indian Policy and Proconsular Power." Ph.D. dissertation, University of California, Los Angeles, 1978.

Harris, Leslie. "British Policy on the North-West Frontier of India, 1889–1901," Ph.D. dissertation, University of London, 1960.

Husain, S. A. "The Organisation and Administration of the India Office, 1910–1924," Ph.D. dissertation, University of London, 1978.

Lydgate, John. "Curzon, Kitchener and the Problem of Indian Army Administration, 1899–1909," Ph.D. dissertation, University of London, 1965.

Malhotra, Piarea Lal. "The Internal Administration of Lord Elgin in India, 1894–1898," Ph.D. dissertation, School of Oriental and African Studies (London), 1966.

Moir, Martin. "A Study of the History and Organisation of the Political and Secret Departments of the East India Company, the Board of Control and the India Office, 1784–1919, with a summary list of records," Archival Administration, University of London, 1966.

Morrow, Margot Duley. "The Origins and Early Years of the British Committee of the Indian National Congress, 1885–1907," Ph.D. dissertation, London University, 1977.

———. "The British Committee of the Indian National Congress as an Issue in and an Influence upon Nationalist Politics, 1889–1901," unpublished paper presented to the Seventh European Conference on Modern Asian Studies, London, 1981.

———. "The Limits of Radical Anti-Imperial Ideology: The Case of the British Committee of the Indian National Congress and the Indian Parliamentary Committee, 1889–1906," unpublished paper presented to the Southern Conference on British Studies, Louisville, 1981.

Moulton, Edward. "William Wedderburn and Early Indian Nationalism," unpublished paper presented to the Seventh European Conference on Modern Asian Studies, London, 1981.

———. "Indian Nationalism and British Radicals: William Wedderburn and the Indian National Congress, 1885–1917," unpublished paper presented to the Western Conference of the Association for Asian Studies, Boise, 1979.

Robb, Peter G. "The Government of India Under Lord Chelmsford, 1916–1921, with special reference to the Policies Adopted towards Constitutional Change

and Political Agitation in British India," Ph.D. dissertation, University of London, 1971.
Ryland, Shane. "The Making of the Government of India Act, 1919," Ph.D. dissertation, Duke University, 1969.
Tate, R. S. "The Home Government of India, 1834–1853," Ph.D. dissertation, University of London, 1972.
Williams, Donovan. "The Formation of Policy in the India Office, 1858–66, with special reference to the Political, Judicial, Revenue, Public and Public Works Departments," D. Phil. dissertation, Oxford, 1962.
———. "The Tyranny of the Past: The India Office, 1858–70," unpublished paper presented to ASPAC Conference, San Diego, 1974.
Zoberi, Z. H. "The Relations between the Home and Indian Governments, 1858–1870," Ph.D. dissertation, University of London, 1949.

Newspapers and Periodicals

Blackwood's Magazine, 1867–1905.
Cornhill Magazine, 1867.
Contemporary Review, 1884, 1913.
Fortnightly Review, 1928.
India, 1890–1921.
Manchester Guardian, 1880–1910.
Nineteenth Century and After, 1911.
North American Review, 1897.
Pall Mall Gazette (London), 1885–1886.
Punch, 1858–1910.
The Times (London), 1880–1910, 1932.

APPENDIX A

Biographical Note on Sir Arthur Godley

John Arthur Godley was born in London June 17, 1847. He was the eldest son of John Robert Godley and Charlotte Godley, the daughter of well-known parliamentarian, G. C. Wynne. An extremely capable man, John Robert had been instrumental in founding the Canterbury Settlement in New Zealand (1849–1852), served as Assistant Undersecretary of State at the War Office (1854–1861), and was touted as a possible Cabinet member before his premature death in 1861.[1] While the father never had his opportunity to rise in public life, his son never sought to, opting instead for a career behind the scenes and without glory, in the India Office. W. E. Gladstone knew them both intimately, and once admitted candidly that he had great difficulty in saying "which was the greater man, the father or the son," and the family today is equally divided as to which man was "the Great Godley."[2]

As a youth, Arthur Godley showed a keen interest in shooting (which he later gave up), nautical matters, and athletics. But these leisure diversions were quickly subordinated to the academic life. By the time Godley started Radley when he was almost ten, he had already acquired a good working knowledge of French. Subsequently Godley was educated at Rugby—to which he was devoted all of his life, spending much of his post-India Office career on the Board of Governors of the school—and at Oxford's Balliol College. At Oxford Godley won the Hertford (1868) and Ireland (1870) scholarships as well as several major prizes for Latin and Greek verse and prose. Although he qualified for a legal career, having won the Eldon law scholarship in 1874 and having been called to the bar at Lincoln's Inn in 1876, Godley never actively practiced law. Instead, in part due to his father's connection with the Grand Old Man of the English Liberal party, and also because of his own distinguished academic career,

Godley became one of Gladstone's junior Private Secretaries between 1872 and 1874, and the Prime Minister's principal Private Secretary between 1880 and 1882.

The Oxford connection also had a great influence on Arthur Godley's subsequent career at the India Office. At Balliol he was under the tutelage of the distinguished Liberal Master of the College, Benjamin Jowett. Jowett's strongest point, according to Godley, was as a trainer of young men, for he imparted to his charges "his high standard of duty and his intolerance of any but the loftiest and at the same time the most practical aims, in whatever was to be undertaken."[3] Godley never deviated from that dictum at the India Office.

Godley's intellectual abilities were quietly but generally acknowledged by his contemporaries. H. H. Asquith, after lunching with the then seventy-seven-year-old Lord Kilbracken, once noted that the former Undersecretary of State for India was "the most distinguished Balliol man of his time," and Algernon West reminisced that Godley was Gladstone's ultimate reference in knotty questions about the classics.[4] West recounted that it had to be "an insoluble problem indeed which [Godley's] ever ripe scholarship cannot answer in a thrice."[5] The "old school tie" system was an important asset for Arthur Godley, as it enabled him to maintain intimacies with influential people, in and out of government, while he was at the India Office. There is an element of truth in the question lightheartedly suggested to Godley by his lifelong friend, Lord Rosebery: "What would Godley have been had he gone to Cambridge instead of Oxford?"[6]

Godley served his political apprenticeship as private secretary to Liberal leaders Gladstone and Lord Granville. He had virtually carte blanche responsibility with regard to the Prime Minister's correspondence.[7] During this service Godley was "saturated with Gladstonian tradition as to the earnestness of work," and in 1882 he was rewarded with his first political office as a Commissioner of Inland Revenue.[8] Since Godley had had close ties with Gladstone since boyhood (when his father was at the War Office), his appointment to Inland Revenue is probably justifiably "pure patronage."[9] Godley, in fact, maintained a lifelong friendship with Gladstone, although he declined to write his biography, recommending instead John Morley for the task. When his own *Reminiscences* (London, 1931) were publicly released (partly to correct some of Morley's work) at the request of Herbert Gladstone, Lord Kilbracken commented that his estimate of the great Liberal leader was "on this side of idolatry."[10]

After brief service at Inland Revenue, Godley was appointed Permanent Undersecretary of State for India at the tender age of thirty-five. Godley recalled having been recommended to the post "severally and independently" by Lords Hartington (Secretary of State for India), Northbrook (former Viceroy of India) and Sir Louis Mallet (the retiring Permanent

Undersecretary). "Mr. Gladstone," Godley later recalled, "had had nothing to do with it and did not even know of the impending vacancy until my name had been submitted to him by Lord Kimberley [Hartington's successor] for his approval."[11] In actuality, Mallet had recommended Sir Evelyn Baring (later Lord Cromer) for the position.[12] Baring, however, was ticketed for Egypt where he would become one of the Empire's great proconsuls, leaving Mallet no option but to endorse Kimberley's offer of the post, *with* Gladstone's previous knowledge and consent, to Godley in May 1883, four months before Mallet's departure from the India Office. Efforts to keep the appointment sub rosa until Godley could actually assume his new office were unsuccessful,[13] and when word leaked out the press immediately attacked the appointment as bearing "all the appearance of a [political] job."[14] In Parliament the appointment was severely criticized by Lord George Hamilton who, ironically enough, was destined to serve as Godley's chief at the India Office for over eight of his twenty-six years as Permanent Undersecretary.[15]

Godley's management of the India Office and his beliefs about the constitutional relationships therein are important for the evolution of that institution. Hence a few comments about Godley's view of his professional role and the relationship of his personal life to it help place his official career in better perspective. This is of special importance because the work of the India Office was so diverse that in a given day the Permanent Undersecretary of State could order a military expedition on India's Northwest frontiers, handle negotiations for a charwoman's salary, or review an architect's designs for map drawers for the Geographical-Records Department. This work was so "extensive and peculiar," that Godley felt completely confident in his abilities to handle it only after eight years in harness.[16]

Paramount among his personal and professional characteristics was Godley's devotion to duty. This attitude was deeply rooted in his relations with Jowett and Gladstone. It was a duty which precluded, as he saw it, his taking any "actor part" in party politics.[17] So even though he was steeped in the Liberal tradition, Godley confessed that, "after 17 years in the public service I find my politics—like those of Sir James Stephen, when he, being Colonial Under Secretary, was asked what party he belonged to—are generally those of a Ministerialist."[18] Nothing, however, could have been more desirable in a permanent official in the late nineteenth century; Godley's determination to stay aloof from English politics enabled him to be a trusted adviser to both the Liberal and Conservative Secretaries of State with whom he had to work. This fact was generally unknown outside the India Office, and after he retired in 1909, the Indian National Congress journal in England, *India*, sarcastically remarked that despite Godley's Liberal background, "there has not been much Liberalism about his administration of this intensely bureaucratic office."[19] Be that as it may—and the Office was intensely bureaucratic—the Permanent Undersecretary was not supposed to have any political preferences, and Godley firmly adhered to that ideal while in office. But this also meant that he knowingly sacrificed any aspirations of a greater, more overt political career. Neither was Godley anxious to shift positions in the Home Civil Service, and he turned down the Permanent Undersecretaryships at the War Office (1893), the Colonial Office (1902–1903) and the Foreign Office (1905). Outside the Civil Service Godley turned down Lord Curzon's offer of the Finance Membership of the Viceroy's Council (1900) and the High Commissionership of South Africa, in succession to Lord Milner (1904).[20] Godley's resolute, decisive character was suited for his post in the India Office; it also restricted his flexibility, and he was more disposed to categorical judgments than lingering reviews. Although mentioned as a possible candidate for the Viceroyalty of India in 1893, Godley's bureaucratic inflexibility made him unsuitable for the post.[21]

Much less is known about Godley's personal life, especially during his India Office career. He was an intensely private man. He was tall, over six feet, with a strong chin and forceful demeanor.[22] After twenty-six years in his office overlooking St. James's Park, he had thinned considerably, sported a distinguished yet closely cropped beard, and had deeply set eyes. A quarter of a century of reading an endless number of papers and accounts had exacted a heavy physical toll on the once vigorous, athletic Godley.

Godley's literary favorites included the Book of Job, Milton, Dante, and Wordsworth. There were also collections of books on natural wildlife, on mysticism, on trains (a favorite hobby), and even a few musical scores in his personal library.[23] But, as befitted his energy and academic training, each favorite was carefully annotated, and in the case of Milton, Godley had computed the author's metrical scheme. There was also a place for authors he disliked, and one finds a carefully critiqued volume of William Morris's writings among Sir Arthur's collection.

While he closely guarded his private life, several events point clearly to an intense dedication to his family, and sensitivities which are never revealed in Godley's official literature. In 1896 Godley's youngest son, Denis, died at the age of six. Godley felt the boy's death deeply, and he prepared a 104-page, privately printed memorandum on the youngster's life. This he read continuously and carefully annotated until his own death thirty-six years later.[24] Many, including Gladstone, wondered if Godley could ever recover from the tragedy and continue his work at the India Office. In fact, Godley felt that only by absorbing himself in his work could he forget Denis's death.[25] In his memoirs Godley referred to the intense work of the period after 1896 as an "invaluable distraction," albeit mostly "pure taskwork."[26] But this was in many ways the Permanent Undersecretary's most active and invigorating period of involvement in Indian affairs, and his reminiscences must be read in light of this private tragedy from which he never fully recovered. Linked in part to this grievous loss, Godley maintained an active interest in his grandchildren's lives after he retired from his official duties.

In 1871 Godley married the Honorable Sara James, daughter of the First Lord Northbourne. She died in 1921, and Godley wrote a short privately printed memoir of his wife.[27] As with the volume on his son, this personal memoir reflects intense dedication in private life, similar in some respects to his dedication to the concept of duty in his official life at the India Office. The two, however, were never mixed.

The circumstances surrounding Godley's retirement from the India Office have been misinterpreted. Morley's estrangement with Godley is a matter of record. In 1907 the Secretary of State expressed his desire "to get rid" of the Permanent Undersecretary because he lacked, in Morley's opinion, initiative and "freshness of mind,"[28] and because he considered Godley too old and conservative.[29] But Morley delayed pressing Godley to retire because he needed the Undersecretary's expertise while he adjusted to his new office. In point of fact, in 1905, even before Morley accepted the Indian seals, Godley had anticipated his retirement in 1907.[30] There is further proof that Godley intended to retire at age sixty in 1907 in the Accountant-General's "Confidential India Office Lists," which show Richmond Ritchie penciled in as Permanent Undersecretary as early as spring 1908.[31] Godley stayed beyond his personally selected retirement date expressly at Morley's request. When it subsequently became obvious that he could no longer work with the Secretary of State, he left office. Above all, Godley desired to "disappear *before* I was kicked out, [and] *before* I became conscious of diminished efficiency."[32]

Godley left the India Office in October 1909. As planned, he was succeeded by Richmond Ritchie, whose appointment was welcomed by the Indian press, which felt the new Permanent Undersecretary was "more human, genial and considerate than his reticent and aloof predecessor Lord Kilbracken."[33] Actually Ritchie received the appointment because he was senior to Arthur Hirtzel in India Office service, and "his supercession would have introduced some discomfort into a peculiarly happy sort of office."[34] After the fact Morley sincerely regretted Godley's departure from the India Office, feeling that it was a "great blow"[35] which brought him "considerable discomfort of mind."[36] Godley left the India Office with a comfortable pension and a firm conviction in a job well done.[37] However, he retained a certain bitterness toward Morley, and after Godley left the office prepared a private memorandum on his estrangement from his last chief which was retained in family records and not Godley's official papers.[38] Hirtzel, Morley's Private Secretary, considered that "the only 'smallness' that J. M. showed at the India Office was in his attitude towards Godley."[39] For his part Godley continued to irritate Morley by persuading William Lee-Warner to retain his Council seat and thus deprive Morley of the opportunity to appoint his own man.[40] This uncharacteristic interference reflected more his personal animosity towards Morley than any conservative attempt to block the Secretary of State's "liberalizing" influence.[41]

Morley contended that Godley was one of those Civil Servants who "prefer power to fame."[42] This suggests that the Permanent Undersecretary had unlimited freedom within his domain. None of the constituent parts of the India Office was unfettered by strict constitutional or conventional limitations. Godley made no attempt to capitalize on his experience politically or even to effect any move within the civil service; he was appointed C. B. in 1882, K. C. B. in 1893, and G. C. B. in 1908. On his retirement from the India Office in 1909, he was raised to the peerage as Baron Kilbracken of Killegar.[43] But even then his subsequent official activity was limited to participation on the Chamberlain Commission on Indian Finance and Currency in 1913, although he remained active on the Board of Governors of Rugby and is credited by many with the preservation and expansion of the school's beautiful green belt and grounds today. Godley was not "as spiritless and disinterested as the machine he managed."[44] His contribution to Indian history far exceeds mere routine work, and his devotion and conduct during his tenure earned him the respect of his subordinates as the "best man in the Civil Service."[45] Although he was far from perfect, the complex business of the India Office was ably administered by Arthur Godley, who for twenty-six years was "a sleepless guardian ever seated in the Permanent Under Secretary's room."[46]

NOTES

1. Lord Kilbracken, *Reminiscences* (London: Macmillan and Co., 1931), p. 5.

2. *The Times* (London), 12 October 1909, p. 4.

3. Kilbracken, *Reminiscences*, p. 55.

4. The Earl of Oxford and Asquith, *Memories and Reflections, 1852–1927* (London: Cassell & Co., 1928), II, 202.

5. H. G. Hutchinson (ed.), *Private Diaries of the Rt. Hon. Sir Algernon West, G. C. B.* (London: John Murray, 1922), p. 52.

6. Rosebery to Kilbracken, 24 September 1917, Kilbracken Papers, BL, Add. MSS. 44,902, f. 58.

7. For details of the complex procedures used in handling Gladstone's mail, see Kilbracken, *Reminiscences*, pp. 87–88. See also Godley to Ampthill, 12 August 1904, Ampthill Papers, IOL, MSS. Eur. E.233/37.

8. Quoted in A. T. Bassett, *The Life of the Rt. Hon. John Ellis, M. P.* (London: Macmillan and Co., 1914), p. 225. Ellis served as Parliamentary Undersecretary of State for India, 1905–1907.

9. Henry Roseveare, *The Treasury* (London: Allan Lane, The Penguin Press, 1969), p. 217.

10. Kilbracken to F. Macmillan, Macmillan Archives [Section s], BL, Add. MSS. 55,245, f. 210. For a further insight into the Godley-Gladstone relationship, see

the reviews of Kilbracken, *Reminiscences*, in *The Times*, 2 and 4 June 1931, and *New York Times Book Review*, 4 October 1931.

11. Kilbracken, *Reminiscences*, p. 155.

12. Bernard Holland, *The Life of the Duke of Devonshire, 1833–1908* (London: Longmans, Green and Co., 1911), I, 381. The Duke of Devonshire, as the Marquess of Hartington, was Secretary of State for India, 1880–82. See also Sir Malcolm Seton, *The India Office* (London: G. P. Putnam's Sons, 1926) and Bernard Mallet, *Life of Sir Louis Mallet* (London: James Nisbet & Co., 1905), p. 108.

13. Kimberley to Gladstone [P. S. dated 4 June 1883], 28 May 1883, Gladstone Papers (Correspondence with Lord Kimberley), BL, Add. MSS. 44,228, f. 76.

14. Extract of an article from *Truth*, entitled "A Political Job?" n.d., Gladstone Papers (Correspondence with Arthur Godley), BL, Add. MSS. 44,223, f. 17.

15. G. B., Parliament, *Hansard's Parliamentary Debates*, 3rd ser., vol. 280 (1883), cols. 562; 1122–23. Hamilton, however, deferred when he was reminded that his own appointment as Parliamentary Undersecretary at the India Office had been at an even earlier age (twenty-nine), and Godley missed his "chance at immortality" in a Gladstonian defence (Kilbracken, *Reminiscences*, p. 156).

16. Godley to Curzon, 13 June 1899, Curzon Papers [hereafter cited as CP], IOL, MSS. Eur. F.111/158.

17. Godley to W. T. Stead, 29 October 1888, Kilbracken Papers, IOL, MSS. Eur. F.102/1.

18. Godley to Curzon, 24 February 1899, CP F.111/158.

19. *India*, 15 October 1909, p. 209.

20. Curzon and Hamilton attributed Godley's refusal to the fact that the Permanent Undersecretary had had for sixteen years "a considerable voice in determining and controlling the policy of the Government of India, and would not leave his...post, except for something where he would be his own master entirely" (Hamilton to Curzon, 2 June 1899, CP F.111/158).

21. Godley had been "shortlisted" as a candidate for the Viceroyalty by the Cabinet (Gladstone Papers [Cabinet Notes], BL, Add. MSS. 44,648, f. 112). Kimberley, however, felt that Godley was "too bureaucratic" to be a viable candidate for India's Governor-Generalship (quoted in "Lord Kilbracken [Obituary]," *The Times*, 28 June 1932, p. 9). See also Hutchinson, *Sir Algernon West*, pp. 197–98.

22. A portrait of Arthur Godley by George Richmond (1872) is in the possession of Sir Arthur's grandson, the Rt. Hon. W. A. H. Godley, Brede, England.

23. I am deeply indebted to Messrs. W. A. H. Godley, Arthur Coleridge, and Patrick A. Rice—Sir Arthur's grandsons—for sharing the former Permanent Undersecretary's library with me.

24. J. Arthur Godley, *D. E. G. 1890–1896* (London: Roehampton, 1898). This small volume had a limited circulation. Sir Arthur had one copy made especially for his own use, with blank pages inserted opposite each printed page. For the thirty-six years following his son's death, Godley continued to write his reminiscences about the boy and family pets, etc. This singularly valuable volume is in the possession of the Rt. Hon. W. A. H. Godley.

25. See Godley to Gladstone, 9 January 1897, Gladstone Papers, BL, Add. MSS. 44,223, ff. 243–44.

26. Kilbracken, *Reminiscences*, p. 233.

27. Lord Kilbracken, *S. K. [Sarah Kilbracken], 1871–1921* (Privately Printed,

1921). This small (nineteen pages) volume is in the possession of Patrick A. Rice, Axminster, England.

28. 13 December 1907, Diary of Frederick Arthur Hirtzel [hereafter cited as HD], IOL, Home Miscellaneous Series, No. 864, II, 105.

29. 3 January 1908, HD III, 9.

30. Godley to Ampthill, 22 November 1905, Ampthill Papers, IOL, MSS., Eur. E.233/14.

31. 1 April 1908, IOR, Accountant-General's Department, L/AG/30/18/25.

32. Godley to Lee-Warner, 26 August 1909, Lee-Warner Papers, IOL, MSS. Eur. F.92/4.

33. P. Leigh-Smith, *Record of Ascent: A Memoir of Sir Richmond T. Ritchie* (Cambridge: Dillon's University Bookshop, 1961), p. 22.

34. See Morley to Minto, 17 October 1909, Morley Papers [hereafter cited as MRP], IOL, MSS. Eur. D.573/4. See also 13 December 1907, HD II, 105; 3 January 1908, HD III, 105; 25 May 1908, HD IV, 50; and 13 September 1909, HD IV, 74.

35. 18 August 1909, HD IV, 66.

36. Morley to Minto, 17 October 1909, MRP D.563/4.

37. When Godley retired, he was granted an additional ten years' service (according to the Superannuation Act, 1859) [L/AG/30/22/41 p. 1489].

38. This memorandum, however, is assumed to have been lost in a small fire at Killegar, according to Patrick Rice, Sir Arthur's grandson, who had seen the work.

39. 11 October 1909, HD IV, 82.

40. See Kilbracken to Lee-Warner, 5 and 7 August 1910, Lee-Warner Papers, F.92/2.

41. See Stanley A. Wolpert, *Morley and India, 1906–1910* (Berkeley and Los Angeles: University of California Press, 1967), p. 53.

42. John Morley, *Recollections* (New York: The Macmillan Co., 1917), II, 153.

43. Ironically, Godley had spent little of his youth at Killegar, and did not really return there after he retired from the India Office. See John Godley, *Living Like a Lord* (London: Victor Gollanez, 1956), pp. 133–50.

44. Wolpert, *Morley*, p. 52.

45. 13 December 1907, HD II, 105.

46. Curzon to Godley, 30 June 1902, CP F.111/161.

APPENDIX B

Biographical Notes

Banerjea, Sir Surendranath (1848–1925): Educated: Doreton College, Calcutta; University College, London; founded Indian Association, 1876; founded Ripon College, Calcutta, 1882; editor, *The Bengalee*; Member, Bengal Legislative Council, 1893–1901; Member, Imperial Legislative Council, 1913–20.

Bayley, Sir Steuart (1836–1925): Educated: Eton and East India Company's College at Hailybury; Junior Secretary to the Government of Bengal, 1862–67; Commissioner of Patna, 1873; C. S. I., 1874; K. C. S. I., 1878; Chief Commissioner of Assam, 1878; Lieut.-Governor of Bengal, 1879; C. I. E., 1881; Home Member, Viceroy's Executive Council, 1882; Lieut.-Governor of Bengal, 1887–90; Political Secretary, India Office, 1890–95; Member, Council of India, 1895–1905; G. C. S. I., 1911.

Brackenbury, Sir Henry (1837–1914): Educated: Eton, Royal Military Academy at Woolich; Military Secretary to Lord Wolseley, Zululand, 1879; various diplomatic appointments in Ireland, Paris, and Cairo, 1880–85; Military Member, Viceroy's Executive Council, 1891–96; Director-General of Ordinance, 1899; C. B., 1880; K. C. B., 1894; K. C. S. I., 1896; G. C. B., 1900; Privy Councillor, 1904.

Brodrick, (William) St. John (1856–1942): Educated: Eton, Balliol College, Oxford; House of Commons, 1880–1906; Undersecretary for War, 1895–98; Undersecretary for Foreign Affairs, 1898–1900; Privy Council, 1897; Secretary of State for War 1900–1903; Secretary of State for India, 1903–1905; K. G., 1916; earldom in 1920; Honorary LL.D. from Trinity College, Dublin, 1922.

Bruce, Victor Alexander, Ninth Earl of Elgin and Thirteenth Earl of Kincardine (1849–1917): Educated: Glenalmond; Eton; Balliol College, Oxford (1873); M. A. in 1877; Treasurer of the Household; First Commissioner of Works, Gladstone

Govt. of 1886; Viceroy of India, 1892–99; K. G., 1899; re-elected Convener of the Fife County Council, 1899; Chairman, Royal Commission Inquiring into Military Preparations for the South African War, 1902; Chancellor of the University of Aberdeen from 1914; Colonial Secretary, 1906–1908.

Burne, Sir Owen Tudor (1837–1909): Educated: Royal Military College and Sandhurst; appointed Military Secretary, Government of India, 1860; Private Secretary to Sir Hugh Rose and Private Secretary to Lord Mayo, 1860–68; Assistant Secretary to the Political and Secret Department of India Office, later to be Secretary and Head of the Department, 1874–1878; Private Secretary to Lord Lytton, 1876; K. C. S. I., 1879 and Colonel in Army; Member, Council of India, 1886–96; G. C. I. E., 1896; Major-General, 1889.

Chirol, Sir (Ignatius) Valentine (1852–1929), traveler, journalist, author: Educated: Sorbonne; clerk in the Foreign Office, 1872–76; correspondent for the *London Standard* and *Levant Herald*, 1880; correspondent of *The Times*, 1892; took charge of the foreign department of *The Times*, 1897; original member of the board of *The Times* Publishing Company, 1908–1912; member of the Royal Commission on the India Public Services, 1912–14; wrote numerous books and acted for Foreign Office in 1915.

Churchill, Lord Randolph Henry Spencer (1849–95): Educated: Eton and Merton College, Oxford; M. P. for Woodstock, 1874 and 1880; Secretary of State for India, 1885–86; Chancellor of Exchequer and leader of House of Commons, 1886; resigned 1886.

Crewe-Milnes, Robert Offley Ashburton, Second Baron Houghton and Marquess of Crewe (1858–1945): statesman: Educated: Harrow and Trinity College, Cambridge; Viceroy of Ireland, 1892–95; P. C., 1892; earldom, 1895; K. G., 1908; Lord President of the Council, 1905–1908 and 1915–16; Lord Privy Seal, 1908–1911 and 1912–1915; leader of House of Lords in 1908; Colonial Secretary 1908–1910; Secretary of State for India, 1910–15; Ambassador to Paris, 1922–28; Secretary of State for War, 1931; leader of Independent Liberals in House of Lords, 1936–44.

Cross, Richard Assheton, First Viscount Cross (1823–1914): statesman: Educated: Trinity College, Cambridge; M. P. for Preston, 1857–62; M. P. for South-West Lancashire, 1868; Home Secretary, 1874–80 and 1885; Secretary of State for India, 1886–92; and made Viscount Cross of Broughton-in-Furness; Office of Privy Seal, 1895–1900; G. C. B., 1880; G. C. S. I., 1892.

Curzon, George Nathaniel, Marquess Curzon of Kedleston (1859–1925): Educated: Eton, Balliol College; M. P. for Lancashire, 1886; wrote *Russia in Central Asia* (1889), *Persia and the Persian Question* (1892), *Problems of the Far East* (1894); Undersecretary at the India Office, 1891–92; Parliamentary Undersecretary for Foreign Affairs and Member of Privy Council, 1895–98; Viceroy of India, 1898–1905; Lord Wardenship of the Cinque Ports, 1904; Chancellor Oxford University, 1907; House of Lords, Irish representative peer, 1908; Lord Rector of Glaslow University, 1907; Lord Privy Seal, 1915; in Charge of Shipping Control Committee,

1916; President Air Board, 1917; member of the War Cabinet, 1916; Foreign Secretary, 1919–25.

Danvers, Frederic Charles (1833–1906), writer of engineering articles: Educated: Kings College, London; Addiscombe; Writer in the Old East India House, 1853; Assistant Secretary, Revenue Department of the India Office, 1877–84; Registrar and Superintendent of Records, India Office, 1884–98.

Danvers, Sir Juland (1826–1902): K. C. S. I., 1886, India governmental official: Educated: King's College, London; entered Home Service, East India Co., 1842; Private Secretary to Sir James Hogg and then Sir Archibald Galloway; Secretary in Railway Department of India Office, 1858; Government Director of Indian Railway Companies, 1861, and with department Secretaryship, Public Works, India Office, 1880–92; retired, 1892.

Digby, William (1849–1904) Anglo-Indian publicist: Subeditor of the *Ceylon Observer*, 1871; editor of the *Madras Times*, 1877; Honorary Secretary in India of the Executive Committee (relief); C. I. E., 1878; editor of the *Liverpooland Southport Daily News*, 1880; editor of the *Western Daily Mercury*, 1879; Secretary of the National Liberal Club, London, 1882–87; Senior Partner: William Hutchinson and Company, 1887; Secretary, Indian Political Agency, 1887–92; Secretary to the British Committee of the Indian National Congress, 1889–1902.

Edge, Sir John (1841–1926): Educated: Trinity College, Dublin (B. A., 1861; LLB., 1862); Chief Justice of the High Court of Judicature for the North-Western Provinces of India at Allahabad, knighted on appointment, 1886; First Vice-Chancellor of University of Allahabad, 1887–93; Chairman of the famine relief committee, India, 1896; Judicial Member, Council of India, 1899–1908; Privy Council, 1909.

Edgerley, Sir Steyning William (1857–1935): Educated: Balliol College, Oxford; Indian Civil Service, 1879; Private Secretary to Governor of Bombay, 1889–95; C. I. E., 1895; K. C. V. O., 1905; Member of Council, Bombay, 1907; Member, Council of India, 1909–16; K. C. S. I., 1916.

Elliot, Gilbert John Murray Kynynmond, Fourth Earl of Minto (1845–1914): Educated: Eton, Trinity College, Cambridge; Governor-General of Canada, 1898–1904; Viceroy of India, 1905–1910; K. G., 1910.

Fowler, Sir Henry Hartley Fowler, First Viscount Wolverhampton (1830–1911): Undersecretary Home Office, 1884; in the Treasury, 1886; member of Privy Council; president of the local government board, seat in Cabinet, 1892–94; Secretary of State for India, 1894–95; G. C. S. I., 1895; Chancellor of the Duchy of Lancaster, 1905; Lord President of the Council, 1908; Honory LL.D from the University of Birmingham, 1909.

Gascoyne-Cecil, Robert Arthur Talbot, Third Marquis of Salisbury (1830–1903): Educated: Eton, Christ's Church, Oxford (1847–1849); Secretary of State for India, 1866–67 and 1874–78; Privy Council, 1866; British Pleniopotentiary to Council in

Constantinople; Foreign Secretary, 1878–80; 1885–86; 1887–92; 1895–1900; K. G., 1878; Prime Minister, 1885–86, 1895–1902.

Godley, Sir Arthur, First Baron Kilbracken (1847–1932): Educated: Radley; Rugby; Balliol College, Oxford (classical scholar of note); assistant private secretary to Gladstone (until 1874); private secretary to Lord Granville; Law Degree; Fellow of Hertford College, 1874–81; principal private secretary to Gladstone, 1880; Commissioner of Inland Revenue, 1882; Permanent Undersecretary of State for India, 1883–1909; C. B., 1882; K. C. B., 1893; G. C. B., 1908; peerage, 1909; chairman of the governing body at Rugby, 1902–1932; a Trustee of British Museum and Director of the P.& O.; Honorary Fellowship at Hertford College (1910) and Balliol (1912); member of Royal Commission on Indian Finance and Currency, 1913.

Hamilton, Lord George Francis (1845–1927): Educated: Harrow; M. P., 1869–1906; Undersecretary of State for India, 1874; Privy Council, 1878; First Lord of the Admiralty, 1885–92 (except 1886); Chairman, London School Board, 1894; Secretary of State for India, 1895–1903; G. C. S. I., 1903; Chairman, Royal Commission on Poor Law and Unemployment; Royal Commission on Mesopotamian Campaign, 1916–17.

Hardie, James Keir (1856–1915), Socialist and Labour leader: Worked as journalist, miners' organizer; National Secretary of Scottish Coal-fields Conference, 1880; secretary of Scottish miners' federation, 1886; ran and owned *The Miner* (1887–89), and the *Labour Leader* (1889–94); elected as Independent Labour Member of Parliament, 1892, for South West Ham until 1895; Chairman of Independent Labour Party, 1893–1900, 1913–15; M. P. for Merthyr Burghs, 1900; first leader of the Labour party in House of Commons, 1906.

Herschell, Lord Farrer, Baron Herschell (1837–1899): Educated: University College, London; Liberal M. P., Durham, 1874–85; knighted and appointed Solicitor-General, 1880–85; Lord High Chancellor with title Baron Herschell of City of Durham, 1886; Lord High Chancellor, 1892–95; died in Washington, at work on Anglo-American Commission, 1899.

Hirtzel, Sir Arthur (1870–1937): Educated: Dulwich College; Trinity College, Oxford (Craven University Scholar); entered India Office, 1894; private secretary to the Secretaries of State, 1903–1909; C. B., 1907; Secretary, Political Department of India Office, 1909–17; K. C. B., 1911; Assistant Undersecretary of State, 1917–21; Deputy Undersecretary, 1921–24; Permanent Undersecretary of State for India, 1924–30.

Hume, Allan Octavian (1829–1912), Indian civil servant and ornithologist: Educated: Haileybury College and London University; C. B., 1860; Secretary in the Revenue and Agricultural Department, Government of India, 1870–79; member of provincial board of revenue; retired from I. C. S., 1882; active in founding Indian National Congress, 1885, and British Committee of I.N.C., 1885–1912.

Jowett, Benjamin (1817–1893): Master of Balliol College, Oxford and Regius Professor of Greek at Balliol College, Oxford; ordained priest, 1845; Public Examiner,

1849, 1850, 1851, and 1853; Vice-Chancellor of Oxford, 1882–86; Honorary Doctor of Theology, Leyden, 1875; L. L. D. Edinburgh, 1884; L. L. D. Cambridge, 1890.

Kaye, Sir John (1814–1876): Military historian: Educated: Eton and Addiscombe; Secretary, Political and Secret Department, East India Company, 1856–58, and India Office, 1858–74; K. C. S. I., 1871; wrote *Administration of the East India Company*, 1853; *The History of the Sepoy War in India, 1857–58*, 3 vols., 1864–71.

Kitchener, Horatio Herbert, First Earl Kitchener of Khartoom & of Broome (1850–1916), Field-Marshall: Educated: Royal Military Academy; Governor-General of Eastern Sudan, 1886; Adjutant-General Egyptian Army, 1888; C. B., 1889; Viscount and O. M., 1902; Commander-in-Chief, Indian Army, 1902–09; Field Marshall, 1909; Secretary of State for War, 1914; K. G., 1915.

Lawrence, Sir Walter, First Baronet (1857–1940): Indian Civil Servant; Settlement Commissioner in Kashmir, 1889–95; Private Secretary to Viceroy, 1889–1903; K. C. I. E., 1903; G. C. I. E., 1906; Chief of Staff to Prince and Princess for India visit, 1905–06; Member, Council of India, 1907–1909; C. B., 1917; G. C. V. O., 1918.

Lee-Warner, Sir William (1846–1914): Educated: Rugby, St. John's College, Cambridge (1869); posted to the Bombay Presidency in1869–71; Political Agent at Kolapur, 1886–1887; Undersecretary in the GOI Foreign Department, 1884; Secretary to the Bombay Government in the political and judicial departments, being promoted to chief secretaryship, 1887; Ex-officio chief commissioner of Coorg, 1895; Education commission, 1882–83 (for India); Secretary of the Political and Secret Department, India Office, 1895; K. C. S. I., 1898; Member, Council of India, 1902–1912; G. C. S. I., 1911.

Mackay, James Lyle, First Earl of Inchcape (1852–1932): Shipowner, Vice-president of Suez Canal Company; President of the Bengal Chamber of Commerce, 1890–93; President of the Indian Currency Association, 1893; head of London Office of the British India Company, 1893; K. C. I. E., 1894; G. C. M. G., 1902; President of the Chamber of Shipping of the United Kingdom, 1903–1918, 1919; Member, Council of India, 1897–1911; Special Commissioner and Pleniopotentiary in the negotiations with China, 1901; peerage: Baron Inchcape of Strathnaver, 1911; Member, Committee for Imperial Defense, 1917; Member, National Economy Committee, 1921–22; Chairman of the Committee on Indian Retrenchment, 1922–23; House of Lords, 1926; G. C. S. I., 1924; Viscount in 1924; President, International Shipping Federation, 1926; Earl of Inchcape and Viscount of Glenapp, 1929.

Maine, Sir Henry James Sumner (1822–88): Jurist; of Christ's Hospital, London and Pembroke College, Cambridge; Regius Professor of Civil Law, 1847–54; Reader of Roman laws and jurisprudence at the Inns of Court, 1852; contributed to the *Saturday Review* (1855 on); Legal Member, Viceroy's Council, 1862–69; Corpus Professor of Jurisprudence, Oxford, 1869–78; K. C. S. I. and appointed to seat on

Council of India, 1871-77; Master of Trinity Hall, Cambridge, 1877; Whewell Professor of International Law, Cambridge, 1887-88.

Mallet, Sir Louis (1823-90): Civil servant and economist; clerk in Audit Office from 1839 to 1847; Board of Trade, 1847; Private Secretary to the President, B. O. T., 1848-52 and 1855-57; C. B., 1866; knighted, 1868; Permanent Undersecretary of State for India, 1874-83; Privy Councillor, 1883; civil servant and economist; published *Free Exchange* (1891) on economic topics.

Montagu, Edwin Samuel (1879-1924): Educated: Trinity College, Cambridge; Liberal M. P. Chesterton division of Cambridgeshire, 1906-22; Private Secretaryship to H. H. Asquith, 1906; Parliamentary Undersecretary of State for India, 1910-14; Financial secretary to the Treasury, 1914; Privy Councillor, 1915 and Chancellor of Duchy of Lancaster (1915); Minister of Munitions, 1916; Secretary of State for India, 1917-22.

Morley, John, Viscount Morley of Blackburn (1838-1923): Educated: University College at Gower Street; Cheltenham College, Lincoln College at Oxford; freelance journalist (1860-63); worked for *Saturday Review*; editor of *Fortnightly Review*, 1867; appointed Editor of the *Morning Star*, 1869; editor of *Pall Mall Gazette*, 1880; M. P. from Newcastle-upon-Tyne, 1883; Chief Secretary for Ireland, 1886; 1896 elected to Parliament from Montrose Burghs; Order of Merit, 1902; Secretary of State for India, 1905-1910; resigned post in India Office but remained in Cabinet as Lord Privy Seal.

Naoroji, Dadabhai (1825-1917): Educated: Elphinstone School and College; Founder, East India Association, 1866; Prime Minister of Baroda, 1874; Member, Bombay Legislative Council, Bombay, 1885; President of Indian National Congress, 1886, 1893, and 1906; first Indian Member of British Parliament, 1892-95.

Newmarch, Sir Oliver Richardson (1834-1920), Major-General, Administrator: Educated: Charterhouse, Merton College, Oxford; entered Bengal Army, 1855; served during Indian Mutiny (awarded medal); Military Secretary, Government of India; Military Secretary, India Office, 1889-99; K. C. S. I., 1894.

Norman, Sir Henry Wylie (1826-1904): Field-Marshall and administrator; 1849, Brigade-Major at Peshawar to Sir Colin Campbell; Deputy Assistant Adjutant-General and A.D.C. to General Abraham Roberts; C. B., 1859: A.D.C. to Queen Victoria, 1863-69, when promoted to Major-General; Assistant Military Secretary to Duke of Cambridge, 1860; First Secretary (Military Department), Government of India, 1862-70; Member, Viceroy's Council, 1870-77; K. C. B., 1873; Lieutenant-General, 1877; Member, Council of India, 1878-83; General, 1882 (Egypt); Governor of Jamaica, 1883; G. C. M. G., 1887 and G. C. B. (1887): Governorship of Queensland, 1889-95; Governor of Chelsea Hospital, 1901; Field-Marshall, 1902; member of South African War Commission, 1903.

Peile, Sir James B. (1833-1906), Indian administrator: Educated: Oriel College, Oxford, 1855; Civil Service of India, 1855 (Bombay Service, 1856); Undersecretary of the Bombay Government, 1859–62; Director of Public Instruction, 1873, (Education, Bombay); Political Agent of Kathiawar, 1878; member of Famine Commission, 1878–80; Secretary and Acting Chief Secretary to the Bombay Government, 1879–82; Member, Bombay Council, 1882; Vice-Chancellor of the University of Bombay, 1884; Member of Viceroy's Council, 1886–87; Member, Council of India, 1887–1902; K. C. S. I., 1888; Royal Commission on Administration of Indian Expenditure, 1895–1900.

Petty-Fitzmaurice, Henry Charles Keith, Fifth Marquess of Lansdowne (1845–1927): Education: Eton, Balliol College, Oxford; House of Lords, 1886; Junior Lord of the Treasury, 1869–1872; Undersecretary for War, 1872–74; Undersecretary of State for India, 1880–83; Governor-General of Canada, 1883–88; Viceroy of India, 1888–94; K. C., 1894; D. C. L. Oxford (honorary); Lord-Lieutenant of Wittshire, 1894; Secretary of State for War, 1895; Secretary of State for Foreign Affairs, 1900–1916; member of inner committee responsible for the conduct of the war, First Coalition Administration, 1915; leader of Conservative Opposition in the House of Lords, 1906–1916.

Pontifex, Sir Charles (1831–1912): Educated: Trinity College, Cambridge (B. A.); Judge, High Court of Judicature, Bengal, 1872–82; Legal Counsel to Secretary of State for India, 1882–92; K. C. I. E., 1892.

Wodehouse, John, First Earl of Kimberley (1826–1902): Education: Eton and Oxford; B. A. 1847; Undersecretary for Foreign Affairs, 1852–56; 1857–61; for India, 1864; Lord Lieut. of Ireland, 1854–66; Earldom, 1866; Lord Privy Seal, 1868–70; Coloniel Secretary 1870–74; 1880–82; Secretary of State for India, 1882–85; 1886; 1892–94; Foreign Secretary, 1894–96.

APPENDIX C

Secretaries of State for India, 1858–1910

Name	Date of acceptance of Seals of Office
Lord Stanley, P.C. (a)	2 Sept., 1858
The Right Hon. Sir Charles Wood, Bart. (b)	18 June, 1859
Earl de Grey and Ripon, P.O. (c)	16 Feb., 1866
Viscount Cranborne (d)	6 July, 1866
The Right Hon. Sir Stafford Northcote, Bart. (e)	8 March, 1867
The Duke of Argyll, K.T., P.C.	9 Dec., 1868
The Marquis of Salisbury, P.C. (2nd time)	21 Feb., 1874
The Right Hon. Gathorne Hardy, P.C., created Viscount Cranbrook, 14 May, 1878 (f)	2 April, 1878
The Marquis of Hartington, P.C. (g)	28 April, 1880
The Earl of Kimberley, P.C.	16 Dec., 1882
Lord Randolph Churchill, P.C.	24 June, 1885
The Earl of Kimberley, K.G., P.C. (2nd time)	6 Feb., 1886

(a) Afterwards (by succession) Earl of Derby; (b) Afterwards (by creation) Viscount Halifax; (c) Afterwards (by creation) Marquess of Ripon; (d) Afterwards (by succession) Marquess of Salisbury; (e) Afterwards (by creation) Earl of Iddesleigh; (f) Afterwards (by creation) Earl Cranbrook; (g) Afterwards (by succession) Duke of Devonshire.

Secretaries of State for India

Name	Date of Appointment
The Right Hon. Sir Richard Assheton Cross, G.C.B., created Viscount Cross, 19 Aug., 1886	3 Aug., 1886
The Earl of Kimberly, K.G., P.C. (3rd time)	18 Aug., 1892
The Right Hon. H.H. Fowler (h)	10 March, 1894
Lord George F. Hamilton, G.C.S.I., P.C.	4 July, 1895
The Right Hon. St. John Brodrick (i)	9 Oct., 1903
The Right Hon. John Morley, O.M. (j) (1st time)	11 Dec., 1905
The Right Hon The Earl of Crewe, K.G. (1st time)	7 Nov., 1910

(h) (by creation) Viscount Wolverhampton, G.C.S.I.; (i) Afterwards (by succession) Viscount Midleton, K.G.: (j) Afterwards (by creation) Viscount Morley of Blackburn O.M.

APPENDIX D

Permanent Undersecretaries of State for India, 1858–1909

Name	Date of Appointment
Sir Russell Clerk, K.C.B.	30 Sept., 1858
Herman Merivale, C.B.	13 April, 1860
Sir Louis Mallet, C.B.	16 Feb., 1874
Arthur Godley, C.B. (a)	30 Sept., 1883
Sir Ritchmond Ritchie, K.C.B.	11 Oct., 1909

(a) Afterwards Sir Arthur Godley, G.C.B., and then Baron Kilbracken.

APPENDIX E

Parliamentary Undersecretaries of State for India, 1858–1910

Name	Date of Appointment
Henry James Baillie, M.P.	30 Sept., 1858
Thomas George Baring, M.P. (a)	25 June., 1859
Earl de Grey and Ripon (b)	21 Jan., 1861
Thomas George Baring, M.P. (a) (2nd time)	31 July, 1861
Lord Wodehouse (c)	25 April, 1864
Lord Dufferin and Clandeboye, K.P., K.C.B. (d)	16 Nov., 1864
James Stansfeld, M.P.	17 Feb., 1866
Sir James Fergusson, Bart., M.P.	6 July, 1866
Lord Clinton	31 July, 1867
M.E. Grant Duff, M.P. (g)	10 Dec., 1868
Lord George F. Hamilton, M.P. (p)	22 Feb., 1874
Hon. Edward Stanhope, M.P.	6 April, 1878
The Marquis of Landsdowne	29 April, 1880
Viscount Enfield (e)	1 Sept., 1880
John Kynaston Cross, M.P.	16 Jan., 1883
Lord Harris	25 June, 1885

(a) Afterwards (by succession) Lord Northbrook, and (by creation) Earl of Northbrook; (b) Afterwards (by creation) Marquis of Ripon; (c) Afterwards (by creation) Earl of Kimberley; (d) Afterwards (by creation) Earl of Dufferin and Ava; (e) Afterwards (by succession) Earl of Stratford;

Name	Date of Appointment
Sir Ughtred Kay-Shuttleworth, Bart., M.P. (f)	7 Feb., 1886
Edward Stafford Howard, M.P. (h)	12 April, 1886
Sir John E. Gorst, K.C., M.P.	4 Aug., 1886
The Hon. G.N. Curzon, M.P. (i)	9 Nov., 1891
G.W.E. Russell, M.P.	19 Aug., 1892
Lord Reay, G.C.S.I., G.C.I.E.	11 March, 1894
The Earl of Onslow, G.C.M.G.	5 July, 1895
The Earl of Hardwick	17 Jan., 1901
Earl Percy, M.P.	18 Aug., 1902
The Earl of Hardwick (2nd time)	12 Oct., 1903
The Marquess of Bath	20 Jan., 1905
John Edward Ellis, M.P.	12 Dec., 1905
Charles E.H. Hobhouse, M.P. (j)	1 Feb., 1907
T.R. Buchanan, P.C., M.P.	16 April, 1908
The Master of Elibank, M.P. (k)	29 June, 1909
Hon. E.S. Montague, M.P. (l)	21 Feb., 1910

(f) Afterwards (by creation) Baron Shuttleworth; (g) Afterwards The Rt. Hon. Sir M.E. Grant Duff, G.C.S.I., C.I.E.; (h) Afterwards K.C.B.; (i) Afterwards (by creation) Marquess Curzon of Kedleston. (j) Afterwards the Rt. Hon. Charles E.H. Hobhouse, M.P.; (k) Afterwards (by creation) the Rt. Hon. Barron Murray of Elibank; (l) Afterwards P.C.

APPENDIX F

Chronological List of Members of the Council of India, 1858–1905

Name	Date of Appointment	Remarks
Charles Mills*	21 Sept., 1858	Resigned, 21 Sept., 1863
John Shepard*	Ditto	Died, 12 Jan., 1859
Sir James Wier Hogg, Bart.*	Ditto	Resigned, 25 Jan., 1872
Elliot Macnaghten*	Ditto	Resigned, 2 Nov., 1871
Ross Donnelly Mangles*	Ditto	Resigned, 1 Sept., 1874
Capt. William Joesph Eastwick*	Ditto	Resigned, 3 Sept., 1868
Henry Thoby Princep*	Ditto	Resigned, 29 April, 1874
Sir Fredk. Currie, Bart.*	Ditto	Died, 10 Sept., 1875
Sir J.P. Willoughby, Bart.*	Ditto	Died, 15 Sept., 1866
Sir H.C. Rawlingson, Bart. K.C.B.*	21 Sept., 1858 Re-appointed, 5 Oct., 1868	Resigned, 16 April, 1859, on appointment as Envoy to Persia. Died, 5 Mar., 1895
Sir R.J.H. Vivian, K.C.B.*	21 Sept., 1858	Resigned, 31 Dec., 1874
Sir H.C. Montgomery, Bart.	On transfer of Government to the Crown in 1858.	Resigned, 13 Nov., 1876
Sir John L.M. Lawrence, Bart., G.C.B.	Ditto Ditto	Resigned 8 Dec., 1863, on appointment as Governor-General of India.

* Formerly Director of the East India Company.

248   Appendix F

Name	Date of Appointment	Remarks
Sir P.T. Cautley, K.C.B.	Ditto Ditto	Resigned, 30 Sept., 1868
W.U. Arbuthnot	Ditto Ditto	Died, 11 Dec., 1874
Col. H.M. Durand, C.B.	18 Jan., 1859	Resigned, 3 Feb., 1861, on appointment as Foreign Secretary to the Government of India.
Sir T.E. Perry, Kt.	8 Aug., 1861	Died, 22 April, 1862
Col. W.E. Baker	18 July, 1861	Resigned, 1 Jan., 1876
Sir G.R Clerk, K.C.B., K.C.S.I.	14 Dec., 1863	Resigned, 28 Nov., 1876
Sir H.B.E. Frere, G.C.S.I.	9 Nov., 1966	Resigned, 1 Mar., 1877
Sir Robert Montgomery, G.C.S.I., K.C.B.	21 Sept., 1868	Died, 28 Dec., 1887
Sir F.J. Halliday, K.C.B.	29 Sept., 1868	Resigned, 31 Dec., 1886
Sir H.J.S. Maine, K.C.S.I., D.C.L.	2 Nov., 1871	Died, 3 Feb., 1888
Sir Louis Mallet, C.B.	8 Feb., 1872	Resigned, 15 Feb., 1874, on appointment as Permanent Under Secretary of State.
Sir G. Campbell, K.C.S.I.	16 Feb., 1874	Resigned, 10 April, 1875, on entering Parliament.
A. Cassels	30 April, 1874	Period of office expired, 29 April, 1884.
Maj. Gen. E.B. Johnson	1 Sept., 1874	Resigned, 6 Feb., 1877 on appointment as Member of Governor-General's Council in India.
Maj. Gen. R. Strachey, C.S.I.	5 Jan., 1875 Re-appointed, 11 Mar., 1879	Resigned, 12 July, 1878, on appointment as President of the Famine Commission in India (Appointment not filled up in interval) Resigned, 2 Oct., 1889, on appointment as Chairman of the East India Railway Company.
Hon. E. Drummond	9 Feb., 1875	Period of office expired, 8 Feb., 1885.
Sir B.H. Ellis, K.C.S.I.	14 July, 1875	Period of office expired, 13 July, 1885.
Col. Hy. Yule, C.B.	23 Oct., 1875	Resigned, 14 May, 1889
Maj. Gen. Sir A.T. Wilde, K.C.B., C.S.I.	1 Jan., 1876	Died, 7 Feb., 1878

Chronological List of Members of the Council of India 249

Name	Date of Appointment	Remarks
Maj. Gen. Sir G.J. Wolseley, G.C.M.G., K.C.B. (Afterwards (by creation) Viscount Wolsely	13 Nov., 1876	Resigned, 24 June, 1878 on appointment as High Commissioner, Cyprus.
Sir W. Muir, K.S.I.	28 Nov., 1876	Resigned, 15 Dec., 1885, on appointment as Principal, Edinburgh University.
R.S. Ellis	17 April, 1877	Died, 9 Oct., 1877
R.A Dalyell, C.S.I.	1 Nov., 1877	Period of office expired, 31 Oct., 1887
Col. Sir W.L. Mereweather, K.C.S.I., C.B.	1 Nov., 1877	Died, 4 Oct., 1880
Lieut. Gen. Sir H.W. Norman, K.C.B.	25 Feb., 1878	Resigned, 30 Nov., 1883, on appointment as Governor of Jamaica.
Maj. Gen. C.J. Foster, C.B.	22 July, 1878	Period of office expired, 21 July, 1888.
B.W. Currie	11 Dec., 1880 (Re-appointed 11 Dec., 1890)	Period of office expired 10 Dec., 1895.
Hon. Sir Ashley Eden, K.C.S.I.	24 April, 1882	Died, 9 July 1887
Maj. Gen. Sir P.S. Lumsden, K.C.B., C.S.I.	1 Dec., 1883	Period of office expired, 30 Nov., 1893
J.R. Bullen-Smith, C.S.I.	6 June, 1884	Died, 5 Jan., 1887
Sir R.H. Davies, K.C.S.I., C.L.E.	3 Mar., 1885	Period of office expired, 2 Mar., 1895.
Sir John Strachey, G.C.S.I., C.I.E.	14 July, 1885	Period of office expired, 13 July, 1895
Gen. Sir D.M. Stewart, Bart., G.C.B., G.C.S.I.	16 Dec., 1885 (Re-appointed 16 Dec., 1895)	Died, 26 Mar., 1900
Col. Sir O.T. Burne, K.C.S.I., C.I.E.	1 Jan., 1887	Period of office expired, 31 Dec., 1896.
R. Hardie	17 Mar., 1887	Period of office expired, 16 Mar., 1897.
Sir A.J. Arbuthnot, K.C.S.I., C.I.E.	1 Nov., 1887	Period of office expired, 31 Oct., 1897.

Name	Date of Appointment	Remarks
Sir J.B. Peile. K.C.S.I.	12 Nov., 1887 (Re-appointed, 12 Nov. 1897).	Period of office expired, 11 Nov., 1902
Sir A.C. Lyall, K.C.B., K.C.I.E.	17 Jan., 1888 (Re-appointed, 17 Jan., 1898.)	Period of office expired, 16 Jan., 1903.
Sir C.A. Turner, K.C.I.E.	21 Feb., 1888	Period of office expired, 20 Feb., 1898.
Lieut. Gen. Sir A. Alison, Bart., G.C.B.	1 Jan, 1889	Period of office expired, 31 Dec., 1898.
Sir Charles H.T. Crosthwaite, K.C.S.I.	3 Mar., 1895	Period of office expired, 2 Mar., 1905.
Sir Steuart C. Bayley, K.C.S.I., C.I.E.	16 Sept., 1895	Period of office expired, 15 Sept., 1905.
F. C. Le Merchant	27 Feb., 1896	Period of office expired, 26 Feb., 1906.
Gen. Sir J.J.H. Gordon, K.C.B.	1 Jan., 1897	Period of office expired, 31 Dec., 1906.
Sir Dennis Fitzpatrick, K.C.S.I.	24 April, 1897	Period of office expired, 23 April, 1907.
Sir J.L. Mackay, K.C.I.E. (Afterwards (by creation) Earl of Inchcape, G.C.S.I., G.C.M.G., K.C.I.E.)	April, 1897	Re-appointed for 5 years 27 April, 1907. Resigned, 12 July, 1911. Died 23 May, 1932.
Sir John Edge, K.C.	30 March, 1898	Period of office expired, 29 Mar., 1908.
Sir P.P. Hutchins, K.C.S.I.	1 Aug., 1898	Period of office expired, 31 July, 1908.
Sir James Westland, K.C.S.I.	8 Aug., 1899	Died, 9 May, 1903
Lieut. Gen. A.B. Babcock, C.B., C.S.I.	26 mar., 1901	Died, 23 Mar., 1907
Sir WIlliam Lee-Warner, K.C.S.I.	12 Nov., 1902	Period of office expired, 11 Nov., 1912

Chronological List of Members of the Council of India 251

Name	Date of Appointment	Remarks
Sir Anthony P. MacDonnell, P.C., G.C.S.I. (Afterwards (by creation) Baron MacDonnell.)	17 Jan., 1903	Resigned, Jan., 1905. Did not act, having held appointment of U.S. for Ireland.
I.F. Finlay, C.S.I.	10 May, 1903	Resigned, 4 Dec., 1906, on appointment as Member of Governor-General's Council in India.
Sir Hugh S. Barnes, K.C.S.I., K.C.V.O.	9 May, 1905	Resigned, 6 Nov., 1913
Lieut. Col. Sir David W.K. Barr, K.C.S.I.	16 Aug., 1905	Period of office expired, 15 Aug., 1915.

APPENDIX G

Committees of the Council of India, 1858–1905

Sept. 1858　　FINANCE, HOME AND PUBLIC　　　POLITICAL AND MILITARY
　　　　　　　WORKS

　　　　　　　Elliot Macnaghten　　　　　　　John P. Willoughby
　　　　　　　Charles Mills　　　　　　　　　William J. Eastwick
　　　　　　　John Shepherd　　　　　　　　　Sir Henry C. Rawlinson
　　　　　　　Col. Sir Proby T. Cautley　　　Maj. Gen. Sir Robert J.
　　　　　　　William Arbuthnot　　　　　　　　H. Vivian

　　　　　　　REVENUE, JUDICIAL, AND LEGISLATIVE

　　　　　　　Sir James Weir Hogg
　　　　　　　Ross D. Mangles
　　　　　　　Henry Thoby Prinsep
　　　　　　　Sir Frederick Currie
　　　　　　　Sir Henry C. Montgomery

Nov. 1859　　 FINANCE　　　　　　　　　　　　MILITARY

　　　　　　　William Arbuthnot　　　　　　　Maj. Gen. Sir. Robert J.
　　　　　　　Elliot Macnaghten　　　　　　　　H. Vivian
　　　　　　　Charles Mills　　　　　　　　　Sir John L.M. Laurence
　　　　　　　Henry T. Prinsep　　　　　　　 Col. Henry M. Durand
　　　　　　　Sir Thomas E. Perry　　　　　　William J. Eastwick
　　　　　　　　　　　　　　　　　　　　　　 Col. Sir Proby T. Cautley

　　　　　　　POLITICAL　　　　　　　　　　　PUBLIC

　　　　　　　Sir John L.M. Laurence　　　　 Sir Henry C. Montgomery
　　　　　　　Henry T. Prinsep　　　　　　　 William Arbuthnot
　　　　　　　John F. Willoughby　　　　　　 John P. Willoughby
　　　　　　　Sir Frederick Currie　　　　　 Maj. Gen. Sir Robert J.
　　　　　　　William J. Eastwick　　　　　　　 H. Vivian
　　　　　　　　　　　　　　　　　　　　　　 Sir James W. Hogg

Committees of the Council of India   253

          PUBLIC WORKS AND RAILWAYS   REVENUE AND JUDICIAL

          Col. Sir. Proby T. Cautley   Ross D. Mangles
          Col. Henry M. Durand   Sir James W. Hogg
          Elliot Macnaghten   Sir Thomas E. Perry
          Charles Mills   Sir Henry C. Montgomery
          Ross D. Mangles   Sir Frederick Currie

Nov. 1860   FINANCE   MILITARY

          William Arbuthnot   Maj. Gen. Sir Robert J.
          Sir Frederick Currie   H. Vivian
          Charles Mills   Sir John L.M. Laurence
          Elliot Macnaghten   Col. Henry M. Durand
          Sir Thomas E. Perry   William J. Eastwick
                                      Col. Sir Proby T. Cautley

          POLITICAL   PUBLIC

          William J. Eastwick   John P. Willoughby
          Sir John L.M. Laurence   Sir James W. Hogg
          Sir Frederick Currie   Ross D. Mangles
          John P. Willoughby   William Arbuthnot
          Henry T. Prinsep   Maj. Gen. Sir Robert J.
                                      H. Vivian

          PUBLIC WORKS AND FINANCE   REVENUE AND JUDICIAL

          Col. Sir Proby T. Cautley   Henry T. Prinsep
          Elliot Macnaghten   Sir Thomas E. Perry
          Charles Mills   Sir James W. Hogg
          Sir Henry C. Montgomery   Sir Henry C. Montgomery
          Sir Henry M. Durand   Ross D. Mangles

Nov. 1861   FINANCE   MILITARY

          Charles Mills   Maj. Gen. Sir Robert J.
          William Arbuthnot   H. Vivian
          Elliot Macnaghten   Sir John L.M. Laurence
          Sir Thomas E. Perry   Col. William E. Baker
          Ross D. Mangles   William J. Eastwick
                                      Col. Sir Proby T. Cautley

          POLITICAL   PUBLIC

          Sir Frederick Currie   Ross D. Mangles
          William J. Eastwick   John P. Willoughby
          Sir John L.M. Laurence   Sir James W. Hogg
          Henry T. Prinsep   William Arbuthnot
          John T. Willoughby   Maj. Gen. Sir Robert J.
                                      H. Vivian

PUBLIC WORKS AND RAILWAYS

Sir Henry C. Montgomery
Elliot Macnaghten
Col. Sir Proby T. Cautley
Charles Mills
Col. William E. Baker

REVENUE AND JUDICIAL

Henry T. Prinsep
Sir James W. Hogg
Sir Thoas E. Perry
Sir Henry C. Montgomery
Sir Frederick Currie

Nov. 1862 FINANCE

William Arbuthnot
Charles Mills
Elliot Macnaghten
Henry T. Prinsep
Sir Thomas E. Perry

MILITARY

Col. William E. Baker
William J. Eastwick
Maj. Gen. Sir Robert J.
  H. Vivian
Sir. John L.M. Laurence
Col. Sir Proby T. Cautley

POLITICAL

Sir John L.M. Laurence
William J. Eastwick
Henry T. Princep
Sir Frederick Currie
John P. Willoughby

PUBLIC

Sir James W. Hogg
Ross D. Mangles
Maj. Gen. Sir Robert J.
  H. Vivian
John P. Willoughby
William Arbuthnot

PUBLIC WORKS AND RAILWAYS

Sir. Proby T. Cautley
Elliot Macnaghten
Charles Mills
Sir Henry C. Montgomery
Col. William E. Baker

REVENUE AND JUDICIAL

Ross D. Mangles
Sir Thomas E. Perry
Sir James W. Hogg
Sir Henry C. Montgomery
Sir Frederick Currie

Nov. 1863 FINANCE

William Arbuthnot
Sir Frederick Currie
Elliot Macnaghten
Charles Mills
Sir Thomas E. Perry

MILITARY

Col. William E. Baker
Col. Sir Proby T. Cautley
William J. Eastwick
Sir John L.M. Laurence
Maj. Gen. Sir Robert J.
  H. Vivian

POLITICAL

William J. Eastwick
Sir Frederick Currie
Sir John L.M. Laurence
Henry T. Prinsep
John P. Willoughby

PUBLIC

Ross D. Mangles
William Arbuthnot
Sir James W. Hogg
Maj. Gen. Sir Robert J.
  H. Vivian
John P. Willoughby

Committees of the Council of India

	PUBLIC WORKS AND FINANCE	REVENUE AND JUDICIAL
	Col. Sir Proby T. Cautley Elliot Macnaghten Col. William E. Baker Charles Mills Sir Henry C. Montgomery	Sir Henry C. Montgomery Sir James W. Hogg Ross D. Mangles Sir Thomas E. Perry Henry T. Prinsep
Nov. 1864	FINANCE	MILITARY
	William Arbuthnot Charles Mills Elliot Macnaghten Ross D. Mangles Sir Thomas E. Perry	Lt. Gen. Sir Robert J. H. Vivian Col. William E. Baker Col. Sir Proby T. Cautley Sir George R. Clerk William J. Eastwick
	POLITICAL	PUBLIC
	Sir Frederick Currie Sir George R. Clerk William J. Eastwick Henry T. Prinsep Sir John P. Willoughby	Sir James W. Hogg Sir Frederick Currie Ross D. Mangles William Arbuthnot Lt. Gen. Sir. Robert J. H. Vivian
	PUBLIC WORKS AND RAILWAYS	REVENUE AND JUDICIAL
	Maj. Gen. William E. Baker Sir Henry C. Montgomery Elliot Macnaghten Charles Mills Col. Sir Proby T. Cautley	Henry T. Prinsep Sir James W. Hogg Sir Thomas E. Perry John P. Willoughby Sir Henry C. Montgomey
Nov. 1865	FINANCE	MILITARY
	William Arbuthnot Elliot Macnaghten Charles Mills Henry T. Prinsep Ross D. Mangles	Maj. Gen William E. Baker Lt. Gen Sir. Robert J. H. Vivian Col. Sir Proby T. Cautley Sir George R. Clerk William J. Eastwick
	POLITICAL	PUBLIC
	Sir George R. Clerk Sir Frederick Currie William J. Eastwick Henry T. Princep Sir John P. Willoughby	Sir John P. Willoughby Sir Thomas E. Perry Lt. Gen. Sir Robert J. H. Vivian Sir James W. Hogg William Arbuthnot

Appendix G

	PUBLIC WORKS AND RAILWAYS	REVENUE AND JUDICIAL
	Sir Henry C. Montgomery Elliot Macnaghten Charles Mills Col. Sir Proby T. Cautley Maj. Gen. William E. Baker	Ross D. Mangles Sir James W. Hogg Sir Thomas E. Perry Sir Frederick Currie •Sir Henry C. Montgomery
Nov. 1866	FINANCE	MILITARY
	William Arbuthnot Elliot Macnaghten Charles Mills Sir Henry Bartle Edward Frere Henry T. Prinsep	Lt. Gen. Sir Robert J. H. Vivian Maj. Gen. William E. Baker Col. Sir Proby T. Cautley William J. Eastwick
	POLITICAL	PUBLIC WORKS
	William J. Eastwick Sir George R. Clerk Sir Thomas E. Perry Henry T. Prinsep Sir Frederick Currie	Sir Henry C. Montgomery Col. Sir Proby T. Cautley Maj. Gen. William E. Baker Sir Bartle Frere Sir James W. Hogg
	RAILWAY AND TELEGRAPH	REVENUE AND PUBLIC AND JUDICIAL
	Maj. Gen. William E. Baker Elliot Macnaghten Charles Mills Ross D. Mangles William Arbuthnot	Sir Frederick Currie Sir James W. Hogg Ross D. Mangles Sir Thomas E. Perry Sir Henry C. Montgomery Lt. Gen. Robert J. H. Vivian
Nov. 1867	FINANCE	MILITARY
	William Arbuthnot Charles Mills Elliot Macnaghten Henry T. Prinsep Sir Thomas E. Perry	Maj. Gen. William E. Baker Lt. Gen. Sir Robert J. H. Vivian Sir George R. Clerk Col. Sir Proby T. Cautley William J. Eastwick
	POLITICAL	JUDICIAL AND PUBLIC
	William J. Eastwick Sir Frederick Currie Sir Bartle Frere Henry T. Princep Sir George R. Clerk	Sir Thomas E. Perry Sir James W. Hogg Sir Frederick Currie Sir Henry C. Montgomery Ross D. Mangles

Committees of the Council of India

PUBLIC WORKS

Col. Sir. Proby T. Cautley
Maj. Gen. William E. Baker
Sir Henry C. Montgomery
Sir Bartle Frere
Lt. Gen. Sir Robert J. H. Vivian

REVENUE

Ross D. Mangles
Sir Henry C. Montgomery
Sir Frederick Currie
Sir Thomas E. Perry
Sir James W. Hogg

RAILWAY AND TELEGRAPH

Elliot Macnaghten
Charles Mills
Ross D. Mangles
Maj. Gen. William E. Baker
William Arbuthnot

SANITARY

Sir Bartle Frere
William Arbuthnot
Col. Sir Proby T. Cautley
Sir Thomas E. Perry
William J. Eastwick

Nov. 1868

FINANCE

William Arbuthnot
Sir Frederick J. Halliday
Elliot Macnaghten
Sir Frederick Currie
Sir Thomas E. Perry

MILITARY

Maj. Gen. Sir Henry C. Rawlinson
Maj. Gen. William E. Baker
Lt. Gen. Sir Robert J. H. Vivian
Sir George R. Clerk
Sir Robert Montgomery

JUDICIAL AND PUBLIC

Sir James W. Hogg
Sir Thomas E. Perry
Henry T. Prinsep
Sir Robert Montgomery
Ross D. Mangles

POLITICAL

Sir Bartle Frere
Sir Robert Montgomery
Sir Frederick Currie
Sir George R. Clerk
Maj. Gen. Sir Henry C. Rawlinson

PUBLIC WORKS

Sir Robert Montgomery
Henry T. Prinsep
Maj. Gen. William E. Baker
Sir Bartle Frere
Lt. Gen. Sir Robert John H. Vivian

REVENUE

Ross D. Mangles
Sir Robert Montgomery
Henry T. Prinsep
Sir Thomas E. Perry
Sir James W. Hogg

RAILWAY AND TELEGRAPH

Maj. Gen. Thomas E. Baker
Elliot Macnaghten
Sir Frederick J. Halliday
Ross D. Mangles
William Arbuthnot

SANITARY

Sir Bartle Frere
William Arbuthnot
Maj. Gen. Sir Henry C. Rawlinson
Sir Thomas E. Perry
Maj. Gen. William E. Baker

Nov. 1869 FINANCE

Sir Frederick J. Halliday
Elliot Macnaghten
Sir James W. Hogg
William Arbuthnot
Sir Frederick Currie

MILITARY

Lt. Gen. Sir Robert J.
　H. Vivian
Maj. Gen. William E. Baker
Maj. Gen. Sir Henry C.
　Rawlinson
Sir Robert Montgomery
Sir George R. Clerk

JUDICIAL AND PUBLIC

Sir Thomas E. Perry
Sir James W. Hogg
Sir Frederick J. Halliday
Henry T. Prinsep
Sir Frederick Currie

POLITICAL

Sir Robert Montgomery
Sir Bartle Frere
Sir Frederick Currie
Maj. Gen. Sir Henry C.
　Rawlinson
Sir George R. Clerk

PUBLIC WORKS

Maj. Gen. William E. Baker
Sir Bartle Frere
Sir Henry C. Montgomery
Sir Thomas E. Perry
Lt. Gen. Sir Robert J.
　H. Vivian

REVENUE

Ross D. Mangles
Sir Thomas E. Perry
Sir Henry C. Montgomery
Sir Robert Montgomery
Henry T. Prinsep

RAILWAY AND TELEGRAPH

William Arbuthnot
Maj. Gen. William E. Baker
Elliot Macnaghten
Ross D. Mangles
Sir Frederick J. Halliday

SANITARY

Sir Bartle Frere
Maj. Gen. Sir Henry C.
　Rawlinson
Henry T. Prinsep
William Arbuthnot
Maj. Gen. William E. Baker

Nov. 1870 FINANCE

William Arbuthnot
Elliot Macnaghten
Sir Frederick Currie
Sir Thomas E. Perry
Sir Frederick J. Halliday

MILITARY

Maj. Gen. Sir Henry C.
　Rawlinson
Lt. Gen. Sir Robert J.
　H. Vivian
Maj. Gen. Sir William E.
　Baker
Sir Robert Montgomery
Sir George R. Clerk

JUDICIAL AND PUBLIC

Sir James W. Hogg
Ross D. Mangles
Henry T. Prinsep
Sir Thomas E. Perry
Sir Henry C. Montgomery

POLITICAL

Sir Frederick Currie
Sir George R. Clerk
Maj. Gen. Sir Henry C.
　Rawlinson
Sir Bartle Frere
Sir Robert Montgomery

Committees of the Council of India 259

PUBLIC WORKS

Maj. Gen. Sir William E.
  Baker
Sir Henry C. Montgomery
Lt. Gen. Sir Robert J.
  H. Vivian
Sir Robert Montgomery
Sir Frederick J. Halliday

REVENUE

Ross D. Mangles
Sir James W. Hogg
Henry T. Prinsep
Sir Henry C. Montgomery
Sir Thomas E. Perry

RAILWAY AND TELEGRAPH

Elliot Macnaghten
William Arbuthnot
Maj. Gen. Sir William E.
  Baker
Sir Bartle Frere
Sir Frederick J. Halliday

SANITARY

Sir Bartle Frere
William Arbuthnot
Henry T. Prinsep
Sir Frederick Currie
Maj. Gen. Sir Henry C.
  Rawlinson

Nov. 1871   FINANCE

William Arbuthnot
Sir Frederick Currie
Sir Thomas E. Perry
Sir Frederick J. Halliday
Sir James W. Hogg

MILITARY

Maj. Gen. Sir William C.
  Baker
Maj. Gen. Sir Henry C.
  Rawlinson
Lt. Gen. Sir Robert J.
  H. Vivian
Sir Robert Montgomery
Sir George R. Clerk

JUDICIAL AND PUBLIC

Sir Thomas E. Perry
Ross D. Mangles
Henry T. Prinsep
Sir Henry C. Montgomery
Sir Henry J.S. Maine

POLITICAL

Maj. Gen. Sir Henry C.
  Rawlinson
Sir Frederick Currie
Sir George R. Clerk
Sir Bartle Frere
Sir Robert Montgomery

PUBLIC WORKS

Maj. Gen. Sir William E.
  Baker
Sir Henry C. Montgomery
Lt. Gen. Sir Robert J.
  H. Vivian
Sir Robert Montgomery
Sir Frederick J. Halliday

REVENUE

Ross D. Mangles
Henry T. Prinsep
Sir Henry C. Montgomery
Sir Thomas E. Perry
Sir Henry J.S. Maine

Appendix G

RAILWAY AND TELEGRAPH

Sir Frederick J. Halliday
William Arbuthnot
Maj. Gen. Sir William E. Baker
Sir Bartle Frere
Sir James W. Hogg

SANITARY

Sir Bartle Frere
William Arbuthnot
Henry T. Prinsep
Sir Frederick Currie
Maj. Gen. Sir Henry C. Rawlinson

Nov. 1872 FINANCE

William Arbuthnot
Sir Frederick Currie
Sir Frederick J. Halliday
Sir Louis Mallet
Ross D. Mangles

MILITARY

Lt. Gen. Sir Robert J. H. Vivian
Maj. Gen. Sir Henry C. Rawlinson
Sir Robert Montgomery
Sir George R. Clerk
Maj. Gen. Sir William E. Baker

JUDICIAL AND PUBLIC

Sir Henry J.S. Maine
Sir Henry C. Montgomery
Henry T. Prinsep
Ross D. Mangles
Sir Thomas E. Perry
Sir Frederick J. Halliday

POLITICAL

Sir Robert Montgomery
Sir Bartle Frere
Sir George R. Clerk
Sir Frederick Currie
Maj. Gen. Sir Henry C. Rawlinson
Sir Thomas E. Perry

PUBLIC WORKS

Maj. Gen. Sir William E. Baker
Lt. Gen. Sir Robert J. H. Vivian
Sir Robert Montgomery
Sir Henry C. Montgomery
Sir Frederick J. Halliday

REVENUE

Ross D. Mangles
Henry T. Prinsep
Sir Henry C. Montgomery
Sir Thomas E. Perry
Sir Henry J.S. Maine
Sir Louis Mallet

RAILWAY AND TELEGRAPH

Sir Frederick J. Halliday
William Arbuthnot
Maj. Gen. Sir William C. Baker
Sir Bartle Frere
Sir Henry J.S. Maine
Sir Louis Mallet

SANITARY

Maj. Gen. Sir William E. Baker
William Arbuthnot
Henry T. Prinsep
Sir Frederick Currie
Maj. Gen. Sir Henry C. Rawlinson

Committees of the Council of India 261

Nov. 1873   FINANCE

    William Arbuthnot
    Ross D. Mangles
    Sir Frederick Currie
    Sir Frederick J. Halliday
    Sir Louis Mallet

MILITARY

    Maj. Gen. Sir William E. Baker
    Lt. Gen. Sir Robert John H. Vivian
    Sir George R. Clerk
    Sir Robert Montgomery
    Maj. Gen. Sir Henry C. Rawlinson

JUDICIAL AND PUBLIC

    Sir Henry J.S. Maine
    Ross D. Mangles
    Henry T. Prinsep
    Sir Henry C. Montgomery
    Sir Thomas E. Perry
    Sir Frederick J. Halliday

POLITICAL

    Maj. Gen. Sir Henry C. Rawlinson
    Sir Robert Montgomery
    Sir Frederick Currie
    Sir Thomas E. Perry
    Sir George R. Clerk

PUBLIC WORKS

    Sir Robert Montgomery
    Maj. Gen. Sir William E. Baker
    Lt. Gen. Sir Robert John H. Vivian
    Sir Henry C. Montgomery
    Sir Frederick J. Halliday

REVENUE

    Sir Bartle Frere
    Sir Henry C. Montgomery
    Sir Thomas E. Perry
    Sir Henry J.S. Maine
    Sir Louis Mallet

RAILWAY AND TELEGRAPH

    Sir Frederick J. Halliday
    William Arbuthnot
    Maj. Gen. Sir William E. Baker
    Sir Henry J.S. Maine
    Sir Louis Mallet

SANITARY

    Maj. Gen. Sir William E. Baker
    Henry T. Prinsep
    Sir Frederick Currie
    William Arbuthnot
    Sir Bartle Frere
    Maj. Gen. Sir Henry C. Rawlinson

Oct. 1874   FINANCE

    William Arbuthnot
    Andrew Cassels
    Sir Frederick J. Halliday
    Sir George Campbell
    Maj. Gen. Edwin B. Johnson

FINANCE
(following the death of Mr. W. Arbuthnot)

    Sir Frederick J. Halliday
    Sir George Campbell
    Andrew Cassels
    Maj. Gen. Edwin B. Johnson

MILITARY

Maj. Gen. Sir William E.
  Baker
Lt. Gen. Sir Robert J.
  H. Vivian
Maj. Gen. Sir Henry C.
  Rawlinson
Maj. Gen. Edwin B. Johnson

JUDICIAL AND PUBLIC

Sir Thomas E. Perry
Sir Henry C. Montgomery
Sir Frederick J. Halliday
Sir Henry J.S. Maine
Sir George Campbell

POLITICAL

Sir Bertle Frere
Sir Frederick Currie
Sir Thomas E. Perry
Sir George R. Clerk
Sir Robert Montgomery
Maj. Gen. Sir Henry C.
  Rawlinson

PUBLIC WORKS AND RAILWAYS

Sir Frederick J. Halliday
Sir Henry C. Montgomery
William Arbuthnot
Maj. Gen. Sir William E.
  Baker
Sir George Campbell
Andrew Cassels

PUBLIC WORKS AND RAILWAYS
(following the appointment
of Sir F. Halliday as
Chairman of the Finance
Committee)

Andrew Cassels
Sir Henry C. Montgomery
Maj. Gen. Sir William E.
  Baker
Sir George Campbell

REVENUE

Sir Henry J.S. Maine
Sir Robert Montgomery
Sir Thomas E. Perry
Sir Bartle Frere
Sir George Campbell

STATISTICS AND COMMERCE

Sir George Campbell
William Arbuthnot
Sir Bartle Frere
Maj. Gen. Sir Henry C.
  Rawlinson
Andrew Cassels

Oct. 1875

FINANCE

The Hon. Edmund Drummond
Sir Frederick Halliday
Andrew Cassels
Maj. Gen. Sir Edwin B.
  Johnson
Lt. Gen. Sir Richard
  Strachey

MILITARY

Maj. Gen. Sir Edwin B.
  Johnson
Sir George R. Clerk
Sir Robert Montgomery
Maj. Gen. Sir Henry C.
  Rawlinson
Col. Henry Yule

Committees of the Council of India 263

JUDICIAL AND PUBLIC

Sir Henry J.S. Maine
Sir Thomas E. Perry
Sir Henry C. Montgomery
The Hon. Edmund Drummond
Sir Barrow H. Ellis

POLITICAL

Sir Robert Montgomery
Sir Thomas E. Perry
Sir George R. Clerk
Sir Frederick J. Halliday
Maj. Gen. Sir Henry C. Rawlinson
Sir Henry J.S. Maine

PUBLIC WORKS AND RAILWAYS

Lt. Gen. Sir Richard Strachey
Sir Henry C. Montgomery
Andrew Cassels
Sir Barrow H. Ellis
Col. Henry Yule

REVENUE

Sir Thomas E. Perry
Sir Henry C. Montgomery
Sir Henry J.S. Maine
The Hon. Edmund Drummond
Sir Barrow H. Ellis

STATISTICS AND COMMERCE

Andrew Cassels
Sir Bartle Frere
Maj. Gen. Sir Henry C. Rawlinson
Lt. Gen. Sir Richard Strachey
Col. Henry Yule

STORES

Andrew Cassels
Lt. Gen. Sir Richard Strachey
The Hon. Edmund Drummond

Oct. 1876   FINANCE

The Hon. Edmund Drummond
Sir Frederick J. Halliday
Andrew Cassels
Maj. Gen. Sir Edwin B. Johnson
Lt. Gen. Sir Richard Strachey

MILITARY

Lt. Gen. Sir Alfred T. Wilde
Sir Robert Montgomery
Maj. Gen. Sir Henry C. Rawlinson
Maj. Gen. Edwin B. Johnson
Col. Henry Yule

JUDICIAL AND PUBLIC

Sir Thomas E. Perry
Sir Frederick J. Halliday
Sir Henry J.S. Maine
Sir Barrow H. Ellis
Sir William Muir

POLITICAL

Sir Henry J.S Maine
Sir Thomas E. Perry
Sir Bartle Frere
Sir Robert Montgomery
Sir Frederick J. Halliday
Maj. Gen. Sir Henry C. Rawlinson
Maj. Gen. Sir Edwin B. Johnson

PUBLIC WORKS AND RAILWAYS

Lt. Gen. Sir Richard
 Strachey
Andrew Cassels
Sir Barrow H. Ellis
Col. Henry Yule
Sir William Muir

REVENUE

Sir Frederick J. Halliday
Sir Thomas E. Perry
Sir Henry J.S. Maine
Sir Barrow H. Ellis
Sir William Muir

STATISTICS AND COMMERCE

Andrew Cassels
Sir Bartle Frere
Lt. Gen. Sir Richard
 Strachey
The Hon. Edmund Drummond
Sir Barrow H. Ellis
Col. Henry Yule

STORES

Andrew Cassels
Lt. Gen. Sir Richard
 Strachey
The Hon. Edmund Drummond
Lt. Gen. Sir Alfred T.
 Wilde

Oct. 1877

FINANCE

The Hon. Edmund Drummond
Sir Frederick J. Halliday
Andrew Cassels
Lt. Gen. Sir Richard
 Strachey
Maj. Gen. Sir Garnet J.
 Wolseley
Sir Barrow H. Ellis

MILITARY

Maj. Gen. Sir Garnet J.
 Wolseley
Maj. Gen. Sir Henry C.
 Rawlinson
Sir Robert Montgomery
Lt. Gen. Sir Alfred T.
 Wilde
Col. Sir William L.
 Mereweather

JUDICIAL AND PUBLIC

Sir Thomas E. Perry
Sir Frederick J. Halliday
Sir Henry J.S. Maine
The Hon. Edmund Drummond
Sir William Muir

POLITICAL

Sir Frederick J. Halliday
Sir Thomas E. Perry
Maj. Gen. Sir Henry C.
 Rawlinson
Sir Robert Montgomery
Sir Henry J.S. Maine
Col. Sir William L.
 Mereweather

PUBLIC WORKS AND RAILWAYS

Col. Henry Yule
Andrew Cassels
Lt. Gen. Sir Richard
 Strachey
Sir Barrow H. Ellis
Robert A. Dalyell

REVENUE

Sir Barrow H. Ellis
Sir Thomas E. Perry
Sir Frederick J. Halliday
Sir William Muir
Robert A. Dalyell

Committees of the Council of India

STATISTICS AND COMMERCE

Andrew Cassels
Lt. Gen. Sir Richard
　Strachey
The Hon. Edmund Drummond
Col. Henry Yule
Sir William Muir

STORES

Lt. Gen. Sir Richard
　Strachey
Andrew Cassels
Lt. Gen. Sir Alfred T.
　Wilde
Maj. Gen. Sir Garnet T.
　Wolseley
Robert A. Dalyell

Nov. 1878　FINANCE

The Hon. Edmund Drummond
Sir Frederick J. Halliday
Andrew Cassels
Sir Barrow H. Ellis
Maj. Gen. Charles J. Foster

MILITARY

Lt. Gen. Sir Henry W.
　Norman
Maj. Gen. Sir Henry C.
　Rawlinson
Sir Robert Montgomery
Col. Sir William L.
　Mereweather
Maj. Gen. Charles J.
　Foster

JUDICIAL AND PUBLIC

Sir Thomas E. Perry
Sir Frederick J. Halliday
Sir Henry J.S. Maine
The Hon. Edmund Drummond
Sir William Muir

POLITICAL

Sir Frederick J. Halliday
Maj. Gen. Sir Henry C.
　Rawlinson
Sir Henry J.S. Maine
Col. Sir William L.
　Mereweather
Sir Robert Montgomery
Sir Thomas E. Perry

PUBLIC WORKS AND RAILWAYS

Sir Barrow H. Ellis
Andrew Cassels
Col. Henry Yule
Lt. Gen. Sir Henry W.
　Norman
Robert A. Dalyell

REVENUE

Sir William Muir
Sir Thomas E. Perry
Sir Frederick J. Halliday
Sir Barrow H. Ellis
Robert A. Dalyell

STATISTICS

Col. Henry Yule
Andrew Cassels
The Hon. Edmund Drummond
Sir William Muir
Robert A. Dalyell

STORES

Robert A. Dalyell
Andrew Cassels
Lt. Gen. Sir Henry W.
Sir William Muir
　Norman
Maj. Gen. Charles J.
　Foster

Appendix G

Nov. 1879   FINANCE

Andrew Cassels
The Hon. Edmund Drummond
Sir Barrow H. Ellis
Sir William Muir
Lt. Gen. Sir Henry W.
  Norman

MILITARY

Lt. Gen. Sir Henry W.
  Norman
Sir Barrow H. Ellis
Maj. Gen. Sir Charles J.
  Foster
Col. Sir William L.
  Mereweather
Sir Robert Montgomery

JUDICIAL AND PUBLIC

Sir Henry J.S. Maine
Roebrt A. Dalyell
Sir Frederick J. Halliday
Sir William Muir
Sir Thomas E. Perry

POILITICAL

Maj. Gen. Sir Henry C.
  Rawlinson
Sir Frederick J. Halliday
Sir Henry J.S. Maine
Col. Sir William L.
  Mereweather
Sir Robert Montgomery
Sir Thomas E. Perry

PUBLIC WORKS AND RAILWAYS

Sir Barrow H. Ellis
The Hon. Edmund Drummond
Maj. Gen. Charles J. Foster
Lt. Gen. Sir Richard
  Strachey
Col. Henry Yule

REVENUE

Sir William Muir
Robert A. Dalyell
Sir Frederick J. Halliday
Sir Henry J.S. Maine
Sir Robert Montgomery

STATISTICS

Lt. Gen. Sir Richard
  Strachey
The Hon. Edmund Drummond
Maj. Gen. Sir Henry C.
  Rawlinson
Col. Henry Yule

STORES

Robert A. Dalyell
Andrew Cassels
Maj. Gen. Charles J.
  Foster
Col. Sir William L.
  Mereweather
Lt. Gen. Sir Richard
  Strachey

Nov. 1880   FINANCE

The Hon. Edmund Drummond
Andrew Cassels
Lt. Gen. Sir Henry W.
  Norman
Lt. Gen. Sir Richard
  Strachey

MILITARY

Lt. Gen. Sir Henry W.
  Norman
Sir Robert Montgomery
Sir Barrow H. Ellis
Col. Henry Yule
Maj. Gen. Charles J.
  Foster

Committees of the Council of India

JUDICIAL AND PUBLIC

Sir Henry J.S. Maine
Sir Thomas E. Perry
The Hon. Edmund Drummond
Sir William Muir
Robert A. Dalyell

POLITICAL

Sir Thomas E. Perry
Maj. Gen. Sir Henry C. Rawlingson
Sir Frederick J. Halliday
Sir Henry J.S. Maine
Sir Robert Montgomery
Lt. Gen. Sir Henry W. Norman

PUBLIC WORKS

Col. Henry Yule
Sir Frederick J. Halliday
Andrew Cassles
Sir Barrow H. Ellis
Lt. Gen. Sir Richard Strachey

REVENUE

Sir William Muir
Sir Thomas E. Perry
Sir Henry J.S. Maine
The Hon. Edmund Drummond
Robert A. Dalyell

STATISTICS

Andrew Cassels
Maj. Gen. Sir Henry C. Rawlinson
Col. Henry Yule
Robert A. Dalyell
Lt. Gen. Sir Richard Stachey

STORES

Lt. Gen. Sir Richard Stachey
Andrew Cassels
Robert A. Dalyell
Maj. Gen. Charles J. Foster

Nov. 1881 FINANCE

The Hon. Edmund Drummond
Andrew Cassels
Bertram W. Currie
Lt. Gen. Sir Henry W. Norman
Lt. Gen. Sir Richard Strachey

MILITARY

Lt. Gen. Sir Henry W. Norman
Robert A. Dalyell
Maj. Gen. Charles J. Foster
Sir Robert Montgomery
Lt. Gen. Sir Richard Strachey

JUDICIAL AND PUBLIC

Sir Henry J.S. Maine
Robert A. Dalyell
The Hon. Edmund Drummond
Sir William Muir
Sir Thomas E. Perry

POLITICAL

Sir Frederick J. Halliday
Sir Barrow H. Ellis
Sir Henry J.S. Maine
Sir Robert Montgomery
Sir Thomas E. Perry
Maj. Gen. Sir Henry C. Rawlinson

PUBLIC WORKS

Sir Barrow H. Ellis
Andrew Cassels
Sir Frederick J. Halliday
Lt. Gen. Sir Richard
　Strachey
Col. Henry Yule

REVENUE

Sir William Muir
Robert A. Dalyell
The Hon. Edmund Drummond
Sir Barrow H. Ellis
Sir Henry J.S. Maine

STATISTICS

Andrew Cassels
The Hon. Edmund Drummond
Maj. Gen. Charles J.
　Foster
Maj. Gen. Sir Henry C.
　Rawlinson
Col. Henry Yule

STORES

Robert A. Dalyell
Bertram W. Currie
Maj. Gen. Charles J.
　Foster
Sir William Muir
Lt. Gen. Sir Richard
　Strachey

Nov. 1882　FINANCE

The Hon. Edmund Drummond
Andrew Cassels
Lt. Gen. Sir Henry W.
　Norman
Lt. Gen. Sir Richard
　Strachey
Bertram W. Currie

MILITARY

Lt. Gen. Sir Henry W.
　Norman
Sir Barrow H. Ellis
Maj. Gen. Charles J.
　Foster
Sir Ashley Eden

JUDICIAL AND PUBLIC

Sir Henry J.S. Maine
Sir Robert Montgomery
The Hon. Edmund Drummond
Sir William Muir

POLITICAL

Maj. Gen. Sir Henry C.
　Rawlinson
Sir Robert Montgomery
Sir Frederick J. Halliday
Sir Henry J.S. Maine
Sir Barrow H. Ellis

PUBLIC WORKS

Lt. Gen. Sir Richard
　Strachey
Sir Frederick J. Halliday
Col. Henry Yule
Robert A. Dalyell

REVENUE

Robert A. Dalyell
Sir Barrow H. Ellis
Sir William Muir
Sir Ashley Eden

STATISTICS

Andrew Cassels
Maj. Gen. Sir Henry C.
　Rawlinson
Col. Henry Yule
Maj. Gen. Charles J.
　Foster

STORES

Maj. Gen. Charles J.
　Foster
Robert A. Dalyell
Bertram W. Currie

Committees of the Council of India

Oct. 1883 FINANCE

Andrew Cassels
Bertram W. Currie
The Hon. Edmund Drummond
Lt. Gen. Sir Richard
  Strachey
Lt. Gen. Sir Henry W.
  Norman

MILITARY

Maj. Gen. Charles J.
  Foster
Maj. Gen. Sir Henry C.
  Rawlinson
Lt. Gen. Sir Henry W.
  Norman
Sir Ashley Eden

JUDICIAL AND PUBLIC

Sir Henry J.S. Maine
Sir Robert Montgomery
Sir Barrow H. Ellis
Sir Ashley Eden

POLITICAL

Maj. Gen. Sir Henry C.
  Rawlinson
Sir Robert Montgomery
Sir Frederick J. Halliday
Sir Henry J.S. Maine
Lt. Gen. Sir Henry W.
  Norman

PUBLIC WORKS

Lt. Gen. Sir Richard
  Strachey
Sir Frederick J. Halliday
Sir William Muir
Col. Henry Yule

REVENUE

Sir Barrow H. Ellis
Sir William Muir
Sir Ashley Eden
Robert A. Dalyell

STATISTICS

Sir William Muir
Andrew Cassels
Col. Henry Yule
Lt. Gen. Sir Richard
  Strachey

STORES

The Hon. Edmund Drummond
Robert A. Dalyell
Maj. Gen. Charles J.
  Foster
Bertram W. Currie

Oct. 1884 FINANCE

The Hon. Edmund Drummond
Sir Barrow H. Ellis
Lt. Gen. Sir Richard Strachey
Bertram W. Currie
James R. Bullen Smith

MILITARY

Sir Ashley Eden
Maj. Gen. Sir Henry C.
  Rawlinson
Maj. Gen. Charles J.
  Foster
Maj. Gen. Sir Peter S.
  Lumsden

JUDICIAL AND PUBLIC

Sir Henry J.S. Maine
Sir Robert Montgomery
Sir Frederick J. Halliday
Robert A. Dalyell

POLITICAL

Maj. Gen. Sir Henry C.
  Rawlinson
Sir Robert Montgomery
Sir Frederick J. Halliday
Sir Henry J.S. Maine
Maj. Gen. Sir Peter S.
  Lumsden

PUBLIC WORKS

Lt. Gen. Sir Richard Strachey
Col. Henry Yule
Sir William Muir
James R. Bullen Smith

REVENUE

Robert A. Dalyell
Sir Barrow H. Ellis
Sir William Muir
Sir Ashley Eden

STATISTICS

James R. Bullen Smith
The Hon. Edmund Drummond
Col. Henry Yule
Robert A. Dalyell

STORES

Sir Barrow H. Ellis
The Hon. Edmund Drummond
Maj. Gen. Charles J.
   Foster
Bertram W. Currie

Oct. 1885

FINANCE

Bertram W. Currie
Lt. Gen. Sir Richard Strachey
James R. Bullen Smith
Sir John Strachey
Gen. Sir Donald M. Stewart

MILITARY

Maj. Gen. Sir Peter S.
   Lumsden
Maj. Gen. Charles J.
   Foster
Sir Ashley Eden
Gen. Sir Donald M. Stewart

JUDICIAL AND PUBLIC

Sir Henry J.S. Maine
Sir Robert Montgomery
Sir Frederick J. Halliday
Robert A. Dalyell

POLITICAL

Maj. Gen. Sir Henry C.
   Rawlinson
Sir Frederick J. Halliday
Sir Henry J.S. Maine
Maj. Gen. Sir Peter S.
   Lumsden

PUBLIC WORKS

Lt. Gen. Sir Richard Strachey
Col. Henry Yule
Sir Ashley Eden
Sir Robert H. Davies

REVENUE

Sir Ashley Eden
Robert A. Dalyell
Sir Robert H. Davies
Lt. Gen. Sir Richard
   Strachey

STATISTICS

Sir John Strachey
Maj. Gen. Sir Henry C.
   Rawlinson
Col. Henry Yule
James R. Bullen Smith

STORES

James R. Bullen Smith
Maj. Gen. Charles J.
   Foster
Bertram W. Currie
Gen. Sir Donald M. Stewart

Committees of the Council of India

Oct. 1886

FINANCE

Bertram W. Currie
Lt. Gen. Sir Richard Strachey
James R. Bullen Smith
Sir John Strachey
Gen. Sir Donald M. Stewart

MILITARY

Maj. Gen. Sir Peter S.
 Lumsden
Maj. Gen. Charles J.
 Foster
Sir Ashley Eden
Gen. Sir Donald M. Stewart

JUDICIAL AND PUBLIC

Sir Henry J.S. Maine
Sir Robert Montgomery
Sir Frederick J. Halliday
Sir John Strachey

POLITICAL

Maj. Gen. Sir Henry C.
 Rawlinson
Sir Robert Montgomery
Sir Frederick J. Halliday
Sir Henry J.S. Maine
Sir Ashley Eden

PUBLIC WORKS

Lt. Gen. Sir Richard Strachey
Col. Henry Yule
Maj. Gen. Sir Peter S. Lumsden
Sir Robert H. Davies

REVENUE

Sir John Strachey
Robert A. Dalyell
Sir Ashley Eden
Sir Robert A. Davies

STATISTICS

Col. Henry Yule
Maj. Gen. Sir Henry C.
 Rawlinson
James R. Bullen Smith
Robert A. Dalyell

STORES

James R. Bullen Smith
Maj. Gen. Charles J.
 Foster
Lt. Gen. Sir Richard
 Strachey
Robert A. Dalyell

Oct. 1887

FINANCE

Bertram W. Currie
Lt. Gen. Sir Richard Strachey
Sir John Strachey
Gen. Sir Donald M. Stewart
Robert Hardie

MILITARY

Gen. Sir Donald M. Stewart
Maj. Gen. Charles J.
 Foster
Maj. Gen. Sir Peter S.
 Lumsden
Sir Alexander J. Arbuthnot

JUDICIAL AND PUBLIC

Sir Henry J.S. Maine
Sir Robert Montgomery
Sir John Strachey
Maj. Gen. Sir Owen T. Burne
James B. Peile

POLITICAL

Maj. Gen. Sir Henry C.
 Rawlinson
Sir Henry J.S. Maine
Gen. Sir Donald M. Stewart
Maj. Gen. Sir Owen T.
 Burne

PUBLIC WORKS

Lt. Gen. Sir Richard
  Strachey
Col. Henry Yule
Sir Robert H. Davies
Robert Hardie

STORES

Robert Hardie
Lt. Gen. Sir Richard Strachey
Maj. Gen. Charles J. Foster
Bertram W. Currie

REVENUE AND STATISTICS

Sir John Strachey
Col. Henry Yule
Sir Robert H. Davies
James B. Peile
Sir Alexander J. Arbuthnot

Oct. 1888   FINANCE

Bertram W. Currie
Lt. Gen. Sir Richard
  Strachey
Sir John Strachey
Gen. Sir Donald M. Stewart
Robert Hardie

JUDICIAL AND PUBLIC

Sir Charles A. Turner
Sir John Strachey
Maj. Gen. Sir Owen T. Burne
Sir James B. Peile
Sir Alfred C. Lyall

PUBLIC WORKS

Lt. Gen. Sir Richard
  Strachey
Col. Henry Yule
Robert Hardie
Sir James B. Peile
Sir Alfred C. Lyall

STORES

Robert Hardie
Lt. Gen. Sir Richard Strachey
Bertram W. Currie
Sir Archibald Alison

MILITARY

Gen. Sir Donald M. Stewart
Maj. Gen. Sir Peter S.
  Lumsden
Sir Alexander J. Arbuthnot
Sir Archibald Alison

POLITICAL

Maj. Gen. Sir Henry C.
  Rawlinson
Gen. Sir Donald M. Stewart
Maj. Gen. Sir Owen T.
  Burne
Sir Charles A. Turner

REVENUE AND STATISTICS

Sir John Strachey
Col. Henry Yule
Sir Robert H. Davies
Sir James B. Peile
Sir Alexander J. Arbuthnot

Committees of the Council of India

Oct. 1889   FINANCE

                 Bertram Currie
                 Sir John Strachey
                 Gen. Sir Donald M. Stewart
                 Robert Hardie

MILITARY

                 Gen. Sir Donald M. Stewart
                 Maj. Gen. Sir Peter S.
                   Lumsden
                 Sir Alexander J. Arbuthnot
                 Sir Archibald Alison

JUDICIAL AND PUBLIC

                 Sir Charles A. Turner
                 Maj. Gen. Sir Owen T. Burne
                 Sir James B. Peile
                 Sir Alfred C. Lyall

POLITICAL

                 Maj. Gen. Sir Henry C.
                   Rawlinson
                 Gen. Sir Donald M. Stewart
                 Sir Owen T. Burne
                 Sir Alfred C. Lyall
                 Sir Charles A. Turner

PUBLIC WORKS

                 Sir Alfred C. Lyall
                 Robert Hardie
                 Sir Alexander J. Arbuthnot
                 Sir James B. Peile

REVENUE

                 Sir John Strachey
                 Sir Robert M. Davies
                 Sir James B. Peile
                 Sir Alexander J. Arbuthnot

STORES

                 Robert Hardie
                 Bertram W. Currie
                 Maj. Gen. Sir Peter S. Lumsden
                 Sir Archibald Alison

Oct. 1890   FINANCE

                 Bertram W. Currie
                 Sir John Strachey
                 Gen. Sir Donald M. Stewart
                 Robert Hardie

MILITARY

                 Gen. Sir Donald M. Stewart
                 Maj. Gen. Sir Peter S.
                   Lumsden
                 Sir Alexander J. Arbuthnot
                 Sir Archibald Alison

JUDICIAL AND PUBLIC

                 Sir Charles A. Turner
                 Sir John Strachey
                 Sir Owen T. Burne
                 Sir James B. Peile
                 Sir Alfred C. Lyall

POLITICAL

                 Maj. Gen. Sir Henry C.
                   Rawlinson
                 Gen. Sir Donald M. Stewart
                 Sir Owen T. Burne
                 Sir Alfred C. Lyall
                 Sir Charles A. Turner

PUBLIC WORKS

Sir Alfred C. Lyall
Robert Hardie
Sir Alexander J. Arbuthnot
Sir James B. Peile

REVENUE

Sir John Strachey
Sir Robert H. Davies
Sir James B. Peile
Sir Alexander J. Arbuthnot

STORES

Robert Hardie
Bertram W. Currie
Maj. Gen. Sir Peter S. Lumsden
Sir Archibald Alison

Nov. 1891 FINANCE

Bertram W. Currie
Sir John Strachey
Gen. Sir Donald M. Stewart
Robert Hardie

MILITARY

Gen. Sir Donald M. Stewart
Maj. Gen. Sir Peter S. Lumsden
Sir Alexander J. Arbuthnot
Sir Archibald Alison

JUDICIAL AND PUBLIC

Sir Charles A. Turner
Sir Owen T. Burne
Sir Alexander J. Arbuthnot
Sir James B. Peile
Sir Alfred C. Lyall

POLITICAL

Maj. Gen. Sir Henry C. Rawlinson
Gen. Sir Donald M. Stewart
Sir Owen T. Burne
Sir Alfred C. Lyall
Sir Charles A. Turner

PUBLIC WORKS

Sir Alfred C. Lyall
Sir John Strachey
Robert Hardie
Sir James B. Peile

REVENUE

Sir John Strachey
Sir Robert H. Davies
Sir Alexander J. Arbuthnot
Sir James B. Peile

STORES

Robert Hardie
Bertram W. Currie
Maj. Gen. Sir Peter S. Lumsden
Sir Archibald Alison

Nov. 1892 FINANCE

Bertram W. Currie
Sir John Strachey
Gen. Sir Donald M. Stewart
Robert Hardie

MILITARY

Gen. Sir Donald M. Stewart
Sir Alexander Arbuthnot
Sir Archibald Alison
Maj. Gen. Sir Peter S. Lumsden

Committees of the Council of India

JUDICIAL AND PUBLIC

Sir Charles A. Turner
Sir Owen T. Burne
Sir Alexander Arbuthnot
Sir James B. Peile
Sir Alfred Lyall

POLITICAL

Maj. Gen. Sir Henry C.
   Rawlinson
Gen. Sir Donald M. Stewart
Sir Owen T. Burne
Sir Alfred Lyall
Sir Charles A. Turner

PUBLIC WORKS

Sir Alfred C. Lyall
Sir John Strachey
Robert Hardie
Sir James B. Peile

REVENUE

Sir John Strachey
Sir Robert H. Davies
Sir Alexander J. Arbuthnot
Sir James B. Peile

STORES

Robert Hardie
Bertram W. Currie
Maj. Gen. Sir Peter S. Lumsden
Sir Archibald Alison

Nov. 1893   FINANCE

Bertram W. Currie
Sir John Strachey
Gen. Sir Donald M. Stewart
Robert Hardie

MILITARY

Gen. Sir Donald M. Stewart
Sir Alexander J. Arbuthnot
Sir Archibald Alison
Sir Owen T. Burne

JUDICIAL AND PUBLIC

Sir Charles A. Turner
Sir Alexander J. Arbuthnot
Sir James B. Peile
Sir Alfred C. Lyall

POLITICAL

Maj. Gen. Sir Henry C.
   Rawlinson
Gen. Sir Donald M. Stewart
Sir Owen T. Burne
Sir Alfred C. Lyall
Sir Charles A. Turner

PUBLIC WORKS

Sir Alfred C. Lyall
Sir John Strachey
Robert Hardie
Sir James B. Peile

REVENUE

Sir John Strachey
Sir Robert H. Davies
Sir Alexander J. Arbuthnot
Sir James B. Peile

STORES

Robert Hardie
Bertram W. Currie
Sir Owen T. Burne
Sir Archibald Alison

Nov. 1894   FINANCE

Bertram W. Currie
Sir John Strachey
Gen. Sir Donald M. Stewart
Robert Hardie

MILITARY

Gen. Sir Donald M. Stewart
Sir Alexander J. Arbuthnot
Sir Archibald Alison
Sir Owen T. Burne

JUDICIAL AND PUBLIC

Sir Charles A. Turner
Sir Alexander J. Arbuthnot
Sir James B. Peile
Sir Alfred C. Lyall

POLITICAL

Maj. Gen. Sir Henry C. Rawlinson
Gen. Sir Donald M. Stewart
Sir Owen T. Burne
Sir Charles A. Turner
Sir Alfred C. Lyall

PUBLIC WORKS

Sir Alfred C. Lyall
Sir John Strachey
Robert Hardie
Sir James B. Peile

REVENUE

Sir John Strachey
Sir Robert H. Davies
Sir Alexander J. Arbuthnot
Sir James B. Peile

STORES

Robert Hardie
Bertram W. Currie
Sir Owen T. Burne
Sir Archibald Alison

Nov. 1895   FINANCE

Bertram W. Currie
Gen. Sir Donald M. Stewart
Robert Hardie
Sir Charles H.T. Crosthwaite

MILITARY

Gen. Sir Donald M. Stewart
Sir Owen T. Burne
Sir Alexander J. Arbuthnot
Sir Archibald Alison

JUDICIAL AND PUBLIC

Sir Charles A. Turner
Sir Alexander J. Arbuthnot
Sir James B. Peile
Sir Alfred C. Lyall

POLITICAL

Sir Alfred C. Lyall
Gen. Sir Donald M. Stewart
Sir Owen T. Burne
Sir Charles A. Turner
Sir Steuart C. Bayley

PUBLIC WORKS

Sir Charles H.T. Crosthwaite
Sir Alfred C. Lyall
Robert Hardie
Sir James B. Peile

REVENUE

Sir James B. Peile
Sir Alexander J. Arbuthnot
Sir Charles H.T. Crosthwaite
Sir Steuart C. Bayley

Committees of the Council of India

STORES

Robert Hardie
Bertram W. Currie
Sir Owen T. Burne
Sir Archibald Alison

Nov. 1896

FINANCE

Francis C. Le Marchant
Gen. Sir Donald M. Stewart
Sir Charles H.T. Crosthwaite
Robert Hardie

MILITARY

Gen. Sir Donald M. Stewart
Sir Owen T. Burne
  (until Dec., 1896)
Gen. John J.H. Gordon
  (until Jan., 1897)
Sir Alexander J. Arbuthnot
Sir Archibald Alison

JUDICIAL AND PUBLIC

Sir Charles A. Turner
Sir Alexander J. Arbuthnot
Sir James B. Peile
Sir Alfred C. Lyall

POLITICAL

Sir Alfred C. Lyall
Gen. Sir Donald M. Stewart
Sir Charles Turner
Sir Steuart C. Bayley
Sir Owen T. Burne
  (until Dec., 1896)
Sir Dennis Fitzpatrick
  (April, 1897)

PUBLIC WORKS

Sir Charles H.T. Crosthwaite
Sir Alfred C. Lyall
Sir James B. Peile
Robert Hardie

REVENUE

Sir James B. Peile
Sir Charles H.T. Crosthwaite
Sir Alexander J. Arbuthnot
Sir Steuart C. Bayley

STORES

Sir Archibald Alison
Robert Hardie
Francis C. Le Marchant
Sir Owen T. Burne (until Dec., 1896)
Gen. John J.H. Gordon (Jan., 1897)

Nov. 1897

FINANCE

Francis C. Le Marchant
Gen. Sir Donald M. Stewart
Sir Charles H.T. Crosthwaite
Sir James L. Mackay

MILITARY

Gen. Sir Donald M. Stewart
Sir Alfred C. Lyall
Sir Archibald Alison
Gen. John J.H. Gordon

Appendix G

JUDICIAL AND PUBLIC

Sir Charles A. Turner
Sir James B. Peile
Sir Dennis Fitzpatrick

POLITICAL

Sir Alfred C. Lyall
Gen. Sir Donald M. Stewart
Sir Charles A. Turner
Sir Steuart C. Bayley
Sir Dennis Fitzpatrick

PUBLIC WORKS

Sir Charles H.T. Crosthwaite
Sir James B. Peile
Sir Alfred C. Lyall
Sir James L. Mackay

REVENUE

Sir James B. Peile
Sir Charles H.T. Crosthwaite
Sir Steuart C. Bayley
Sir Dennis Fitzpatrick

STORES

Sir Archibald Alison
Francis C. Le Marchant
Gen. John J.H. Gordon
Sir James L. Mackay

Nov. 1898

FINANCE

Francis C. Le Marchant
Gen. Sir Donald M. Stewart
Sir Charles H.T. Crosthwaite
Sir James L. Mackay

MILITARY

Gen. Sir Donald M. Stewart
Sir Alfred C. Lyall
Sir Archibald Alison
Gen. Sir John J.H. Gordon

JUDICIAL AND PUBLIC

Sir John Edge
Sir James B. Peile
Sir Dennis Fitzpatrick
Sir Philip Hutchins

POLITICAL

Sir Alfred C. Lyall
Gen. Sir Donald M. Stewart
Sir Steuart C. Bayley
Sir Dennis Fitzpatrick

PUBLIC WORKS

Sir Charles H.T. Crosthwaite
Sir James B. Peile
Sir Alfred C. Lyall
Sir James L. Mackay

REVENUE

Sir James B. Peile
Sir Charles H.T. Crosthwaite
Sir Steuart C. Bayley
Sir Dennis Fitzpatrick
Sir Philip Hutchins

STORES

Sir Archibald Alison
Francis C. Le Marchant
Gen. Sir John J.H. Gordon
Sir James L. Mackay

Committees of the Council of India 279

Oct. 1899   FINANCE

Francis C. Le Marchant
Gen. Sir Donald M. Stewart
Sir Charles H.T. Crosthwaite
Sir James L. Mackay
Sir James Westland

MILITARY

Gen. Sir Donald M. Stewart
Sir Alfred C. Lyall
Gen. Sir John J.H. Gordon
Sir James Westland

JUDICIAL AND PUBLIC

Sir John Edge
Sir James B. Peile
Sir Dennis Fitzpatrick
Sir Philip Hutchins

POLITICAL

Sir Alfred C. Lyall
Gen. Sir Donald M. Stewart
Sir Steuart C. Bayley
Sir Dennis Fitzpatrick
Sir John Edge

PUBLIC WORKS

Sir Charles H.T. Crosthwaite
Sir James B. Peile
Sir Alfred C. Lyall
Sir James C. Mackay

REVENUE

Sir James B. Peile
Sir Charles H.T. Crosthwaite
Sir Steuart C. Bayley
Sir Dennis Fitzpatrick
Sir Philip Hutchins

STORES

Francis C. Le Marchant
Gen. Sir John J.H. Gordon
Sir James L. Mackay
Sir James Westland

Nov. 1900   FINANCE

Francis C. Le Merchant
Sir Charles H.T. Crosthwaite
Sir James L. Mackay
Sir James Westland

MILITARY

Sir Alfred C. Lyall
Gen. Sir John J.H. Gordon
Sir James Westland

JUDICIAL AND PUBLIC

Sir John Edge
Sir Dennis Fitzpatrick
Sir Philip Hutchins
Sir James B. Peile

POLITICAL

Sir Alfred C. Lyall
Sir Steuart C. Bayley
Sir Dennis Fitzpatrick
Sir John Edge

PUBLIC WORKS

Sir Charles H.T. Crosthwaite
Sir James B. Peile
Sir Alfred C. Lyall
Sir James L. Mackay

REVENUE

Sir James B. Peile
Sir Charles H.T. Crosthwaite
Sir Steuart C. Bayley
Sir Dennis Fitzpatrick
Sir Philip Hutchins

STORES

Francis C. Le Marchant
Sir James Westland
Sir James L. Mackay
Gen. Sir John J.H. Gordon

Nov. 1901   FINANCE

Francis C. Le Marchant
Sir Charles H.T. Crosthwaite
Sir James L. Mackay
Sir James Westland
Lt. Gen. Alexander R.
  Badcock

MILITARY

Sir Alfred C. Lyall
Gen. Sir John J.H.Gordon
Sir James Westland
Lt. Gen. Alexander R.
  Badcock

JUDICIAL AND PUBLIC

Sir John Edge
Sir James B. Peile
Sir Dennis Fitzpatrick
Sir Philip Hutchins

POLITICAL

Sir Alfred C. Lyall
Sir Steuart C. Bayley
Sir Dennis Fitzpatrick
Sir John Edge
Lt. Gen. Alexander R.
  Badcock

PUBLIC WORKS

Sir Charles H.T. Crosthwaite
Sir James B. Peile
Sir Alfred C. Lyall
Sir James L. Mackay

REVENUE

Sir James B. Peile
Sir Steuart C. Bayley
Sir Dennis Fitzpatrick
Sir Philip Hutchins

STORES

Francis C. Le Marchant
Sir James Westland
Sir James L. Mackay
Gen. Sir John J.H. Gordon

Nov. 1902   FINANCE

Francis C. Le Marchant
Sir Charles H.T. Crosthwaite
Sir James L. Mackay
Sir James Westland
Lt. Gen. Alexander R.
  Badcock

MILITARY

Gen. Sir John J.H. Gordon
Sir Alfred C. Lyall
Sir James Westland
Lt. Gen. Alexander R.
  Babcock
Sir William Lee-Warner

JUDICIAL AND PUBLIC

Sir John Edge
Sir Charles H.T Crosthwaite
Sir Dennis Fitzpatrick
Sir Philip Hutchins

POLITICAL

Sir Alfred C. Lyall
Sir Steuart C. Bayley
Sir Dennis Fitzpatrick
Sir John Edge
Lt. Gen. Alexander R.
  Badcock

Committees of the Council of India

    PUBLIC WORKS

    Sir Charles H.T. Crosthwaite
    Sir Alfred C. Lyall
    Sir Steuart C. Bayley
    Sir Philip Hutchins

    REVENUE

    Sir Dennis Fitzpatrick
    Sir Steuart C. Bayley
    Sir Philip Hutchins
    Sir William Lee-Warner

    STORES

    Sir James Westland
    Francis C. Le Marchant
    Gen. Sir John J.H. Gordon
    Sir James L. Mackay

Nov. 1903   FINANCE

    Francis C. Le Marchant
    Sir Charles H.T. Crosthwaite
    Sir James L. Mackay
    Lt. Gen. Sir Alexander R. Badcock
    James F. Finlay

    MILITARY

    Gen. Sir John J.H. Gordon
    Lt. Gen. Sir Alexander R. Badcock
    Sir William Lee-Warner
    James F. Finlay

    JUDICIAL AND PUBLIC

    Sir John Edge
    Sir Charles H.T. Crosthwaite
    Sir Dennis Fitzpatrick
    Sir Philip Hutchins

    POLITICAL

    Sir Steuart C. Bayley
    Sir Dennis Fitzpatrick
    Sir John Edge
    Lt. Gen. Sir Alexander R. Badcock
    Sir William Lee-Warner

    PUBLIC WORKS

    Sir Charles H.T. Crosthwaite
    Sir Steuart C. Bayley
    Sir James L. Mackay
    Sir Philip Hutchins

    REVENUE

    Sir Dennis Fitzpatrick
    Sir Steuart C. Bayley
    Sir Philip Hutchins
    Sir William Lee-Warner

    STORES

    Sir James L. Mackay
    Francis C. Le Marchant
    Gen. Sir John J.H. Gordon
    James F. Finlay

Nov. 1904   FINANCE

    Francis C. Le Marchant
    Sir Charles H.T. Crosthwaite
    Sir James L. Mackay
    Lt. Gen. Sir Alexander R. Badcock
    James F. Finlay

    MILITARY

    Gen. Sir John J.H. Gordon
    Lt. Gen. Sir Alexander R. Badcock
    Sir William Lee-Warner
    James F. Finlay

JUDICIAL AND PUBLIC

Sir John Edge
Sir Charles H.T. Crosthwaite
Sir Dennis Fitzpatrick
Sir Philip Hutchins

POLITICAL

Sir Steuart C. Bayley
Sir Dennis Fitzpatrick
Sir John Edge
Lt. Gen. Sir Alexander R. Badcock
Sir William Lee-Warner

PUBLIC WORKS

Sir Charles H.T. Crosthwaite
Sir Steuart C. Bayley
Sir James L. Mackay
Sir Philip Hutchins

REVENUE

Sir Dennis Fitzpatrick
Sir Steuart C. Bayley
Sir Philip Hutchins
Sir William Lee-Warner

STORES

Sir James L. Mackay
Francis C. Le Marchant
Gen. Sir John J.H. Gordon
James F. Finlay

Oct. 1905

FINANCE

Francis C. Le Marchant
Sir James L. Mackay
Lt. Gen. Sir Alexander R. Badcock
James F. Finlay

MILITARY

Gen. Sir John J.H. Gordon
Lt. Gen. Sir Alexander R. Badcock
James F. Finlay
Sir David W.K. Barr

JUDICIAL AND PUBLIC

Sir John Edge
Sir Dennis Fitzpatrick
Sir Philip Hutchins
Sir William Lee-Warner

POLITICAL

Sir William Lee-Warner
Sir Dennis Fitzpatrick
Sir John Edge
Lt. Gen. Sir Alexander R. Badcock
Sir Hugh S. Barnes
Sir David W.K. Barr

PUBLIC WORKS

Sir James L. Mackay
Sir Philip Hutchins
Sir Hugh S. Barnes
Sir David W.K. Barr

REVENUE

Sir Dennis Fitzpatrick
Sir Philip Hutchins
Sir William Lee-Warner
Sir Hugh S. Barnes

STORES

James F. Finlay
Francis C. Le Marchant
Gen. Sir John J.H. Gordon
Sir James L. Mackay

Index

Abyssinia, 112
Accountant-General, 14, 18
Admiralty, 114
Afghanistan, 69, 91, 148, 160
Africa, 112, 113. See also Egypt; South Africa
Agency theory, 145, 146, 147
Agricultural policies, 72, 73
All-India Congress Committee, 174
Ampthill, Baron (A. O. V. Russell), 77, 146–47, 148, 149–50
Amrita Bazar Patrika, 166
Anderson, H. L., 16
Anglo-Russian entente, 142
Arbuthnot, Sir Alexander, 55
Ardagh, Colonel John, 176
Argyll, 8th Duke of (George Douglas Campbell), 64, 127–28, 129, 143
Arundel, Sir A. T., 79
Asquith, H. H. (Earl of Oxford and Asquith), 6, 95, 96
Auditor, 14
Australia, 113–14

Babington-Smith, H., 149, 176
Balfour, Arthur, 42, 74, 150
Banerjea, S. N., 161, 164, 170, 235
Bayley, C. S., 169
Bayley, Sir Steuart, 235

Bengal: partitioning of, 142, 164, 180; press in, 179, 180
Bengalee, 161
Bhavnagri, M. M., 168
Birkmyre, William, 44–45, 104, 105, 106, 161
Blunt, W. S., 170
Board of Trade, 114
Boer War, 110–11. See also South Africa
Bolton, C. W., 169
Bombay Presidency Association, 161
Bonnerjee, W. C., 161
Bourdillon, E. D., 16
Brackenbury, Sir Henry, 135, 235
Bradlaugh, Charles, 161
Bright, John, 37, 160, 161
British Army in India, 110, 133, 200
British Committee of the Indian National Congress, 20, 159, 160, 166, 172; on contagious diseases act, 200; on currency crisis, 198; and elections of 1895, 163, 164; finances of, 168, 169; founded, 162; and Hume, 161–62; v. India Office, 165, 167, 170, 174; journal of (see *India*); loses support, 164, 168, 169, 173; members of, 162; and Parliament, 163, 171; on simultaneous exams, 163–

64; usefulness of, 173–74; and Wedderburn, 167
Brodrick, St. John (Lord Midleton), 44, 113, 150, 235; on control of press, 178; and Council of India, 75, 76; and Curzon, 74–77, 147–48; on Curzon-Kitchener debate, 76; Godley on, 75, 77; on Indian army, 74; at War Office, 74, 111
Brussels Conference, 198
Buck, G. S., 176–77
Buckle, G. E., 178
Bureaucracy, 5, 6, 11, 18, 19, 191, 192
Burne, Owen Tudor, 45, 66–67, 175–76, 236

Cabinet: on foreign policy, 140; v. Government of India, 140; and Indian policy, 114–15; pressures/influences India Office, 89, 102, 196, 200; pressures/influences Secretaries of State, 73, 81, 92–101, 131; on Viceroy, 94–95; v. Viceroy, 140, 141, 143, 148
Caine, W. S., 162, 164
Campbell, Sir George, 103
Campbell-Bannerman, Sir Henry, 93
Canning, Charles John (1st Earl), 123
Cantonment legislation, 14, 132–38; British Committee of Congress on, 200; Council of India on, 70, 133, 200, 201; Cross on, 69, 132–33; Elgin on, 133–34, 135, 137; Fowler on, 134; Government of India on, 72, 132, 133, 135, 199, 201; Hamilton on, 72; Indian press on, 137; India Office on, 133, 134, 135, 199–201; Kimberley on, 70, 133; Miller on, 133, 134, 135, 136; Viceroy's Council on, 133–34, 135, 137, 138
Carrington, Lord (Charles Wynn-Carrington), 94, 95
Cell, John W., 192, 193
Central Registry, 19
Chatterji, P. K., 35
Chirol, Valentine, 177, 178, 236
Churchill, Lord Randolph, 66–68, 90, 91, 93, 236

Civil and Military Gazette, 175
Civil Procedure Bill, 124, 127
Civil Service, 3; and India Office, 5, 23–24, 26, 114
Clerk, Sir George Russell, 12, 13, 52
Cobden Club, 44–45, 104, 105, 106, 161
Colonial Office, 3, 5, 113–14, 192, 193
Communications, 5, 23, 124, 191. *See also* Telegraph
Connaught, Duke of (Arthur William Albert), 90
Conservative Party, 93, 168
Contagious diseases legislation, 14, 200. *See also* Cantonment legislation
Coronation expenses, 73, 91
Correspondence Departments, 14–15, 16–17, 18, 52; Political and Secret Department of, 14, 19, 38, 40, 45–46
Cotton, Sir Henry, 162, 166, 170, 173
Cotton duties crises, 130–33, 138, 199; Council of India overruled on, 70, 131; Elgin and, 130, 131–32, 136; Fowler on, 134; Godley and, 71, 131; Government of India on, 72, 128, 131–32, 135–36, 137; Hamilton on, 71, 72; Indian press on, 132, 137; India Office on, 131, 132; Kimberley on, 70, 131; Morley on, 170; Northbrook on, 131; Salisbury on, 131; Viceroy's Council on, 131–32, 136; Westland on, 131, 136
Council of India, 11, 35–61, 124; Act of 1858 on, 35–36, 40, 41, 42, 48, 52, 193; Act of 1869 on, 39–40, 41, 42, 53; as advisory board, 37, 39, 40, 81, 193; appointments to, 36, 51; Birkmyre on, 104, 105, 106; and Brodrick, 75, 76; on cantonment legislation, 70, 133, 200, 201; as check/balance, 37; and Churchill, 67, 68; Clerk to, 14; committees of, 5, 12, 13, 15, 45, 46, 47–48, 50, 52–53, 54, 55, 56, 68, 79–80, 82, 192, 193, 194; on correspondence, 17, 45, 46–48, 49, 50, 56, 72; on cotton duties, 70, 131; Cross and, 69, 133; on

Index

currency crisis, 197, 199; Curzon on, 42, 43, 75, 76, 105–6, 138, 139–40, 141; on Curzon-Kitchener dispute, 76; dissents in, 48–49, 56; East India Company influences, 36, 53; established, 35, 36, 103, 104; factions in, 39, 193; on famine relief, 109; financial powers of, 40–42, 43, 56; "forward" group in, 64, 67; Fowler and, 70; function/role of, 15, 26–27, 35, 36, 38, 52, 194, 195; Godley and/on, 42–43, 44, 51, 53, 54, 55, 69, 71, 75, 194, 195; v. Government of India, 43, 72, 73, 125, 139; Hamilton and, 55, 66, 71, 72–73, 75, 140, 194; independence of, 103–4; and Indian Civil Service, 51; Indian experience of members of, 15, 36–37, 50, 51, 81, 194, 196; on Indian National Congress, 195; on Indian troops, 111; and India Office, 5, 13, 15, 16, 26, 27, 35, 37, 45–48, 52, 53, 54–55, 82, 194, 202; Kimberley and, 64, 65–66, 68, 70, 131, 163–64; meetings of, 48; membership of, 26, 36–37, 39–40, 50–51, 53–54, 81–82, 90, 105–6, 128, 177, 193, 194–95; Monarchy on, 36; Morley and, 78–80, 81; Muslim bloc in, 80; and Mysore succession, 39; paperwork by, 51–52, 53, 54, 55, 193; Parliament on, 35–36, 38, 39–40, 41, 44–45, 64, 102, 103–4, 163; and Permanent Undersecretary, 44, 51, 71 (see also Godley, Arthur); policy formed by, 5, 15, 26–27, 35, 36, 38, 49, 51, 55–56, 64, 102, 191, 194–95; Political Committee of, 45, 46, 47–48; politics within, 52–53; powers of, 38–39, 43, 44, 105; press on, 39; pressure groups within, 64; procedures of, 49–50, 54, 69; public opinion on, 44–45; Queen Victoria on, 37; reorganization of, 39, 52, 53, 54, 69; Salisbury on, 39; and Secretaries of State, 35–36, 37, 38–40, 41–42, 43, 44, 45, 46–47, 48, 49, 52, 56, 63–88, 106, 131, 133, 163–64, 192, 194, 195, 200, 201; on sedition, 45, 46–47; specialization in, 55, 194; Stanley on, 36; veto power of, 40, 42–43, 44, 56; Viceroy and, 51, 69, 138–39, 195

Council of India (Reduction) Act (1889), 54, 68
Council of India Act (1907), 54
Cranborne. See Salisbury, 3rd Marquis of
Cranbrook, 1st Earl of (Gathorne Gathorne-Hardy), 64
Creagh, General Sir O'Moore, 109–10
Crewe, Marquess of (R. O. A. Crewe-Milnes), 195, 236
Criminal Investigation Department, 46, 168, 169
Cross, Richard A. (Viscount Cross), 24, 94, 105, 236; on cantonment, 69, 132–33; Godley on, 68, 69; on ICS age limits, 69; overrules Council of India, 69, 133
Croswaithe, Charles, 198
Crown. See Edward VII; Monarchy; Victoria, Queen
Currency crisis, 131, 197–99
Currie, Bertram, 198
Curzon, George Nathaniel (1st Marquess), 20, 124, 236–37; on Afghan policy, 148; on Ampthill, 146–47; on Brodrick, 74–77; Brodrick on, 147–48; v. Cabinet, 140, 141, 148; on Council of India, 42, 43, 75, 76, 105–6, 138, 139–40, 141; on Elgin, 138; on famine policy, 109; v. Foreign Office, 110; and Godley, 77, 149, 150; Godley on, 140, 141, 148; and Government of India, 43, 178; on Government of India Act revised, 42–43, 76, 105–6; and Hamilton, 71, 72, 73, 74, 139, 140; on Indian army, 112, 113; on Indian emigration, 113; on Indian National Congress, 170; on India Office, 43, 105, 106, 138–41; v. Kitchener, 76, 142, 146, 148, 151, 178; leave of absence of, 146–48; on Persian Gulf, 110; on press, 175, 176, 179, 180; on private correspondence, 91; resigns,

141, 148, 178; travels in India, 19, 105; and Viceroy's Council, 139; on Viceroy's rights, 141; on War Office, 111

Dalhousie tradition, 46
Danvers, Frederic C., 17, 19, 237
Danvers, Juland, 17, 237
Dawkins, Clinton, 73, 76
Dictionary of National Biography, 50, 130, 132
Digby, William, 161, 162, 164, 166, 167, 168, 237
Dilke, Sir Charles, 171
Dilks, David, 197
Dufferin and Ava, 1st Marquess of (Frederick Temple Blackwood), 66, 67, 148–49
Dunlop Smith, Sir J. R., 78, 145, 176

East India Association, 160
East India Company, 4, 12, 18, 41, 160, 191; Court of Directors of, 15, 36, 45; dissolved, 36; influences Council of India, 36, 53; influences India Office, 6, 15, 45, 192, 193; and Parliament, 106
The Economist, 199
Edge, Sir John, 47, 237
Edgerley, Sir Steyning, 81, 237
Edward VII, 89, 91, 92, 95. *See also* Monarchy
Egypt, 110, 111–12
Elgin, 9th Earl of (Victor Alexander Bruce), 42, 68, 94, 95, 123, 124, 129–38, 140, 143, 151, 235–36; on cantonment legislation, 133–34, 135, 137; and cotton duties crises, 130, 131–32, 136; and currency crisis, 198; Curzon on, 138; *Dictionary* on, 130, 132; difficulties of, as Viceroy, 129–32, 133–38; on famine policy, 109; and Fowler, 71, 133, 134, 137–38; and Godley, 71, 149; and Hamilton, 71–72; on Indian army, 112; on Indian emigration, 114; Indian press on, 71, 130; mandate theory of, 136–37, 145; on private correspondence, 91; reputation/credibility of, 129–30, 132, 137, 138; on tariff legislation, 134; on "urgent" legislation, 130; and Viceroy's Council, 130, 131–32, 133–34, 135, 136, 137; on Viceroy's position, 137, 138
Ellis, J. E., 77
Elphinstone, Mountstuart, 178–79
England. *See* British Army in India; Great Britain
The Englishman, 78
English Opinion on India, 177

Famine policies, 72, 73, 109
Fawcett, Henry, 40, 160
Finance Department, 14, 199
Foreign Office, 3, 5, 109–10, 112
"Forward" policy, 64, 67, 93
Foster, William, 4
Fowler, Henry (Lord Wolverhampton), 65, 69–71, 91, 143, 237; on cantonment legislation, 134; on cotton duties, 134; and Council of India, 70; Elgin and, 71, 133, 134, 137–38; Godley on, 69, 70; on Home v. Indian government, 70, 132, 134–35, 136, 138; Indian press on, 71; and lobbies, 70; on public opinion, 70
Fowler Committee (on currency), 198, 199
Fraser, Lovat, 144, 177
Free traders, 71
Frontier policy, 68, 72, 73, 109

Gandhi, Mohandas K., 114, 173
General Post Office, 114
German East Africa, 113
Ghose, Motilal, 166
Giffen, Sir Robert, 199
Gladstone, William Ewart, 26, 66, 93; and Godley, 6, 77, 227, 228; on honors, 96, 101; and Morley, 77, 78
Godley, Sir Arthur (Lord Kilbracken), 12, 124, 138, 191, 238; on Accountant-General, 18; on Act of 1858, 42; and Ampthill, 149–50; biography of, 227–34; on British public opin-

ion, 174–75; on Brodrick, 75, 77; and Churchill, 66, 67; on Correspondence Departments, 18; and cotton duties crises, 71, 131; and Council of India, 42–43, 44, 51, 53–54, 55, 69, 71, 75, 194, 195; on Cross, 68, 69; and Curzon, 77, 140, 141, 148, 149–50; described, 6; on discretion, 17–18, 20; discretion of, 150; duties of, 14, 17, 18, 75; and Elgin, 71, 149; on Fowler, 69, 70; Gladstone influences, 6, 77, 227, 228; on Imperial policies, 112; on Indian army, 111–12; on Indian lobbies, 168; on Indian press, 179; on Indian public opinion, 179–80; on India Office, 49, 89; and India Office appointments, 15; on India Office employees/staff, 13, 17, 22–23, 24, 26; India Office reorganized by, 13, 19–20, 21–23, 42, 107, 169; influence of, 5–7, 18, 107, 196–97; on insiders v. outsiders, 15, 196; on Kimberley, 65; on Kitchener, 77, 79; as liaison, India Office-Council of India, 54–55, 63, 71, 75; as liaison, India Office-Government of India, 77, 148–50; as liaison, India Office-Viceroys, 125, 140, 142; and Minto, 150; on Monarch's private correspondence, 91, 92; and Morley, 77–78, 80, 171, 231–32; paper flow and, 17, 18, 63, 72; on Parliament, 19–20, 104–5, 106–7; politics of, 6, 229–30; retires, 231; on Russo-Japanese War, 180; on salaries, 24; and Secretaries of State, 64–65, 69, 71, 75, 145–46, 150–51, 171; on secret correspondence, 47–48; on Stores Department, 18; and/on Viceroys, 71, 96, 136, 146, 147, 148–50

Gokhale, G. K., 164, 167, 168, 170, 171, 172, 173

Gold Exchange Standard, 199

Gold Standard Defence Association, 197, 198

Gopal, S., 132

Gorst, Sir John, 13–14

Government of India, 26, 76, 109; v. Cabinet, 140; in Calcutta, 5, 39, 69, 159; on cantonment legislation, 132, 133, 135, 199, 201; on Civil Procedure Bill, 124; composition and function of, 125–26; on constitutional questions, 124–25; on coronation expenses, 73; on cotton duties, 72, 128, 131–32, 135–36, 137; and Council of India, 39, 43, 72, 73, 125, 139; on currency crisis, 197; and Curzon, 178; departments in, 126–27; disseminates news, 175, 176; on famine policy, 73; finances of, 132; foreign policy of, 110, 140; Godley and, 77, 148–50; Governor-General as head of, 124, 125–26 (see also Viceroy and Governor-General); independent action by, 130; on Indian army, 74, 113; on Indian National Congress, 169; on Indian representation, 194; and India Office, 5, 70, 71, 72, 77, 115, 123–58, 171, 181, 192, 196, 200; on leaving acts to operation, 125; on legislation, 124, 127–28, 129, 143, 179; Legislative Council in, 126, 127, 128, 131, 133, 135–36, 137; policy-making role of, 178; portfolio system of, 126; Presidency-Governors in, 91, 146; and press, 132, 137, 144, 175, 176, 179, 180; on previous sanction, 124, 128; proposes reform, 79; on railways, 139; v. Secretaries of State, 72, 77, 92, 93, 124, 125, 127–28, 129, 146; on secret correspondence, 45, 46, 47; on sedition, 46, 47, 143; on tariffs, 124; on Viceroy's Council, 125; on Viceroy's position, 125

Government of India Act (1858), 45, 47, 101, 161, 162; on Council of India, 35–36, 40, 41, 42, 48, 52, 53, 193; Godley on, 42; on India Office, 24; intent of, 37; on Parliament's role in Indian affairs, 102–3; revised, 42–43, 76, 105–6; on Secretary of State's powers, 40, 48

Government of India Act (1869), 39–40, 41, 42, 53
Government of India Act (1919), 125
Government of India Act (1935), 54
Governor-General. *See* Viceroy and Governor-General
Governor-General in Council, 124, 125–26
Great Britain: administration of, 3 (*see also* Cabinet; Parliament); communications to, 23, 124; Indian lobbies in, 161–65, 170, 171–72, 173, 174 (*see also* British Committee of the Indian National Congress; Indian Political Agency); Indian radicals in, 178; pledge to India of, 162; press in, 78, 160, 167, 169, 175, 176, 177, 178, 181; public opinion in, 159, 160, 172, 174–75
Griffen, Sir Lepel, 67

Hamilton, Lord George, 46, 47, 71–74, 150, 238; on agricultural policies, 72, 73; on Brodrick, 74; v. Cabinet, 73; on cantonment legislation, 72; on cotton duties, 71, 72; and/on Council of India, 55, 66, 71, 72–73, 75, 140, 194; and Curzon, 71, 72, 73, 74, 139, 140; on Digby, 167; and Elgin, 71–72; on famine policy, 72, 73, 109; on frontier policy, 72, 73; v. Government of India, 72, 91; on Indian army, 111, 112–13; Indian press on, 71, 73, 84 n.41; on Indian press, 169; on India Office, 11, 108; v. Parliament, 73; on plague policy, 72, 73; on private correspondence, 72
Hardie, James Keir, 10, 105, 171, 173, 238
Hardinge, Charles (Baron of Penshurst), 95, 96
Harris, 4th Baron (George Robert Canning), 68
Hartington, Marquess of (Spencer Compton Cavendish), 5, 41, 64
Hectography, 30 n.52
Herschell, Lord Farrer, 94, 238
Herschell Committee on Indian Finance, 198
Hindoo Patriot, 137
Hindu, 65, 166
Hirtzel, Arthur, 80, 142, 172, 238
Hobhouse, Arthur, 128
Home charges, 163, 197
Home Government of India. *See* India Office
Honors, 37, 96, 101, 146
Hume, Allan O., 161–62, 164, 165, 166, 238
Husain, S. A., 3
Hyndman, Henry, 170

Ilbert Bill, 64
Imperial Famine Grant, 109
Imperial needs/policies, 92, 93, 110–13, 196, 199, 201, 202
India: communications in, 23, 124; contagious diseases legislation for (*see* Cantonment legislation); currency in, 131, 197–99; emigration from, 113–14, 178; English press in, 175–76, 177; English public opinion on, 174–75; finances of, 40, 108, 112, 113, 164; foreign policy of, 140, 142; frontier policy for, 68, 72, 73, 109; as home question, 160; and Ireland, 160, 180; lobbies, 20, 69, 161–74 (*see also* British Committee of the Indian National Congress; Indian Political Agency); and Monarchy, 89, 90, 91, 92; nationalism in, 44, 160–61, 164–65, 177–78, 194, 195, 202; Parliament on, 19–20, 44, 102–4, 108, 109, 132–33, 138, 160, 162, 163–64, 165–66, 197, 201; policy for, 4, 11–12, 66, 69, 89, 92, 93, 107, 123, 127, 128–29, 143, 159, 177–78, 201; press in, 71, 73, 84 n.41, 130, 132, 137, 164, 166, 169, 175, 176, 177, 178–79, 180, 181; press controls in, 178, 180; public opinion in, 159, 178–81; sedition in, 143; trade policy for, 68, 124 (*see also* Cotton duties crises)
India, 71, 162, 168, 169, 173, 174, 177

Index

India Council. *See* Council of India
Indian army: Commander-in-Chief of, 74, 90, 93–94, 126; on foreign soil, 74, 110–11, 112–13; in World War I, 111
Indian Civil Service, 26, 51, 69, 103, 114, 163, 167
Indian Councils Acts (1861), 127
Indian Councils Acts (1909), 80
Indian Currency Association, 197
Indian Exchequer, 109
Indian National Congress, 20, 26, 44; on Bengal partitioning, 164; and British public opinion, 174; Churchill on, 68; on currency crisis, 198; Curzon on, 170; on England's pledge to India, 162; Extremists in, 173, 180; Gandhi leads, 173; goal of, 163; and Government of India, 169; and India Office, 169, 170, 180, 181; lobby of, 103 (*see also* British Committee of the Indian National Congress); organ of (see *India*); Surat split in, 165, 168, 172, 173; and Svadeshi movement, 164
Indian Parliamentary Committee, 20, 161, 163, 165, 169–70, 171; and election of 1895, 168; and India Office, 159, 160, 167; M.P.s on, 170; in retreat, 173
Indian Police, 114
Indian Political Agency, 161, 162, 166
India Office: Act of 1858 on, 24; appointments in, 15; Assistant Undersecretary in, 14; as bureaucracy, 5, 6, 11, 18, 19, 191, 192; Cabinet influences, 89, 102, 196, 200; on cantonment legislation, 133, 134, 135, 199–201; Central Registry of, 19; on Civil Procedure Bill, 124; and Civil Service Commission, 5, 23–24, 26, 114; constitutional struggles within, 40, 48; controls information flow, 19–20, 38, 165, 177–78, 198, 199; on cotton duties, 131, 132; and Council of India, 5, 13, 15, 16, 26, 27, 35, 37, 45–48, 52, 53, 54–55, 63, 71, 75, 82, 191, 194, 202; and currency crisis, 197–99; Curzon on, 43, 105, 106, 138–41; departmental organization of, 5, 6, 13, 14, 15, 18, 20, 21, 50, 56, 195, 196 (*see also individual departments by name*); East India Company influence in, 6, 15, 45, 192, 193; funding for, 3, 4, 24, 26, 197; Government of India subordinate to, 5, 70, 71, 72, 77, 115, 123–58, 171, 181, 192, 196, 200; Hamilton on, 11, 108; head of (*see* Secretary of State for India); and imperial policies, 199, 201, 202; independence of, 5, 108–9, 180; and Indian emigration, 113–14; on Indian legislation, 124, 127–28, 129, 143; and Indian National Congress, 169, 170, 180, 181; and Indian nationalism, 202; insiders and outsiders in, 15, 16, 196; internal investigations of, 53–54, 105; Judicial and Public Department of, 46; on leaving acts to operation, 125; and lobbies, 5, 20, 159, 160, 161, 165, 167, 169, 170, 174, 180, 181, 196; Monarch influences, 37–38, 89–92, 93, 96, 102, 114, 142, 180; and other departments of state, 5, 24–26, 89, 108–14, 115, 165; paper flow in, 5, 11, 14, 15–16, 17, 18–19, 20, 21–22, 23, 26, 38, 124, 192, 195–96; and Parliament, 5, 19–20, 73, 89, 103, 104, 105, 106, 107, 114, 165, 180, 192, 196, 198, 200, 201; Permanent Undersecretary in (*see* Godley, Arthur); on Persian Gulf, 109, 110; policy-making role of, 3–5, 6, 14, 15, 16, 19–20, 26–27, 38, 46, 64, 107, 124, 142, 159, 177–78, 191, 192, 195, 196, 197, 198, 201; and press, 5, 17–18, 60, 169, 175–76, 177, 178–79, 180, 198, 199; on previous sanction, 124, 128; printing office of, 20; promotions in, 23, 24, 26, 108; and public opinion, 44–45, 151, 178–79, 180–81, 201; reorganized/reformed/modernized, 13, 15–16, 19–20, 21–23, 37, 39, 42, 63, 64, 65, 68, 77, 79,

107, 169, 192, 193, 196–97; salaries in, 24, 25, 26, 108; on secret correspondence, 17, 45, 46–48; security in, 20, 21, 22, 171; staff of, 5, 11, 13, 15, 16–17, 18, 21, 22–23, 24, 25, 26, 108, 195–96; and Viceroys, 43, 105, 106, 125, 138–41, 142, 146–47; and Viceroy's Council, 70, 71, 125, 126, 133, 134, 135, 199; working conditions in, 14, 20–21, 22, 23; in 1860s, 12
India Reform Society, 160
"India's Appeal to the British Voter," 161
Ireland, 160, 180
Iyer, G. S., 164

Jowett, Benjamin, 6, 228, 238–39

Kaye, Sir John, 4, 13, 16, 45, 239
Kilbracken. *See* Godley, Arthur
Kimberley, 1st Earl of (John Wodehouse), 11, 14, 23, 64–66, 69, 241; v. Cabinet, 93–94, 95, 96, 101, 131; on cantonment legislation, 70, 133; on committee system, 68; on cotton duties, 70, 131; Council of India overruled by, 65–66, 70, 131, 163–64; Godley on, 65; on Ilbert Bill, 64; on Indian Civil Service, 163–64; on India Office, 17, 22, 65, 68, 105; lobbies and, 131; Parliament and, 65; press on, 65
Kitchener, 1st Earl of, 239; v. Curzon, 76, 142, 146, 148, 151, 178; Godley on, 77, 79; and Indian army, 74, 113; and India Office, 142, 145–46; press on, 95
Knight, Robert, 175
Knight Grand Cross of the Order of the Bath (G.C.B.), 96
Knight of the Garter, 96, 101

Labour Party, 170
Lamb, Charles, 23
Lansdowne, 5th Marquess of (Henry Petty-Fitzmaurice), 38, 69, 93, 94, 96, 101, 149, 175, 176, 241

Lawrence, John, 52
Lawrence, Sir Walter, 75, 177, 239
Leaving acts to operation, 125
Lee-Warner, William, 17, 46, 47, 55, 239
Liberal Party, 78, 93, 114, 163, 170
Lobbies, 69; currency, 197; Fowler and, 70; India Office and, 5, 20, 159, 160, 165, 167, 169, 170, 174, 180, 181, 196; Kimberley and, 131; Morley and, 170–73; on Parliament, 20, 103, 105, 107, 173–74, 180 (*see also* British Committee of the Indian National Congress; Indian Political Agency)
London Indian Society, 160
Lumsden, Sir Peter, 67
Lyall, Sir Alfred, 51–52, 55, 65, 79, 146, 194
Lytton, 1st Earl of (Edward Robert Bulwer), 66, 67, 138

Macgregor, J. C., 176
Mackay, Sir James Lyle, 55, 96, 194, 198, 239
Mackenzie, Sir A., 176
Mackenzie Wallace, Donald, 176, 177
McLaren, W. S. B., 162
Maine, Sir Henry, 41, 47, 128, 239–40
Majoribanks, Edward, 94
Malaviya, M. M., 170
Malcolm tradition, 46
Mallet, Sir Louis, 12, 13, 64, 240
Mandate theory, 136–37, 145
Markham, C. R., 16
Mayo, 6th Earl of (Richard Bourke), 123, 127, 128
Mehta, Pherozeshah, 170, 172, 173
Melville, J. R., 16
Merivale, John H., 12, 13
Midleton. *See* Brodrick, St. John
Mill, John Stuart, 36
Miller, Sir Arthur, 133, 134, 135, 136
Minto, Countess of (Mary Elliot), 144–45
Minto, 4th Earl of (Gilbert John Elliot), 4, 124, 141, 151, 237; and Godley, 150; on military administra-

tion, 79; v. Morley, 77, 79, 91, 92, 142, 143, 144–45, 146; and press, 176–77; private correspondence of, 91, 92; on Secretary of State's powers, 145; and Viceroy's Council, 143; on Viceroy's role, 144
Monarchy: appointments by, 36, 37, 89, 94–95, 126; v. India Office, on Indian policy, 37–38, 89–92, 93, 96, 102, 114, 142, 180; and Prime Minister, 93; private correspondence of, 90–92; and Secretaries of State, 37, 90–92, 94, 95, 96. *See also* Edward VII; Victoria, Queen
Montagu, Edwin, 144, 145, 147, 240
Montagu-Chelmsford Report, 106, 138, 164
Moore, A. W., 67
Morality legislation, 132–33. *See also* Cantonment legislation
Morley, John (Viscount Morley), 5, 77–81, 138, 168, 240; on Anglo-Russian entente, 142; on Bengal partitioning, 142; and Cabinet, 81, 95, 96; on Campbell, 103; on cotton duties, 170; and Council of India, 78–80, 81; and Gladstone, 77, 78; and Godley, 77–78, 80, 171, 231–32; on Gokhale, 172; and Indian members, 170–72; on India Office, 21; and lobbies, 170–73; on military administration, 79, 95; v. Minto, 77, 79, 91, 92, 142, 143, 144–45, 146; on Muslims, 80; press on, 78, 80, 81; on previous sanction, 143; on public opinion, 180; reform efforts by, 77, 79, 143–44, 145; on Viceroy's Council, 143
Mysore succession, 39

Nair, S., 170
Naoroji, Dadabhai, 161, 162, 163, 164, 240
Natal, 113
Nationalism, 44, 160–61, 164–65, 177–78, 194, 195, 202
National Review, 81
Natu brothers, 46

Newmarch, Sir Oliver, 240
New Zealand, 113
Nightingale, Florence, 160
Norman, Sir Henry, 94, 129, 240
Northbrook, 1st Earl of (Thomas George Baring), 13, 128–29, 131
Northcote, Sir Stafford, 39, 64, 91, 128, 134, 135, 146
Northwest Frontier Bill, 73
Norton, Eardley, 161, 164

Parliament: Act of 1858 empowers, 102–3; on Contagious Diseases Act, 200; on Council of India, 35–36, 38–40, 41, 44–45, 64, 102, 103–4, 163; and East India Company, 106; Godley on, 19–20, 104–5, 106–7; Hamilton and, 73; on home charges, 163; on Indian affairs, 19–20, 37, 44, 102–4, 106, 109, 138, 160, 162, 163–64, 165–66, 197, 201; on Indian budget, 108; Indian committee within, 161, 163; Indian members in, 163, 167, 170–72, 180; and India Office, 5, 19–20, 73, 89, 103, 104, 105, 106, 107, 114, 165, 180, 192, 196, 198, 199, 200, 201; Kimberley and, 65; lobbied, 20, 103, 105, 107, 159, 160, 161, 162, 163, 164, 171, 173–74, 180; on morality legislation, 132–33; and press, 160; and Secretaries of State, 37, 38, 44, 102, 103, 104, 105, 163; on tariffs, 131
Parliamentary Returns and Questions, 13, 19, 107, 165
Parliamentary Undersecretary, 12, 13, 14, 19
Paul, Herbert, 163
Peile, Sir James, 55, 240–41
Permanent Undersecretary, duties of, 13, 18, 63, 192. *See also* Godley, Arthur
Persian Gulf, 109, 110
Plague: policy, 72, 73; riots, 91
Playfair, Patrick, 131
Political and Secret Department. *See* Correspondence Departments, Political and Secret Department of

Ponsonby, Sir Henry, 90
Pontifex, Sir Charles, 241
Poona plague riots, 91
Presidency-Governors, 91, 146. *See also* Government of India
Press: in Bengal, 179, 180; in Calcutta, 175; on cantonment legislation, 137; on cotton duties, 132, 137; controlled, 178, 179, 180, 198, 199; on Council of India, 39; Curzon and, 175, 176, 179, 180; Digby and, 166; Elgin and, 71, 130; English, 5, 78, 160, 167, 169, 175, 176, 177, 178, 181; English, in India, 175–76, 177; foments unrest, 177, 179, 180; on Fowler, 71; Godley on, 179; and Government of India, 132, 137, 144, 175, 176, 179, 180; on Hamilton, 71, 73, 84 n.41; in India, 5, 71, 74, 84 n.41, 130, 132, 137, 164, 166, 169, 175, 176, 177, 178–79, 180, 181; and India Office, 5, 17–18, 160, 169, 175–76, 177, 178–79, 180, 198, 199; on Kimberley, 65; on Kitchener, 95; Lansdowne on, 175, 176; and Minto, 176–77; on Morley, 78, 80, 81; and Parliament, 160; and Viceroys, 176–77, 179; Wedderburn on, 167
Previous sanction, 128, 129, 138, 143
Pritchard, Sir Charles B., 131, 136, 137
Privy Council, 114
Prostitutes, licensed, 132, 199, 200
Public opinion, 70; British, 159, 160, 172, 174–75; Indian, 159, 178–81; India Office and, 44–45, 151, 178–79, 180–81, 201
Punch, 95

Rai, Lala Lajpat, 143, 170
Rationalization, 5, 191
Records and Registry Department, 14, 18–20; Parliamentary Branch of, 19–20, 45, 107, 169
Reid, R. P., 161, 163
Reuter's, 176–77

Ridley Commission on the Civil Service, 23–24, 26, 108
Ripon, 1st Marquess of (George Frederick Robinson), 5, 66, 114, 123, 124, 138–39
Ritchie, Richmond, 231
Roberts, Sir Frederick, 67, 90, 93, 94
Robinson, William, 23
Rosebery, 5th Earl of (Archibald Primrose), 94, 95, 101
Russell, G. W. E., 14, 201
Russo-Japanese War, 180

Salisbury, 3rd Marquess of (R. A. T. Gascoyne-Cecil), 39, 40, 64, 90, 143, 237–38; on cotton duties, 131; on Council of India, 39; on Indian appointments, 93; on Indian legislation, 128–29
Seccombe, Thomas, 16
Second Afghan War, 160
Secretary of State for India, 5, 11, 14; appointment power of, 40, 50–51, 52, 126, 128, 142, 146; authority of, 38, 102, 145–46, 162; Cabinet pressures, 73, 81, 92–101, 131; constraints on, 38; and Council of India, 35–36, 37, 38–40, 41–42, 43, 44, 45, 46–48, 49, 50–51, 52, 56, 63–88, 106, 192, 194, 195; Council of India overruled by, 40, 48, 65–66, 69, 70, 72–73, 81, 131, 133, 163–64, 200, 201; duties/functions of, 38, 123; Godley aids, 63, 64–65, 69, 71, 75, 77, 125, 140, 142, 145–46, 150–51, 171; and Government of India, 72, 77, 92, 93, 124, 125, 127–28, 129, 146; on honors, 96, 101, 146; Indian legislation formed by, 127, 128–29; and India Office, 56, 63; and Monarchy, 37, 90–92, 94, 95, 96; on Mysore succession, 39; and Parliament, 37, 38, 44, 102, 103, 104, 105, 163; party issues and, 92, 93, 95–96, 101; on private correspondence, 90–92, 142, 145, 146; salary of, 102, 103, 104, 105, 163, 171; and secret correspondence, 45,

46–48; and Secret Department, 40, 46; and Viceroys, 72, 125, 128–29, 131, 139, 140, 142, 143, 145; and Viceroy's Council, 126, 128, 146. *See also* Brodrick, St. John; Churchill, Lord Randolph; Cross, Richard A.; Fowler, Henry; Hamilton, Lord George; Kimberley, 1st Earl of; Morley, John; Stanley, Edward Henry; Wood, Sir Charles
Secretary of State in Council, 36, 38, 39, 49, 53, 56, 82, 103, 104, 139, 144, 200. *See also* Council of India
Sedition, 45, 46–47, 143
Selborne, Earl of (William Waldegrave Palmer), 110
Sepoy Mutiny, 35, 81, 193
Seton, Sir Malcolm, 3
Simla, 69, 145, 159; Clique, 162
Singh, S. N., 3, 35, 72, 80–81
Slagg, John, 44, 103–4, 105, 106, 161
South Africa, 74, 110–11, 112–13, 114
Stanley, Edward Henry (Earl of Derby), 15–16, 36, 52, 64
Stansfeld, James, 200, 201
The Statesman, 175
Stewart, Sir D. M., 55, 90, 94
Stores Department, 14, 18
Strachey, Sir John, 55, 124, 144, 194
Strachey, Gen. Sir Richard, 55, 194, 198
Stuart, James, 200, 201
Suez Canal, 23
Surat split, 165, 168, 172, 173
Svadeshi movement, 164

Tariff legislation, 129, 132, 134. *See also* Cotton duties crises
Telegraph, 23, 47, 191
Telephone in Whitehall, 22
Thuggee and Dacoity, Department of, 46, 169
Tilak, Bal Gangadhar, 173
The Times, 175; on Council of India, 39; on Government of India, 144, 176; and India Office, 176, 177, 178; on Morley, 80, 81
Times of India, 137, 177

Transvaal Registration Bill, 114
Transvaal War Fund, 109
Treasury, 3; on currency crisis, 198; and India Office, 5, 24–26, 108–9, 165
Treveylan, Sir Charles, 123–24
Typewriters in India Office, 20–21

Upper Burma, 93
Urgent legislation, 111, 128, 129, 130, 143

Venereal diseases, 133, 200; control of, 132, 199, 200 (*see also* Cantonment legislation)
Viceroy and Governor-General, 5, 123; acting, 146–47, 148, 149–50; appointment as, 37, 94–96, 126; and Cabinet, 94–95, 140, 141, 143, 148; on cotton duties, 131; and Council of India, 51, 69, 138–39, 195; difficulties of, 129–30, 133–38; Godley and, 71, 96, 136, 146, 147, 148–50; Government of India and, 125; and his Council (*see* Viceroy's Council); on Indian legislation, 128–29; India Office and, 43, 105, 106, 125, 138–41, 142, 146–47; position/authority of, 51, 125, 128, 129, 135, 136, 137, 138, 141, 143, 144, 146–47, 151; press and, 176–77, 179; private correspondence of, 91, 92; and Secretaries of State, 72, 125, 128–29, 131, 139, 140, 142, 143, 145; on urgent legislation, 128, 129, 130, 143. *See also* Curzon, George Nathaniel; Elgin, 9th Earl of; Lansdowne, 5th Marquis of; Minto, 4th Earl of; Ripon, 1st Marquis of
Viceroy's Council, 38, 71, 129; on cantonment legislation, 133–34, 135, 136, 137, 138; Commander-in-Chief on, 126; on cotton duties, 131–32, 136; and currency lobby, 197; Curzon and, 139, 143; Elgin and, 130, 131–32, 133–34, 135, 136, 137; Government of India Act, 1919, on, 125; on Indian legislation, 143; India

Office over, 70, 71, 125, 126, 133, 134, 135, 199; Minto and, 143; Morley on, 143; role/position of, 125, 133, 134; Secretary of State and, 126, 128, 146

Victoria, Queen: on Council of India, 37; and Gladstone, 93; on honors, 37, 96, 101; on Indian policy, 37, 89; and India Office, 90–91, 93, 96; on Muslims, 91; on plague riots, 91; private correspondence of, 90, 91; Viceroy appointments by, 37, 94, 95

Wacha, D. E., 164
Walpole, Horace, 14
War Office, 3, 44, 74, 110–12, 113
Waterfield, Henry, 17

Weber, Max, 5, 191–92
Wedderburn, William, 160, 162, 163, 167–69, 173
Welby, Sir Reginald, 24, 108
Welby Commission, 26, 104, 105, 164
Westland, Sir James, 131, 136
White, Sir George, 93, 94
Williams, Donovan, 3, 4, 35, 37, 46, 50, 125
Wilson, Sir Arthur, 47
Wolpert, Stanley, 80
Wolverhampton. *See* Fowler, Henry
Wood, Sir Charles (Viscount Halifax), 13, 14, 37, 127; on Council of India, 36; on Indian legislation, 129; reforms India Office, 15–16, 52, 64
Woodman, J. V., 176

About the Author

ARNOLD P. KAMINSKY is a Lecturer in Asian Studies at California State University, Long Beach. He has contributed articles to *The Journal of Indian History*, *The Indian Economic and Social History Review*, *Asian Profile*, *Military Affairs*, and *British Imperial Policy in India and Sri Lanka, 1858-1912: A Reassessment*, edited by Robert I. Crane and N. G. Barrier.

Recent Titles in
Contributions in Comparative Colonial Studies
Series Editor: Robin W. Winks

Constraint of Empire: The United States and Caribbean Interventions
Whitney T. Perkins

Toward a Programme of Imperial Life: The British Empire
at the Turn of the Century
John H. Field

European Colonial Rule, 1880–1940: The Impact of the West on India, Southeast Asia, and Africa
Rudolf von Albertini, with Albert Wirz
Translated by John G. Williamson

An Empire for the Masses: The French Popular Image
of Africa, 1870–1900
William H. Schneider

Western Women in Colonial Africa
Caroline Oliver

The Emergence of Modern South Africa: State, Capital, and the Incorporation of Organized Labor on the South African Gold Fields, 1902–1939
David Yudelman

The Second British Empire: Trade, Philanthropy, and Good Government,
1820–1890
John P. Halstead

Completing a Stewardship: The Malayan Civil Service, 1942–1957
Robert Heussler

Double Impact: France and Africa in the Age of Imperialism
G. Wesley Johnson, ed.

The Selling of the Empire: British and French Imperialist Propaganda, 1890–1945
Thomas G. August

The Transition to Responsible Government: British Policy in British North America, 1815–1850
Phillip A. Buckner